PEACE BE STILL

PEACE BE STILL

MODERN BLACK AMERICA FROM

WORLD WAR II TO BARACK OBAMA

MATTHEW C. WHITAKER

University of Nebraska Press | Lincoln and London

© 2013 by the Board of Regents of the University of Nebraska
Portions of chap. 1 were previously published in the author's
Race Work: The Rise of Civil Rights in the Urban West (Lin-
coln: University of Nebraska Press, 2005), 63–87. © 2005 by
the Board of Regents of the University of Nebraska.
Portions of chap. 6 were previously published in *Hurricane
Katrina: America's Unnatural Disaster*, edited by Jeremy I.
Levitt and Matthew C. Whitaker (Lincoln: University of
Nebraska Press, 2009), 1–10. © 2009 by Jeremy I. Levitt and
Matthew C. Whitaker.

Publication of this volume was assisted by the Virginia
Faulkner Fund, established in memory of Virginia Faulkner,
editor in chief of the University of Nebraska Press.

Library of Congress Cataloging-in-Publication Data
Whitaker, Matthew C.
Peace be still: modern black America from World War II to
Barack Obama / Matthew C. Whitaker.
pages cm
Includes bibliographical references and index.
ISBN 978-0-8032-4693-5 (cloth: alk. paper)
ISBN 978-0-8032-4964-6 (paperback: alk. paper)
1. African Americans—History—1877–1964. 2. African
Americans—Social conditions—20th century. 3. African
Americans—Social conditions—21st century. 4. African
Americans—Politics and government—20th century. 5. Afri-
can Americans—Politics and government—21st century.
6. Civil rights movements—United States—History—20th
century. I. Title.
E185.6.W57 2013
973'.0496073—dc23
2013029667

Set in Minion Pro by Laura Wellington.
Designed by A. Shahan.

I dedicate this book to the person who put me on the path and set me free, my mother, Covey L. Whitaker.

Contents

Illustrations ix

Acknowledgments xi

Introduction: American History as
African American History 1

1. "Make Way for Democracy," 1939–1954 7

2. "Let Your Motto Be Resistance," 1954–1961 53

3. "Deep Rumbling of Discontent," 1961–1968 85

4. "So Let It Be Done," 1968–1980 133

5. "To the Break of Dawn," 1980–2000 169

6. "The Audacity of Hope," 2000–2008 213

7. Contemporary Black America 247

8. Hope and Change: The New Millennium
and Freedom's Promise 279

Appendix 1: Excerpts from the
U.S. Constitution (1787) 307

Appendix 2: Executive Order #8802 (1941) 309

Appendix 3: *Brown v. Board of Education
of Topeka* (1954) 311

Appendix 4: The Civil Rights Act of 1964 313

Appendix 5: The Voting Rights Act of 1965 317

Appendix 6: Fair Housing Act (1968) 321

Appendix 7: "A More Perfect Union" (2008) 323

Appendix 8: African American Population as
a Percentage of the Total Population, 1870–2008   333

Appendix 9: Distribution of the African American
Population by Region, 1870–2008   335

Appendix 10: Black Population in the Twenty
Largest U.S. Cities, 2008   337

Notes   339

Bibliography   349

Index   375

Illustrations

1. Dorie Miller   16
2. First black members of the Women's Army Corps   20
3. Tuskegee Airmen   26
4. Jackie Robinson   45
5. George E. C. Hayes, Thurgood Marshall, and James M. Nabrit   50
6. Mamie Till   57
7. Rosa Parks   61
8. Martin Luther King Jr.   65
9. Malcolm X   78
10. Freedom Riders   81
11. Martin Luther King Jr. at the March on Washington   96
12. Fannie Lou Hamer   101
13. Muhammad Ali   111
14. Tommie Smith and John Carlos   113
15. Angela Davis   114
16. Sidney Poitier   116
17. The Black Panther Party   121
18. Stokely Carmichael   123
19. James Brown, the "Godfather of Soul"   124
20. Richard Pryor   148
21. Clarence Thomas   173
22. Anita Hill   176
23. Michael Jackson and Quincy Jones   186
24. Jesse Jackson   192

25. Nelson Mandela   197

26. Colin Powell and Condoleezza Rice   205

27. Barack Obama   229

28. New Orleans after Hurricane Katrina   232

29. Oprah Winfrey   239

30. Michael Jordan   240

31. Toni Morrison   250

32. Russell Simmons and Sean "Diddy" Combs   261

33. John Hope Franklin   264

34. Barack Obama, 2009 presidential inauguration   285

35. New York protestors   288

36. Eric Holder   300

37. Barack Obama, 2011 State of the Union address   302

Acknowledgments

Favor is priceless. I have benefited from the good deeds of many people, and if my wealth were determined by the goodwill they have given me, my buying power would rival that of Bill Gates. Indeed, I am truly beholden to many institutions, colleagues, friends, and family for enabling me to write this book. I thank the following people at Arizona State University for encouraging my research, writing, teaching, and service-based intellectual life: Michael M. Crow, president; Elizabeth Capaldi, executive vice president and provost of the University; Frederick Corey, vice provost and dean, University College; Elaine Sweet, assistant dean, University College; Robert Page, vice president and dean, College of Liberal Arts and Sciences; Neal A. Lester, associate vice president, Office of Knowledge Enterprise Development; Norma Villa, manager of the School of Historical, Philosophical, and Religious Studies; Marjorie Zatz, director of the Justice and Social Inquiry Program; Jewell Parker Rhodes, Virginia C. Piper Chair of Creative Writing; and colleagues Thomas J. Davis, Paul Hirt, Pat Lauderdale, Stephen Marc, Brooks D. Simpson, Pamela Stewart, and Mark von Hagen. I also appreciate the support of the School of Letters and Sciences and the intellectually stimulating collaboration with Deborah Cox and Sarah Herrera that I have experienced in asu's Center for the Study of Race and Democracy.

I am truly indebted to the following scholars at other universities throughout the United States for their considerable assistance and support: Gordon Bakken, California State University–Fullerton; Albert S. Broussard, Texas A&M University; William Jelani Cobb, University of Connecticut; Ronald G. Coleman, University of Utah; Pero Dagbovie, Michigan State University; Eric Duke, University of South Florida; Darlene Clark Hine, Northwestern University; Peniel E. Joseph, Tufts University;

Robin D. G. Kelley, University of California, Los Angeles; Wilma King, University of Missouri–Columbia; Nell Irvin Painter, Princeton University; Vicki Ruiz, University of California–Irvine; Quintard Taylor Jr., University of Washington; Joe William Trotter Jr., Carnegie Mellon University; Rhonda Y. Williams, Case Western Reserve University; and Yohuru Williams, Fairfield University.

I am particularly obliged to Patricia Etter (retired) and Chris Marin of the Department of Manuscripts and Special Collections at the Hayden Library and to the staff of the Government Documents Division at Arizona State University. Individuals at the Planning Department of the City of Phoenix, Arizona, also contributed greatly to the completion of this book. The Michigan Historical Collection at the University of Michigan, Ann Arbor; the New York Public Library's Schomburg Center for Research in Black Culture; the Charles H. Wright Museum of African American History in Detroit, Michigan; the DuSable Museum of African American History in Chicago, Illinois; the National Civil Rights Museum in Memphis, Tennessee; and the Martin Luther King Center in Atlanta, Georgia also provided me much needed access to both primary and secondary sources that helped inform this synthesis of modern African American history.

I must invoke the names of, and pay respect to, my predecessors and mentors (direct and indirect), whose trailblazing work gave rise to and advanced the field of African American history. The following historians and their work made this book possible: George Washington Williams, Carter G. Woodson, Lorenzo J. Greene, W. E. B. Du Bois, Charles Harris Wesley, John Henrik Clarke, Walter Rodney, Herbert Aptheker, August Meier, Elliott Rudwick, John Hope Franklin, Lerone Bennett, Jr., Nathan Irvin Huggins, Mary Frances Berry, George Frederickson, Eric Foner, Nell Irvin Painter, Darlene Clark Hine, Manning Marable, Leon Litwack, Joe William Trotter Jr., George Lipsitz, V. P. Franklin, David Levering Lewis, Clayborne Carson, Deborah Gray White, Earl Lewis, and Robin D. G. Kelley.

I am grateful to my students, the torchbearers who will push the study of African American history to a new level of sophistication and relevance in the twenty-first century. *Peace Be Still* benefited from their critical support, fresh ideas, and encouragement. I am particularly grateful for the assistance of current and former graduate students Monica Butler and Elyssa Ford. A special note of thanks is due to Megan Falater, whose passion, intelligence, and commitment enhanced the quality of this book.

I must also acknowledge my good friends: Robert Hackett, Jason B. "Sugar Bear" Harris, Carole Coles Henry, Lasana O. Hotep, Alonzo Jones, John L. Jones, Jeremy I. Levitt, Robert Robertson, Dan Robbins and Kristi Rutz-Robbins, and Michael A. Smart. They continue to remind me that intellectual life and fun are not antithetical and that the "ivory tower," like life, is often what you make of it. To Jill Schiefelbein, your keen eye greatly improved the quality of this work. This book would not have been possible without the support and counsel of Carolyn Kaluzniacki and Art Newman. They reminded me that "every shut eye ain't sleep, and every goodbye ain't gone."

Finally, for giving me inspiration and sustaining me with love and affection, I thank Cassondra "Lovey" Blackwell; my doting, elegant, and astonishingly patient mother, Covey L. Whitaker; my razor-sharp, witty, and shrewd late grandmother, Doris V. Whitaker; my daughter, Anastacia, whose stirring confidence is surpassed only by her unyielding humanity; and my son, Jackson, whose creativity and passion renew my hope for a brighter future.

PEACE BE STILL

INTRODUCTION

American History as African American History

"Moses, my servant, is dead. Therefore arise and go over Jordan."
There are no deliverers. They're all dead. We must arise and go over
Jordan. We can take the promised Land.
—NANNIE BURROUGHS, "Unload Your Toms," *Louisiana Weekly*,
December 23, 1933

History exists within the past and the present. Although we tend to view
the past as complete and fixed regardless of the passage of time, it is far
from static. If you consider how many things occurred in the lives of
individuals, peoples, and nations at any given moment in history, you
will realize that the historian is compelled to select that which is important from these myriad events in order to ascertain the meaning of what
happened. These distinctions between the important and the unimport-
ant are of course made in the present. We do not identify that which we
believe is essential knowledge if history delves into an impenetrable and
irrelevant knot of minutiae. Chronicling and evaluating the past is the
vocation of historians, who craft "historical narrative" with the aim of
offering readers a sound account of the past that is understandable in the
present. Historical narrative, therefore, inevitably empowers some individuals and events with historical significance and neglects, overlooks,
and repudiates the historical value of others.

In any event, historical narrative evolves constantly, as what we yearn
to know about the past changes in relation to what is important to us now
and what will be important to us in the future. You do not have to look
very far into our American past to see that such changes have unfolded.

Indeed, before the modern civil rights movement of the 1950s and 1960s, American history was viewed almost entirely as the history of white people. Most white Americans simply believed that there was nothing of interest to investigate or note in African American history. This has changed. African American history is now one of the most vibrant subfields in the discipline. The same can be said of women's history. Before the feminist movement of the 1970s, American history was primarily the story of men. This is no longer the case. The last thirty years have witnessed in an explosion of literature devoted to women's history. In both subfields and in many others, more changes are on the horizon and the chronicling of history continues to progress.

As historians are continually challenged by new issues and questions, the past constantly yields new insights and discoveries. This is why African American history written even a generation ago is less suited to address all of the concerns of today's readers. In the last quarter century much has happened, so those who study African American history are asking different questions of the past. Today we want to know what black men *and* women did, what Sly Stone's "everyday people" were thinking and doing, the role culture played in black people's daily lives, the role class played in black communities, how black people interacted with other people of color, how region has factored into the evolution of African American communities, even how rap music and hip-hop have shaped African Americans and, ostensibly, recent American history and life.

Peace Be Still, a concise history of African Americans since World War II, addresses these questions. In doing so, it will argue that the history of African Americans since 1941 is nothing short of a remarkable story of a people who worked hard to give meaning to their freedom and reconstruct the United States into a nation that delivers to *all* of its people that which is promised in its documents of freedom. Inasmuch as modern American history has been greatly influenced and at times defined by the history and lives of people of African descent, this book will turn things around, casting the history of the United States in the mid-twentieth and early twenty-first centuries within the experiences of Americans of African descent. Finally, *Peace Be Still* offers considerable coverage of the arts and culture of modern black America, distinguishing it from other histories that adopt a linear approach and focus almost exclusively on politics and resistance.

"During the past twenty-five years, African American history has become an established field of intellectual inquiry. Not only is it one of the most vibrant subfields in American history, answering some of the most pressing questions of the hour and hosting some of the most stimulating historical debates, but it is also changing the way in which we view American history as a whole. African American history is not merely the addition of black people to a larger American historical narrative; it has its own issues and concerns."[1]

Like most recent studies of black history and life, *Peace Be Still* is not simply a story of victimization, despite the indignities and acts of terrorism African Americans have endured. Instead, it chronicles the history of a people who dared to fight the forces that sought to dehumanize and oppress them, who fashioned a dynamic culture of artistic and religious expression, educational and professional advancement, in addition to resistance to oppression and marginalization. It examines black intellectualism and professionalism and emphasizes the prominence and interconnectedness of black institutions and interracial alliances. Most important, *Peace Be Still* offers readers a vibrant and accessible history of African Americans since World War II, encouraging them to reconsider the "consensus" view of American history by highlighting the extent to which African American history illuminates the promise, conflicts, contradictions, hopes, and victories that all Americans share.[2]

The narrative begins by examining the powerful influence World War II had on the United States, particularly how it stirred African American activism and electrified the modern civil rights movement. "Roused by generations of discrimination, buoyed by a swelling population, and inspired by World War II and America's renewed promise of democracy, African Americans seized the time to quicken their longstanding quest for equality."[3]

Although World War II intensified activism and replenished hope in black communities, the war's ultimate impact on African Americans was mixed. "While World War II ushered in a period of unprecedented progress in black employment, mobility, and professional activism, America's crusade in the name of freedom and democracy failed to reach millions of its black citizens at home. White supremacy and racial discrimination flourished in the United States during the war." Black leaders called for the 'Double V': African Americans' fight against fascism abroad, and their battle against white supremacy at home."[4]

"Like World War I, World War II generated employment opportunities for blacks and stimulated another phase in what historians have labeled the Great Migration of African Americans from the South to the North and West. Masses of black migrants again flooded some of America's largest northern and western cities in search of the 'promised land,' only to find racial segregation, financial distress, and limited upward mobility. Even successful blacks were targeted by unhappy and racist whites who abhorred black competition in the workplace and did not welcome black people as neighbors. Racial conflict often led to violence, as discord between white and black workers and their communities triggered white terrorism and race riots in cities throughout the United States."[5]

World War II permanently changed the African American experience. The war and postwar years brought new employment opportunities and an enhanced self-awareness to black people. At the same time, African Americans no longer tolerated second-class citizenship in the face of their recent sacrifices for the nation and repudiated as hypocritical U.S. rhetoric, policy, and actions that sought to end the reign of murderous, racist dictators while maintaining discriminatory and segregationist practices not only in the South, but in many other parts of the nation.[6]

The wartime experiences of black people, both overseas and on the home front, and the adversarial climate of the Cold War that followed set the stage for the peak years of the civil rights movement. Black World War II veterans returned from the war determined to make *their* America safe for democracy, too. Extremely sensitive about its image abroad during the Cold War, the United States felt pressure to live up to its lofty ideals regarding justice and equality at last. The racial friction that came to a head during World War II foretold an even more intense period of racial discord and progress between 1946 and 1970. World War II laid bare the longstanding inconsistencies between America's rhetoric and the truth about its denial of social and economic equality to its black citizens. Black people committed themselves to ensuring that America delivered on its promise of freedom and democracy for all. They also worked to connect the era's black freedom struggle to liberation movements around the world. If the efforts of African Americans to seek justice and equality have caused historians to label this story "the long civil rights movement," the renewal of those efforts during and after World War II gave birth to "the modern civil rights movement."[7]

Rallying support for black liberation and racial equality from churches, mutual aid societies, fraternal organizations, and everyday people, activists within the modern civil rights movement devised creative strategies for the liberation of black people in America. African Americans of every persuasion, young and old, rich and poor, educated and untaught, organized to strike out against the edifice of white supremacy and racial inequality. They often met staunch resistance from government officials and from most white Americans. African Americans possessed different ideas about how the movement should be conducted, even though they often shared a communal desire for liberation and racial equality.[8]

The black freedom struggle of the 1960s and the various protest movements it spawned developed techniques and organizations that finally brought America face to face with the conflict between its democratic ideals and the somber realities of racism, sexism, and elitism. Throughout the decade, activists squared off against the fierce resistance of white supremacists, sexists, and defenders of the economic status quo. The activism of these insurgent forces forced three presidents, Congress, and leaders of the private sector to respond and take action. The black power movement instilled a greater sense of pride and self-determination in black Americans, and an unprecedented number of African American leaders were elected to high-ranking political offices. In 1972, congresswoman Shirley Chisholm mounted a bid for the presidency itself.[9]

By 1970, despite the assassinations of Martin Luther King Jr. and of Robert F. Kennedy, a presidential hopeful who supported civil rights, economic opportunity and the withdrawal of U.S. troops from Vietnam, many African Americans were optimistic about the possibility of a brighter future. The ranks of the black middle class swelled, corporate America diversified, and relatively large numbers of well-to-do black people moved to ever-expanding suburbs. The majority of African Americans, however, did not fare so well over the next four decades. Enormous economic and political changes severely retarded many of the gains black Americans had made between 1946 and 1970. Deindustrialization, outsourcing, downsizing, reductions in federal spending on inner cities, attacks on affirmative action, underfunded and poorly administrated schools, and the reemergence of deliberate acts of racism led to high rates of African American unemployment, increases in black poverty, and decreases in African American social and political capital.[10]

African Americans responded to these complex challenges in ways that reveal the heterogeneity and dynamism of a black community and culture marked by diverse and sometimes conflicting elements including a resurgent black nationalism, committed black feminisms, black neoconservatism, African and Caribbean immigration, and the global domination of hip-hop. In short, African Americans continue to resist marginalization, seek equality, confront intraracial differences and hostilities, and deeply influence American life in search of their promised land.

1

"MAKE WAY FOR DEMOCRACY," 1939–1954

> Be not dismayed in these terrible times. You possess power, great
> power. Our problem is to hitch it up [to] action on the broadest,
> daring, and most gigantic scale.
>
> —A. PHILIP RANDOLPH, Detroit, Michigan, September 26, 1942

African American life during the Great Depression and World War II created the framework for the development of the modern civil rights movement. Forged to destroy both legal and extralegal racial discrimination
and segregation, the civil rights movement was profoundly embedded
in the sustained transformation of average black people into agents of
their own liberation. This movement was also linked with the growth of
the black middle class, the ascendance of community-based institutions,
and watershed legal victories in federal courts against institutionalized
racial discrimination. In addition, black Americans made use of political
and social changes to advance their agenda. These changes included the
advent of television, the global decolonization movement, and America's
claim on leadership of the "free world" during the Cold War. The civil
rights movement grew out of a bevy of local grassroots struggles, yet black
people also created new organizations and fashioned local and regional
events into a broader national, and ultimately international, movement.
Although African American activists encountered massive white resistance and struggled with serious internal disputes, activists eventually
secured support from a critical mass of white supporters and some other
people of color, and together they advanced the fight for full citizenship
and equality that had been initiated one century earlier. In short, World
War II helped ignite the modern civil rights movement, which was, in
essence, America's second Reconstruction.

As the Great Depression lingered and the world economy struggled throughout the 1930s, powerful forces emerged from the abyss of destruction and despair in Europe and Asia to pose serious challenges to peace and prosperity around the globe. Adolf Hitler in Germany and Benito Mussolini in Italy rose to power during the 1920s and 1930s, exploited the fears and vulnerability of their citizenries, and formed an imperialist alliance known as the Axis. This fascist collaboration championed a fanatical nationalism that censored domestic resistance and employed terrorism, coercion, and violence to expand its empires beyond the borders of their nation-states. For his part, Hitler was a staunch white supremacist, one committed to ridding the world of people of color. Fiercely antisemitic, he held Jews responsible for Germany's many economic and social problems. Hitler's Nazi Party also abhorred gypsies, homosexuals, and people of African descent. Just as Hitler initiated a genocidal campaign to "cleanse" Germany of all Jews, so too did he develop and execute plans to discriminate against, torture, and murder gypsies, homosexuals, and black people. His hatred of black people led him to label jazz music as "nigger" music and prohibit the playing of jazz in German cities.

Through political pressure and military force, Germany came to dominate much of Europe during the 1930s, with Great Britain and France seemingly unwilling or unable to stop it. In August 1939, the Soviet Union signed a nonaggression pact with Germany, which gave Hitler a free hand to invade Poland on September 1, 1939. Although the Soviet Union was not part of the Axis powers (Germany, Japan, and Italy), it invaded Finland shortly thereafter. Britain and France, both allies of Poland, could no longer ignore the situation. They declared war on Germany, and World War II had begun. At virtually the same time, Japan moved to expand its empire in Asia. The Japanese government had long opposed the incursions of British, French, Dutch, and American colonial interests in the Far East and South Pacific. Japan also had collided with the Soviet Union in Manchuria and fought with China throughout the 1930s.

The United States allied itself with China and denounced Japan's association with Nazi Germany and Fascist Italy. The United States also declared its intentions to support Britain, doing what it could to send supplies to the beleaguered British after the fall of France to Hitler in the spring of 1940. In June 1941, a third nation joined the alliance. That month Germany invaded the Soviet Union, and the United States and Great Britain chose to extend the hand of friendship to the Russians. However, the United States refrained from formal entry into the conflict as a full-fledged participant until the Japanese attacked Pearl Harbor, Hawaii on December 7, 1941, an event that stunned the nation and left America's premier Pacific military base and much of the Navy's Pacific fleet severely damaged. Within days, the United States was at war with Germany and Italy as well.

Honor, Duty, and Deception: African Americans in World War II

The American entry into World War II, which followed the attack on Pearl Harbor, changed the nation forever. It emerged from the conflict as the world's wealthiest and most industrialized military power. As before, waging war ushered in an era of significant change, challenge, and opportunity for African Americans. If it meant unprecedented progress in employment, mobility, and professional activism for many African Americans, America's grand crusade to make the world safe for democracy and free peoples everywhere from racist dictators failed to reach millions of its own black citizens, who still lacked access to freedom and democracy themselves. Without a doubt, white supremacy and Jim Crow segregation thrived in the United States during the war, but black Americans resisted their oppression at home even as they defended the nation abroad.

Many black people became politically active during the war, both domestically and internationally, as they drew inspiration from other people of African descent and from black nation states around the world. Ethiopia, Haiti, and Liberia were the only three black-governed nations in the world at the time, and their independence uplifted black people throughout the world. When Italy invaded Ethiopia in 1935, black people throughout America watched with anger and frustration. The black press covered the brutality of the invasion and the horrors perpetrated against Ethiopians. African Americans responded by holding rallies and fundraisers in support of the "Ethiopian cause." Although the Ethiopians fought bravely, Italy defeated them using every means at its disposal, including toxic gas. The Ethiopian struggle motivated many black Americans to pay close attention to the unfolding of World War II, Africa, and the racial tyranny associated with fascism.

African Americans who subscribed to leftist ideas and politics were also stirred, between 1936 and 1937, by a civil war between the Spanish government and a fascist insurgency orchestrated by General Francisco Franco, an ally of Germany and Italy. Approximately one hundred black Americans served in Spain with the Abraham Lincoln Battalion, a multiracial unit of three thousand American volunteers. Many of the black people who joined the Abraham Lincoln Battalion did so as an expression of a Marxist notion of internationalism, but, for the great majority of African Americans, the nation's massive mobilization for World War II enlisted them in the cause of ending fascism abroad and destroying Jim Crow and racial injustice at home.

Although mobilization put millions of Americans back to work and gave the U.S. economy a powerful boost, wartime industry did not create immediate opportunities for African Americans. Between 1939 and 1941, expenditures on armaments effectively ended the Great Depression. While white wartime laborers experienced a boom in employment opportunities, most black Americans found factory doors shut to them. The majority of American manufacturers refused to employ blacks in anything other than menial labor positions, even if the applicants were qualified to perform highly skilled labor. In addition, many locals of the American Federation of Labor (AFL) entered into "closed-shop" contracts with employers who forbade the hiring of African American workers on the grounds that they were not already union members, neatly skirting the fact that the AFL denied membership to black people in the first place. The president of North American Aviation communicated the feelings of white business and labor leaders across the nation when he professed, "Regardless of their training as aircraft workers, we will not employ Negroes. It is against our policy." A top oil company official also refused to hire African Americans, arguing that the drilling and producing of oil wells was a "white man's job" and that it was "going to stay that way."[1]

Despite President Franklin D. Roosevelt's efforts to include black people in New Deal programs, the federal government did nothing to discourage discriminatory practices as the nation mobilized for war. In its own training and placement programs, the U.S. Employment Service (USES) submitted to the racial customs of white neighborhoods by acquiescing to the demands of businesses for "whites only." In a flagrant instance of organized racism, the leading USES training site, located in Inglewood, California, considered any black person on or near city streets after sunset eligible for apprehension and incarceration; in other words, only black people at the training facility were under curfew. Even the U.S. military, after admitting black men in numbers that corresponded to their percentage of the population, continued to segregate them and consigned them to service and support positions. The Army Air Corps initially rejected

African Americans completely. Black women often fared even worse; they were rarely allowed to work in defense industries, with many companies arguing that they were best suited for domestic work.

White supremacy and racial discrimination in the armed forces endured even as military leaders fiercely repelled calls for integration. Among the African Americans who took on these conditions was A. Philip Randolph, who had come to national prominence as the founder of the Brotherhood of Sleeping Car Porters, the first African American labor union formally recognized by the AFL. Pullman porters, dissatisfied with their treatment by the Chicago-based Pullman Company, sought the assistance of Randolph and others in organizing their own union in 1925. By 1942, the Brotherhood of Sleeping Car Porters was one of the largest and most powerful predominantly black organizations in America.

The black press also called attention to the persistence of segregation and exclusion of African Americans in the war effort. On January 31, 1942, the *Pittsburgh Courier*, founded in 1907 and once the country's most widely circulated black newspapers, published a letter written to Robert Vann, the newspaper's editor, that helped to alter the trajectory of African American history. James C. Thompson of Wichita, Kansas, communicated his yearning for African Americans to "keep defense and victory in the forefront so that we don't lose sight of our fight for true democracy at home." He reasoned that if the Allied nations used the "V" for Victory sign to rally citizens in opposition to aggression, imperialism, and tyranny, then black Americans should embrace the "double V": victory over fascism abroad and victory over white supremacy at home. The *Pittsburgh Courier* adopted Thompson's notion, creating the phrase "Double V" for "Double Victory." Soon all the black press, as well as civil rights leaders and organizations, had embraced the concept. The Double V campaign inspired black people and organizations to intensify their protests against racist practices in the military. Walter White of the National Association for the Advancement of Colored People (NAACP), T. Arnold Hill, chairman of the National Urban League (NUL), Lester Granger, also of the NUL, black New York Congressman Adam Clayton Powell Jr., Robert Vann, and Mabel K. Staupers of the National Association of Colored Graduate Nurses (NACGN) joined Randolph in leading the protest. They helped mobilize African American workers, women's groups, college students, officials, and interracial alliances to resist inequality.

At a time when American officials, generals, and editors presented the nation to the world as a shining example of freedom and equality, African Americans forced those same officials, generals, and editors to acknowledge the glaring inconsistencies rooted in their declared principles and behaviors. White supremacy persisted during the course of the war, but the efforts of the black rank-and-file and protest organizations—along with the continuing need of the military for soldiers and industry for laborers—eventually weakened the institution of segregation.

The March on Washington Movement

A. Philip Randolph prepared African American communities to engage the U.S. government directly. On September 27, 1940, Randolph, along with Walter White and T. Arnold Hill, met with President Roosevelt in the Oval Office. Roosevelt greeted the black delegation and engaged them in polite small talk, asking Randolph, "Which class were you in at Harvard?" Randolph, who graduated from Cookman Institute in Florida and attended evening classes at New York City College, responded flatly, "I never went to Harvard, Mr. President." Randolph grew more impatient by the moment, as Roosevelt proceeded to speak cordially with White and Hill. Finally, Randolph snapped. "Mr. President, time is running on," he said. "You are quite busy, I know, but what we want to talk to you about is the problem of jobs for Negroes in defense industries." The meeting ended with Roosevelt having promised nothing.[2]

Randolph prepared to confront the federal government publicly. After months of deliberation and preliminary planning, he announced the creation of the March on Washington Movement (MOWM) on January 25, 1941. Some one hundred thousand African American protestors would march to the steps of the nation's capital if Roosevelt refused to take meaningful action on behalf of racial equality. There was only one way to avoid such an embarrassing confrontation. Randolph demanded that the president issue an executive order to outlaw racial discrimination in companies that signed government contracts, eradicate the exclusion of blacks from defense training programs on the basis of race, and order the USES to place workers in jobs on a nondiscriminatory basis. Randolph also called for the end of segregation in the military, asking the president to endorse legislation that would withhold any resources associated with the National Labor Relations Act from unions that denied membership to black Americans.

Randolph's actions constituted a radical shift from the strategies of most contemporary civil rights organizations. For example, the MOWM called for a massive grassroots effort to mobilize ordinary people, not just intellectual and political elites. Randolph also perceived the march as an independent action orchestrated by black people that would bar the participation of white people, which represented a departure from the interracial work of many other organizations. Randolph's populist rhetoric and grassroots efforts garnered major support from black people who felt largely ignored by middle class–controlled organizations, such as the NAACP. A week before the march was to begin, on July 1, 1941, a distressed Roosevelt yielded and issued Executive Order #8802, (appendix 2, page 000) establishing the Fair Employment Practices Commission (FEPC). The order declared, "There shall be no discrimination in the employment of workers in defense industries or government because of race, creed, color, or national origin."[3] The order also empowered the FEPC to investigate complaints and take action against employers who continued to discriminate.

In return for the order, Randolph cancelled the march. However, the MOWM quickly became the most militant and important force in African American politics. Its call for nonviolent civil disobedience was unacceptable to mainstream African American organizations, however, and the NAACP withdrew its support of MOWM activities. The hopes of MOWM members that the FEPC would become an independent investigative body were dashed in June 1942 when Roosevelt placed the commission under congressional oversight, and before long the FEPC and the MOWM lost most of their momentum and effectiveness. Randolph found it difficult to secure additional victories on behalf of racial justice between major opposition from government agencies, southern congressmen, and white people who were unwilling to address racial issues during wartime. But at its zenith, between 1941 and 1942, the MOWM had demonstrated unity, power, and the ability of African Americans to engage in direct grassroots politics. It served as the model for the highly celebrated March on Washington in 1963, during which Martin Luther King Jr. gave his famous "I Have a Dream" speech. The militant politics of the MOWM also presaged the black power movement of the late 1960s.

Discrimination on the Frontline and Home Front

The FEPC fostered modest changes to the status quo. The lure of defense industry jobs and the promises of the FEPC triggered an enormous migration of African Americans from the South to northern defense plants, even if the majority of African Americans employed by these plants held only the most menial of jobs. Some defense industries refused to comply with the order altogether, arguing that simply hiring African Americans would be forcing them to integrate their entire workforce. This proved to be a major problem in the South. Roosevelt's executive order also failed to address racial discrimination within labor unions. The FEPC's rhetoric was eloquent and noble, but the commission had no means to enforce its provisions. In 1943, after learning that some employers were violating the spirit of the new order, Roosevelt decided to strengthen the FEPC. As a result, he increased the FEPC budget to nearly $500,000 and replaced the part-time Washington DC staff with a professional full-time one that was deployed throughout the nation.

By the end of World War II, black Americans held an unprecedented number of defense jobs. Black civilians occupied 8 percent of defense industry jobs, up from 3 percent on the eve of the war. In addition, two hundred thousand black people were employed by the federal government, tripling prewar numbers. Still, the majority of those employed in the defense industry or by the federal government worked in menial positions.

African Americans had an even more difficult time making progress in the armed forces. Even as black men were once again called upon to make the world safe for democracy, they found themselves consigned to segregated units, restricted to noncombat duties, and denied opportunities to become commissioned officers. In short, the military reflected U.S. society's acceptance of white supremacy.

In 1925 the American War College released the findings of a study that reflected the racism that permeated the armed services. The report argued that black Americans were intellectually inferior, amenable to white supremacy, prone to mob violence, physically unfit for combat, and difficult to command because of an inherent laziness. The War Department accepted the so-called findings uncritically; in 1941 it officially segregated African American soldiers and placed most of them in noncombat units. These actions disregarded the stellar performance of black soldiers in previous wars, as well as the valor shown by black servicemen in the earliest stages of World War II.

Indeed, blacks in military service sacrificed for their country from the very beginning of U.S. engagement in the conflict. On the morning of

December 7, 1941, Doris "Dorie" Miller (1919–1944) (see fig. 1), an African American sailor, was doing laundry abroad the battleship USS *West Virginia* in Pearl Harbor. As "Mess Attendant, second class" Miller gathered the laundry, he heard a loud and urgent summons to battle. Emerging from below deck, he saw Japanese fighter planes attacking U.S. naval forces, the harbor already engulfed in flames. He hurried to an antiaircraft station, only to find it shattered by a Japanese torpedo. Concerned for his crewmates, Miller pulled the captain and several others to safety under heavy enemy fire. He was an exceptionally strong man, having been a star football player in his hometown of Waco, Texas and a heavyweight boxing champion in West Virginia. After moving his fellow sailors out of harm's way, Miller returned to the bridge and commandeered a .50-caliber machine gun, despite having never before fired the weapon. Before the attack had ended he managed to shoot down at least two, and perhaps as many as six, enemy aircraft. "It wasn't hard," Miller recalled, "I just pulled the trigger and she worked fine."[4] On May 27, 1942, the U.S. Navy honored him for "distinguished devotion to duty, extraordinary courage and disregard for his own personal safety," and awarded him the Navy Cross. Thereafter, the Navy saw fit to "promote" Miller to "Cook, third class," moving him from the laundry room to the galley.

Miller's experience is emblematic of the Jim Crow mindset and policies of the U.S. military early in the war. Military bases offered little sanctuary from Jim Crow and white racism. Many commanding officers banned black newspapers on base, some resorting to burning these papers to isolate black servicemen from their community. African American soldiers were given fewer supplies and inferior food. They lived in the worst areas on base and were refused admission to officers' clubs, recreational facilities, and stores. Making matters worse, most military training camps were located in the South, where local residents mocked, discriminated against, or outright attacked both on-base and off-base African American soldiers. For these trainees, venturing off base, even in uniform, was taking their lives into their hands.

Many black soldiers who left base encountered life-threatening situations. When Air Corps cadet Lincoln J. Ragsdale drove his parents' car, a 1940 Buick, off base to a service station in Tuskegee, Alabama, he was followed, forced off the road, and removed from his car by three white police officers. "Blinded by the pitch darkness of a rainy night in Alabama," Ragsdale remembered, he "heard the cold steel click of a shotgun being

FIG. 1. Admiral Chester W. Nimitz pins the Navy Cross on Dorie Miller, the first Negro to win the award, in a ceremony aboard a warship at Pearl Harbor. © Bettmann/Corbis/AP Images (4206101448).

cocked."[5] A police officer shouted, "Let's get that nigger!" The policemen charged Ragsdale, knocked him down, and beat him within an inch of his life. As one of the officers prepared to fire the shotgun into the body of the overpowered and prone Ragsdale, one of them said, "Naw, let's just scare him." The men continued to beat Ragsdale until they grew too tired to continue, leaving him alone by the side of the road, face down in the mud, beaten, bruised, and frightened. He was hardly the only black soldier, however, to face such abuse. In a "white only" waiting room in a railroad station in Kentucky, three black soldiers were beaten by white civilian policemen for not deferring to white women when ordered to do so. Another African American soldier had his eyes gouged out by a white policeman in an altercation in South Carolina, and a white bus driver in North Carolina was found not guilty of murder after he killed a black soldier following an argument.

Even bodily harm did not top the list of infuriating aspects of black life in a white supremacist army. Perhaps most aggravating was the case of white German prisoners, whom the army treated better than its own black soldiers. Dempsey Travis, a black soldier from Chicago, was shocked to witness "German prisoners free to move around the camp, unlike black soldiers who were restricted. The Germans walked right into the doggone places like any white American. We wearin' the same uniform, but were excluded."[6] African Americans were treated so poorly that when Walter Winchell, the well-known newspaper columnist and radio commentator, asked a young black woman how Adolf Hitler should be punished, she answered "Paint him black and bring him over here."[7]

The majority of black soldiers were placed in auxiliary units, especially in the engineering and transportation corps. The transportation corps was nearly one-half black, and those who served in it loaded and carried supplies to the front lines. When U.S. forces pushed toward Germany in 1944 and 1945, black soldiers in the transportation corps withstood enemy fire to bring ammunition, fuel, and other essential items to soldiers on the front lines. African American combat units, including highly effective tankers in Europe, distinguished themselves in battle and were a source of pride for black people on the home front. African American engineers built roads, erected camps, and constructed ports. Black soldiers worked hard at and excelled in these duties because they truly wished to serve their country, yet they were subjected to unfair and often brutal discipline. In Europe, for instance, African American soldiers were executed in far greater numbers than white soldiers, despite the fact that black Americans constituted only 10 percent of all U.S. troops.

This type of treatment was also present in the Navy. One example is the treatment of African American soldiers at its Port Chicago base north of San Francisco. On July 17, 1944, munitions being loaded for transport to the Pacific theater exploded, killing 320 American sailors, 202 of whom were black. Following the incident, 328 of the surviving black soldiers stationed at the port were ordered to relocate to another ship to again load ammunition, of whom 258 protested and were summarily arrested. Around 50 of the dissenting soldiers were named as organizers of what became known as the "Port Chicago Mutiny." The men were charged with mutiny, convicted, and sentenced to prison terms as long as fifteen years, despite a brief filed in their defense by Thurgood Marshall, a young attorney for the NAACP.

Discontent was particularly intense among black military personnel in the Southwest. On Thanksgiving night, in 1942, in a café in Phoenix, Arizona, a black soldier from the 364th Infantry Regiment, who was stationed at the nearby Papago Park Army base, struck a black woman over the head with a bottle during a dispute. When white military policemen attempted to arrest the soldier, he brandished a knife and fought back vigorously. When the military policeman hurt the soldier after firing upon him, black servicemen in the café erupted in angry disapproval and broke ranks. Military policemen soon rounded up about one hundred and fifty random black soldiers, most of whom had nothing to do with the incident, and returned them to Papago Park. Buses were secured to transport the group. Before the groups boarded the buses, however, a jeep full of armed blacks, including soldiers and civilians, descended upon the area. The black soldiers became inflamed and broke rank. A "lone shot from somewhere" was fired, according to accounts; the source of the shot was never determined, but it ignited a riot. "This does it," one observer shouted, "now all hell will pop." The soldiers ran in all directions as handguns, rifles, and high-caliber automatic weapons furiously "snapped and barked." A "hunt" for everyone who fled the scene ensued.[8]

Phoenix's law enforcement authorities summoned all available police officers, ordering them to join the military police in apprehending the suspects. Twenty-eight blocks were cordoned off and searched. Several of the "hunted" soldiers hid in the homes of friends in the area. To "flush them out," the military police drove armored personnel carriers through the streets. An anonymous observer later recalled, "They'd roll up in front of these homes and with the loudspeaker they had on these vehicles, they'd call on him to surrender. If he didn't come out, they'd start potting the house with these fifty-caliber machine guns that just made a hole you could stick your fist through."[9] Before the tumultuous ordeal ended, three men died and eleven were wounded. Most of the men arrested and jailed were soon released, but some of those who bore arms during the riot were eventually court-martialed and sent to military prisons.

Disturbances occurred at other military bases in the Southwest as well, including Fort Huachuca, a military installation in the Southern Arizona desert. During the late nineteenth century, Fort Huachuca had been home to the all-black 9th and 10th Cavalries, the Buffalo Soldiers. During World War II, the fort housed the largest concentration of black soldiers in the nation, particularly after the army elected, in 1942, to establish the U.S. 93rd Infantry Division by combining the 25th, 368th, and 369th regiments with various field companies and battalions. The Buffalo Soldiers had been led by white officers; the 93rd, however, had nearly three hundred black officers. By December 1942, the 32nd and 33rd companies of the Women's Auxiliary Army Corps (WAAC) joined the men of the 93rd in the Sonoran desert (see fig. 2). These women served as postal clerks, stenographers, switchboard operators, truck drivers, and typists, freeing the men from these duties so they could train for combat. Despite their numbers and myriad duties, however, all black soldiers at Fort Huachuca were subjected to harassment and racial discrimination from white superiors. In 1942, black soldiers stationed at the fort protested after Arizona governor Sidney P. Osborn requested the Army's help in picking Arizona's long-staple cotton due to a farm labor shortage in the state. "I am sure there are many thousands of experienced cotton pickers at Huachuca," Osborne declared, "and I am sure that they could be put at nothing more necessary, essential or vital at this particular moment than aiding in the harvesting of this crop." African American soldiers at the fort reported the slight to the NAACP and the black press. Osborne defended his request as benign. The protests were heard, however, and the Army eventually postponed any plans to use troops in the cotton fields. Black soldiers were ridiculed and discriminated against for their stance, nonetheless, which aggravated racial tensions on the base.[10]

Gravely unhappy with the treatment of African American servicemen and servicewomen, William Hastie, the first African American judge of a federal District Court (Virgin Islands) and dean of the Howard University School of Law, A. Philip Randolph, Walter White, T. Arnold Hill, Lester Granger, Adam Clayton Powell Jr., Robert Vann, Mabel K. Staupers, and other prominent civil rights advocates organized black workers, women's groups, students, and interracial alliances to counter and upend discrimination in the military. They pushed the federal government and

FIG. 2. Maj. Charity E. Adams and Capt. Abbie N. Campbell inspect the first contingent of black members of the Women's Army Corps assigned to overseas duty, England, 1945. National Archives and Records Administration.

the military to address racial inequality at a time when both institutions were keenly interested in putting forth a unified face for the world to see.

Black Americans not only questioned their role in World War II, but they also tended to view Nazism and European imperialism in the same light as white supremacy in the United States. As historian Nell Irvin Painter has noted, columnist George Schuyler, writing for the *Pittsburgh Courier*, "likened German expansion in Europe to British colonialism in Africa." He argued that black Americans had no place in this conflict, asking, "Why should Negroes fight for democracy abroad when they were refused democracy in every American activity except tax paying?"[11] Dizzy Gillespie, the famous bebop trumpeter, responded to a summons by his local draft board by reminding the panel that he did not know what a German looked like, and was uncertain as to whom he would point his gun at if he were in battle:

> "In this stage of my life here in the United States whose foot," he queried rhetorically, "has not been in my ass?" At the same time, a play in New York City had a black soldier proclaim he would "fight Hitler, Musso-

lini, and the Japs all at the same time, but I'm telling you I'll give those crackers down South the same damn medicine." A black observer in North Carolina claimed, "No clear thinking Negro can long afford to ignore the Hitlers here in America."[12]

Many black activists sought to support African American troops by challenging their mistreatment by the federal government. In 1942, Randolph suggested that a national campaign of civil disobedience might be required to dramatize the plight of black Americans fighting battles for freedom on multiple fronts at home and abroad. He cautioned his fellow blacks not to sublimate the needs of African American communities to those of the nation; he wanted all black people to disregard the advice that W. E. B. Du Bois had issued to rally African American support for World War II.

Du Bois, a Harvard educated scholar, activist, and cofounder of the NAACP, had called upon blacks to fight for equal rights, the right to vote, and opportunities for higher learning. Racial parity, he argued, would only come through political organization, resistance, and protest. Anything less, he reasoned, confined African Americans to subservience and poverty. Du Bois encouraged African Americans to enlist and fight during World War I to "make the world safe for democracy." "Let, us, while this war lasts," he wrote, "forget our special grievances [with American racism] and close our ranks."[13]

Activists, such as Randolph, rejected Du Bois's call to arms in World War I and in World War II. "Negroes made the blunder of closing ranks and forgetting their grievances in the last war," Randolph stated. "We are resolved that we will not make that blunder again." Du Bois never questioned his own leadership during World War II, but he did admit that the so-called Great War "did not bring us democracy." Right after the bombing of Pearl Harbor, Du Bois reminded black people that progress would only arise through struggle: "We close ranks again but only, now as then, to fight for democracy, not democracy for white folks but for yellow, brown and black."[14] Although few blacks shared Du Bois's transnational and transracial vision of democracy, many did contemplate the conflict's effects on Africans and Asians.

The federal government grew particularly sensitive to any type of black resistance to the war effort, and it came down hard on anyone suspected of disloyalty. In 1942, a Red Scare–like crackdown by the Federal Bureau of Investigation (FBI) arrested more than eighty black critics of the military draft and the war. Among those arrested were leaders of the Nation of Islam (NOI), who had publicly refused to submit to the draft and fight in what they called a "white man's war." NOI leader Elijah Muhammad and many of his followers languished in prison for three years. In 1943, Bayard Rustin, a black activist and advocate of passive resistance who collaborated with Randolph on the MOWM, was arrested and sentenced to three years in prison when he failed to submit to induction.

Such threats did not deter prominent African Americans from protesting racism. Black movie star Lena Horne stopped one of her performances at Fort Riley, Kansas when she noticed German prisoners of war seated in the front rows and black American soldiers in the back, where they had been segregated by force. Horne left the stage, walked to the back of the hall, and sang directly to the black soldiers, to the consternation of white military personnel. African American soldiers also resisted second-class treatment. Jackie Robinson, a second lieutenant in the U.S. Army and a former star athlete at the University of California, Los Angeles (UCLA), was court-martialed, although eventually acquitted, for refusing to sit in the back of a segregated bus near Camp Hood (now Fort Hood), Texas in 1944. Although President Roosevelt had issued Executive Order #8802 back in 1941, racism in the armed forces persisted throughout the war. African American media and leftist organizations released myriad reports of black soldiers fighting racial prejudice at military installations across the nation.

African American Women

In 1942, the *Crisis,* the primary organ of the NAACP, noted:

[T]he colored woman has been a more potent factor in shaping Negro society than the white woman has been in shaping white society because the sexual caste system has been more fluid and ill-defined than among whites. Colored women have worked with their men and helped build and maintain every institution we have. Without their economic aid and counsel we would have made little if any progress.[15]

Black women played a critical role in protesting the U.S. military's racist policies and in opening up the armed services for black female participation. Their agitation led to their admittance into the Women's Auxiliary Corps, created as an extension of the armed services during the initial stages of the war. African American women's critical role in the military during World War II stood in stark contrast to the all-male military of preceding wars and conflicts and set the stage for the permanent involvement of black women in the nation's services.

Perhaps the most significant step forward for black women at the time was the trailblazing work of Mabel K. Staupers (1890–1989), who served as executive director of the National Association of Colored Graduate Nurses (NACGN). Staupers led the NACGN in a successful fight to end the quota system in the U.S. Army Nurse Corps. Despite the fact that many African American nurses volunteered to serve during World War II, the Army observed a strict quota and only admitted a very small number of African American women; the Navy rejected them altogether. Bold and determined, Staupers denounced these policies as discriminatory, and in November of 1944, she took her case directly to Eleanor Roosevelt. She explained to the First Lady that 82 black nurses were serving a mere 150 patients at Fort Huachuca, Arizona, at a time when the Army faced an acute nursing shortage and was considering the institution of a draft of white nurses. Even more insulting to Staupers were the instances in which black nurses were tasked to care for German prisoners of war at a higher percentage than white nurses. Staupers considered this situation unacceptable and an insult to the patriotism of black women. "When our women hear of the great need for nurses in the Army and when they enter the service," she stated, "it is with the high hopes that they will be used to nurse sick and wounded soldiers who are fighting our country's enemies and not primarily to take care of these enemies."[16]

Early in 1945, Staupers, the NACGN, and female nurses of all races responded to the War Department's claim of a continued shortage of nurses by protesting the exclusion and discriminatory treatment of black nurses in the Army and Navy Nurse Corps. Public support for their efforts to eliminate quotas was strong, as American citizens soon showered the War Department with correspondence condemning quotas and similar prohibitions. Quickly succumbing to this pressure in January of 1945, the Army and Navy desegregated the Nurse Corps of their respective branches and revised military policies to forbid discrimination on the basis of race. Shortly after this landmark policy change, Phyllis Daley became the first black woman accepted into the Navy Nurse Corps. More than three hundred African American women would ultimately serve in the Army Nurse Corps during World War II.

The military soon opened new doors to black men as well. By 1944 the Navy reluctantly began training black men as officers. Likewise, the Army gradually opened officer-training schools for black men and women. But the most impressive and celebrated example of the wartime history of black military advancement and resistance to white supremacy is the formation of the Army Air Corps fight school at Tuskegee Institute in Alabama. Many white people continued to believe that black people were not intelligent enough to operate technologically sophisticated machines, and certainly not airplanes. Despite the military establishment's lingering opposition to black people rising to the status of officer, factors such as the daring acts of early-twentieth-century pilots Bessie Coleman and Hubert Julian, pressure by black leaders, and the urgency of war finally led to the establishment of an all-black flight-officer training school in 1941. It was located at the predominantly black Tuskegee Institute, which had been founded on July 4, 1881 by Booker T. Washington, celebrated nineteenth-century African American champion of industrial education, self-sufficiency, and entrepreneurship. Capitalizing on the school's segregated yet established aeronautical engineering program, the Army Air Corps created the flight school, Tuskegee Army Airfield, for black men only.

At a time when African American men were believed, by most, to lack intelligence, skill, courage, and patriotism, the Tuskegee Airmen became America's first black military airmen. These men came from every section of the country, with large numbers coming from New York, Washington DC, Los Angeles, Chicago, Philadelphia, and Detroit. Each possessed a strong desire to serve the United States and show his quality. Most were college graduates or undergraduates. Others displayed their academic qualifications through comprehensive entrance examinations. Those who demonstrated intellectual acumen and physical strength were accepted as aviation cadets, trained initially as single-engine pilots, and later trained as twin-engine pilots, navigators, or bombardiers.

The first class of thirteen flying cadets of the 99th Pursuit Squadron began its training at Tuskegee on July 19, 1941. Cadets at Tuskegee received a grueling and rigorous education as they prepared for combat; they also endured the frustrations of being black in a training locale heavily populated by southern white officers who possessed deep-seated notions of white supremacy. As a consequence, most cadets "washed out," or dropped out, before graduation. Dogged by the physical and mental rigors of their training, intense competition, and institutional racism, successful cadets had to be intellectually formidable, strong communicators, and remarkably resilient.

Most of the cadets who "washed out" simply could not handle the intense psychological stress associated with their service and training and were not already oriented to military discipline or the intensity of military drilling. Those cadets from the North, particularly, clashed with abusive white southern officers. Some enlisted men, such as cadet Jimmy Moore, also succumbed to the constant abuse. Throughout most of his training, Moore patiently endured the harsh environment of the flight school. Then, just one day before his graduation, he "snapped," lashing out verbally at a white superior officer who had just hit him with a barrage of racial slurs. This incident abruptly ended Moore's military career.

The first class of Tuskegee cadets produced five graduates in March 1942: Captain Benjamin O. Davis Jr., George S. Roberts, Lemuel Custis, Charles De Bow, and Mac Ross. Davis Jr., the first black graduate of West Point in the twentieth century, was the son of Benjamin O. Davis Sr., the only senior black officer in the Army, who had become a brigadier general in 1941. Between March and September of 1942, thirty-three pilots received their wings. They were soon followed by additional officers eager to see action. These men quickly demonstrated their loyalty to their country and their ability to perform at the highest levels their training allowed. Dubbed the "Lonely Eagles" by the black press because of their small numbers and segregated status and "Red Tails" for the distinctive markings on their planes, these combat pilots came to be known by the entire nation as the "Tuskegee Airmen" (see fig. 3).

Once given the opportunity to fight, the Tuskegee Airmen proved themselves to be proficient in battle. The 99th Pursuit Squadron, which became the 332nd Fighter Group, was deployed in April 1943 to North Africa, where it flew its first combat mission against Italian and German forces on the island of Pantelleria on June 2, 1943. Davis Jr., who had been promoted to the rank of colonel, was placed in command of the 332nd Group when it was dispatched to Italy in January 1944. Davis Jr., like his father, would later rise to the rank of brigadier general. The Tuskegee fighters' duties included escorting bombers and participating in many other missions. The 332nd was instrumental in sinking an enemy destroyer in the Adriatic Sea, and it also protected the 15th Air Force bombers as they attacked strategically critical oil fields in Rumania (modern Romania).

FIG. 3. Tuskegee Airmen at the Negro Training Center examine a map before taking off in a biplane for a training exercise. *Left to right*: Lt. John Daniels of Chicago, Cadet Clayborne Lockett of Los Angeles, Cadet Lawrence O'Clark of Chicago, Cadet William Melton of Los Angeles, and civilian instructor Milton Crenshaw of Little Rock. © Bettmann/Corbis/AP Images (110928085577).

Under the command of Davis Jr., the fighter group won the admiration of African Americans throughout the United States and the respect of many officials in the Air Corps.

The Tuskegee Airmen flew more than 15,500 sorties and completed 1,578 missions. The 332nd demonstrated their impressive skill again as they escorted heavy bombers into Germany's Rhineland in two hundred separate missions without losing one fighter to enemy fire. It destroyed 409 enemy aircraft, sank 1 enemy destroyer, and eliminated myriad ground installations with strafing runs. On January 27, 1944, the 99th, commanded by William W. Momyer, shot down 5 enemy aircraft in less than four minutes, despite being outnumbered nearly two to one. In recognition of their service to their country, the Tuskegee Airmen collected 150 distinguished Flying Crosses, 1 Legion of Merit, 1 Silver Star, 14 Bronze Stars, and 744 Air Medals.

The Tuskegee Airmen were in good company. Nearly half a million other African American soldiers also distinguished themselves overseas. The 761st Tank Battalion, which served in six European nations and fought in the 1944 German counteroffensive known as the Battle of the Bulge, was cited for its courage under enemy fire. By the end of the war, many such units were given presidential citations for their role in the Allied victory. Furthermore, three African Americans earned the Navy Cross and eighty received the Distinguished Flying Cross. The success of the Tuskegee Airmen and their fellow black troops so impressed a military advisory board that its members recommended in 1944 that the armed services discard the general policy of withholding black soldiers from battle. During the final months of the European war, Allied Supreme Commander Dwight D. Eisenhower authorized an "experimental" departure from the military's segregationist policy when he permitted nearly forty black soldiers to serve as replacements in white units that had suffered heavy losses. In addition, 2,500 black volunteers were allowed to serve in platoons assigned to predominantly white infantry units. In a subsequent study of this experiment, white officers reported that the black troops performed "very well" in combat; unfortunately, top military officials at the time disparaged the study's conclusions and prevented its release to the public.

As a result of their participation in the war, many African Americans developed a renewed sense of self-esteem and devotion to the struggle for racial equality and black liberation. They were better educated than their predecessors in World War I, and more of them had entered the service with "radical" ideas of racial equality. They were self-assured and tended to compromise less than earlier generations of black soldiers. Sociologists St. Clair Drake and Horace Cayton commented on this transformation, explaining:

> At least half of the Negro soldiers who fall into this class were city people who had lived through a Depression in America's Black Ghettoes, and who had been exposed to unions, the Communist movement, and to the moods of racial radicalism that occasionally swept American cities. Even the rural southern Negroes were different this time, for the thirty years between the First and Second World War has seen a great expansion of school facilities in the South and distribution of newspapers and radios.[17]

Lincoln Ragsdale, one veteran of World War II, believed that it was his "Tuskegee experience" that emboldened him and gave him direction. "It gave me a whole new self-image," he maintained. He "remembered when we [Tuskegee Airmen] used to walk through black neighborhoods right after the war, and little kids would run up to us and touch our uniforms. 'Mister, can you really fly an airplane' they'd ask. The Tuskegee airmen gave blacks a reason to be proud."[18] Their service also gave the 2.5 million black veterans of World War II incentive to believe that they could achieve much more in their communities and the nation.

On the Home Front: A New Resolve, Migration, and Labor

African Americans fought for democracy and racial equality on the home front as well. The war fundamentally changed the consciousness of the nation's black community. Black laborers and volunteers produced goods and purchased bonds for the war effort, while transformations engendered by the war created new problems and aggravated old ones. At times, this volatile mix of unprecedented change and trouble erupted into violence in cities throughout the United States. Protest groups, African American leaders, and the black press fought employment discrimination, political exclusion, and segregation for the duration of the war.

The fight to preserve democracy abroad deeply affected black communities, even shifting their regions of residence. The war most significantly altered the African American West, as black people flocked to the region seeking jobs in desegregated military industries such as shipyards and munitions factories. Other African Americans first came west upon their assignment to western military bases. During the 1940s, the West's black population grew by 443,000, or 33 percent. The largest urban areas of the region hosted increases in the African American population, ranging from 168 percent in the city of Los Angeles to an incredible 798 percent in San Francisco. Increases were not as striking in the Hawaiian Islands and the Southwest, but cities in both regions also witnessed rising black populations. The number of black Phoenicians surged from 4,263 in 1940 to 5,217 in 1950. These growing populations ushered in social, economic, and political change. The majority of the black migrants of this decade hailed from Oklahoma, Texas, Louisiana, and Arkansas. Fifty-three percent of the migrants were women, most of whom were married. The rise of the black population in the West, and a smaller rise in the North, mirrored a reduction of the black southern population, which fell from 77 percent in 1940 to 68 percent by 1950. The most significant rise in a single area's African American population occurred in Southern California, where the aeronautical industry, the hard work of protest groups, and the federal government's enforcement of antidiscrimination labor statutes all helped the black community of greater Los Angeles (city and suburban municipalities) grow by 340,000 during World War II.[19]

Nevertheless, before and after the war, the majority white population in the American West expected African Americans to remain socioeconomically subordinate. White supremacy and Jim Crow were, unfortunately, alive and well in Southwestern cities such as Phoenix, where race relations, if they were not as rigid, volatile, and capricious, still resembled those in the South.

African American migrants brought to the West a less conciliatory approach to racism than had previously existed in the west, and also a desire for positive change. Pressure from black activists, for example, pushed the California legislature to consider bills that would outlaw racial discrimination in workplaces and public accommodation by 1943. In Denver, black protesters eliminated legal segregation in theaters. Victories over job discrimination and Jim Crow were more elusive in the Southwest, however. In Phoenix, for example, segregation endured. Still, the prospect of good jobs and dreams of a freer life increased the black western population tenfold and intensified the region's burgeoning civil rights movement.

The war also quickened the migration of black people from rural to urban areas in the South and North. Despite an improving farm economy, the lure of high-paying defense jobs, as well as the accoutrements of urban life, prompted many black farmers to relocate. Moreover, recent advances in global competition and agricultural technology greatly diminished the need for black laborers in many rural areas. By the end of the war, a mere 28 percent of black men worked on farms, which constituted a reduction of 13 percent since 1940 alone. Wartime needs and government pressures had prompted industry to hire more black workers in urban areas, creating additional reasons to migrate. The number of African American workers in nonagricultural jobs rose from 2.9 million to 3.8 million during the war, as thousands of black people secured jobs not previously available to them. With so many black men in the military, new employment opportunities particularly benefited black women, who took positions outside the purview of domestic work in unprecedented numbers. Across the nation six hundred thousand black women, of whom four hundred thousand were former servants, transitioned into industrial work.

Organized labor also became more welcoming to blacks during the war. African American union membership increased from 200,000 to 1.25 million between 1940 and 1945. Unions affiliated with the Congress of Industrial Organizations (CIO), chiefly the United Automobile Workers (UAW), were particularly open to accepting black workers. AFL affiliates, however, continued to refuse admission to African Americans. Greater involvement in unions, although it was not without problems, helped black Americans establish significant networks that would aid in their fight against lingering racial discrimination in the workplace.

As they had in the past, African American leaders looked to the federal government for support in their battle against racial inequality. Randolph and his supporters were disappointed with the ineffectiveness of the FEPC during the early stages of the war. Randolph urged the MOWM to respond with plans for another protest. Once again, President Roosevelt avoided a public confrontation by issuing Executive Order #9346 in May 1943. In several important ways, this order built upon the foundation laid by Executive Order #8802. Executive Order #9346 placed the FEPC within the Office of Emergency Management (OEM), forerunner of the Federal Emergency Management Agency (FEMA), and the OEM was beholden only to Roosevelt in his office as President. The order itself required that (a) all government contracts, and not simply military contracts, include a nondiscrimination clause, and that (b) the number of FEPC committee members and their salaries be increased. Roosevelt appointed Malcolm Ross, a fiery white liberal, to chair the committee. Ross presided over hearings for cases involving allegations of discrimination in a wide range of industries, but especially in railroads and shipping. The hearings were fairly successful. Between 1943 and 1946, more than fourteen thousand complaints were filed with the FEPC, of which more than five thousand were resolved successfully. The committee encountered staunch resistance, however, particularly in the South. In some cases, it was not uncommon for the FEPC to acquiesce to long-established southern racial mores regarding the treatment of laborers.

Randolph and his contemporaries were not the only people fighting for African Americans at this time. The war years witnessed the emergence of an increasing number of younger black activists who embraced and developed more direct methods to challenge racial injustice. In 1942, Pauli

Murray joined the Fellowship of Reconciliation (FOR), an international pacifist group founded in 1914. That year, the FOR unveiled its nonviolent methods on the campus of Howard University, which Murray attended as a law student. She knew that black FOR members were studying and incorporating the strategies of Mahatma Gandhi to confront racial segregation. James Farmer, an alumnus of Howard's school of religion and the FOR's "race relations secretary," united the organization in 1943 with an interracial group of activists in Chicago to found the Committee of Racial Equality (CRE). Murray also developed a close relationship with Bayard Rustin, also of the FOR. Like Murray, Rustin was a veteran of the leftist activism of the Great Depression era. After becoming disillusioned with the Young Communist League, to which he had previously belonged, Rustin looked to the FOR as his political activist outlet. Murray and Rustin were also intimately aware of the stigma, trauma, and frustration associated with discrimination on several inextricably linked fronts. Murray experienced bigotry as an African American and as a woman, whereas Rustin was victimized as a black man and a homosexual during an era when homophobia was not acknowledged, let alone confronted.

Murray's activism and devotion to Gandhian principles were soon tested. In June 1944, Howard students protested the arrest of three black female students who had refused to leave a lunch counter at an all-white café adjacent to campus. Murray served as an unofficial legal advisor for the students as they considered the legal ramifications of their civil disobedience and the legal options available to the arrested students. Eventually the students were released on bail, and the charges were dropped as a result of Murray's representation and mounting pressure from the black community. During the spring of 1943 she also participated in a student protest of the Little Palace Cafeteria near Howard, marching alongside picketers who bore signs that read; "We Die Together, Why Can't We Eat Together?" Protestors made their way into the diner; when they were refused service, they took their empty trays, sat down in open seats, and read their school books. The students staged these famous "sit-downs," which foreshadowed the "sit-ins" of the 1960s, for three days. On the final day, the owner of the restaurant relented and permitted black people to eat at his establishment. Murray recalled feeling "jubilant" after their victory. She believed that the protest "proved that intelligent, imaginative action could bring positive results." She also noted that twelve of the nineteen protestors were black women. "We women," she stated, "reasoned that it was our job to help make the country for which our black brothers were fighting a freer place in which to live when they returned from wartime services."[20]

Racial friction remained high during the war, and some tensions were not eased through nonviolent civil disobedience. Indeed, the eruption of racial violence in numerous cities nationwide during the summer of 1943 quickly muted the optimism that Murray felt following her successful protest against white supremacy in Washington DC. One of the most violent and deadly race riots in U.S. history unfolded in Detroit that summer. Murray argued that "few Negroes were surprised" by the explosion of violence, as "the racial tension that produced it had been building steadily throughout the war."[21]

The unrest in Detroit emerged from a unique context. During the war the city's highly productive factories churned out everything from tanks to airplanes. Detroit's booming industry attracted fifty thousand black Americans between 1942 and 1950. Overcrowding in the city's neighborhoods and fierce competition for jobs and resources undermined the hope for interracial coalition building fostered by the integrated CIO. Thousands of white UAW members walked out of a factory to protest the promotion of eight black workers, all of whom were also members of the UAW. Similarly, employers at the Packard plant organized a "hate strike" in opposition to the hiring of three black women as drill operators. In addition, three African American families tried to move into the federally funded, all-white Sojourner Truth Housing Project in Detroit in February 1942, only to be greeted by an angry mob of white people, comprising young and old, male and female. Many members of the mob wielded guns, knives, or bats. The white mob attacked the black families and any African American they could find in the area. Black residents fought back with guns, knives, and any weapons they could get their hands on. Some seventeen hundred National Guardsmen were summoned to reestablish order. The threat of more violence, however, engulfed the city, prompting city leaders to assure white residents that future housing projects would adhere to established racial demographics of area neighborhoods, so as not to introduce more African Americans into white communities. This procedure was quickly implemented in cities across the nation to preserve de facto and de jure residential segregation.

Back in Detroit, frustration again boiled over into outright violence. On June 20, 1943, a riot ensued after a fist fight broke out between a black man and a white man at the sprawling Belle Isle Amusement Park along the banks of the Detroit River. The fight quickly escalated into a melee between warring factions of blacks and whites, and spilled into the city. The rioters looted and burned buildings, most of them in and around Paradise Valley, one of the oldest and poorest neighborhoods in Detroit. As the violence intensified, blacks dragged whites out of cars and destroyed white-owned shops in Paradise Valley, while whites overturned and burned black-owned automobiles and assaulted blacks on streetcars and in major intersections. The predominantly white Detroit police did little to stop the bloodshed. In fact, many police officers joined white rioters in attacking blacks, including those attempting to flee the carnage.

The Detroit riot of 1943 ended only after President Roosevelt, at the request of Mayor Edward Jeffries Jr., ordered six thousand federal troops to enter and occupy the city on June 21, by which time twenty-five blacks and nine whites lay dead. Perhaps most disturbingly, of the twenty-five African Americans who perished, seventeen died at the hands of the police. Detroit law enforcement argued that the shootings were justified because the victims had been caught looting stores. In remarkable contrast, none of the whites who died were killed by the police. Some seven hundred people were injured in the violence, and the city suffered upward of $2 million in property damage. Many white residents of Detroit blamed the riot on the black press and the NAACP, arguing that black Detroiters had pushed too hard for economic and political equality and had been unduly influenced by communist agitators. Conversely, black leaders, leftist trade unionists, other racial and ethnic groups, and Jewish organizations blamed the riot on a plethora of white supremacist groups and terrorist outfits, such as the Black Dragon Society, the KKK, the Christian Front, the Knights of the White Camelia, the National Workers Leagues, and the Southern Voters League.

Although African American leaders were unified in their denunciation of the violence in Detroit and the racism that spawned the riot, they increasingly disagreed on how they should proceed to confront racial injustice. The NAACP, whose numbers swelled from 50,000 in 1940 to 450,000 by 1945, benefited greatly from the "Double V" campaign and the far reach of the *Crisis*. Dissension existed in the ranks, however. Members argued over the merits of integration versus black nationalism or self-segregation. Some black people also questioned the efficacy of mounting legal challenges to segregation on behalf of job applicants, students, and the middle class and urged NAACP leadership to turn their attention to poor and working-class African Americans instead. The newer civil rights organizations beckoned younger, more militant blacks, persons attracted by the new groups' strategy of direct action against white supremacy. Meanwhile, existing organizations retooled. In 1944, southern white liberals united with black people to forge the Southern Regional Council (SRC). Initially founded in 1919 as the Commission on Interracial Cooperation, the reconstituted SRC immediately declared its intention to combat "the intractable issue of racial injustice in the South." The interracial SRC fought against lynchings, stereotypical black roles in Hollywood, and other issues "most important to race and democracy." The SRC published academic works focusing on race and racism, and challenged racial injustice in the media. The most vociferous group to emerge during this era, however, was an offshoot of the CRE, the Congress of Racial Equality (CORE).

As an interracial group of activists in Chicago founded the Committee of Racial Equality (CRE) at Howard University, some in the newly created CRE also worked to establish a national civil rights organization. That vision jelled in the Congress of Racial Equality (CORE) founded in 1942 by Bernice Fisher, James R. Robinson, Joe Guinn, George Houser, Homer Jack, and James Farmer. Many of these students, including Farmer, were members of the Chicago branch of the FOR. Like those who created FOR, CORE's founders were deeply influenced by the nonviolent resistance teachings of Gandhi. CORE began as a "non-hierarchical, decentralized organization funded entirely by the voluntary contributions of its members."[22] Farmer and George Houser, a white University of Chicago student, served as the organization's first leaders.

CORE members worked to challenge racial inequality. Initially the organization protested segregation in public accommodations. Farmer traveled to states in the Midwest with Bayard Rustin, who was serving as FOR's field secretary and primary recruitment officer. Farmer and Rustin successfully recruited many white college students, primarily from the Midwest. Despite the quick growth of the organization, CORE did not present a unified front to the nation, for its officers and members believed that bringing local chapters under national control would contradict their opposition to hierarchy. The lack of centralized national leadership, however, resulted in ideological differences among chapters. For example, some chapters embraced pacifism whereas others sought out opportunities for direct action. This tension permeated CORE throughout its early existence.

Nevertheless, over time, CORE successfully integrated some places of public accommodation in the North and South by engaging in nonviolent sit-ins and pickets. As CORE continued to grow, its membership decided they needed an energetic leader to link the goals and tactics of local chapters with a unified national agenda: Farmer was elected the organization's National Director in 1953.

Seeking to end racial discrimination, white and black people established other new organizations throughout the United States. In 1943 activists of various racial and ethnic backgrounds in Los Angeles established the Council on Civic Unity, which championed interracial understanding and contested racial injustice. The Los Angeles–based group was duplicated in several western cities. In Arizona, for example, a similar organization was founded in the late 1940s.

African Americans' various approaches to the race problem were as heterogeneous as black people themselves. Black women founded political councils and protest organizations in African American neighborhoods throughout the South and Midwest to aid in efforts to fight racial segregation. Other African American women addressed injustice through their art and literary works. Still others, such as Rosa Parks, an active member of the Montgomery, Alabama NAACP during the 1940s, and Ella Baker, the NAACP's national field secretary during the same period, would go on to become revered civil rights leaders during the 1950s and 1960s.

African American students, especially those who attended predominantly black colleges, began to protest the segregated environments of their cities and towns on a regular basis. The protest led by Murray and FOR in 1943 helped ignite a groundswell of student insurgency that reverberated for the next two decades. The reach of Murray's work extended as far west as Phoenix, where sixteen-year-old Opal Ellis, a black female student at Phoenix's segregated George Washington Carver School and a member of the local NAACP's Youth Auxiliary, led a sit-in at the city's segregated Woolworth's store, one of the first sit-ins west of the Mississippi River.

Yet as World War II came to a close, an expanding and more dynamic movement for racial justice was tempered by the staggering reality of demobilization. Ultimately, the Double V campaign proved to be bittersweet: sweet because African Americans had made many socioeconomic advances, but bitter because, despite these gains, African Americans remained subjected to economic oppression and segregation in schools, places of public accommodation, and residential areas across the nation.

Following the surrender of Germany and then Japan in 1945, the United States shifted from war mobilization to peacetime demobilization. Many of the inroads that black people had made during the war were erased when soldiers were discharged and factories returned to their prewar discriminatory practices. By 1945, however, things had changed. No longer would African Americans accept second-class citizenship. Instead, black people stood poised and ready to fight, willing to adopt new strategies for advancement in the postwar world.

African Americans and the Cold War

The relationship between the United States and the international community remained complicated well after the war ended. In 1945 the United Nations, formed in San Francisco in June of that year, began to shape the postwar world. Before long, the diverging interests of the world's new "superpowers," the United States and the Soviet Union, developed into a decades-long period of disagreement and hostility known as the Cold War. These two nations could not reconcile their ideological differences regarding religious beliefs, individual rights, and human rights. The United States was an unapologetic capitalist society built upon the notion of individual freedom and democracy, whereas the Soviet Union was a communist nation forged by principles of collectivism and social control. The defeat of the German and Japanese empires created large vacuums of power that both America and Russia sought to fill. Simultaneously, the destruction of Western Europe and the inability of its nations to retain their colonial possessions in Asia, Africa, and Latin America led to revolutions that created newly independent nations that both superpowers hoped to influence, if not to control outright. The Cold War world, therefore, was an unpredictable and volatile world in which global tensions framed domestic and foreign policy.

American leaders followed a policy of "containment," an attempt to stop the spread of the Soviet Union's power and communist ideology. In 1949, the United States played a key role in founding the North Atlantic Treaty Organization (NATO), which it hoped would serve to offset Soviet power in Eastern Europe while simultaneously shielding Western Europe as these nations rebuilt from the devastation of war. When Asian and African countries secured their independence from occupation and colonial rule during the 1950s and 1960s, the United States fought to restrict Soviet influence on these new nations as well. The American government executed this agenda through the auspices of the Marshall Plan (1941–1947), a financial and humanitarian effort aimed at creating a stronger economic and social foundation for European countries. It also sought to stabilize Western Europe, Japan, and the newly independent nations through secret operations carried out by the recently created Central Intelligence Agency (CIA) and through military force.

Throughout the Cold War, America generated state-sponsored propaganda that attempted to persuade the so-called Third World that the United States was, indeed, an exemplar state to follow and befriend. The Cold War influenced the worldview of all Americans at this time. At the same time, the launch of the most productive stage of the long struggle for civil rights challenged the nation to finally fulfill its promises of freedom and democracy to all its citizens. Indeed, the connections between the Cold War and the civil rights movement are profound. The United States was so wrapped up in promoting its self-image of a bastion of unfettered freedom, under siege by evil communists abroad and recalcitrant black people at home, that it created an atmosphere of paranoia (McCarthyism, a subset of the Red Scare). Meanwhile, its treatment of African Americans undercut its own ideals and its efforts to present itself as a beacon of democracy.

The Cold War also coincided with the rise of the U.S. military-industrial complex, which established the United States as the most powerful military state in the world. The federal government maintained this new massive power through the direct employment of millions of Americans and appropriations that covered an unprecedented number of government contracts to construction companies and weapons manufacturers. This expansion in the size and budget of the federal government resulted in a shift of regional power. In particular, the power that southern politicians held over the national government weakened, which also led to a decline in the control that these politicians wielded over national race relations. By virtue of the sheer numbers of people of color who resided in emerging nations in Africa, Asia, and Latin America, American foreign policymakers were now compelled to be mindful in their dealings with regard to race and culture, both at home and abroad. Indeed, some foreign nations viewed the exploitation of African Americans as an indication that the U.S. government was not, in fact, the bastion of freedom it claimed to be. To make a case for communism and elevate its status in the world, the Soviet Union loudly questioned America's commitment to freedom and democracy, eager to draw attention to the unjust ways in which the United States treated it citizens of color. Therefore, throughout the Cold War, pressures from abroad fortified movements to advance the cause of civil and human rights within the United States.

In this way, the Cold War provided black leaders with opportunities to comment on international affairs. W. E. B. Du Bois and Ralph Bunche, for example, offered divergent perspectives on the role that the United States should play during the period. Du Bois had long believed that the destinies of Africans and African Americans were inextricably linked. By 1945, many people considered him the "Father of Pan-Africanism." That year, he presided over the fifth Pan-Africanist Congress, held in Manchester, England. Du Bois and many of the Africans who attended the meeting, the latter newly radicalized by World War II and the ensuing decolonization movements, called for the denunciation of Western imperialism. Du Bois believed that the United States enabled colonialism, proclaiming, "We American Negroes should know [that] until Africa is free, the descendants of Africa the world over cannot escape their chains. The NAACP should therefore put in the forefront of its program the freedom of Africa in work and wage, education and health, and the complete abolition of the colonial system."[23]

Bunche approached foreign policy very differently, and he elected to work within established American systems of governance and diplomacy. Bunche, an American political scientist, diplomat, and civil rights advocate, played an instrumental role in the formation and administration of the United Nations; he served as the assistant to the United Nations Special Committee on Palestine, and thereafter as the principal secretary of the UN Palestine Commission. Most of all, he played a major role in establishing a peace agreement between Israel and the Arab states in 1949, for which he was awarded the Nobel Peace Prize in 1950. He felt great concern for the condition of people of African descent in America and abroad. Always conscious of the status of people of African descent, he argued:

> Today, for all thinking people, the Negro is the shining symbol of the true significance of democracy. He has demonstrated what can be achieved with democratic liberties even when grudgingly and incompletely bestowed. But the most vital significance of the Negro to American society is the fact that democracy which is not extended to all of the nation's citizens is a democracy that is mortally wounded.[24]

In contrast to Bunche, Du Bois, with his confrontational nature, did not win any peace prizes. Rather, his forceful critique of American imperialism, combined with the paranoia of millions of Americans, landed him in a web of anticommunist suspicion and anger. In the sobering American environment of the Cold War, black Americans with connections to the Communist Party of America (CPUSA), as well as those who denounced the United States for virtually any reason, were singled out for distrust and interrogation. Celebrated writers Langston Hughes and Richard Wright were forced to defend their patriotism before the House Un-American Activities Committee (HUAC), whereas even established civil rights leaders such as Thurgood Marshall and Walter White, persons with no communist connections whatsoever, took great care to support the federal government's anticommunist rhetoric and actions explicitly to protect themselves from the witch hunt. These men and other leaders of African American communities were particularly careful to align themselves with the pro–civil rights efforts of Harry S. Truman, who, as vice president, assumed the presidency upon Roosevelt's death on April 12, 1945.

From the beginning, the Truman administration was swept up in the whirl of anticommunist fear and panic that was consuming the nation. Truman endorsed loyalty programs in which government employees were fired when suspected (by virtually anyone willing to accuse them) of disloyalty to the United States. This environment of paranoia regarding the spread of communism soon developed into so-called "red-baiting" within the government itself. The charge came to be embodied by Senator Joseph McCarthy (R-WI), who used the Senate Permanent Subcommittee on Investigations to hunt for communists and turned "McCarthyism" into a popular movement to glorify himself, crusade against the notion of communist sympathy, and root out anyone identified as communist sympathizers. McCarthy's targets eventually spread to the entire U.S. citizenry, with a particular focus upon those in Hollywood and the entertainment industry. Outspoken and elderly scholars were targeted by HUAC as well; the eighty-three-year-old Du Bois was indicted on February 8, 1951, and called an "agent of a foreign principal" for his collaboration with the Peace Information Center. Although HUAC had dismissed the charge by November 1951 due to lack of evidence the indictment, nonetheless, castigated Du Bois for his activism and shed light on his difficult relationships with other black activists. Indeed, many African Americans failed to defend his name following the indictment, both out of fear that they themselves might be the next target by HUAC and because many of them had long been criticized by Du Bois and were not particularly interested in defending him now.

Other prominent African Americans, including the outspoken singer and actor Paul Robeson, were also brought before HUAC. Robeson, unlike many of those dragged before HUAC, had worked with the CPUSA during the 1930s. He had also traveled at one time to the Soviet Union as one of a wave of liberal activists who initially supported the rise of communism in the Soviet Union. Most of his fellow travelers ended their support of the Soviet Union either upon learning of the pact between the Soviet Union and Germany in 1939, or later, when the genocide and state-sponsored violence the Soviet government used to maintain the Soviet state and its satellites became known. Robeson, however, did not end his support of the Soviet Union, and continued to speak publicly on the nation's behalf in the United States. He argued, for example, that "it is unthinkable that American Negroes would go to war on behalf of those [United States] that have oppressed us for generations against a county [the Soviet Union] which in one generation has raised our people to full human dignity of mankind." In the highly charged atmosphere of the Cold War, the general public was quick to criticize Robeson's views and denounce him for them. For instance, a Robeson concert, held on August 27, 1949, in Peekskill, New York, was disrupted by crowds of local whites who, before Robeson arrived, attacked concertgoers with baseball bats and rocks. At another Robeson concert, in Peekskill, on September 4, 1949, marauding groups of protesters burned crosses on a nearby hill, and a jeering crowd threw rocks and chanted, "Dirty commie" and "Dirty kikes." Robeson, who was on his way to perform, made more than one attempt to get out of the car and confront the mob but was restrained by his friends.[25] Given the fear-mongering of HUAC at the time, it is not surprising that Robeson soon found himself before the committee. In 1950 the State Department revoked his passport, and he was consequently unable to leave the United States legally until 1958, when the U.S. Supreme Court declared this and other travel bans unconstitutional. As a performer and artist with an international following, Robeson found revocation of his passport to be particularly punitive. During another HUAC investigation into Robeson, in 1956, the activist and artist refused to pledge, in writing, that he was no longer a member of the CPUSA. These investigations contributed mightily to the end of Robeson's long and successful career.

The persecution of Robeson illustrates the conservative maneuvering that undermined progressive influences in the black freedom struggle. By 1948, African Americans constituted a critical political constituency. Their needs emerged as inescapable issues for anyone seeking public office to address, particularly those desiring the office of the presidency. African Americans' rising political influence, coupled with their country's budding fidelity to emerging nations and the rise of the civil rights movement, facilitated major changes in the federal government's relations with black people. Furthermore, a Communist coup in Czechoslovakia in February 1948 reignited tensions between the United States and the Soviet Union. Many officials in both countries believed a war between the superpowers was imminent. Ranking leaders in the U.S. military worried about the nation's ability to prosecute such a war, in part because black Americans had already voiced their opposition to ever serving again in racially segregated armed services. In response to Truman's move to resuscitate the draft, Randolph threatened the federal government with massive black resistance to induction.

Randolph meant what he said, and he wasted no time preparing to battle the segregation of the U.S. military. In 1947, he had formed the League for Non-Violent Civil Disobedience against Military Segregation (NCDAMS). Through this organization, in 1948, he warned America that African Americans would not comply with a racially segregated draft. From his pulpit and his seat in Congress, the outspoken Adam Clayton Powell Jr., a fearless, dashing, and highly controversial minister and Harlem, New York activist, championed Randolph's stance. Indeed, Powell proclaimed that the United States did not possess enough jails to accommodate all of the black people who would refuse to serve. On June 24, 1948, pressure increased on the Truman administration when the Soviet Union instituted a military blockade on the divided city of Berlin in Germany. Truman viewed this action as a potential precursor to war, and he could ill afford to be drawn into a volatile and protracted conflict with African Americans on the eve of a potential conflict with the Soviet Union.

To appease Randolph and his black constituency, Truman publicly recognized the need for progress in American race relations when he created a special commission on civil rights. Its report, entitled *To Secure These Rights*, called on the federal government to deliver what the NAACP and other groups had begun requesting decades earlier: a federal antilynching law; equal opportunity in education, employment, and housing; the end to all poll taxes that limited a citizens' ability to vote; and the end of racial segregation in the military. Upon receiving the report, Truman asked for the instantaneous execution of these requests in a special address to Congress on July 26, 1948. Southern Senators filibustered the measures, prompting Truman to issue Executive Order #9981, which desegregated the U.S. Armed Forces. Although the power of southern senators prevented many of the report's recommendations from becoming law, Truman's action had been bold and clear. Following the issuance of the executive order, Randolph and Grant Reynolds, cochair of NCDAMS, dissolved the organization and canceled all planned protests against the military and federal government.

Though Truman courted black voters with his pro–civil rights overtures and executive order, a large number of black and white leftists threw their support behind Henry Wallace, the Progressive Party's presidential candidate in the election of 1948. Wallace campaigned aggressively throughout the South for black civil rights. He endeared himself to African Americans with his down-to-earth style and wit, and he impressed them by refusing to address segregated gatherings. Those who supported Wallace included a number of persons affiliated with the CPUSA, including Hosea Hudson, a well-known Alabama Communist. These controversial associates eventually destroyed Wallace's chances for election. Moreover, the Democratic presidential nominating convention embraced a civil rights platform as well. This prompted many progressives to support Truman as the Democratic Party candidate. Many blacks also supported Truman because he was a member of the same political party as Senator Hubert Humphrey, whom they thought well of in light of his support for civil rights. The Democrats also benefited because they lacked Wallace's political baggage. In the end, foreign and domestic pressures, as well as political dynamics and transformations, led to the Democratic Party's support for the civil rights of black Americans and its selection of Truman as its candidate. At the same time, however, support for black rights hurt the Democrats in the South, commencing the white shift to the Republican Party. In 1948, a group of white right-wing Democrats organized by southerners who objected to the Democrat's Civil Rights Platform formed the Dixiecrat Party in Birmingham, Alabama. The Dixiecrat Party nominated Governor Strom Thurmond of South Carolina for President in 1948. In the general election he received more than 1 million votes and carried four states.

African Americans continued to make advances in the worlds of arts, sports, and entertainment during the Cold War. Though the big bands of the swing era struggled to survive by the late 1940s, popular singers such as Ella Fitzgerald, Nat "King" Cole, Sarah Vaughn, and Billie Holiday continued to have successful careers. Increasingly static and often overly orchestrated swing music inspired young jazz artists, such as saxophonist Charlie Parker, trumpeter Dizzy Gillespie, and pianist Thelonious Monk, to create their own more fluid and dynamic style of music. These musicians abandoned big bands for small, concentrated, experimental ensembles, known for playing a new, more popular genre called bebop. Although bebop quickly became a popular new genre of music, gospel music and "race music," which would soon come to be known as rhythm and blues (R&B), became more popular and long-lasting. By 1950 African American gospel was featured at Carnegie Hall when Joe Bostic produced the Negro Gospel and Religious Music Festival. Black gospel and white gospel quickly emerged as distinct genres, with specific audiences. Black gospel artists, such as the celebrated Mahalia Jackson, found success among black and white listeners. Most black gospel artists, however, were shunned by the predominantly white gospel mainstream. "Race music," a fusion of African American music genres such as blues, jazz, and gospel, soon coalesced into a distinct genre called rhythm and blues. Song writers and recording artists such Little Richard, Ike Turner, and Ray Charles combined the music of the black church and southern blues clubs, or "juke joints," to forge the bedrock of R&B.

Writers also met with continued success. The highly acclaimed poet Gwendolyn Brooks, for example, garnered numerous awards and honors for her work, including Guggenheim Fellowships in 1946 and 1947 and a Pulitzer Prize for poetry for "Annie Allen" in 1950. She was the first African American ever to receive a Pulitzer in any category. Black film stars also found new opportunities. Lena Horne, Ethel Waters, Eddie Robinson, Butterfly McQueen, and Bill Robinson starred in films such as *Cabin in the Sky* (1943) and *Stormy Weather* (1943), which boasted all-black casts and played to large black and interracial audiences. These stars often lamented the fact that Hollywood film makers had pigeonholed black actors and actresses, largely limiting them to stereotypical roles such as "Mammies" and "Uncle Toms." Many black people today, however, view these actors as pioneers who made the most of the limited opportunities offered to them.

Jackie Robinson (1919–72), a professional athlete and advocate for black freedom, is perhaps the most iconic figure of black pride during the Cold War years (see fig. 4). Jack Roosevelt Robinson was born in Cairo, Georgia, where he was reared in destitution as the first of five children born to a single mother. Not long after Jackie's father abandoned his family, his mother, Mallie Robinson, joined the exodus of African Americans leaving the South and moved her children and extended family of thirteen west to Pasadena, California. Jackie attended John Muir High School, then Pasadena Junior College, where he proved himself an exceptional athlete capable of playing football, basketball, and baseball, as well as running track. In 1938 he was named the region's Most Valuable Player in baseball. He remained in school, however, at the University of California, Los Angeles, where he made history by becoming the first student to collect varsity letters in four sports. As previously mentioned, Robinson was drafted by the U.S. Army in 1942, but his service ended promptly (he was honorably discharged), when he refused to submit to the Army's policies of racial segregation. His courageous protest of Jim Crow in the military presaged his impact on professional baseball and American society.

Following his discharge from the Army in 1944, Robinson played in the Negro Leagues, his first experience with professional baseball. Soon thereafter, something momentous happened: Robinson was selected by Branch Rickey, a vice president with the Brooklyn Dodgers, to integrate major league baseball. In preparation for the move, Rickey signed Robinson to the Montreal Royals, a farm team for the Brooklyn Dodgers, in 1945. Rickey knew that Robinson would face difficult times as a young black athlete in professional baseball, which was then wholly dominated by whites. In fact, Rickey made Robinson promise to keep his composure when he became the target of white racism. As Rickey had expected, Robinson was tested the minute he stepped onto the field. Many of his white teammates shunned and harassed him, and fans jeered, cursed, spat, and threw things at him. He and his family even received death threats on a daily basis.

Despite the racial abuse he endured, Robinson distinguished himself as a professional athlete and was brought up to the Dodgers the next year. He took the field on April 15, 1947, becoming the first African American to play in baseball's major leagues. Players on rival teams said that they would

FIG. 4. Jackie Robinson talking to his son Jackie Robinson Jr., February, 20, 1950. AP Photo (500220049).

not play against the Dodgers because of Robinson's presence. Even some of his Brooklyn Dodgers teammates threatened to sit out games in which Robinson played. However, not all of Robinson's teammates shared the same opinion. League President Ford Frick and Baseball Commissioner Happy Chandler put their administrative support behind Robinson, as did Hank Greenberg and Dodgers captain Pee Wee Reese, two popular players. Reese, in particular, showed a physical act of support by putting his arm around Robinson after fans continually heckled and yelled racist insults. In spite of the harassment from fans and certain teammates,

Robinson stood courageous on the field and resisted the temptation to respond to his hecklers, either verbally or otherwise. He more than proved his worth on the field, hitting twelve home runs in his first year alone, leading the league in stolen bases, and helping the Dodgers win the National League pennant. He was also selected as Rookie of the Year. Robinson tallied an outstanding .342 batting average during the 1949 season, again led the National League in stolen bases, and earned the National League's Most Valuable Player (MVP) award. By 1955, he was one of the National League's best players and had led the Dodgers to a successful trip to the World Series.

Robinson's winning personality and success as an athlete soon endeared him to Americans of all colors. He became the highest-paid player in Dodgers history, and his achievements in major league baseball paved the way for other black players who, at the time, had been relegated to the Negro Leagues, including such superstars as Satchel Paige, Willie Mays, Monte Irvin, Larry Doby, and Hank Aaron. Robinson was not only a leader on the field, but he was also a vocal supporter of other black athletes and of black civil rights. In July 1949, he boldly went before HUAC to testify about discrimination, and he publicly denounced the Yankees as a racist organization in 1952, citing the team's failure to desegregate even five years after he had personally broken the "color line" in the major leagues with the Dodgers. Robinson connected himself to other black activists, consulting with civil rights leaders, such as Thurgood Marshall and Adam Clayton Powell Jr., often lending his support to their efforts to combat racial injustice.

The Push for Civil Rights

During and after World War II, African Americans continued to influence American society and local and national politics. In 1943 William L. Dawson (D-IL) won election to the U.S. House of Representatives, where he joined Adam Clayton Powell Jr., as the only black representatives in Congress. By 1950 Powell and Dawson had sufficient seniority in Congress to wield considerable power on behalf of African Americans. The NAACP opened itself up to new ideas and collaborations, allying with leftist politicians, labor unions, and Jewish groups in a broad coalition that became the Leadership Conference on Civil Rights in 1950. The NAACP was still unable to fulfill its decades-old quest to secure a federal antilynching bill, but black attorneys, benefiting from the foundational work of Charles

Hamilton Houston, used the organization's precedent-setting cases of the 1930s through 1950, including *Missouri ex rel. Gaines v. Canada* (1938), *Sipuel v. Oklahoma* (1946), *McLaurin v. Oklahoma* (1950), and *Sweatt v. Painter* (1950), to move the nation increasingly closer to the eradication of racial segregation in education. These cases, addressing graduate and professional education, rested on the argument that although states had provided separate arrangement for black educational opportunities, those institutions were not equal to their white counterparts. The courts agreed: the strategy of using the doctrine of "separate but equal," offered by the Supreme Court in *Plessy v. Ferguson* (1896) to demolish separate but unequal educational opportunities worked wonders.

The students that Houston trained at Howard University Law School, as well as others who were inspired by his painstaking attack on the legality of racial segregation, continued to advocate for black civil rights. Thurgood Marshall, Constance Baker Motley, Oliver Hill, Robert L. Carter, Robert Ming, James Nabrit Jr., Louis Redding; Jewish attorney Jack Greenberg; historians John Hope Franklin, C. Vann Woodward, and Alfred Kelley; and psychologist Kenneth Clark, through the auspices of the NAACP's Legal Defense and Educational Fund (NAACP-LDEF), attacked the heart of racial segregation and the nation's "separate but equal" doctrine by arguing that "separate" is inherently unequal, period. Although they were often ignored, mocked, threatened, or assaulted, these men and women traversed the entire nation, alone and in groups, building their cases. In 1950, this crack team of antisegregation crusaders took on a suit filed by Harry Briggs, a Navy veteran, and twenty-four other residents of Clarendon County, South Carolina, who objected to the treatment their children faced in public school. These black children were forced to walk eighteen miles round trip, each day, to a segregated black school that offered no heat, electricity, or bathrooms. The case, known as *Briggs v. Elliot* (1952), was the first legal challenge to elementary school segregation in the South.

As the *Briggs* case attempted to attack school segregation in the South, civil rights activists in other regions of the country waged their own battles against school segregation. One such battle proved to be an extremely important front in the larger war against sanctioned racism in American schools. By 1953 members of the NAACP and other activist groups in Phoenix, Arizona were successful in ending segregation in secondary education in *Phillips v. the Phoenix Union High School District*. The ruling in *Phillips* was the first in the United States to declare racial segregation in public schools unconstitutional, and it set an important precedent that would aid Marshall in his fight against school segregation nationally. In the South, the *Briggs* case fused with three others in Delaware, Virginia, and Kansas that were also making their way through the federal courts.

The most famous such case involved Linda Brown, a seven-year-old African American girl in Topeka, Kansas, who, every day, had to walk one mile, crossing a dangerous railroad yard, to a bus station where she waited for more than an hour to board a bus that took her to a "black elementary school" that was farther away from her home than the nearby "white elementary school." Oliver Brown, Linda's father, opposed school segregation and was appalled by the racist circumstances in which his daughter attended school. He and thirteen other black parents, in turn, tried to enroll their children in the local "white schools" in the summer of 1950, but were turned down because they were black. The parents solicited help from the NAACP and, together, they filed suit against the Topeka Board of Education under the equal protection clause of the Fourteenth Amendment to the U.S. Constitution. The case was named after Oliver Brown because he was the first parent listed in the lawsuit. After losing the case at the state level, the NAACP merged the case with those in Virginia and Delaware and appealed to the United States Supreme Court on October 1, 1951. Together, these cases would constitute the famous *Brown v. Topeka Board of Education* case that would strike a death blow to *Plessy* and the "separate but equal" doctrine.

The arduous work of the NAACP Legal Defense team would ultimately pay off. Marshall and his fellow civil rights attorneys and professionals faced a formidable legal team headed by John W. Davis, a former U.S. solicitor general from South Carolina who had argued many cases before the Supreme Court, more than any other attorney of his era. When arguments for the case commenced on December 9, 1952, the Supreme Court's chambers were filled to capacity. Arguing on behalf of the students from South Carolina, Marshall was direct, logical, and poised. He appealed to the Court to confront the *Plessy* dogma directly, proclaiming that de jure segregation was arbitrary and capricious. He argued that *Plessy* was a "legal aberration, the faulty conception of an era dominated by provincialism, by intense emotionalism in race relations, and by the preaching of a doctrine of racial superiority that contradicted the basic concept upon which our society was founded." He also posited that Americans in the twentieth century had demonstrated, by virtue of their fighting two world wars to "make the world safe for democracy" and by combating tyranny at home, that the racist principles upon which *Plessy v. Ferguson* rested "obviously tend to preserve not the strength but the weakness of our heritage."[26]

Brown v. Topeka Board of Education (appendix 3, page 311) captured the attention of all Americans and stimulated intense debate. Even as Marshall made his arguments, most black people and their allies reached relative consensus on the value of racial integration. However, most white people supported school segregation at that time, and they hoped the Supreme Court would issue a quick ruling that affirmed just such a position. The Court, however, remained deeply divided, as well as doubtful of its ability to enforce a ruling mandating desegregation. The delay was, in some ways, a blessing. Earl Warren, the former Republican governor of California, was appointed on September 30, 1953 by newly elected President Dwight D. Eisenhower to fill the vacancy left by the death of Chief Justice Fred Vinson. Warren worked diligently to persuade the justices to rule on behalf of desegregation. Some speculated that the former governor used this case to make a principled amends for his complicity in the internment of Japanese Americans during World War II; he was committed to repudiating racial injustice this time around.

The ruling in *Brown v. Board of Education* came on May 17, 1954. That day, Marshall stood before the justices as Warren announced a unanimous decision that "in the field of public education the doctrine of 'separate but equal' has no place" in schools. (See fig. 5.) The court had determined that a designation based wholly upon race was a violation of the equal protection clause of the Fourteenth Amendment to the United States Constitution. Segregation in public schools was abolished. The *Brown* ruling led to the unraveling of the entire legal edifice of Jim Crow (though unofficial structures remained) which had governed the lives of African Americans since Reconstruction. It also provided a powerful precedent to inform future constitutional crises involving race. In this sense, the case benefited not only African Americans, but also millions of other people of color in America.

Conclusion

Between 1939 and 1954, African Americans made major gains by organizing and using their unique culture of struggle, which deployed their spiritual, intellectual, artistic, athletic, and rhetorical skills in the service of their quest for freedom, and by challenging the United States to fulfill its

FIG. 5. George E. C. Hayes (*left*), Thurgood Marshall (*center*), and James M. Nabrit celebrate outside the U.S. Supreme Court in Washington DC on May 17, 1954, immediately after legal segregation in public schools was abolished. Library of Congress.

promise of freedom and democracy to all. Despite facing overwhelming odds, they intensified their calls for racial justice, revamped their activist organizations, and forged new alliances. They took steps forward against the backdrop of World War II, one of the most violent and complex conflicts in modern history, and the ensuing Cold War. Blacks merged their fight for racial equality with the growing struggle for political, economic, and social progress at home and abroad. Their efforts forced President Roosevelt to issue Executive Order #8802 and compelled President Truman to issue Executive Order #9981. These orders reflected major victories for black workers, who could now seek redress for discrimination in defense industries, and for African American service personnel, who sought equal treatment when they risked their lives for their country. These measures, coupled with the landmark *Brown* decision, significantly improved the lives of African Americans.

The success of black civil rights leaders, performers, and athletes embodied the realization of dreams long deferred and provided hope for millions of other African Americans. Ralph Bunche's Nobel Peace Prize, Ella Fitzgerald's music, Gwendolyn Brooks's poetry, and Jackie Robinson's integration into professional baseball uplifted black people amid the ever-present reality of racial subordination. The Cold War ushered in an era of suspicion, distrust, and suppression, and particularly limited the freedom available to militant voices such as Robeson and Du Bois. More moderate groups, such as the NAACP-LDEF, however, fought for racial healing by utilizing universal principles of freedom and equality and the structural mechanisms of the state. The forthcoming modern civil rights movement would both build upon and transcend these monumental advancements. The black freedom struggle would soon reach its high point and become the most dynamic, powerful, and effective movement to combat white supremacy in history.

2

"LET YOUR MOTTO BE RESISTANCE," 1954–1961

One's own struggle is individual, but it is not unique. All of life is involved; struggle is an inescapable aspect of life.

—HOWARD THURMAN, *Meditations of the Heart*, 1953

For most white Americans, the period between 1954 and 1963 brought unparalleled prosperity. The wealthy among them, as well as many middle-class whites, escaped the integration of public schools and the decaying urban industrial economy by fleeing to all-white suburbs characterized by an emerging technology-based economy and carefully planned communities. Indeed, by 1960, 52 percent of U.S. citizens, most of whom were white, owned their own homes. Many whites would later wistfully recall this period as a golden era of solid nuclear families untainted by drugs, violence, and rabble-rousing.

For most African Americans, however, the mid-1950s to the mid-1960s was a decade darkened by continued segregation, economic disparity, and violence. The entire nation remained divided along racial lines: in the South, Jim Crow and white violence continued to disfranchise millions of African Americans. Most black Americans simply were not buoyed by the postwar financial boom. Residents of densely populated urban areas saw factory jobs grow scarce as the industrial economy began shifting from being based on manufacturing to being based on technology and services, a situation for which many workers lacked skills. Black people, who were generally less educated, mobile, and experienced than their white counterparts, suffered higher unemployment rates in the new economy than did any other community of color in the nation, and even when blacks did make gains, white workers resented the competition they appeared to present. As urban communities deteriorated and racial discrimination persisted, black people refused to accept their circumstances, setting the stage for an eruption of discontent, anger, and, ultimately, for significant changes.

In the Wake of Brown

One year after the *Brown* decision in 1954, the Supreme Court handed down a second ruling, popularly known as *Brown II*, to mollify supporters of racial segregation and alleviate racial tensions. This ruling addressed the speed and manner with which schools should desegregate; the high court stressed that states should quickly comply with their 1954 ruling. Indeed, the first ruling declared that the desegregation of schools should be carried out with "all deliberate speed." Most African Americans understood this phrase to mean that the courts had mandated that desegregation occur immediately. Most whites, on the other hand, interpreted the same phrase to mean that desegregation should occur sometime in the distant, unde- fined future. President Dwight D. Eisenhower supported racial segrega- tion, objected to both rulings, and failed to deploy the power of his office to pressure states to adhere to the court's mandate. In fact, Eisenhower pledged to James Byrnes, then governor of South Carolina, that he would be sure to "make haste slowly" in ensuring enforcement of the ruling.

Such lackadaisical leadership emboldened segregationists. Politicians, religious leaders, and local business captains responded to *Brown* by orga- nizing and supporting myriad efforts to undermine the law. White Citizens Councils were established in many southern cities to oppose integration and racial pluralism, and to maintain the prevailing racial hierarchy of the South through intimidation and terrorism. These councils included ministers, professionals, law enforcement officers, and powerful business- men. Extreme prosegregation views were not limited to white suprem- acists; they supported by white moderates as well as highly respected leaders. For instance, Jerry Falwell, a young Virginia preacher, argued that African Americans were descendants of Noah's son Ham, and were consequently cursed by God to be perpetual servants. Falwell also pro- claimed that the Supreme Court's *Brown* rulings were influenced by the USSR. Falwell argued that the attorneys who argued for the desegrega- tion of America's schools, and the organizations they represented, were enlisted, supported, and paid by "Moscow." Senator James O. Eastland of Mississippi labeled the *Brown* ruling a "monstrous crime." Other leaders took action to challenge the Supreme Court's decision. The Virginia legislature shuttered all the schools in Prince Edward County to avoid integration. Further, on March 12, 1956, ninety-six southern congressmen, led by Senator Sam Ervin Jr. from North Carolina, made public "The Southern Manifesto," a pact that promised to maintain racial segregation and the "sacred heritage of the South." The Manifesto denounced the *Brown* decision as an "unwarranted exercise of power by the court, contrary to the Constitution."[1]

Seeking places to lay blame, critics of *Brown* mercilessly attacked black southern organizations, particularly chapters of the NAACP, an organization that some white supremacists were now determined to destroy. By 1957 nine southern states had filed suit to purge the south of the group's presence. Some states even made NAACP membership unlawful, accusing the group of collaborating in a global communist conspiracy. NAACP membership dropped from 128,716 during the mid-1940s to 79,677 in 1960, with the organization forced to close 246 chapters in southern states. As a result, the integration of public schools became nothing more than an abstract notion throughout much of the South. Massive white resistance called into question the power of the highest court of the land, and likewise cast doubt on the possibility that those who advocated for civil rights might ever secure justice solely through the legal process.

The extent to which many southern whites went to suppress the emerging confidence of black people became painfully clear in 1955. That year, the brutal lynching of fourteen-year-old Emmett Till demonstrated white supremacists' continued desire to thwart racial progress. Till's murder, however, also created shockwaves that helped ignite the burgeoning modern civil rights movement. Till, a fun-loving, energetic teenager, had traveled from his home in Chicago to visit his great-uncle, Mose Wright, and his family in Money, Mississippi. Although Mamie Bradley, his mother, warned him to be careful while down south, Till did not fully understand the nuanced, retrograde nature of southern racial etiquette. In response to a dare from his friends, Till entered a local grocery store to buy candy. As he departed, he said, "Bye, baby," to Carolyn Bryant, the white wife of the store's owner, who was behind the counter.

Three days later, Carolyn's husband Roy Bryant and his half-brother, J. W. Milam, entered Mose Wright's home in the middle of the night and kidnapped a terrified Till at gunpoint. Till's body was later found floating in the Tallahatchie River. Roy Bryant, Milam, and perhaps several other assailants brutally lynched Till; they tortured him, gouged out one of his eyes, shot him through the head, and tied a seventy-five-pound cotton gin fan around his neck before throwing his mutilated body into the river. Young Emmett's remains were returned to Chicago. At the request of Mamie Bradley, the body was displayed in an open casket so that, in her words, "everyone could see what they did to my baby" (see fig. 6). Till's mutilated body was viewed by thousands of mourners: nearly fifty thousand people attended the funeral. Yet despite overwhelming evidence and the courageous testimony of Mose Wright, who risked his life by appearing in the courtroom, an all-white jury acquitted Bryant and Milam. In 1956, Till's killers sold their declaration of guilt to *Look*, a magazine, for $4,000. In this published interview, Bryant and Milam celebrated their ability to get away with murder. Till's lynching and his mother's courageous decision to share the brutality of his death with the world marked a turning point in African American history. The murder exposed the unjust and brutal nature of race relations in America for all to see, both in the United States and the world at large, and it helped forge the race consciousness of an entire generation of black activists. Mamie Bradley spoke to groups around the nation who felt called to action by the murder of her son. Myrlie Evers, who became a leading member of the civil rights movement, recalled her feelings when she heard Bradley speak. "I bled for Emmett Till's mother," she remembered. "I know when she came to Mississippi and appeared at the mass meetings how everyone poured out their hearts to her, went into their pockets when people had only two or three pennies, and gave."[2] Till's murder galvanized African Americans and their allies, and ushered in a new chapter in the struggle for black liberation and racial equality.

Martin Luther King Jr. and the Civil Rights Movement

Robust local communities, drawing on the strength and courage of a highly devoted cadre of leaders, served as the crucibles of the civil rights movement. One such community was Montgomery. In hindsight we can see that Montgomery's forty-five thousand black citizens were primed and ready to lead America into a new era of black activism and racial progress. Martin Luther King Jr., who had just moved to Montgomery with his bride, Coretta, arrived just in time to play a critical role in the movement, and soon cast himself and the black freedom struggle into the spotlight.

Born and raised in Atlanta, Georgia, in 1929, King was the first son of Martin Luther King Sr., a leading Baptist minister, and his wife, Alberta

FIG. 6. Mamie Till, supported by (*right to left*) Bishop Louis Henry Ford, Gene Mabley, and Bishop Isiak Roberts, collapses upon the arrival of her murdered son's remains in Chicago, September 2, 1955. © Bettmann/Corbis.

Williams King, whose father had founded Montgomery's Ebenezer Baptist Church. By the time Martin Jr. was born, Martin Sr. was serving as Ebenezer's senior pastor. Young Martin demonstrated tremendous promise from an early age. A highly intelligent child, he entered Morehouse College, one of the most prestigious historically black colleges in the United States, at the age of fifteen. He thrived at Morehouse, where he distinguished himself as facilitator of dialogue and intellectual exchange. King had long believed that his future was intertwined with the uplift of black people and the church. When he was eighteen, before his graduation with a BA in sociology from Morehouse, his father ordained him as a minister. Eschewing a future in the academy, medicine, or law, the younger King devoted his life to the ministry. His vision of religious service combined his father's style, which was pious, deliberate, and powerful, with that of Benjamin Mays, the highly respected president of Morehouse. Mays was deeply introspective, cerebral, polemical, and unwavering in his commitment to "Morehouse men" and social justice. King endeavored to model himself after both men.

After graduating from Morehouse and entering the ministry, King enrolled in the racially integrated Crozer Theological Seminary, known as the "bastion of the social gospel," in Chester, Pennsylvania. By this time King was already developing his own presence and style, independent of his father's practice and that of his predominantly white Crozer classmates. Easily the most popular student, his rhetorical skills clearly had blossomed, and his professors and peers marveled at his eloquence. When asked how he was doing, King often said that he was "cogitating with cosmic universe."[3] No one knew what this meant or if it meant anything at all, but it helped solidify King's reputation as an uncommon, if not thoughtful, student.

While at Crozer, King fell in love with a young white woman. After having talked cautiously of marriage, he ended the relationship after at least one of his mentors warned him of the "terrible problems" an interracial marriage would create for him. Like many other young black people from his era, King rejected a life to the attainment of status and worldly possessions in favor of one dedicated to service and justice. He graduated from Crozer in 1951 as valedictorian and received a full financial scholarship to earn a PhD at Boston University. Believing that a doctorate would enable him to fuse his passion for academic life with the Christian ministry, he accepted the scholarship and moved to Boston.

It was there that he met Coretta Scott. Like Martin, Coretta Scott was intimately aware of the injustice and violence associated with white supremacy in the South. Indeed, she had witnessed firsthand the beating of her own family by racist whites. Scott was born in Heiberger, Alabama, in 1927 and was raised on the farm of her parents, Bernice McMurry Scott and Obadiah Scott. Coretta was an excellent student, and she was especially good in music. Her intelligence and talents earned her the title of valedictorian of her 1945 graduating class at Lincoln High School. She received a scholarship and chose to attend Antioch College in Yellow Springs, Ohio. As an undergraduate, she gravitated toward the fledgling civil rights movement; becoming a charter member of the Antioch chapter of the NAACP, and the college's Race Relations and Civil Liberties Committees. She earned a BA in music and education from Antioch and earned a scholarship to study "concert singing" at New England Conservatory of Music in Boston, Massachusetts.

Not long after she arrived in Boston, she met Martin and the two began dating. Their shared interests in religion, the arts, and social justice helped to fuel their romance, and on June 18, 1953, they were married by the Rev. Martin Luther King Sr. Hoping to avoid the horrors of southern racism, at least for a time, Coretta was not eager to leave Boston and return to the South after her marriage and the completion of her and Martin's studies in Boston. Although Martin entertained job offers in the North, he chose to return to the South, arguing, "The South, after all, was our home. Despite its shortcomings we loved it as home."[4] Like the generations of blacks who preceded them, Martin and Coretta King acquiesced to a time-honored tradition that called upon educated young black southerners to go back to their region of origin to help liberate it from the clutches of racial injustice.

The Montgomery Bus Boycott

In the spring of 1954 Martin Luther King Jr. accepted a position as pastor of Dexter Avenue Baptist Church in Montgomery, Alabama. Known as "the cradle of the Confederacy," Montgomery was the city in which Jefferson Davis was sworn in as president of the newly formed slaveholding republic in 1861. By the time King became the leader of Dexter's largely middle-class congregation, the city's black population was poised to make history. By no means did this movement begin with the church's new pastor; instead it grew out of a long history of organizing and strategizing among the city's black activists and civil rights groups. As early as 1949 grassroots activists and religious groups had collaborated with the city's two black colleges to forge a formidable protest infrastructure.

One of the most engaged and efficient organizations in Montgomery was the Women's Political Council (WPC). Mary Frances Fair Burks, chair of the Alabama State College English Department, founded the WPC in 1946 when the city's all-white League of Women Voters refused to allow her and other black women to participate in its activities. The WPC was chaired by the dynamic and vocal Alabama State College professor Jo Ann Gibson Robinson, whom King later tapped to head Dexter's Social and Political Action Committee. The WPC created voter registration drives, agitated against racial segregation, and protested the discriminatory treatment that black people endured in the city.

Although the WPC had only forty members by 1954, all of whom were black middle-class women, the organization's leaders were willing to stand up to the powerful white elite. The council also worked with a local chapter of the NAACP led by E. D. Nixon, who also headed the Alabama chapter of the Brotherhood of Sleeping Car Porters. Nixon's activist career was already a storied one; he created the Montgomery Voters League in 1943 to help black people register to vote in Alabama in the face of strong and often violent white resistance. The Reverend Ralph Abernathy, pastor of Montgomery's First Baptist Church, also played a key role in the city's movement. He, like many younger activists, was unwilling to wait any longer for substantive change. He and his cohorts sought an immediate end to Montgomery's racist environment. He recalled:

> Many of the older clergy were in favor of sweeping social change, but they were willing for it to come about slowly, when white society was ready to accept it. Those of us in our twenties were less patient and less afraid of making trouble. As we talked with one another, we began saying that we were willing to help tear down the old walls, even if it meant a genuine uprising.[5]

After World War II these individuals and the organization that united them developed a number of methods to rally blacks in Montgomery to fight white supremacy. Robinson and the WPC routinely brought their concerns before the Montgomery City Council; following King's arrival in the city, the WPC regularly called upon him to accompany them to lend his calm demeanor, sophistication, quick wit, and passion for justice to their petitions for equal treatment. King's and Abernathy's passion and youth, Nixon's connections, and the WPC's experience and creativity set the stage for change.

Just four days after the *Brown* ruling, Robinson wrote a letter to Montgomery's mayor on behalf of the WPC, communicating black citizens' objections to the discriminatory policies on the city's buses. She ended her letter with a call for action, warning the city council of a planned boycott of the buses. "Please consider this plea," Robinson wrote, "for even now plans are being made to ride less, or not at all, on our buses."[6] The mayor dismissed her warning and the buses remained segregated. African American attorneys and Montgomery's NAACP chapter, however, engineered a precedent-setting case to challenge segregation on Montgomery buses. On March 2, 1955, fifteen-year-old Claudette Colvin was arrested for refusing to give up her seat on a bus to a white person. The WPC and black lawyers were prepared to use this incident to spark the threatened bus boycott. Nixon, however, believed that Colvin, who was pregnant and unmarried, would not elicit the requisite amount of sympathy and respect to serve as an effective symbol around which the movement could build. He and Montgomery's other activists elected to wait for a more promising opportunity.

FIG. 7. Rosa Parks is fingerprinted by police lieutenant D. H. Lackey in Montgomery, Alabama, two months after refusing to give up her seat on a bus for a white passenger, February 22, 1946. Library of Congress.

On December 1, 1955, Montgomery's civil rights leaders got that opportunity. Rosa Parks, an inspirational woman who had already established herself as a committed activist and opponent of racial segregation, proved an ideal symbol around which to mount a protest (see fig. 7). Modest and soft-spoken at age forty-two, Parks had worked for a decade as a secretary of the Montgomery NAACP chapter, led voter registration drives, and coordinated the local NAACP Youth Council. A veteran protester, she had even been thrown off other city buses in the past when she chosen to sit in the white sections in the front. In fact, her reputation was already so established that many of the city's bus drivers recognized her and refused to stop for her. Parks had also studied in the interracial Highlander Folk School in Tennessee, which, under the leadership of activists such as Septima Clark, a longtime education and civil rights activist, trained attendees to help bring about positive social change through antiracist lectures, readings, and training in the ways of nonviolent protest. Parks also encouraged whites and blacks to become involved in the racial transformations that were occurring throughout the United States.

Though Parks had protested before by sitting in white sections of the bus, she had not planned to mount a protest when she boarded a bus on December 1, 1955. She made the decision on the spot to refuse to give up her seat to a white male passenger. She later recalled:

> I would have to know once and for all what rights I had as a human being and a citizen. I was so involved with the attempt to bring about freedom from this kind of thing, I felt just resigned to give what I could to protest against the way I was being treated, and felt that all of our meetings, trying to negotiate, bring about petitions before the authorities, really hadn't done any good at all.[7]

Therefore, she felt compelled to refuse that day when told to vacate her seat; consequently, she was arrested for violating Montgomery's transportation codes. When the arresting police officer asked her why she had not heeded the driver's command, she said, "I didn't think I should have to. Why do you push us around?"[8] Parks was taken to the police station and booked.

Word of Parks's arrest spread quickly, galvanizing the black community of Montgomery. Learning that Parks was in jail, Nixon secured her release, using his own home as collateral to post bail. He then urged Parks to allow activists to use her arrest to inspire a comprehensive protest of segregation on Montgomery's buses. Despite her husband's concerns that "white folks will kill you," Parks bravely agreed. Nixon immediately notified other local leaders of their plans, including Jo Ann Gibson Robinson, who enlisted two of her students to work throughout the night of December 1, 1954, making seventy-five thousand flyers to notify the rest of the city's black community of Parks's arrest and call on them to show their solidarity by boycotting the city's buses. By the morning of December 2, less than a day after the arrest, Robinson had organized two hundred volunteers to disseminate the leaflets. "Another Negro woman has been arrested and thrown in jail because she refused to get up out of her seat on the bus for a white person to sit down," the flyer warned. "This has to be stopped. Negroes have rights too, for if Negroes did not ride the buses, they could not operate. The next time it may be you or your daughter or mother."[9]

On December 5, 1955, not one African American in Montgomery rode the buses. Encouraged by this overwhelming proof of the boycott's initial success, Nixon and other local activists quickly established the Montgomery Improvement Association (MIA) to direct the burgeoning protest. King, then twenty-six years old, was installed as the group's president despite initial protest and hesitation on his part.

On the evening of December 5, the MIA held a mass meeting of the black community at the Holt Street Baptist Church to decide the future direction of the boycott. The crowd that gathered was so dense and excited that those who had called it could barely push their way into the building. Despite the enthusiasm and passion of the crowd, Joe Azbell of the *Advertiser*, one of a handful of white reporters at the scene, was taken aback both by the kind way in which he was treated and the focused nature of the throng of people, writing, "The meeting was much like an old-fashioned revival with loud applause added. It proved beyond any doubt that there was discipline among Negroes that many whites doubted. It was almost a military discipline combined with emotion."[10]

The leadership of the young King (see fig. 8), then relatively unknown, gave shape to the MIA meeting. He set forth the purpose of the boycott, and in doing so framed the strategy and goals of the last and most powerful phase of the civil rights movement. King grounded his calculated yet passionate treatise in the fundamental American values of freedom and democracy, Judeo-Christian teachings of love and brotherhood, and the insurgent language of liberation and justice:

> We are here this evening for serious business. We are here in a general sense because first and foremost we are American citizens, and we are determined to apply our citizenship to the fullness of its means. . . . You know, my friends, there comes a time when people get tired of being trampled over by the iron feet of oppression. There comes a time, my friends, when people get tired of being flung across the abyss of humiliation where they experience the bleakness of nagging despair. . . . And we are not wrong, we are not wrong in what we are doing. If we are wrong, then the Supreme Court of this Nation is wrong. If we are wrong, the Constitution of the United States is wrong. If we are wrong, God Almighty is wrong. If we are wrong, Jesus of Nazareth was merely a Utopian dreamer and never came down to earth. If we are wrong, justice is a lie. And we are determined here in Montgomery to work and fight until justice runs down like water and righteousness like a mighty stream.[11]

Inspired by King's electrifying speech, the assembled black community rose, sang "My Country 'Tis of Thee," cheered, and voted unanimously by acclamation to continue their protest, a boycott that was to last 381 days. During this time life for virtually all African Americans in Montgomery changed dramatically. King's faith and leadership were tested during the ordeal: on January 30, 1956, shortly before the protest came to an end, King and his family narrowly escaped from harm's way when their home was bombed. The terrorist attack thrust him and the Montgomery movement onto the front pages of every major newspaper in the country, thereby burning King and the bus boycott into the consciousness of Americans of all races. In the face of threats and violent acts, the boycotters courageously endured. Upwards of seventeen thousand black people participated in the boycott initially, and by its end, King claimed that forty-two thousand African Americans had taken to the streets at one time or another to protest Montgomery's discriminatory bus system.

Though men were more visible among MIA leadership, black women played critical roles in framing and executing the protest. Almost every black woman in Montgomery, most of whom depended on city buses to get to work, refused to ride. As a consequence, many of these women had to walk more than a dozen miles a day. Others were aided by their white female employers, who drove them to and from work in their personal automobiles to retain their service as domestic workers. Over time, however, the number of whites who provided such transportation support dwindled under pressure from their peers, who objected to these collaborations. In response, black women developed an intricate carpool system that helped the boycott to function. They attended mass meetings every evening to support each other. Robinson started the MIA newsletter and circulated it widely, while other women aided the effort by preparing meals and hosting bake sales to raise the more than $2,000 per week needed to keep the carpools operational.

Boycott leaders quickly realized that they would have to engineer an even more highly organized alternative transportation system if the boycott were to succeed for an extended period. Churches bought cars and station wagons specifically for this purpose, while funeral parlors let their drivers use their hearses to chauffer black boycotters to and from work. The organizers designated pick-up points on established routes throughout the city. The carpool system became an efficient, cost-effective means of transportation for Montgomery's black community.

FIG. 8. Martin Luther King Jr., 1966. Lyndon Baines Johnson Library and Museum, photo by Yoichi Okamoto.

The boycott severely damaged the profit margin of the bus company, eliminating a whopping 65 percent of its business and forcing it to eliminate routes, fire drivers, and raise fares. White business owners also suffered because black patrons cut back on their shopping to help defray the cost of the boycott. Nonetheless, city leaders remained resolute, and white politicians who wished to stay in office succumbed to pressure to denounce the boycott and support segregation. On February 10, 1956, eleven thousand whites gathered for a White Citizen's Council rally in Montgomery to cheer the mayor and police chief for not having given in to the demands of the MIA.

When it became clear that the black residents of Montgomery had no intention of capitulating, white leaders resorted to intimidation to disrupt the boycott. The most glaring case came in February 1956, when the Montgomery grand jury indicted, arrested, and released on bond almost one hundred MIA boycott leaders, including King, Parks, Abernathy, and other black ministers who participated in the movement. The charges brought against these leaders were based on an old state statute from 1921 that barred boycotts initiated without "just cause." Such intimidation only strengthened the resolve of MIA leaders, however, and intensified the national media's coverage of the movement and King. When intimidation failed, white supremacists resorted to violence by attempting to assassinate MIA leaders Nixon, Abernathy, and Fred Shuttlesworth, who was pastor of the Bethel Baptist Church in Birmingham, by bombing their homes on January 30 and December 25, 1956 and January 10, 1957, respectively. The home of white Lutheran minister Robert Graetz, a committed ally and the only white member of the MIA board, was bombed twice. Graetz and his congregation, which was predominantly black, were targeted as punishment for Graetz's unyielding support of African Americans and civil rights.

The Montgomery movement drew support not only from black and white people in the South, but also benefited from the aid of allies in the North. Some northerners donated large sums of money to the MIA cause. Others, such as Bayard Rustin of CORE and Stanley Levison, a prominent Jewish businessman and King advisor, also took direct action. When King and his fellow ministers were indicted on conspiracy to disrupt the busing system in Montgomery, Rustin immediately came to the city and pleaded with MIA leadership to adhere to Gandhian principles by allowing the police to arrest them without protest. Rustin recalled that many of the leaders responded to his request without objections, and others had already begun to submit without being prompted:

> Many of them did not wait for the police to come but walked to the police station and surrendered. Nixon was the first. He walked into the station and said, "You are looking for me? Here I am." This procedure had a startling effect on both the Negro and the white communities. White community leaders, politicians, and police were dumbfounded. Negroes were thrilled to see their leaders surrender without being hunted down. Soon hundreds of Negroes gathered outside the police station and applauded the leaders as they entered, one by one.[12]

Because of his support, Rustin became an unofficial advisor to King on the principles of passive resistance, and the two developed a deep and abiding friendship after the Montgomery movement ended.

During the Montgomery boycott, new alliances were formed that raised the Cold War antennae of the federal government. Levison and Ella Baker formed In Friendship, which was an organization primarily purposed to raise money for the boycott. The involvement of Levison and Rustin indirectly connected the boycott to the Communist Party. Levison was a former CPUSA member, while Rustin was a longtime radical activist and organizer. Though King was never a communist, his association with Rustin and Levison attracted the attention of the FBI, which had already developed an irrational fixation with African American leaders and black-led associations. J. Edgar Hoover became obsessed with King, whom he hated viscerally, calling him "the most dangerous man in America."[13] Hoover used all of his resources to connect King with communism and discredit the civil rights movement as a byproduct of a Moscow-led effort to undermine white supremacy and, with it, America. Hoover began wiretapping King's telephone and hotel rooms during the Montgomery boycott. He would later use some of the information he acquired through these wiretaps to threaten King with the public disclosure of his extramarital affairs unless the civil rights leader committed suicide. King ignored the threats, and the FBI retaliated by failing to warn him about potential threats to his life of which the agency was aware.

Intimidation, however, failed to deter black boycotters. Threats and attacks merely encouraged them to press on with their work. National and international pressure to end Montgomery's segregationist ways rose to a fever pitch as well, though the national and international communities seemed to exercise little influence with the city's government. The unwillingness of white political and business leaders to negotiate, combined with the terrorist acts of white supremacists, prompted the MIA to seek justice through the court system. In consultation with local and national NAACP lawyers, the MIA filed suit to challenge the constitutionality of the segregated bus system in Montgomery. With this case, *Gayle v. Browder* (1956), the MIA and the NAACP moved beyond their earlier desire for "a more humane form of segregation" to a new desire to end segregation in Montgomery's public transportation.

The legal strategy of the MIA succeeded, as Alabama's racial segregation on buses was ruled unconstitutional in federal district court on June 4, 1956. Montgomery buses remained segregated, however, as an appeal of the June 1956 decision worked its way through the courts. As the boycott neared its one-year anniversary, King and the other participants found reason to believe that their efforts would end in failure. Indeed, in November 1956, Alabama state courts stood poised to pronounce carpools illegal. Such a ruling would of course break the back of the boycott. Yet on November 13, 1956, the Supreme Court upheld the lower court's ruling, ordering the city to end its buses' segregationist and discriminatory practices.

On the evening of the ruling, a fleet of forty cars carried members of the Ku Klux Klan through Montgomery's black community in yet another attempt to intimate black residents and remind them of "their place" in the social hierarchy. Having just secured a major victory for justice, Montgomery blacks were not intimated in the least. No black people ran into their homes or shuttered their windows in response to the caravan. Rather, the black residents of Montgomery stood firm and looked the terrorists in the eye. Some even waved. The Klan members, befuddled and unsure of what to do next, simply drove away. In a mass meeting held on December 20, 1956, to call an official end to the boycott, King, who was now an internationally known prophet of justice and peace, addressed the crowd:

> I'm not telling you something that I don't live. ["That's right!" a congregant shouted.] I'm aware of the fact that the Ku Klux Klan is riding in Montgomery. I'm aware of the fact that a week never passes that somebody's not telling me to get out of town, or that I'm going to be killed next place I move. But I don't have any guns in my pockets. I don't have any guards on my side. But I have God of the Universe on my side. I'm serious about that. I can walk the streets of Montgomery

without fear. I don't worry about a thing. They can bomb my house. They can kill my body. But they can never kill the spirit of freedom that is in my people.[14]

The next morning King, Abernathy, and other MIA activists boarded the first desegregated bus in Montgomery, thereby ushering in the end of one phase of the struggle and inaugurating a new one. The boycott was the first victory of the modern civil rights movement, and it gave King the moral authority and media attention that made him arguably the movement's most recognized and influential leader. "Old Man Segregation is on his death bed," King announced as the Montgomery bus boycott ended. He was quick to point out that the struggle was far from over: "History has proven that social systems have a great last-minute breathing power, and the guardians of a status quo are always on hand with their oxygen tents to keep the old order alive." White supremacy endured, King proclaimed, "in the South in its glaring and conspicuous forms [and] in the North in its hidden and subtle forms. But if democracy is to live, segregation must die."[15] He and other activists, therefore, turned their attention to new challenges, including voter registration and the desegregation of educational institutions and places of public accommodation.

Beyond Montgomery

Energized by the Montgomery bus boycott, many other black communities began their own protests and created other activist organizations. These protests remained under local control and were unaffiliated with King, the NAACP, or other national organizations. When the NAACP was legally banned from the state of Alabama, black residents in 1956 organized the Alabama Christian Movement for Human Rights, appointing Shuttlesworth as its leader. Later that year Shuttlesworth's home was bombed. Another bus boycott was initiated in Tallahassee by students attending Florida A&M University in May 1956. This boycott also drew support from a local pastor and the Tallahassee Inter-Civic Council, a civil rights organization. The pastor, Reverend C. K. Steele, was among those activists arrested in December 1956 for their efforts to physically desegregate buses by boarding them.

King and other leaders in the South knew of these protests, and they determined that a regional organization would provide greater centralization and regional support to local communities. Sixty black leaders met in Atlanta in January 1957, though King and Abernathy left the meeting prematurely to address the bombing of four black churches, one of which housed Abernathy's congregation. The remaining attendees organized the Southern Christian Leadership Conference (SCLC), selecting King as its head. They also recruited King to draft a "Statement to the South and Nation" that would link the civil rights movement with the black and other diasporas. King wrote:

> Asia's successive revolts against European imperialism, Africa's present ferment of independence, Hungary's death struggle against communism, and the determined drive of Negro Americans to become first class citizens are inextricably bound together. They are all vital factors in determining whether in the Twentieth Century mankind will crown its vast material gains with the achievement of liberty and justice for all, or whether it will commit suicide through lack of moral fibre.[16]

King, who understood the power of the international attention drawn towards him, used his newly acquired celebrity to speak out against white supremacy within and beyond the United States. An early participant in and supporter of antiapartheid campaigns in South Africa, he also championed decolonization movements in Africa and Asia.

International leaders responded to King. Kwame Nkrumah, responsible for freeing Ghana from colonialism (the first African nation to make that transition), invited King to Ghana in March 1957. Nkrumah, who graduated with a BA in 1939 and two MA degrees in 1942 from U.S. colleges, was already influenced by African American culture. King accepted Nkrumah's invitation, traveling to Ghana with Randolph, Powell, and Bunche. The independence ceremonies that King witnessed on this trip resonated with him: "I knew about all of the struggle, and all of the pain, and all of the agony that these people had gone through for this moment." While continuing his visit in Ghana, King met Vice President Richard Nixon, who was traveling on behalf of the U.S. government. Addressing Nixon, King said, "Mr. Vice President, I'm very glad to meet you here, but I want you to come visit us down in Alabama where we are seeking the same kind of freedom [Ghana] is celebrating."[17] King's comments secured him a meeting with Nixon when the two returned to the United States.

When King did return to America, amid his meteoric rise, he faced a blistering schedule as he canvassed the nation to raise funds for the SCLC. The SCLC was particularly important, he declared, because it served as a centralized organization for affiliate groups. Rather than seeking the membership of individuals, it supported local organizations, including the MIA. The SCLC provided training to community and student activists. It also promoted the principles of nonviolence and created citizenship schools in varied communities. The organization's campaign to register voters, combat racial segregation, secure employment opportunities, and fight for adequate housing were underscored by its focus on nonviolence and civil disobedience. Although the SCLC also combated racial segregation in transportation in cities throughout the South, its primary focus became black voting rights. The NAACP, however, did not place much faith in the methods of the SCLC, and the former was reluctant to redirect resources from important legal cases to defend SCLC protestors. NAACP leaders also took exception to King's connections to activists on the radical left. Though the NAACP and SCLC did collaborate in some instances, the two organizations often differed in temperament and tactics.

While the SCLC and the NAACP waged their fight against segregation, activists from these organizations also pressured the federal government to step up its commitment to civil rights. Despite President Eisenhower's lack of support for civil rights and the plight of African Americans, he, with Representative Powell, House Speaker Sam Rayburn, and Senator Lyndon B. Johnson, moved Congress and the nation one step closer to a more just system through the enactment of the Civil Rights Act of 1957. The act established the Commission on Civil Rights, a six-member bipartisan commission that possessed the power to "investigate allegations that certain citizens are being deprived of their right to vote" as well as to study other denials of equal protection of the laws. The act made it unlawful for an individual to interfere with another person's right to vote, and it gave the attorney general the power to prevent racist judges from interfering with African American's attempts to vote by using federal injunctions. The act also mandated the appointment of a new assistant attorney general, one who would oversee a new division of the Justice Department devoted strictly to civil rights enforcement. Nevertheless, the Civil Rights Division matured slowly and had little direct impact on voting rights. During the division's first two years, it initiated only three actions of enforcement, one each in Georgia, Alabama, and Louisiana. Surprisingly, the division did not enforce voting rights in Mississippi, even though the rate of voter registration among blacks in the state was a mere five percent. It eventually furthered access to the ballot during the John F. Kennedy administration, under the leadership of Burke Marshall and John Doar. Later still it became a more effective watchdog, and its reports helped set the stage for new and more meaningful civil rights legislation in the 1960s.

Though Eisenhower was not particularly interested in using the power of the presidency to assist black people in their fight for freedom and equality, the rebelliousness of Orville Faubus, governor of Arkansas, gave him no choice but to act on behalf of integration. Across the South, public school districts had begun developing desegregation strategies in the wake of *Brown*, but school officials in Little Rock, Arkansas chose to defy the ruling.

"On May 24, 1955, in Little Rock, Arkansas," according to the Little Rock High School National Historic Site, "the local school board adopted a plan for gradual integration, known as the Blossom Plan (also known as the Little Rock Phase Program). The plan called for desegregation to begin in the fall of 1957 at the City's Central High School, and filter down to the lower grades over the next six years. Under the plan, students would have been permitted to transfer from any school where their race was in the minority, thus ensuring that the black schools would remain racially segregated, because many people believed that few, if any, white students would opt to attend predominantly black schools. Federal courts upheld the Blossom Plan in response to a lawsuit by the NAACP."[18]

On September 3, 1957, nine black teenagers, schooled in nonviolent resistance by leaders of the local NAACP, attempted to integrate Central High School in Little Rock. When fifteen-year-old Elizabeth Eckford arrived, alone, at the campus at the intersection of 14th and Park Streets, she was confronted by an angry mob of white segregationists who tried to terrorize her into going away. She tried in vain to enter the front of the building, but was ordered back to Park Street by National Guardsmen who were sent to the scene by Faubus to deny African Americans entrance and maintain order. Surrounded by the jeering and malicious crowd, she made her way to a nearby bench on Park Street, where she sat quietly for the city bus that eventually took her to her mother's job. Eckford later said of her ordeal, "I tried to see a friendly face somewhere in the mob, someone who maybe would help. I looked into the face of an old woman and it seemed a kind face, but when I looked at her again, she spat on me." Others among the "Little Rock Nine," including Ernest Green, Jefferson Thomas, Terrence Roberts, Carlotta Walls, Minnijean Brown, Gloria Ray, and Thelma Mothershed, arrived at the school later in the afternoon and congregated at the "south, or 16th Street corner, where they and an integrated group of local ministers who were there to support them were also turned away."[19]

"The Nine remained at home for more than two weeks, trying to keep up with their schoolwork as best they could," according to the National Park Service. "Meanwhile, Faubus reluctantly removed the guardsmen from in front of the school, after a federal court directed him to stop interfering with its order." On September 23, the Nine entered the school for the first time, while the wrathful crowd outside chanted, "two, four, six, eight / we ain't gonna integrate!" Others in the mob chased, captured, and beat black reporters who were covering the events in the streets in full view of local police, who did nothing. "The Little Rock police," the historic site explains, "fearful that they could not control the increasingly unruly mob, removed the Nine later that morning." They returned home again. Eisenhower, characterizing the mob's actions "disgraceful," ordered "1,200 members of the U.S. Army's 101st Airborne Division, the 'Screaming Eagles' of Fort Campbell, Kentucky, to the scene, and placed the Arkansas National Guard under federal control." On September 25, 1957, with federal troops escorting them, the Nine were taken back to the school, entered the building, and completed their first full day of classes. "After three full days inside Central," Melba Pattillo recalled, "I know that integration is a much bigger word than I thought."[20]

Gaining access to the school was bittersweet. The Nine successfully integrated the school legally, but they did not integrate it socially. They were treated horribly by the majority of their white peers and teachers. The Nine were harassed, mocked, scorned and beaten. After a few days in the school, they had to be escorted almost everywhere on campus, at all times, by soldiers. Their military guards, however, could not follow them into the bathrooms and locker rooms, where the Nine were often ambushed, made to drink toilet water, and beaten. "Although all of the Nine endured verbal and physical terrorism during their year at Central, Minnijean Brown was the only one to resist aggressively. She was suspended for dropping a bowl of chili on the heads of two white students during a lunch break, and she was expelled for referring to a student who hit her as 'white trash.' Of her experience, she later said, 'I just can't take everything they throw at me without fighting back.' The other eight students remained at Central until the end of the school year. On May 27, 1958, Ernest Green became Central's first black graduate. Martin Luther King Jr. attended his graduation ceremony. Green later told reporters, 'It's been an interesting year. I've had a course in human relations first hand.' The others were forced to attend other schools or take correspondence classes the next year when voters opted to close all four of Little Rock's high schools to prevent further desegregation efforts."[21]

The New Guard: Student Action

Throughout the nation, students soon began to protest discrimination. African American college students embraced and adapted the "sit-in" strategy practiced by sixteen-year-old Opal Ellis in Phoenix in 1945, advanced by FOR and CORE, and employed by passionate black activists in Wichita, Kansas, in 1958. By the early 1960s sit-ins had taken the nation by storm, having become the tactic du jour for young, increasingly militant black activists. They quickened the civil rights movement, making it more direct and unmasking some of the most virulent manifestations of white supremacy before the watchful eyes of the entire nation.

The sit-in campaigns most closely associated with the modern civil rights movement began on February 1, 1960, in Greensboro, North Carolina. On that day, four African American students from North Carolina A&T College sat down at the Woolworth's lunch counter in downtown Greensboro. Joseph McNeil, Ezell Blair, Franklin McCain, and David Richmond entered the store, purchased merchandise, and sat down at the "whites-only" counter. A white server asked them to leave the counter, but they politely refused. They were surprised when police officers failed to arrive and place them under arrest. The protesters remained seated, undisturbed, until the store closed for the day. The next day, nearly two dozen protesters crowded into the Woolworth's to stage another sit-in. Though there was no conflict or violence at the second sit-in, the protest attracted the local media. By the third day of the protest, the participants had founded the Student Executive Committee for Justice, which synchronized protest efforts and led to an antisegregation march of several thousand students. The majority of the black community in Greensboro, seeking a nonviolent end to the protests, convinced the students to cease their protest while city council members searched for "a just and honorable solution."[22] As the movement in Greensboro unfolded, African American students began sitting in at lunch counters throughout the nation. By March 1, sit-ins were under way in more than thirty cities in seven states.

One such student led effort was launched in Nashville, Tennessee. There James Lawson, an African American who attended Vanderbilt Divinity

School, taught the principles of nonviolence to other students. John Lewis, Diane Nash, and Marion Berry, who would later become leaders in their own right, received training from and worked with Lawson in protests that demanded much from those who participated in them, and resulted in hundreds of arrests, tirades of insults, beatings, and even torture in jail. The protests did result in the desegregation of local lunch counters, however, in May 1960. Students counted this protest as a victory for their independent activism.

Student sit-ins also accelerated in Atlanta. In March 1960 two hundred students representing the city's six historically black colleges, inspired by the leadership of Spelman College freshman Ruby Doris Smith and Atlanta University students Julian Bond and Lonnie King, organized sit-ins at local lunch counters to protest the racial segregation practiced in the city. The students also created the Committee on Appeal for Human Rights and sought to negotiate with the owners of the lunch counters where protests were held. After the negotiations brought no results, the students asked King to become involved, hoping that his notoriety would bring more attention to their cause. The Atlanta campaign broadened, now demanding the desegregation of all places of public accommodation, the enforcement of voting rights, and equal access to educational and employment opportunities. The students' efforts lasted for more than one year before white and black leaders in the city met to negotiate the protest and segregation. These leaders decided to desegregate the lunch counters and to initiate the desegregation of Atlanta's schools the following school year, 1961. The protesting students complained about the decision, though they ultimately submitted to the settlement.

Despite students' ties to NAACP youth groups, conflicts between the younger people and the national organization quickly grew. The independence and defiance of the student-led sit-in movement manifested a substantive and timely critique of the limitations of the NAACP's legal strategy and the SCLC's authoritarian structure. Many young activists believed that the nation's oldest civil rights organization had become too hierarchal, static, and predictable—in short, out of touch. They also pointed out that the SCLC was controlled by black ministers, men who demanded deference instead of action from younger activists. NAACP and SCLC leaders publicly backed the sit-ins, although they had secretly questioned the value and efficacy of student-led civil disobedience. By the fall of 1960, notwithstanding the consternation of members of the NAACP and SCLC, the civil rights movement was profoundly transformed by the fiercely independent student protest movement. Those who participated in sit-ins planned to continue the direct-action tactics that effectively wrested the reins of the movement away from older, more guarded groups such as the NAACP and King's SCLC.

The Rise of the Nation of Islam

As Americans fixed their eyes on an intensifying civil rights movement in the South, they missed the growing number of African Americans in northern and western cities, including Chicago, Detroit, Los Angeles, New York, and Phoenix, who were drawn to the Nation of Islam (NOI). The NOI fielded immaculately dressed black men in suits and bow ties and black women in long white dresses who quickly became fixtures in urban industrial America. Followers of the NOI were calm, stately, articulate, and disciplined practitioners of the brand of Islam fashioned by Wallace Fard Muhammad and directed by Elijah Muhammad. Elijah Muhammad and the NOI preached a custom-made brand of Islam that mixed declarations of black supremacy, including the notion that whites were inferior "devils" created by a mad scientist named Yacub, with elements of orthodox Islamic teachings and the black liberation theology associated with black Baptist and African Methodist Episcopal tradition.

Though many Americans, black and white, considered the NOI a radical cult, its members adhered to very conservative values and customs. The organization endeavored to "uplift" urban blacks by emphasizing the virtues of cleanliness, discipline, self-help, and entrepreneurship. It required its followers to be model citizens, and barred them from dancing, gambling, using profanity, viewing films featuring sex or "coarse speech," engaging in premarital sex, drinking alcohol, taking drugs, and using tobacco. Even George Schuyler, the black conservative editor of the *Pittsburgh Courier*, was impressed by the NOI's ability to recruit dispossessed and delinquent black people, whom it then converted into to self-sufficient, law-abiding citizens. "Mr. Muhammad may be a rogue and a charlatan," Schuyler wrote in 1959, "but when anybody can get tens of thousands of Negroes to practice economic solidarity, respect their women, alter their atrocious diet, give up liquor, stop crime, juvenile delinquency and adultery, he is doing more for the Negro's welfare than any current Negro [l]eader I know."[23]

The NOI eschewed overt political activity, opting instead to focus on the spiritual reclamation of black people by creating a black substitute for the "white man's religion." Unlike their Christian counterparts, however, members of the NOI did not subscribe to the philosophy of "turning the other cheek" when wronged. Instead, the NOI practiced self-defense and did not shy away from confrontation, even creating a paramilitary wing of "soldiers" named the Fruit of Islam (FOI) who were trained in the martial arts. The FOI provided security at NOI events, served as bodyguards for Muhammad, who was also known as "the Messenger," and were willing to sacrifice their lives if necessary to protect the religious organization. The NOI recruited heavily among America's black prison population in particular. Among the many convicts that the NOI recruited and converted was Malcolm Little, whose name was later changed to Malcolm X by Elijah Muhammad.

Malcolm X

Malcolm X (1925–1965), who became one of the most influential black leaders of the twentieth century (see fig. 9), was born in Omaha, Nebraska to Earl Little, a Georgia native and itinerant Baptist preacher, and Louise Norton Little, who was born on the West Indian island of Grenada. Not long after Malcolm's birth, his family moved to Lansing, Michigan, where his father joined Marcus Garvey's Universal Negro Improvement Association (UNIA). Earl Little publicly advocated black nationalist beliefs after joining the UNIA, and local white supremacists responded to his rhetoric and independence by setting fire to the family's home. Earl was killed by a streetcar shortly after this incident in 1931. Authorities determined that his death was a suicide, but the Little family believed he was murdered by white supremacists. Growing up without his father, Malcolm revealed himself to be a gifted student. He dropped out of high school, however, after a teacher mocked his desire to become an attorney, and descended into a rudderless life of delinquency. When his nine other siblings, three older and six younger, were separated following his mother's mental breakdown and commitment to a mental institution in 1937, he moved to Boston's Roxbury district to live with Ella Little Collins, an older half-sister. After working odd jobs in Boston for a while in 1943, Malcolm moved to Harlem, where he fell into an underworld of drug dealing, pimping, gambling and various other forms of "hustling." He avoided military service during World War II when he announced to his draft board that he planned

FIG. 9. Malcolm X. Library of Congress.

to organize black soldiers to attack white servicemen, at which point the board classified him as "mentally disqualified for military service."[24]

Malcolm was arrested and convicted for burglary in Boston in 1946 and sentenced to ten years in prison. While jailed he began to follow NOI teachings; he also educated himself in history, religion, philosophy, and literature. When Malcolm was paroled in 1952, Elijah Muhammad summoned him to Chicago and changed his surname to "X," as is the custom with all NOI members. The name change was a repudiation of Malcolm's "slave name" as well as a symbol of African Americans' inability to claim their ancestral African names. Muhammad, who recognized Malcolm's organizing ability, natural leadership skills, remarkable rhetorical talents, and fiery passion, dispatched the young ex-convict to Boston to become the Minister of Temple No. 11. Malcolm exceeded expectations as a leader in Boston, and was quickly reassigned to Temple No. 7 in Harlem in 1954. Through speaking engagements, television appearances, and by founding *Muhammad Speaks*, a newspaper that became the NOI's official organ, Malcolm X quickly became a national public figure. In 1959, the NOI was introduced to the American mainstream when CBS aired "The Hate That Hate Produced," a documentary hosted by Mike Wallace. The program illuminated the perspectives and practices of the NOI, using Malcolm as the religion's principal spokesperson, and suggested that the members' views were in complete opposition to those of other, better established black leaders of the era. Malcolm X criticized prominent civil rights leaders during the interview for seeking integration rather than focusing their energies on black institution-building and self-defense. Although he disagreed with other leaders over tactics, one should not overlook that he often agreed with them on the basic social, economic, and political needs of black people.[25]

While Malcolm X often toed the NOI line, he possessed an independent mind and sometimes disagreed with official NOI ideas and positions. For instance, during the late 1950s he secretly ridiculed Elijah Muhammad's interpretation of the origin of the "white race," and he appeared to be uneasy with the notion that every white person was literally a devil. More important, perhaps, Malcolm X flatly objected to the NOI's policy of political neutrality. He believed that political participation was obligatory and disregarded NOI rules by lending his support and name to boycotts and other forms of dissent.

Like other black leaders of the time, Malcolm X also worried about the status of people of African descent throughout the Black Diaspora during the 1950s and early 1960s. As anticolonial movements throughout the black world reached their acme, he spoke out in favor of self-governance in America and abroad, with Africa becoming his chief political concern outside of the United States. In this regard his views were not new, as African Americans had long understood their fight as but one theater in the international drama of the global black freedom struggle. Even as fierce leaders such as Malcolm X and more militant young activists transformed the civil rights movement into a more aggressive struggle for freedom and equality, they realized that their efforts constituted one front in an international fight for the freedom and equality of people of African descent.

SNCC, the Freedom Rides, and Decentralization

Ella Baker, who appreciated the promise and power of youth activism and direct action, understood the national and international significance of the American civil rights movement and the role of youth within it. She believed that young people, and especially students, should take more active roles in its execution. Fearing that student action would dissipate without proper support and guidance, Baker took steps to harness the talents and passion of students who placed themselves on the front lines of the black freedom struggle. She organized a conference for 150 students at Shaw University in Raleigh, North Carolina, her alma mater, between April 15 and 18, 1960. Baker, who was dissatisfied with the all-male executive leadership of the SCLC, for which she served as operations manager, envisioned a more decentralized organization that embraced participatory democracy. Her critique of the SCLC and its entrenched leadership resonated with students. At the conference in Raleigh, delegates from fifty colleges and high schools representing thirty-seven communities in thirteen states gathered to discuss their roles in the movement, and also to examine how they could build on its momentum. Baker, who offered her support and guidance, facilitated the birth of an entirely new organization of activists; those in attendance named their organization the Student Nonviolent Coordinating Committee (SNCC). SNCC's first chairman was Nashville college student and political activist Marion Berry. Like other civil rights groups, SNCC principally advocated nonviolence, but it also called for action, and even militancy, when necessary. Many established African American leaders did not approve of SNCC's more provocative methods, which they considered to be antithetical to peace and therefore also to racial progress.

Taking advantage of the effectiveness of student-led sit-ins, an interracial group of activists, led by James Farmer, a longtime civil rights activist and the executive director of CORE, coordinated "freedom rides" through the South in 1961 (see fig. 10). The freedom rides were intended to begin

FIG. 10. Freedom Riders, sponsored by the Congress of Racial Equality, gather outside a burning bus in Anniston, Alabama, May 14, 1961. Photograph by Joe Postiglione, Library of Congress.

in Washington DC and end in New Orleans, Louisiana, and be similar to the "journey of reconciliation" planned by the same organization in 1946. During these rides, activists rode interstate buses in interracial groups to test the enforcement of the Supreme Court's decision in *Morgan v. the Commonwealth of Virginia* (1946), which outlawed segregation in interstate travel. The rides quickly learned that the *Morgan* decision went unenforced, as they were arrested by police in North Carolina. The freedom rides of 1961 continued the same strategy, as an interracial group of civil rights advocates traveled on interstate buses to test the recent U.S. Supreme Court decision in *Boynton v. Virginia* (1960), which reaffirmed the *Morgan* decision.

The freedom rides of 1961 were soon met by violence at the hands of white southerners. On May 4, 1961, black freedom rider John Lewis was severely beaten in the presence of white police officers when he attempted to enter a white waiting room in the Greyhound bus terminal in Rock Hill, South Carolina. Another white mob firebombed a bus carrying freedom riders through Anniston, Alabama. As the terrified young people fled the flames and smoke that engulfed the bus, the mob physically assaulted them. Allies quickly came to the aid of these freedom riders: a contingent of blacks, led by Shuttlesworth, arrived at the scene and transported many of the injured and stunned riders to Birmingham. CORE canceled the freedom rides when it became apparent that no protesters would have access to police protection, and most of the activists left Alabama. SNCC members in Nashville refused to stop their protest, however, and traveled to Birmingham on May 20 to resuscitate the rides and continue their trek to Montgomery. When they arrived, an angry mob of a thousand whites awaited them in Montgomery. The riders were brutally beaten, all of them sustaining injuries that required hospitalization, including Department of Justice administrative assistant John Seigenthaler, who was knocked unconscious when he attempted to protect two females riders, Susan Wilbur and Susan Hermann.

The widely televised attack only strengthened the resolve of the freedom riders, but it greatly embarrassed officials in the U.S. government, who now decided that the conflict had gone too far. Attorney General Robert Kennedy dispatched four hundred federal marshals to "restore law and order" in Montgomery. King and Abernathy entered the fray on May 21, as 1,200 activists gathered in Abernathy's church to shield themselves from a mob of angry whites. Only after federal marshals surrounded the building did John Patterson, governor of Alabama, order the National Guard and state troopers to protect those inside. Farmer arrived soon afterward to lead freedom riders who were still present and willing to carry on to Jackson, Mississippi. Law enforcement officials shielded them from harm until they reached their destination. Once they arrived, however, police officers arrested the interracial group for violating a recently passed "reach of the peace" statute, a charge of which they were quickly convicted and fined $200 each. The judge sentenced each one of them to ninety days in jail when the activists refused to pay. To further terrorize them, Mississippi officials transferred the male and female riders, who numbered nearly one hundred, to the state penitentiary at Parchman, where they were beaten, abused, repeatedly strip-searched, forced to sleep on concrete floors, fed spoiled food, and denied access to bathrooms. When other activists arrived in Jackson, they too were arrested, sent to Parchman, and forced to endure similar conditions. By summer's end, more than three hundred women and men were held in Parchman under the worst possible circumstances.[26]

Not all activists, or NAACP leaders for that matter, embraced nonviolent civil disobedience. Like Malcolm X, Robert F. Williams, leader of the Monroe, North Carolina chapter of the NAACP, came to reject nonviolence and embrace self-defense in the face of white terrorism and violence. Many residents of Monroe, the regional headquarters of the Ku Klux Klan, intimidated and violated black people at will. After the Klan perpetrated a number of violent acts against the city's black community, Williams and other members of the local NAACP grew more militant. When two underage black boys were found guilty of rape and sentenced to indefinite terms in reform school for merely kissing a white girl, Williams lost all faith in the ability and willingness of whites to deal fairly with blacks. International pressure eventually led to the release of the boys, but Williams had already determined that African Americans must be prepared to defend themselves from white people and institutions. He armed himself and squads of black people, directing them to fight off any attacks from the Klan and other white supremacists.

Williams's militancy greatly influenced the views of black people through the United States, particularly when direct action proved to be highly effective. Williams later wrote, "The Afro-American is a 'militant' because he defends himself, his family, his home, and his dignity. He does not introduce violence into a racist social system, the violence is already there, and has always been there. It is precisely this unchallenged violence that allows a racist social system [to exist]."[27] When freedom riders arrived in Monroe in 1961, Williams and other black residents welcomed their support but refused to take their oath of nonviolence. When racist mobs attacked the freedom riders and massed for an assault against the black community, Williams, sheltered a lost white couple in his home during the storm of racial tension that engulfed the town. For his efforts, he was accused of having kidnapped the couple. Williams and his wife Mabel were forced to flee Monroe and live in exile. While the FBI launched a nationwide hunt for them, they found refuge in Cuba, where they lived for five years. From Cuba, the couple advocated for armed self-defense and black liberation through their Radio Free Dixie radio broadcasts and their Crusader newsletter. Both the broadcasts and the newsletter reached U.S. soil from Cuba. While in Cuba, Williams also wrote *Negroes with Guns*, which helped inspire the rise of the black nationalist movement in the second half of the 1960s.

As historian Dwayne Mack argues, the national and international attention the freedom rides engendered, in Monroe as well as in other cities and foreign countries, forced President John F. Kennedy to pressure the Interstate Commerce Commission (ICC) to outlaw racial segregation in interstate travel once again. On November 1, 1961, the new order went into effect across the nation. Unlike its response to the earlier Supreme Court rulings, which white supremacists readily dismissed, the ICC immediately levied sanctions and penalties for violation of its order. The freedom rides not only revealed the courage and determination of young black and white activists and the promise of interracial collaboration, but also inspired African Americans in the rural South to view civil disobedience as a legitimate strategy for ensuring their ability to exercise their civil rights.[28]

Even though African Americans were still dogged by de jure segregation, economic inequality, and the ferocity of white supremacy by the early 1960s, the freedom rides demonstrated their commitment to the struggle for positive change. Still, racial oppression continued to affect the American social landscape. Millions of African Americans, particularly in the South, continued to suffer under the yoke of disfranchisement and mob rule. Despite the post–World War II economic boom, the majority of black Americans were left behind by a generation of upwardly mobile whites. Deindustrialization, white flight from urban areas, unequal educational opportunities, fewer job opportunities, and racial segregation in expanding suburban communities left most African Americans behind socially, economically, and politically. When black people did make inroads, whites often repudiated them as aberrant, inferior and unwelcomed. This context, coupled with an increasingly aggressive civil rights struggle, laid the foundation for unprecedented conflict and more substantial changes.

3

"DEEP RUMBLING OF DISCONTENT," 1961–1968

What we are seeing now is a freedom explosion . . . The deep
rumbling of discontent that we hear today is the thunder of the
disinherited masses, rising from dungeons of oppression to the
bright hills of freedom . . . All over the world, like a fever, the
freedom movement is spreading in the widest liberation in history.

—MARTIN LUTHER KING JR., "Quest for Peace and Justice,"
Nobel Lecture, December 11, 1964

Between 1961 and 1965, the civil rights movement cultivated highly effective systems and organizations that forced the U.S. government and its
citizens to confront the contradictions between its democratic rhetoric
and the racism that permeated every sector of its society. During this
period, the black freedom struggle confronted white supremacy and racial
injustice on a daily basis. Advocates of the status quo and virulent racists
fought against integration and racial unity. The nation reached a boil-
ing point, forcing the president and Congress to take action in support
of protesters. White supremacists feared the power that an empowered
black voting bloc, the first since the days of the first Reconstruction, could
wield. Within African America lay the ability to exert great influence on
the balance of political power in the United States. As advocates of civil
rights continued to challenge racial segregation, others set their sights
on securing access to the ballot. CORE and SNCC continued to overpower
the strategies of segregationists, and President Kennedy proved more
sympathetic to issues of racial justice than his predecessor. Black activists seized this moment to empower African American voters throughout the United States.

The presidential election of 1960, which featured candidates John F. Kennedy and Richard M. Nixon, was one of the most competitive in U.S. history. This was also an election in which King and the civil rights movement played a critical role. At the start of the campaign, most black people supported Nixon, the Republican Party's nominee. Nixon supported civil rights legislation and many people considered him more in touch with working-class Americans. In contrast, Senator John F. Kennedy of Massachusetts, the Democratic nominee, had demonstrated virtually no interest in black people or the civil rights movement. As the campaign unfolded, however, Kennedy offered words of sympathy and support for the black freedom struggle while Nixon receded from his previous support of the movement and did an about-face, courting the votes of white southerners by refusing to speak about civil rights. At the time, Republicans had a modest record of supporting civil rights, but the 1960 election saw this tradition erode as Nixon pandered to white supremacists in an effort to secure desperately needed votes. This strategy was soon to be known as the "southern strategy," a title that refers to the largely Republican tactic of carrying southern states and white voters by using race as a wedge issue on matters such as desegregation and exploiting racial fears among white voters of the South.

Meanwhile, Kennedy revealed himself as receptive to matters of racial justice during the course of the campaign. He interceded when King was arrested, convicted, and jailed on a probation violation for his participation in an Atlanta lunch counter sit-in. Acting on the advice of others, including his brother Robert F. Kennedy, Kennedy called Coretta Scott King to offer his support and used his political power to secure her husband's release from Reidsville Prison in Georgia. African Americans were moved by Kennedy's show of support, and the majority of them ended up voting for him. On Election Day, Kennedy defeated Nixon by less than 1 percent of the popular vote, a razor-thin margin of victory that highlighted the importance of his African American support. In Illinois, for instance, where black voters cast 250,000 ballots for Kennedy, the Democrats won the state by a narrow margin of 9,000 votes.

Even though Kennedy opposed racial injustice on the campaign trail, he proceeded cautiously with respect to civil rights after the election. When King and other civil rights leaders called for federal intervention during the freedom rides, Kennedy was slow to respond. The crises and conflicts roused by activists eventually forced the new president and the federal government to step in and offer protection. Kennedy's primary motivation was to prevent unrest and cast the United States in the best possible light during the Cold War. In addition, white supremacists wielded tremendous power in Congress, which limited Kennedy's options for intervention.

Though he faced numerous challenges, Kennedy assisted the civil rights movement at important times. He issued Executive Order #11063, which ordered government agencies to cease discriminatory practices in federally funded housing. He also nominated Thurgood Marshall to the Second Circuit Court of Appeals, appointed journalist Carl Rowan as deputy assistant secretary of state, and selected Vice President Lyndon B. Johnson to chair the newly formed Committee on Equal Employment Opportunity. In addition, Kennedy's administration included more than forty African Americans, including George L. P. Weaver, assistant secretary of labor; Mercer Cook, ambassador to Norway; and Robert Weaver, director of the Housing and Home Finance Agency. When Robert F. Kennedy was appointed attorney general by his brother, he strengthened the Civil Rights Division of the Justice Department by hiring a cohort of highly intelligent, creative, and aggressive attorneys.

The Albany Movement

President Kennedy's support for civil rights took a step backward, however, during an extremely confrontational struggle between civil rights advocates and white supremacists in Albany, Georgia. In fact, historian Lee W. Formwalt argues that

> Although the struggle for civil rights in Albany can be said to have started during Reconstruction, when thousands of politically active black men elected fellow African Americans to local and state offices, the roots of the modern movement can be traced to the 1920s Jim Crow era, when fewer than thirty African Americans were registered to vote in Albany. In the immediate wake of World War I and World War II, however, C. W. King founded a local branch of the NAACP in Albany, at which he helped middle-class blacks organize voter registration drives. Others petitioned local governments to make improvements in the infrastructure of African American neighborhoods.[1]

Despite their efforts, however, white supremacy in Albany was entrenched and black people who organized against it were often terrorized.

When Charlie Ware, a black field worker in Albany, was attacked and shot three times in the neck by white Baker County Sheriff L. Warren Johnson on July 10, 1961, however, the cauldron of Albany's racial antagonisms boiled over. It was Ware, not Johnson, who ended up in jail, charged with assaulting a sheriff. Georgia's Colored Ministerial Alliance, the NAACP, SNCC, and other civil rights groups formed a coalition to defend Ware. This coalition, which elected Dr. W. G. Anderson as its president, came to be known as the "Albany movement." Hoping to extend the gains made by the sit-ins and freedom rides, the Albany movement aimed to end all forms of racial segregation in the city,[2] focusing primarily on "bus and train stations, libraries, parks, hospitals, buses, jury representation, public and private employment, and police brutality."[3] Albany movement participants, like protestors in Montgomery, deployed myriad methods of nonviolent civil disobedience, including large demonstrations, jail-ins, sit-ins, boycotts, and litigation.

The protests in Albany continued through the end of 1961, though they did not always make obvious progress. Albany's police chief, Laurie Pritchett, was keenly aware that activists wished to provoke vitriolic opposition and even white violence in order to garner national and international attention for their cause. Pritchett did not want to do anything that might generate negative publicity for townspeople or officials or sympathy for the protesters. The police chief responded to the demonstrations with mass arrests that were genteel in comparison to the brutal treatment that civil rights protestors received elsewhere. The media consequently lost interest in the Albany movement, and the protesters found their goals stymied. By December 1961, negotiations with city officials stalled after more than five hundred activists were jailed.

In an effort to resuscitate the movement, Anderson asked King to come to Albany and lend his talents and considerable media following to the cause. Many local activists and grassroots organizers opposed the invitation to King, believing that his presence would "steal their thunder" and undermine their autonomy. Others also believed that his sometimes controlling, often messianic actions would ultimately damage the movement's ability to advance without him should he fall victim to an assassin's bullet. Members of SNCC were particularly tired of King's figurehead status. Their organizers scoffed at King derisively when he and Abernathy traveled to Albany, labeling him "De Lawd" for "miraculously appearing at their campaigns and assuming to speak for the movement."[4]

When King arrived in December 1961, nothing in his behavior dispelled the perception of his kingpin status. Within days he and more than 250 protestors were arrested and jailed (alongside the over 500 activists already incarcerated) after a King-led protest of segregation in the city. Their goal was to remain in jail in order to, as one protestor stated, "break the system down from within. Our ability to suffer was somehow going to overcome their ability to hurt us."[5] For his part, King promised to stay in jail until Albany desegregated. Pritchett, however, had already instructed his officers to use nonviolent means of arrest and made arrangements for up to 2,000 protestors to be jailed in adjacent municipalities if necessary. The Albany police chief cleverly evaded violent clashes and federal intervention. A mere two days after King's jailing, he and city leaders reached a controversial settlement. In return for the termination of the civil rights protests in Albany, the city agreed to waive the cash bonds (but not drop the charges) and free the jailed activists, adhere to the desegregation ruling of the Interstate Commerce Commission, and resume biracial negotiations in sixty days. No formal document was signed, as Pritchett and Albany officials refused to acknowledge the negotiations publicly. A number of Albany movement members, including SNCC operatives, were livid that King had negotiated an armistice without their input or approval.

King blamed the 1961 failure in Albany on the overly wide scope of the protest, and prepared to move forward with the civil rights movement. He argued later in a 1965 interview, "The mistake I made there was to protest against segregation rather than against a single and distinct facet of it. Our protest was so vague that we got nothing, and the people were left very depressed and in despair." He continued, "What we learned from our mistakes in Albany," however, "helped our later campaigns in other cities to be more effective." Indeed, the Albany movement prepared activists for the Birmingham campaign that followed less than a year later.[6]

Federal Assistance: Too Little, Too Late

Although President Kennedy had done had done nothing to assist activists in Albany, he did help to draw attention to the issue of disfranchisement in the South. His backing of the federally funded Voter Education Project in 1962 helped raise and distribute funds to civil rights organizations that performed voter education and registration work in the region.

Kennedy also reaffirmed the federal government's commitment to civil rights by assisting James Meredith as he desegregated the University of Mississippi in 1961. Initially denied admission to "Ole Miss," Meredith sued and cited racial discrimination as the reason the university had not accepted him. The first rulings in the case were against Meredith, but the would-be student appealed to the U.S. Fifth Judicial Circuit Court. This court ordered his admission to the school and confirmed that Meredith was initially turned down because of racial discrimination. On October 1, 1962, Meredith became the first black student at the University of Mississippi. His enrollment, which was bitterly opposed by white supremacist Governor Ross Barnett, sparked white mob violence on the Oxford campus. The rioting left two people dead, including French journalist Paul Guihard. At the behest of the president, U.S. Attorney General Robert Kennedy dispatched federal marshals to quell the violence, protect Meredith, and uphold the court order granting the black student admission to school. The rioting continued: forty-eight soldiers were injured and another thirty federal marshals were shot. Barnett was fined $10,000 and sentenced to jail for contempt. He neither paid the fine nor served time. Meredith's actions were regarded as a pivotal moment in the civil rights movement. He graduated from the University of Mississippi in 1963, only two years later, with a degree in political science.

Birmingham

The signature catalyst for increased federal involvement in the civil rights movement was the Birmingham campaign of 1963. Birmingham, Alabama, was considered by many to be one of the most segregated and racially oppressive cities in America, and the movement's leadership, particularly King, believed it to be the ideal location for the next stage of the struggle. After joining with Shuttlesworth's Alabama Christian Movement of Human Rights (ACMHR), King and the SCLC collaborated with the Alabama group to launch a massive direct-action campaign against racial segregation in the city. They expected the Birmingham campaign to be the most difficult battle of the civil rights movement to date, but they also believed that Birmingham would set a precedent for desegregation at the national level. SNCC chairman John Lewis argued:

> Our goal in Birmingham was larger than ending segregation in one Southern city. It was our hope that our efforts in Birmingham would

dramatize the fight and determination of African-American citizens in the Southern states and that we would force the Kennedy administration to draft and push through Congress a comprehensive Civil Rights Act, outlawing segregation and racial discrimination in public accommodations, employment and education.[7]

The campaign in Birmingham, named "Project C" for "Confrontation" by the protestors, began with a series of mass meetings and direct actions, including sit-ins, marches on City Hall, and a boycott of segregated downtown businesses. The ever-increasing number of volunteers meant that the scope of the project quickly expanded. Volunteers participated in sit-ins at libraries, publicly supported voter registration drives, and even held kneel-ins at churches. The city responded to the protests on April 10, 1963, by using a court injunction to demand a cessation of insurgent activities. King and the SCLC disregarded the court order. "We cannot in all good conscience obey such an injunction," King declared. "Injunction or no injunction, we're going to march. Here in Birmingham, we have reached the point of no return."[8] King was arrested two days later when he continued to protest in Birmingham. City authorities sought to levy extra punishment upon him by placing King in solitary confinement. There he received a letter signed by eight Birmingham ministers who denounced his protest as "unwise and untimely."

Using a pen he had smuggled into jail and scraps of paper he had managed to gather, King composed his eloquent "Letter from Birmingham Jail" to the clergymen who had denounced his protest. In his treatise, which was ultimately published and read widely, King rejected the arguments of those who expected African Americans to remain patient in the face of discrimination: "I guess it is easy for those who have never felt the stinging darts of segregation to say, 'Wait.'" That was no longer good enough for him. "Freedom," he declared, "is never voluntarily given by the oppressor; it must be demanded by the oppressed. Nonviolent direct action seeks to create such a crisis and foster such a tension that a community which has consistently refused to negotiate is forced to confront the issue. It seeks so to dramatize the issue that it can no longer be ignored. " He concluded, "Any law that degrades human personality is unjust. All segregation statutes are unjust because segregation distorts the soul and damages the personality. It gives the segregator a false sense of superiority and the segregated a false sense of inferiority."[9]

King's letter was hailed as a milestone in American history, but it did little to advance the Birmingham campaign. With King still in solitary confinement, Coretta Scott King feared for his life. She contacted the president and the attorney general, and the Kennedy brothers persuaded Birmingham officials to allow the civil rights leader to call home. Celebrated singer, actor, and activist Harry Belafonte provided $50,000 to secure King's release on April 19, thereby revitalizing the campaign. Following King's release, activist James Bevel of the SCLC suggested that they incorporate more young students into the protest. Most people, including many of the activists present in Birmingham, decried the notion that youngsters should be used in this manner. King and other leaders, however, believed their presence was necessary to dramatize the desperate nature of black people's status, as the young people would surely be subjected to ridicule and violence by racist authorities and average white citizens. King and others believed that such racist retaliation would guarantee the success of the protest. On May 2 and 3, 1963, thousands of young persons, some as young as six years old, marched through the streets of Birmingham.

This new strategy of the Birmingham movement infuriated many people on the scene, and none more than Eugene "Bull" Connor, Birmingham's public safety commissioner, and his officers. Unlike Chief Pritchett of Albany, Connor was a man prone to violence and known for his temper, a trait that King and his peers hoped to exploit. Connor's response exceeded their wildest expectations. The police not only apprehended the children in the march, but also beat them and turned attack dogs loose on them. Firefighters sprayed the protesting children with powerful water hoses that shredded their clothes, sliced their flesh, and sent many of them rolling down the street in agony. The attack was so vicious that the children and their parents abandoned nonviolence in the ensuing days, fighting back with rocks, sticks, bottles, and anything else they could reach. The violence directed against black people by the city's government, and the resolve of the black community in the face of it, forced Birmingham's white establishment to negotiate a truce. Alarmed at the ugly turn of events, President Kennedy sent Burke Marshall, assistant attorney general for civil rights, to the city to supervise the discussions. To prevent further negative publicity, Birmingham's white business leaders agreed to end racial segregation in their establishments and to hire African Americans.

The announcement of the agreement in Birmingham was met, however, with violent retaliation. The Ku Klux Klan bombed the A. G. Gaston Motel, which housed the SCLC's headquarters, as well as the home of the Reverend A. D. King, Dr. King's brother. Black residents responded to this latest round of violence in kind, burning cars and buildings and attacking police officers. An exasperated Kennedy ordered three thousand federal troops into position near Birmingham and made preparations to federalize the Alabama National Guard. Martin Luther King and other leaders staved off a full-fledged riot by assuring the black community that the deal would stick. Ultimately the white people who agreed to the deal kept their word, effectively preparing for the destruction of Jim Crow segregation in Birmingham.

The momentum generated by the Birmingham victory fueled similar protests throughout the U.S. in 1963. The South alone hosted eight hundred marches, sit-ins, and other acts of civil disobedience. Southern whites retaliated, however: ten activists were murdered and twenty thousand jailed. One of the most heartbreaking killings to follow the successful Birmingham campaign was the vicious assassination of Medgar Evers by white supremacist Byron de la Beckwith in Jackson, Mississippi, on June 12, 1963. Evers, the executive secretary of the Mississippi NAACP and the most influential leader in the Jackson desegregation movement, was one of the most passionate and respected civil rights leaders of his era. His murder reaffirmed the depth of white racism and the need for the civil rights movement to press on.

The Birmingham campaign seared disturbing and unforgettable images of hatred and violence into the minds of all Americans, and ongoing civil rights demonstrations dramatized the need for national solutions and healing. The urgency of the moment inspired President Kennedy to speak out in support of racial progress on June 11, 1963:

> We face . . . a moral crisis as a country and a people. It cannot be met by repressive police action. It cannot be left to increased demonstrations in the streets. It cannot be quieted by token moves of talk. It is a time to act in the Congress, in your state and local legislative body, and above all, in all our daily lives. A great change is at hand, and our task, our obligation, is to make that revolution . . . peaceful and constructive for all.[10]

Kennedy then advanced the most comprehensive civil rights bill in American history. Although the American people in general were becoming convinced that segregation was a problem that must be addressed, Southern congressmen stymied the President's efforts to push the civil rights legislation through Congress.

The SCLC, NAACP, SNCC, and National Urban League (NUL) supported Kennedy's civil rights legislation. They resuscitated Randolph's March on Washington Movement in an effort to pressure the bill through Congress. In 1961, Randolph and Rustin had recommended that activists march to protest the astronomical rate of African American unemployment, but few people answered the call. After the Birmingham victory, however, many activists believed that the time was right to embrace Bayard Rustin's idea. Randolph, who sought to capture the history and new hope of the Civil Right Movement, christened the planned event "The March on Washington for Jobs and Freedom." This march was held on August 28, 1963. More than 250,000 demonstrators descended upon the U.S. capital in what was, at that point, the largest public protest in American history. Leaders of the march were unable to agree upon a unified platform, and some of them clashed over the content of the speeches slated for delivery. Randolph and the Negro American Labor Council wanted to underscore the extreme poverty that scourged black America, while more radical elements in the movement, led by the SNCC and CORE, were frustrated with what they considered Kennedy's tepid and forced support for civil rights and racial equality. These young activists viewed the march as an opportunity to express their discontent with American race relations and pressure the administration to develop measurable goals for social, economic, and political equality.

For his part, Kennedy was concerned that the enormous march would lead to the unraveling of his civil rights legislation. He consequently pressured Roy Wilkins, then executive secretary of the NAACP, and Whitney Young, head of the NUL, to restrict the march's agenda so that the only message communicated by marchers was support for the pending civil rights bill in Congress. Anything more, in Kennedy's view, would derail the bill. Kennedy, Wilkins, and Young worked hard to ensure that the speeches delivered at the march would be measured and nonconfrontational. These efforts to make the march "respectable," acceptable to the Kennedy administration, and tolerable for most whites shifted the original focus away from economic opportunity and equality. John Lewis, a veteran of the freedom rides and sit-ins, and chairman of SNCC, was forced to rewrite his speech, which originally described Kennedy's civil rights legislation as "too little" and "too late." The fiery Malcolm X, who was not involved in the march, argued that the plans were merely a symbolic diversion orchestrated by black leaders who failed to confront white supremacy head-on. He labeled the event the "Farce on Washington."

Although tensions over tactics within the movement raged on behind the scenes, the March on Washington itself was a monumental success. The protest culminated in a rally at Lincoln Memorial, where King delivered his historic "I Have a Dream" speech (see fig. 11). In it, with unsurpassed ardor and passion, King stated:

> I say to you today, my friends, so even though we face the difficulties of today and tomorrow, I still have a dream. It is a dream deeply rooted in the American dream. I have a dream that one day this nation will rise up and live out the true meaning of its creed: "We hold these truths to be self-evident: that all men are created equal." I have a dream that one day on the red hills of Georgia the sons of former slaves and the sons of former slave owners will be able to sit down together at the table of brotherhood. I have a dream that one day even the state of Mississippi, a state sweltering with the heat of injustice, sweltering with the heat of oppression, will be transformed into an oasis of freedom and justice. I have a dream that my four little children will one day live in a nation where they will not be judged by the color of their skin but by the content of their character. . . . And when this happens, when we allow freedom to ring, when we let it ring from every village and every hamlet, from every state and every city, we will be able to speed up that day when all of God's children, black men and white men, Jews and Gentiles, Protestants and Catholics, will be able to join hands and sing in the words of the old Negro spiritual, "Free at last! Free at last! Thank God Almighty, we are free at last!"[11]

The March on Washington was a groundbreaking reflection of the ability of the civil rights movement to mobilize hundreds of thousands of Americans, across race lines, in opposition to racism and injustice.

The march and King's powerful speech were not enough to end the unyielding opposition of many white southerners to black equality. On September 15, 1963, less than one month after the march, white extremists bombed the 16th Street Baptist Church in Birmingham, killing four

FIG. 11. Martin Luther King Jr. waves to a crowd of 250,000 following his historic "I Have a Dream" speech, August 28, 1963. AP Photo/File (6308280301).

little black girls who were attending Sunday School. Despite his grief and anger, Chris McNair, the father of the youngest of the victims, called on the black community to remain peaceful and strategic in its response. "We must not let this change us into something different than who we are," he declared. "We must be human." King echoed McNair's remarks, arguing, "The innocent blood of these little girls may well serve as the redemptive force that will bring new light to this dark city. Indeed, this tragic event may cause the white South to come to terms with its conscience."[12] The great majority of American citizens were shocked and outraged by the murders. By the next month, when John F. Kennedy was also assassinated on November 22, 1963, U.S. citizens manifested an unprecedented desire for peace and reconciliation. This new shift paved the way for substantive socioeconomic changes in the United States.

LBJ and the Civil Rights Acts

The first major change brought about by the 16th Street Church martyrdoms, argues historian Aldon Morris, was the Civil Rights Act of 1964 (appendix 4, page 000). Lyndon B. Johnson, a white Southerner who succeeded Kennedy as president, defied his region's anti–civil rights tradition by working relentlessly to pass the bill initiated by JFK. Johnson signed the act, which represented the zenith of the civil rights movement at the time, into law on July 2, 1964. The new law prohibited discrimination based on race, color, religion, or national origin in public establishments, by employers, and by labor unions. In conjunction with subsequent legislation, the Civil Rights Act of 1964 also made discrimination in colleges and within employment unlawful, laying the groundwork for future Supreme Court cases. It also aided African Americans and other people of color by making the federal government more responsible for protecting citizens from discriminatory treatment. The act restated some of the protections outlined in constitutional amendments enacted during Reconstruction, but it also expanded the reach of federal regulatory powers. For example, it enabled government agencies to withhold funding from any office or program that engaged in discriminatory behavior. Though the act furthered the civil rights movement, it did not by any means mark the end of it, as SNCC and the SCLC next turned their attention to voting rights. Following the passage of the Civil Rights Act, President Johnson communicated his preliminary support of black voting rights:

Much can be done, and must be done, if the potential freedoms affirmed by the Civil Rights Act of 1964 are to be translated into practice and meaningful progress. The most direct responsibility of each citizen is to participate in the affairs of his nation, state and community by exercising his right to vote. Every qualified citizen must register and vote if we are to be worthy of the freedoms we enjoy and hope to obtain.[13]

Freedom Summer

Activists were ahead of Johnson, however, and had begun registering southern black people to vote well before Congress passed the Civil Rights Act of 1964. Members of CORE and SNCC understood that while segregation was undergoing systematic destruction, African Americans would not truly secure political power, a more just judiciary, an end to mob violence and police brutality, or a more equal educational system without true access to and benefit of the franchise. Robert "Bob" Moses, who began registering black voters in Mississippi in 1961, played a key role in drawing attention to black political exploitation in the state. He was also one of the founders of the Council of Federated Organizations (COFO), which was organized in 1962 to assist the NAACP, CORE, SCLC, and SNCC in Mississippi. Activism in Mississippi and black voter registration in the state were quickly halted, however, by white supremacists who intimidated and attacked civil rights operatives in Mississippi in late 1963.

A wise strategist, Moses instituted a program he called Freedom Summer by recruiting a thousand northern white activists, most of whom were college students, to bring fresh energy and national attention to civil rights groups in Mississippi during the summer of 1964. These volunteers, black and white, worked with CORE and SNCC in particular. Moses and COFO believed that only a large-scale interracial voter registration movement would liberate blacks in Mississippi from the stranglehold of Southern white political domination. Freedom Summer was a departure from COFO's emphasis on black self-determination, but council leaders believed that the presence of privileged white students in the underbelly of the white supremacist South would draw media attention to the cause of African American voting rights. Any violence perpetrated against activists and the students of the Freedom Summer by white supremacists would, in Moses's opinion, pressure the federal government to take action on behalf of African Americans in the state. Moses and the council also aimed to forge a grassroots political network that would sustain itself long after student activists left Mississippi at the close of the summer.

The southern civil rights activists and northern volunteers who participated in Freedom Summer met white supremacy and the very real threat of violence in Mississippi with incredible bravery. Training for volunteers began in June 1964 at the Western College for Women in Oxford, Ohio. Certainly the members of SNCC and other activists appreciated the enthusiasm of the northern volunteers and the national attention they attracted to the cause. The established activists understood, however, that this national attention would imply that these predominantly white volunteers were more valuable to American institutions such as the media than were black people, whether they were activists themselves or ordinary citizens. They also understood that the federal government was more likely to respond to violence against white volunteers than it would to black activists or black southern residents. These expectations of how the media and federal government would respond if white northern volunteers were attacked sadly proved prescient. On June 21, 1964, James Chaney, a black activist from Mississippi, and Michael Schwerner and Andrew Goodman, two white Jewish volunteers from New York, disappeared. The three men had been traveling to and from Philadelphia, Mississippi, to talk to residents about the recent burning of a black church. Cecil Price, the deputy sheriff of the town, pulled the activists off the road and wrote them up on speeding charges. The officer then left them stranded on the isolated roadside, where at least a dozen Klansmen were lying in wait to seize them. After beating the three young men with chains, the Klansmen shot them to death. Months later, after a massive search, one of the Klansmen, enticed by a $30,000 reward, took investigators to the spot where the mob had buried the young men.

The murders of Chaney, Goodman, and Schwerner brought white supremacy and terrorism in Mississippi under a national microscope, and what the national community found was displeasing. During the Freedom Summer, more than a thousand volunteers were arrested, thirty-five were shot at, eighty were beaten, and six were murdered. Moreover, thirty homes and thirty-seven churches were bombed or burned. Reeling from the violent onslaught of white terrorism, many SNCC operatives renounced King's devotion to nonviolence, the presence of whites within the movement, and the righteousness of integration. Still, in the face of these internal and external issues, Freedom Summer moved forward. The campaign established forty-one "Freedom Schools," in which more than three thousand young blacks took classes in traditional subjects but also studied African American history, the philosophy of nonviolent civil disobedience, and leadership. These efforts helped educate and empower black communities, igniting future local movements for political power throughout Mississippi and the entire South.

Political Ascendency

Freedom Summer also led to the organization of the Mississippi Freedom Democratic Party (MFDP). The MFDP, established as an interracial alternative party, demanded entrance to the 1964 Democratic National Convention in Atlantic City, New Jersey. MFDP leaders sought to dramatize the systematic denial of black voting rights in Mississippi. Many delegates to the national convention wanted to seat the civil rights delegation, but President Johnson, who was running for reelection, did not want to ostracize southern whites and push them into the camp of his adversary, Republican Barry Goldwater of Arizona. To curry the favor of the Credentials Committee, the delegation, which included Fannie Lou Hamer (1917–1977) (figure 12), a former cotton field worker, grassroots organizer, and powerful speaker, and activists Victoria Gray, Annie Divine, and Aaron Henry, testified about the discrimination that black people routinely faced at the polls in Mississippi. When Hamer, the daughter of sharecroppers, delivered to the committee a moving, televised speech, Johnson hastily called a press conference to shift attention away from her and the MFDP in Atlantic City. Despite Johnson's actions, Hamer's stirring 1964 remarks struck a chord with the American people. The subsequent outpouring of national sympathy pressured Johnson, as well as Johnson's running mate, Senator Hubert H. Humphrey from Minnesota, to seek a compromise with the MFDP. When Johnson and Humphrey offered the MFDP two "at large" seats for members Aaron Henry and Ed King, without offering the delegates any official votes, MFDP leaders rejected the compromise. King, Rustin, and other African American leaders urged the MFDP to accept the offer, however, arguing that Johnson and the Democrats had largely delivered upon their promises to support civil rights, and that, if elected, Barry Goldwater would place a moratorium on civil rights legislation. For her part, Hamer repudiated the compromise, stating flatly, "We didn't come here for no two seats when all of us is tired."[14] This process proved

FIG. 12. Fannie Lou Hamer at the Democratic National Convention in Atlantic City, New Jersey, August 1964. Library of Congress.

upsetting to many young activists as well; some members of SNCC, for example, came to completely reject interracial collaboration of any kind.

Selma

Although the Civil Rights Act of 1964 included stipulations to assist African Americans in the voter registration process, southern whites' defiance undermined the law's effectiveness. To address black disfranchisement and push the federal government to protect black voters, King and the SCLC planned a major protest in Selma, Alabama, in early 1965, after the presidential election. The timing of the march would make it easier for Johnson to act without fear of backlash. Black people who tried to register to vote in Alabama were stymied by the deliberate slowness, sometimes as long as nine months or more, with which state agents completed the registration process and literacy tests. These issues were not specific to Alabama: they characterized black voter registration throughout the South. The selection of Selma, however, provided a particularly stark case for the movement: of the 15,000 eligible black adults residing in Selma and the surrounding county of Dallas in 1965, fewer than 350 of them were actually registered to vote. This protest would serve multiple ends for King and the SCLC. It would publicize the miserable status of black people in Alabama, but it would also embolden the federal government to address the issue of equal voting rights through legislation.

The activist descent upon Selma in early 1965 was carefully organized. SNCC, the SCLC, and the Dallas County Voters League registered eligible black people to vote and protested throughout the city. The protesters soon encountered violence at the hands of law enforcement officers. State troopers attacked a group of demonstrators in Marion, a town near Selma, on February 18. The state troopers shot Jimmie Lee Jackson, a twenty-seven year old unarmed activist, as he sought to protect his mother from their onslaught.

In response to the slaying of Jackson, civil rights workers organized a march for Sunday, March 7, from Selma to Montgomery, the capitol of Alabama. John Lewis and Hosea Williams led the marchers, traveling as far as the Edmund Pettis Bridge, just outside of Selma. The marchers were not able to cross the bridge, for none other than the governor of Alabama, George Wallace, had ordered state troopers and other officials to halt the march. But even with the bridge blocked, the marchers did not disband, as they remained determined to reach the capitol steps in Montgomery.

In response to the marchers' resolve, Major John McCloud, who commanded the blockade, ordered state troopers to attack the protesters with tear gas and clubs. Having unleashed the violence, local officials chased the protesters off the bridge.

The violent attack on the marchers on the Edmund Pettis Bridge soon became known as "Bloody Sunday:" it attracted national and even international attention. More determined than ever, civil rights workers assembled in Selma organized a second march to occur two days later on March 9. Worried by the possibility of a second march and more violence, President Johnson pushed his administration to draft a voting rights bill. Administration officials also asked King to postpone the march. On the morning of March 9, a federal district court judge barred the event from proceeding until a federal hearing could take place. Despite Johnson's request and the court order, King did not try to stop the march and participated in it so as not to draw the ire of the other civil rights workers. The group of over one hundred protesters walked out to the Edmund Pettis Bridge, where they knelt in prayer. Following the prayer, King led them back to Selma. Though the marchers had not known of King's plans, the civil rights leader had compromised earlier that day with his federal government contacts. His actions greatly angered those activists who believed they were evidence of his personal manipulation of the civil rights movement.

Despite King's compromise and the limited second march, the violence in Alabama continued. On that same day white men from Alabama brutally beat James Reeb, a white Unitarian minister from Massachusetts, near a black church in downtown Selma. He died two days later. This escalation drew further national attention to the state. Days later, a distressed Johnson held a press conference in which he noted:

> We all know how complex and how difficult it is to bring about basic social change in a democracy, but this complexity must not obscure the clear and simple moral issues. It is wrong to do violence to peaceful citizens in the streets of their town. It is wrong to deny Americans the right to vote. It is wrong to deny any person full equality because of the color of his skin.[15]

Two days after the press conference, the President addressed a joint session of Congress and called for passage of a voting rights bill.

The events of Selma soon reached their zenith. Activists organized a third march for March 21, 1965. This time, with the protection of nearly two thousand National Guardsmen, the civil rights advocates reached the state capitol after approximately four days of travel on foot. The rally on the capitol grounds attracted about twenty-five thousand people. At it King declared: "The end we seek is a society at peace with itself, a society that can live with its conscience."[16]

Nearly five months later, on August 6, Johnson signed the Voting Rights Act of 1965 (appendix 5, page 000). It outlawed educational requirements for citizens seeking to vote. It also created new powers for the Department of Justice, which could now work in conjunction with federal registrars to help raise the number of registered voters. U.S. Attorney General Nicholas Katzenbach seized upon this opportunity quickly, dispatching multiple federal registrars to the South to register voters; these workers registered eighty thousand people in a matter of months. The increase was particularly striking in certain areas of the South. In 1964 only 28,500 black people were registered to vote; by 1968 this number had exploded to 251,000. Successful voter registration effectively challenged white supremacy in the voting booth.

The victory in Selma was bittersweet for King, whose reputation in the civil rights community continued to decline. By this point younger black people and organizations, including SNCC, were embracing new, more radical ideas and tactics. Indeed, after the MFDP's failure in 1964, many black people realized that they could not depend on the federal government to come to their rescue. A younger cadre of activists, therefore, argued that black people needed more than white allies: they needed power. It was at this time that Stokely Carmichael (figure 18), later known as Kwame Ture, emerged as the leading voice of militancy and nationalism within SNCC.

Stokely Carmichael (1941–98) was born in Port of Spain, Trinidad, and moved to New York City at the age of eleven. A successful student, he attended the predominantly white Bronx High School of Science beginning in 1956. He enrolled at Howard University and joined SNCC in 1960, and he participated in the group's sit-ins and freedom rides. Despite his heavy activist duties, he graduated from Howard in 1964. Together with other young SNCC activists, Carmichael criticized the relationship between black civil rights workers and white liberals. He also became disenchanted with nonviolence as a means of protest. Following the MFDP failure, Carmichael and several other SNCC activists began to carry guns to protect themselves. Young, more militant black activists like Carmichael were also greatly influenced by the radicalism of Robert F. Williams and Malcolm X.

Malcolm X's career continued through 1965. His rejection of integration and "turning the other cheek" resonated with Carmichael and his peers, allowing Malcolm to influence a younger generation of activists. "The day of nonviolent resistance is over," Malcolm proclaimed. In 1964, he also argued, "Revolutions are never based upon love-your-enemy, and pray-for-those-who-despitefully-use-you. And revolutions are never waged by singing 'We Shall Overcome.' Revolutions are based on bloodshed." It was at this time, however, that Malcolm X's connections to the NOI splintered. Elijah Muhammad suspended him from the Nation for having described the assassination of JFK as an instance of "chickens coming home to roost,"[17] which meant, in other words, that Kennedy was a victim of the same violence that terrorized African Americans. Many members of the NOI were also jealous of Malcolm's meteoric popularity. Malcolm broke with the NOI and founded Muslim Mosque, Inc. in 1964. That same year he went on a pilgrimage to Mecca that expanded his world view: he changed his name to El-Hajj Malik El-Shabazz and founded the Organization for Afro-American Unity, which he modeled after the Organization of African Unity. He also denounced the NOI philosophy that all white people are devils, and he worked toward unifying his message and work with that of civil rights efforts in the South and anticolonialism in Africa. Malcolm X's militant disposition, independence, fearlessness, and steadfast criticism of white supremacy in the United States made him the enemy of many Americans, including powerful forces within the NOI, FBI, and CIA. Abruptly, on February 14, 1965, assassins connected to the NOI, and some would say to the FBI and CIA, murdered El-Hajj Malik E-Shabazz as he spoke at the Audubon Ballroom in Harlem. His murder stunned African Americans and sent many black people into a deep depression. Others erupted in anger, taking to the streets to riot and loot in a cathartic rage.

Malcolm X was viewed by many people as the personification of black manhood. He said things that most black people thought, but were too afraid to say. The famed black actor, Ossie Davis, who delivered the slain leader's eulogy, described Malcolm X as African America's "shining black prince" who sacrificed his life "because he loved us so."[18] Despite the tremendous outpouring of affection and gratitude that most black people demonstrated in the aftermath of Malcolm X's murder, most within the NOI denounced him as a "Benedict Arnold" and a traitor, including his most promising protégé, the young and dynamic Minister Louis Farrakhan. Most black people, however, especially young African Americans, embraced his militant support of self-defense and his work in "overturning systems"[19] that marginalized and dehumanized black people radicalized other African American leaders, including Stokely Carmichael.

Still reeling from Malcolm X's assassination, Carmichael was elected to replace John Lewis as SNCC chairman in May 1965. This change in leadership formalized the shift from moderate to militant activist ideology in the organization.[20] That same year, Carmichael led the campaign that established the Lowndes County Freedom Organization (LCFO). The LCFO organized a militant voter registration drive, held rallies, and led marches on behalf of black civil rights in the Deep South. The LCFO, an organization with only black members, adopted the symbol of the black panther, which they believed conveyed power in the spirit of Malcolm X, who advocated self-defense in response to threats from violent white people. Registration efforts continued in 1966, when James Meredith launched his one-man "march against fear" from Tennessee to Jackson, Mississippi, to inspire African American southerners to register to vote. Not long after his march began, white terrorists shot and seriously injured Meredith. Carmichael and SNCC joined with other groups, including the SCLC, to finish the march. As the activists made their way through Alabama, Carmichael popularized the motto "Black Power." This slogan quickly became SNCC's motivational maxim. Carmichael put it, "We been saying freedom for six years and we ain't got nothin'. What we gonna start saying is Black Power." Carmichael, however, was careful to explain what black power meant:

> In Lowndes County [Mississippi], for example, black power will mean that if a Negro is elected sheriff, he can end police brutality. If a black man is elected tax assessor, he can collect and channel funds for the building of better roads and schools serving black people thus advancing the move from political power into the economic area. Politically, black power means what it has always meant to SNCC: the coming together of black people to elect representatives and to force those representatives to speak to their needs. It does not mean merely putting black faces into office.[21]

The slogan and Carmichael's subsequent work on behalf of black power made him a media darling and a lightning rod for more moderate black leaders. Some accused Carmichael of "reverse racism," but the SNCC leader maintained that he only advocated racial pride and self-determination. As provocative as the phrase black power was, it was not as divisive and disruptive to the dynamics and further progress of the struggle as sexism (Carmichael once said that "the only position for women in SNCC is prone"),[22] sex between black men and white women, and disputes over integration versus segregation. By 1968, CORE had followed in SNCC's footsteps. It expelled its white members, even though by doing so it lost a corresponding degree of social and financial capital. Both SNCC and CORE were diminished as a result of these tactical decisions. By the end of the 1960s, SNCC was virtually nonexistent.

King felt rather ambivalent about the mantra of black power. He applauded its emphasis on African American socioeconomic potency, cultural pride, and intellectual independence, but he worried that these ideas, reduced to a motto, would be misused. A misunderstanding of black power might privilege black versus white, which King rejected as "a nihilistic philosophy born out of the conviction that the Negro can't win." He also disapproved of the ideology's "implicit and often explicit belief in black separatism."[23]

In May 1967, Hubert G. Brown, otherwise known as H. Rap Brown, succeeded Carmichael as the leader of SNCC. Brown intensified the radicalism of what became known as the black power movement by calling white people "honkies" and police officers "pigs." He declared, "Violence is as American as apple pie." In August 1967, Brown told an audience in Cambridge, Maryland, that "black folks built America, and if America don't come around, we're going to burn America down."[24] A few hours after these comments, a fire was ignited in the middle of the city's African American community. White firefighters refused to put out the blaze, and police charged Brown with inciting a riot and committing arson. After posting bail, the leader of SNCC fled the city. Brown was not to blame for the riot, and the charges were eventually dropped. As cities across America exploded in similar racial violence, many people began to seek the underlying causes of the frustration and anger that led to these violent eruptions. One did not have to dig too deep to find that the segregation, poverty, dislocation, and hopelessness that gripped many urban communities created ideal conditions for social unrest. The militancy and desperation that marked these events reflected a corresponding transformation in the black freedom struggle. The black power movement had supplanted the civil rights movement in visibility and urgency. Laws had been changed to provide racial equality on paper, but black militants wanted social, economic, and political equality, and they were unwilling to wait.

The religious community was also transformed by the civil rights and black power movements. As early as 1946, the Federal Council of Churches, which included Catholics, Protestants, and Jews, promised to forge a "non-segregated church and a non-segregated society."[25] Between 1963 and 1965, the National Council of Churches (NCC) provided financial and spiritual support to the modern civil rights movement. In 1963, the NCC also created a Commission on Religion and Race. The NCC participated in the March on Washington and supported the Civil Rights Act of 1964 and the Voting Rights Act of 1965. In 1965, Benjamin Payton, a black graduate of Harvard Divinity School and Yale University's graduate school, was appointed director of the Commission on Religion and Race. Under his leadership, the commission was placed under the Division of Christian Life and Mission, which ultimately became the NCC's Department of Social Justice. A staunch supporter of black economic growth and autonomy, Payton created the National Commission on Black Churchmen in 1966, which endorsed black power principles and tactics.

The group grew into a major ecumenical organization. Indeed, white churches were influenced by the black power movement, as evidenced by their creation of black committees within their congregations. By 1970 these black caucuses of white churches included the Black Methodists for Church Renewal, the Black Presbyterians United, and the Episcopal Union of Black Clergy and Laity. Black Roman Catholics also challenged their faith, insisting that it too become more racially inclusive. These efforts primed the religious community for James Forman's "Black Manifesto." Indeed, in April 1969, Forman, a black man who had worked as a teacher in Chicago but became well known by virtue of his work in SNCC, called upon white churches to pay $500 million in reparations for their role in and profit from black slavery and discrimination. Forman made his demand at the National Black Economic Development Conference in Detroit, which was funded by the Interreligious Foundation for Community Organizations, an entity in turn funded largely by white churches. Forman's scathing analysis of white spirituality prompted many white religious institutions simply to abandon the black freedom struggle. These white leaders were deeply insulted by Forman's uncompromising demands and Marxist rhetoric. From that point forward, the relationship between African Americans and Jews, which never had been particularly strong, deteriorated. Many black people considered Jewish people guilty of paternalism and racism, and many Jews charged African Americans with being ungrateful for their support and antisemitic.

By 1967 the number of radicalized adherents of black power had swelled significantly. Angela Yvonne Davis (1944–), who became a living icon of black radicalism and power, played a critical role in the black power movement. Davis was born and raised on "Dynamite Hill" in Birmingham, Alabama, so named because the neighborhood was routinely bombed by the Ku Klux Klan to intimidate blacks and "keep them in their place." Davis's mother, nonetheless, was an active member of the local NAACP. After relocating to New York City with her mother as a teenager, Davis moved to Massachusetts to attend Brandeis University. During her junior year Davis studied philosophy in Germany and the French language in France. In 1965 she graduated magna cum laude from Brandeis with a bachelor's degree in French literature. Three years later she earned a master's degree from the University of California at San Diego, where she also became a member of the Communist Party. Davis was drawn to Marxist ideals, in part because they offered her systemic answers for many of the problems that plagued black people. Indeed, she maintained that Marxism helped her understand U.S. society:

> What had seemed a personal hatred of me, an inexplicable refusal of Southern whites to confront their own emotions, and a stubborn willingness of blacks to acquiesce, became the inevitable consequences of a ruthless system which kept itself alive and well by encouraging spite, competition and oppression of one group by another. Profit was the word: the cold and constant motive for the behavior, the contempt, and the despair I had seen.[26]

Davis also had become involved in black power politics during her time at the UCSD, years in which the black community and nation experienced sweeping change. This was a time when leading figures in civil rights organizations such as H. Rap Brown were calling for revolution and a comprehensive change in black attitudes and race relations in the United States. Using passionate and confrontational rhetoric, Carmichael and Brown inspired militant grassroots organizing on college campuses throughout America. They were joined in their radical leadership by Congressman Adam Clayton Powell Jr., whose support for young, more militant black activists, combined with his efforts to contest his expulsion from Congress following his refusal to pay a libel suit penalty, had motivated many militant black people to speak out and advocate for black power.

The escalation of the Vietnam War and the continuation of the military draft further fueled the era's atmosphere of antiauthoritarianism. The war and the draft personally affected a great many black people, perhaps most famously in the case of Muhammad Ali, then the heavyweight boxing champion of the world, who, as a conscientious objector, refused his induction into the armed services. In his refusal, Ali symbolized the convergence of black radicalism and opposition to the war.

Muhammad Ali (1942–) was born Cassius Marcellus Clay Jr. in Louisville, Kentucky. He captured America's imagination during the turbulent 1960s, evoking images of athletic excellence and black militancy that transformed him into an enduring legend. Raw physical ability made him the three-time heavyweight champion of the world, but Ali's good looks and riveting charisma captivated legions of fans who held up the champ as a modern-day hero. Ali's compelling qualities also inspired revulsion in millions of other Americans who saw him as a Janus-faced warrior who betrayed the nation through his embrace of a foreign religion and adoption of a peculiar sounding name.

Cassius Clay first came into public consciousness when he won the gold medal for the United States at the Olympic Games in Rome in 1960. After turning pro in 1960 and amassing many victories, he defeated the mysterious and seemingly unbeatable Sonny Liston. "I shook up the world," Ali shouted right after he claimed the title (fig. 13), "I'm pretty! I'm a bad man!"[27] Immediately following the fight, which had attracted international attention, he again stunned the world by announcing that he had joined the highly controversial NOI and changed his name to Cassius X. This change was a rejection of his surname, which he identified as a remnant of colonialism and his ancestors' enslavement. Mentored by Malcolm X, the boxer was directed by Elijah Muhammad. Cassius X was soon given the name Muhammad Ali by Elijah Muhammad, who explained that the name Muhammad meant "worthy of all praise," and that Ali meant "most high."[28]

The adoption of Ali's name signified his new identity as a Muslim and presaged his emergence as a powerful spokesperson for and symbol of freedom, self-determination, and black pride. His religious conversion, coupled with his increasingly visible black nationalism, race consciousness, and boastful personality, quickly eroded his unsolicited "Golden Boy"

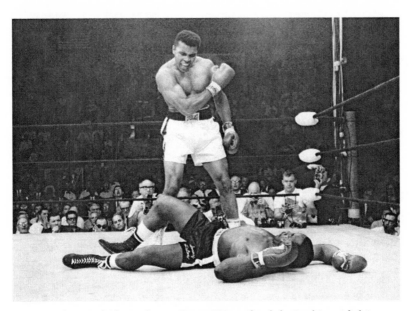

FIG. 13. Muhammad Ali stands over Sonny Liston after defeating him and claiming the Heavyweight Championship of the world, February 15, 1964. AP Photo/John Rooney (6505250172).

image. When he refused to be inducted into the military or to serve in Vietnam in 1966, the U.S. government and millions of Americans labeled him a "draft-dodger." He proclaimed, "I refuse to be inducted into the armed forces of the United States because I claim to be exempt as a minister of the religion of Islam [and because] I ain't got nothing against them Vietcong." When Ali made his controversial statements about the war, he made no direct link between it and racial issues. It was not until Carmichael appropriated Ali's comments in an effort to rally black opposition to the war that Ali began to speak of the connections between white supremacy in the United States and America's involvement in Vietnam. "Why," Carmichael asked, "should black folks fight a war against yellow folks so that white folks can keep a land they stole from red folks? We're not going to Vietnam. Ain't no Vietcong ever called me nigger!" Carmichael's more reflective comments resonated with Ali, and after hearing them, Ali himself often told reporters and listeners that "no Vietcong ever called me nigger" when pressed to explain his antiwar stance.[29]

Ali's radicalism inspired other black athletes to use sporting events as platforms for protest on behalf of African Americans. A group of Olympic athletes led by San Jose State professor Harry Edwards, who was a former athlete, formed the Olympic Project for Human Rights. Edwards recognized the increasing number of African Americans in collegiate and professional sports, and he believed that these individuals could, if unified, wield significant power. Black athletes at San Jose State, motivated by Edwards, threatened to boycott the school's football team if university officials failed to punish fraternities and other university groups that discriminated against people of color. For their part, the Olympic Project encouraged black athletes to boycott the 1968 Olympics in Mexico City in order to dramatize the plight of black Americans. A boycott of this Olympic Game would also demonstrate athletes' opposition to the stripping of Ali's heavyweight championship because of his refusal to serve in the military. Lew Alcindor (later Kareem Abdul-Jabbar), the highly visible star center of the UCLA basketball team, was one of a handful of sports stars who refused to participate in the 1968 Olympics.

The majority of black athletes who qualified for those same Olympics, however, elected to participate. The 1968 Games began as scheduled in Mexico City not long after police killed hundreds of young people who had been protesting the Mexican government's treatment of its poor and indigenous people. In this highly charged atmosphere, Olympic organizers declared that they would respond swiftly and harshly to any protests held during the event. Despite such warnings, Tommie Smith and John Carlos, two track and field athletes from San Jose State, staged an unscripted demonstration of black power and solidarity with people of African descent in struggle. Taking the gold and silver in the 200-meter sprint, Smith and Carlos, after having received their medals, stood tall on the winner's podium and each of them held one fist high overhead in a black power salute (fig. 14) as the U.S. national anthem played in the background. For their protest, Smith and Carlos were removed from the U.S. team and banished from Mexico.

Radical organizations other than the NOI also interacted with the ideas engaged by Ali and other athletes. Indeed, Ali's problack, antiwar stance inspired many people who appropriated his rhetoric and positions regularly. "Become a member of the world's highest paid black mercenary army!" read once SNCC poster. In southern California, Angela Davis (figure 15) became involved with SNCC, and its members not only assumed the political disposition of the national organization but also adopted the prevailing cultural expressions of black power politics. Like many black

FIG. 14. Tommie Smith (*center*) and John Carlos (*right*), give the black power salute in Mexico City, October 10, 1968. AP Photo/File (68101601865).

FIG. 15. Angela Davis. AP Photo (730403014).

students, Davis distinguished herself by studying black history and wearing African-inspired clothes and "natural" or "Afro"-styled hair. Like her peers, she was roused by politically charged music such as Nina Simone's "Mississippi Goddam" and James Brown's "Say It Loud, I'm Black and I'm Proud!" Even more mainstream artists such as Marvin Gaye and the Supremes still performed songs with recognizable black stylistic ethos. Black cultural nationalists such as Harold Cruse, who established himself as a literary critic and writer, denounced black leftist politics, however, and declared in works such as *The Crisis of the Negro Intellectual* (1967) that African American political activism should be based upon African and African American values; he believed that African American leftists of the 1930s and 1940s had been manipulated by white, primarily Jewish leaders of the Communist Party. A former member of the CPUSA, Cruse believed at he himself had been thus misled, and that black people had since failed to forge political institutions that drew primarily on black community culture.

Davis, who rejected Cruse's position, became a member of the CP's Che Lumumba Club in 1968, even as her primary political and cultural identity were being shaped by the militant black philosophies of the day. Neither Davis's leftist ideas nor Cruse's cultural nationalism, however, represented the whole of black political activism during this period. As many (mostly younger) black people embraced radical political and economic solutions to their problems, others gravitated to more traditional civic engagement. As Carmichael and Brown rose to power in SNCC, Thurgood Marshall was named to the U.S. Supreme Court by President Johnson. Similarly, Edward Brooke of Massachusetts became the first black U.S. senator since Reconstruction; Carl Stokes of Cleveland, Ohio, and Richard Hatcher of Gary, Indiana, became the first African American mayors of major cities; and the Supreme Court struck down laws criminalizing interracial marriage in *Loving v. Virginia*.

Artists also expressed (through their work and words) the political ideologies of the black community. By 1967, African American actor Sidney Poitier (1927–) (fig. 16) was a highly successful leading man in Hollywood in films, some of which challenged racial stereotypes and beliefs that one's race could pose an insurmountable barrier. Poitier's movie debut came in 1950 in *No Way Out*, in which he played a physician charged with caring for a white supremacist. In 1951, he played a South African minister and political activist in *Cry, the Beloved Country*. Ten years later, in 1961, he earned a Golden Globe nomination for his role in the film adaptation of *A Raisin in the Sun*, originally written by Lorraine Hansberry. In 1963 Poitier became the first African American to win the Academy Award for Best Actor, which he received for his leading role in *Lilies of the Field*. In 1967, he starred with Spencer Tracy and Katherine Hepburn in *Guess Who's Coming to Dinner*, a film that boldly, if humorously, explored the taboo issue of interracial marriage. Later that year, he received rave reviews for his role in *In the Heat of the Night*. In this film, Poitier's character, a Philadelphia detective named Virgil Tibbs, ended up having to assist a racist Mississippi sheriff, played by Rod Steiger, in solving a homicide. Steiger won the Academy Award for Best Actor for his role, and the film won the Oscar for Best Picture of the year. The actor's talent, independence, dignity, and support of the civil rights movement and black upward mobility reflected both the civil rights and black power movements in their aims to secure respect and equality for black people.

FIG. 16. Sidney Poitier with his Oscar for Best Actor for his performance in the 1963 film *Lilies of the Field.* © AP/Corbis.

Just as Poitier reached the pinnacle of his career, largely by dramatizing the many problems associated with racism in America, Angela Davis's more radical and direct approach to the struggles of black people took her down a decidedly troubled path. Following her graduation from UCSD, she was hired by UCLA as an assistant professor of philosophy, where her involvement in radical antiracist and anticapitalist organizations soon led to her ouster. During the summer of 1970, Davis provided legal and strategic advice to the imprisoned George Jackson, Fleeta Drumgo, and John Clutchette, a trio known as the "Soledad brothers" (after Soledad Prison, where they were imprisoned), who were on trial for murder. On August 7, 1970, Jonathan Jackson, George's seventeen-year-old brother, collaborated with two associates to interrupt George Jackson's trial in order to distract law enforcement officers in the building, thus assisting in the escape of their friend James McClain from another part of the Marin County Hall of Justice. McClain was being held and tried for attempted murder. In the courthouse, Jonathan Jackson and his associates stood up, directed everyone present to "freeze" at gunpoint, and escorted the judge, prosecuting attorney, and several jurors into a van parked outside. As they attempted to flee the scene of the crime, Jonathan Jackson and William Christmas, one of his accomplices, were killed in a shootout with police. Judge Harold Haley was killed by his captors with a shotgun blast, and prosecutor Gary Thomas was paralyzed after being hit by a shot fired by a police officer during the incident. The shotgun used by the alleged perpetrators to kill Judge Haley was registered in Davis's name, which implicated her in the botched escape attempt. A warrant was issued for her arrest, and she was charged as an accomplice to conspiracy, kidnapping, and homicide. Davis went underground for several months, was placed on the FBI's most wanted list, and became the target of an intense search. The FBI eventually captured and arrested her. She was tried on the charges associated with the kidnapping and killings, and was ultimately acquitted in one of the most notorious trials in modern U.S. history.

Radical leaders were not the only African Americans whose views shifted during the 1960s. Even Martin Luther King Jr. felt compelled to reevaluate his leadership in light of the influence of the black power movement and continued racial violence. Deeply concerned about the rising tide of restlessness in black communities, he worked hard to promote moderation within the civil rights movement and foster collaboration between black power advocates, including Brown and Carmichael, and traditional leaders such as Roy Wilkins and Whitney Young. King lamented the fact that his disconnect with SNCC's leaders was widely known, observing, "This debate might well have been little more than a healthy internal difference of opinion, but the press loves the sensational and it would not allow the issue to remain within the private domain of the movement."[30] Though he eventually spoke forcefully about the injustices associated with the war in Vietnam, he was not inclined to do so early on in the conflict.

King formally announced his opposition to the Vietnam War during the ninth annual SNCC convention in August 1965, marking a turning point in his career. At the conference, King called for negotiations with the Vietnamese National Liberation Front and an immediate cessation of hostilities. His words drew criticism from federal officials and from many of his peers in the SCLC, who failed to see the link between King's vision of peace and justice in America and the war in Vietnam. In the wake of that criticism, many encouraged King to remain silent on the Vietnam question going forward. In addition, King was reticent to speak out again because he did not want to alienate President Johnson or undermine federal support for the enforcement of civil rights legislation. But when Johnson announced in 1966 his intention to reallocate funds from his "War on Poverty" to the prosecution of the war in Vietnam, King could no longer contain his feelings concerning Vietnam.

Moreover, as the United States stepped up its bombing of targets in Vietnam and increased the number of troops assigned to the region and the media brought devastating images of burning and injured children (not to mention the scores of injured and dead soldiers, many of whom were African American) to televisions in homes across the nation, King was moved to issue a public statement outlining his opposition to what he considered to be an unjust, imperialistic war. He explained, "I knew that I could never again raise my voice against the violence of the oppressed in the ghettos without having first spoken clearly to the greatest purveyor of violence in the world today: my own government." He warned, "A nation that continues year after year to spend more money on military defense than on programs of social uplift is approaching spiritual death."[31]

On April 4, 1967, King issued a public and critical statement against the war to a crowd of 3,000 in Riverside Church in New York City. In this powerful speech entitled "Beyond Vietnam," he indicated that U.S. involvement in the war was "taking the young black men who have been crippled by our society and sending them 8,000 miles away to guarantee liberties in Southeast Asia which they had not found in southwest Georgia."[32] King credited Vietnam's destruction to "deadly Western arrogance," declaring, "We are on the side of the wealthy, and the secure, while we create a hell for the poor."[33] Describing the war in Vietnam as a malignant manifestation of American colonialism, he called for an immediate and unilateral ceasefire.

King's comments on the war in 1966 and 1967 met with a mixed reception. He did receive the support of some prominent activists. John Lewis, the former SNCC chair who attended King's speech at Riverside Church, described it as his "greatest." Carmichael renewed his faith in King's leadership after listening to him deliver the address again at Ebenezer Baptist Church in Atlanta, and white antiwar activists were similarly inspired by King's position on the war. Most who heard King's speech, however, roundly denounced his comments. The majority of his fellow civil rights activists were among the first to reject his speech publicly and distance themselves from their leader. Roy Wilkins of the NAACP rejected King's position, arguing that it would undermine the civil rights movement. Thurgood Marshall also encouraged King to abandon his antiwar rhetoric, while FBI Director J. Edgar Hoover wrote a letter to Johnson in which he described the civil rights leader as "an instrument in the hands of subversive forces seeking to undermine our nation."[34] King was unmoved by such threats and criticism. "The ultimate measure of a man," he stated, "is not where he stands in moments of convenience, but where he stands in moments of challenge, moments of great crisis and controversy."[35] Indeed, just two weeks after his April 4 speech, he led thousands of demonstrators on an antiwar march to the United Nations headquarters in New York City.

King believed that the civil rights movement should broaden to include economic justice as well. A 1966 attempt to shed light on the salience and injustice of poverty in Chicago convinced him of the inextricable link between economic and racial inequality: he also came to understand that drawing attention to the former was often as unwelcome and dangerous as were challenges to the latter. King and the SCLC had descended upon Chicago in January 1966 to confront economic exploitation in urban slums. The civil rights legend believed that the use of nonviolent direct action in Chicago "could arouse the conscience of this nation to deal realistically with the northern ghetto." Through an effort code-named Operation Breadbasket, King and the SCLC focused on housing discrimination and racist hiring practices in the city. Not long after the campaign's kick-off rally at Soldier Field on July 10, 1966, race riots erupted on Chicago's West Side. Young blacks responded with violence when they were attacked by enraged whites as they marched through the all-white Chicago neighborhood of Cicero on August 5. King, who had moved to Chicago temporarily with his family, was struck by a rock during the march. "Bottles and bricks were thrown at us," he recalled. "I've been in many demonstrations all across the South, but I can say that I had never seen, even in Mississippi, mobs as hostile and as hate-filled as [those] in Chicago."[36]

Throughout the summer of 1966, King faced the insurmountable challenges of unifying Chicago's diverse African American communities and confronting working-class whites who opposed the racial integration of housing. He noted, "Many whites who opposed open housing would deny they were racist. They turn to sociological arguments without realizing that criminal responses are environmental, not racial." By late August, however, Mayor Richard J. Daley cleverly outmaneuvered King by publicly endorsing the civil rights leader's goals while doing little to realize them. Though Operation Breadbasket, led by former North Carolina Agricultural and Technical State University student activist Jesse Jackson, made minor inroads in employment desegregation and the creation of business opportunities for blacks in the city, the Chicago campaign was largely unsuccessful. By September, Daley struck an inconsequential deal with King, the SCLC, and many housing boards. In the so called Summit Agreement, the Chicago Housing Authority committed to build "non-ghetto low-rise" public housing, and the Mortgage Bankers Association agreed to provide low-interest loans on a nondiscriminatory basis. King left Chicago, and the city continued to practice "business as usual." He showed his frustration in trying to assess the failure. "The city's inaction," he argued, "[was] another hot coal on the smoldering fires of discontent and despair that are rampant in our black communities."[37]

As King puzzled over economic inequality and its connection to racism, other organizations addressed similar issues. The most institutionalized expression of black militancy and disaffection was the Black Panther Party for Self-Defense (BPP), founded by Huey P. Newton and Bobby Seale in Oakland, California in October 1966 (fig. 17). The BPP mixed Marxist-Leninist philosophies with black nationalist doctrines. In collaboration with white leftists, the Black Panthers endeavored to establish a revolutionary movement to destroy capitalism and eliminate police brutality. Eldridge Cleaver, the Panthers' minister of education, played a key role in developing the organization's guiding principles. Cleaver was a convicted rapist: while in prison, he studied the teachings of Malcolm X. In his autobiographical manifesto entitled *Soul on Ice* (1968), he argued that people of African descent were not simply oppressed Americans, they were victims of colonization. In his view, therefore, integration was not a viable solution to black suffering. African Americans, he argued, needed liberation from

FIG. 17. A Black Panther Party poster (late 1960s) featuring Robert George "Bobby" Seal and Huey Newton. Library of Congress.

white supremacy and American imperialism. "To achieve these ends," he proclaimed, "we believe that political and military machinery that does not exist now and has never existed must be created. We need functional machinery that is able to deal with these two interrelated sets of political dynamics which, strictly speaking, make up the total political situation on the North American continent."[38] Reflecting the group's radicalism, the party eliminated the term "Self-Defense" from its name in 1968.

Black rage and the ascendency of the BPP affirmed King's belief that racial tensions were spiraling toward a violent end. "Those who would make a peaceful revolution impossible," he argued, "will make a violent revolution inevitable."[39] His words were prophetic. During the summer of 1965, the Watts neighborhood of East Central Los Angeles exploded in racial violence. This overwhelmingly black section of the city had long been overcrowded, plagued by underemployment, without sufficient health care facilities, virtually devoid of public transportation, consumed by crime and drug addiction, mired in poverty, and besieged by police brutality. The riots in Watts, which some classify as a rebellion, began on August 11, 1965, when Los Angeles Highway Patrol officers stopped two African American brothers, both of whom were residents of Watts and one of whom was home from college for his summer vacation, for speeding.

A crowd of black people gathered to observe the officer issue the driver a ticket. One of the brothers expressed his belief that he was stopped without provocation. The police officer objected, the young man became angry, and bystanders sensed that something unfair was happening to the young black men. The officer called for reinforcements: not long afterward police back-up arrived from the Los Angeles Police Department (LAPD). Fearful that the episode might escalate, an LAPD officer drew his gun, arrested the detainees, and took them into custody. Hundreds of Watts residents protested as the police departed the scene. Less than one hour later, African Americans in Watts took to the streets, smashing windows, looting, burning buildings, shooting, and engaging police officers in physical combat in a revolt that lasted for five days and involved 30,000 people. The riot finally ended when 14,000 National Guard troops arrived and occupied Watts. In the wake of the violence, 34 persons lay dead, 1,032 were injured, 4,000 had been arrested, and the areas had suffered $40 million in property damage.

Violent riots continued through the remainder of the 1960s. During the summer of 1967, black communities across the nation erupted in racially charged violence. One of the most brutal episodes occurred in Newark, New Jersey, on July 13, after a crowd of blacks began throwing rocks at the police to protest the arrest of an African American taxi driver. Rioting ensued for six days, resulting in major property damage, more than 1,000 injuries, and 23 deaths. Not long after the Newark riot, Detroit exploded. When police officers raided a Detroit afterhours club named the "Blind Pig" on July 22, local black people attacked the arresting officers, igniting

FIG. 18. Stokely Carmichael (Kwame Ture). Library of Congress (LC-USZ62-114815).

another of the worst episodes of urban violence in American history. Over the course of five days and nights, 33 blacks and 10 whites were killed, 1,189 people were injured, and more than 7,200 people were arrested and jailed. In addition, nearly 2,500 stores were looted and property damage reached $32 million. As police could not stop it, the riot did not end until the National Guard and army paratroopers arrived to reclaim the city.

King worried that such racial violence would embolden those black power leaders who rejected his nonviolent methods. He bemoaned the publication of radical books such *Black Power: The Politics of Liberation in America* (1967), a book written by Carmichael and black political scientist Charles Hamilton which, like Cleaver's *Soul on Ice*, likened black Americans to a colonized people. Carmichael and Hamilton argued that

FIG. 19. James Brown, the "Godfather of Soul," 1979. © Neal Preston/Corbis.

black power was "the last reasonable opportunity" for America "to work out its racial problems short of prolonged destructive guerilla warfare."[40] Despite King's firm belief in nonviolence, he too believed that violence was unavoidable given the current state of U.S. race relations. He, however, blamed America's inaction for the racial violence consuming the nation, noting that "the nation waited until the black man was explosive with fury before stirring itself even to partial concern."[41] Although King remained committed to nonviolence, it became difficult for him to compete with the rising influence of black power leaders.

Maintaining his belief that the slogan "black power" was incendiary, King refused to participate in the National Conference on Black Power that convened in Newark following the riot in July, 1967. One thousand delegates attended the conference, including Brown and people from King's SCLC, the NUL, and the NAACP, but it was black nationalists from the North's urban ghettos who made the biggest impact at the meeting. Imamu Amiri Baraka, a poet hailing from Newark, greatly influenced the gathering when he arrived bandaged and bruised following a beating from police. Standing before the assemblage, he called for continued black resistance and self-reliance.

Born Everett Leroi Jones, Imamu Amiri Baraka changed his name when he converted to the Kewadia sect of Islam in the late 1960s. He attended Rutgers and Howard Universities before serving three years in the U. S. Air Force. Between 1960 and 1968, he became increasingly active in leftist, militant black struggles, which followed his visits to Cuba as member of a delegation of writers. His first book of poetry, entitled *Preface to a Twenty Volume Suicide Note*, was published in 1961. He received critical acclaim for his play *The Dutchman* (1964), which featured a deadly incident on a New York subway involving Clay, a young upwardly mobile black man tormented by latent rage and Lulu, a beautiful yet vicious white woman who triggered Clay's rage. Greatly influenced by the assassination of Malcolm X in 1965, Baraka divorced his Jewish wife, became a fervent black nationalist, and moved to Harlem. There, Baraka funded the Black Arts Repertory Theater School. "Black Arts," one of his poems, helped inspire the burgeoning Black Arts Movement of the late 1960s. Just before the Newark conference, Baraka had also embraced the cultural nationalist views of Maulana Karenga, the former UCLA graduate student who later became the founder of Kwanzaa, a week-long holiday observed from December 26 to January 1 to honor African American and Pan-African heritage. In 1968, Baraka founded the Black Community Development and Defense Organization.

Although black power advocates viewed themselves as righteous voices of black frustration and anger, many white critics, including Maryland Governor Spiro Agnew and Hoover, argued that they were nothing more than purveyors of conflict and violence. Following the riots of 1967, Hoover pressured President Johnson to begin a clandestine counterintelligence program (COINTELPRO) "to expose, disrupt, misdirect, discredit, or otherwise neutralize the activities of black nationalists, hate-type organizations and groupings, their leadership, spokesmen, membership, and supporters and to counter their propensity for violence and civil disorder."[42] COINTELPRO specifically targeted CORE, SNCC, BPP, NOI, and the Louisiana-based Deacons for Defense and Justice. Although it was not a primary target, King's SCLC was also singled out for intelligence gathering.

Even as federal, state, and local authorities moved to crush the black militancy associated with the Watts, Newark, and Detroit riots, President Johnson established the National Advisory Commission on Civil Disorders, led by Illinois governor Otto Kerner, to ascertain the root causes of the urban violence in America. The commission boasted two black members out of eleven, namely Republican senator Edward W. Brooke and Roy Wilkins of the NAACP. In its final report, released in 1968, the Kerner Commission cited white racism as the primary cause of the riots and declared that the United States was "moving toward two societies, one white, one black, separate and unequal." The report further noted, "Negroes firmly believe that police brutality and harassment occur repeatedly in Negro neighborhoods. This belief is unquestionably one of the major reasons for intense Negro resentment against police." The report asked the federal government to invest heavily in urban areas, public housing, schools, jobs, and a "national system of income supplementation."[43] All but consumed by the ever-expanding war in Vietnam, and heavily influenced by conservative white southerners in Congress, Johnson did very little to act upon the commission's recommendations.

The Vietnam War and the race riots of the late 1960s undermined Johnson's genuine commitment to the black freedom struggle and his massive effort to fight poverty in the United States. Johnson's campaign, known as "the Great Society," sought to eradicate poverty through social programs and direct aid. Although Johnson's Great Society enacted Medicare and Medicaid programs, giving the elderly and disabled access to medical care in 1964 and early 1965, the heart of his Great Society legislation was born in late 1965 with the implementation of programs for educational improvements, urban renewal, the development of impoverished areas, and crime prevention. Johnson stated his commitment to "an unconditional war on poverty" when he outlined a new direction for his administration:

> It is not enough to just open the gates of opportunity. All our citizens must have the ability to walk through the gates. This is the next and more profound stage of the battle for civil rights. We seek not just freedom but opportunity—not just legal equity but human ability—not just equality as a right and a theory, but equality as a fact and as a result.[44]

Johnson, who hailed from humble beginnings, truly identified with the marginalized and downtrodden. An ardent supporter of Franklin Roosevelt's New Deal as a member of the House of Representatives, LBJ boldly refused to support the Southern Manifesto as a senator, and he had skillfully surmounted the filibustering of southern senators to steer through Congress the passage of the 1957, 1960, and 1964 Civil Rights Acts, as well as the 1965 Voting Rights Act.

Perhaps the most important piece of Great Society legislation, however, was the Economic Opportunity Act of 1964. The act established an Office of Economic Opportunity that oversaw a number of programs: Head Start to assist poor preschool children; Upward Bound to prime indigent high school students for college; and Volunteers in Service to America (VISTA) to enable citizen volunteers to work as a domestic peace corps to serve the poor, illiterate, and unrepresented. Neighborhood administrative boards, which included African Americans (thus providing them with valuable political experience), implemented these programs at the local level. Johnson's War on Poverty created the first government programs that allowed black people to play a substantive role in creating and supervising programs that served their own communities. The New Careers program, for instance, helped the poor secure work as teachers' assistants, daycare workers, and community organizers. The program thus provided social, economic, and political capital to those who had none. In doing so, it educated and inspired many black people to assume leadership roles in their community.

Perhaps most controversial among the War on Poverty programs were the Community Action Programs (CAPs), which fought poverty on a local level through a massive infusion of federal funds into afterschool programs, community centers, childcare, skills development, and job training. Despite differences in communities throughout America, CAPs shared certain features: "nonprofit corporation status; local governing boards; racially heterogeneous staffs composed of professional social workers, academics, and para-professionals; and collective funding from many sources, including foundations and local governmental agencies as well as federal agencies."[45] What distinguished CAPs and made these local organizations controversial were the massive amount of funds the federal government promised to invest in the program, the speed with which CAPs were created and made operational, and the statutory mandate that all programmatic decisions made by CAPs include input from local residents.

Johnson's Great Society programs faced many critics, including local leaders who were loath to relinquish some of their power and control to those who were previously marginalized and disfranchised. Racists and bigots went so far as to suggest that Johnson's efforts merely rewarded idle, criminal, and otherwise unworthy blacks and other poor people with government handouts. African Americans looked to the Great Society with hope, only to have their expectations undercut by white opposition to funding programs adequately. Many have argued that if Johnson had been given the proper resources, the War on Poverty might have proven a worthy fight. Yet appropriations that could have funded the War on Poverty were diverted to the U.S. role in the war in Vietnam. Funding for the War of Poverty amounted to $10 billion, while the war in Vietnam cost $140 billion.

As funding for the Great Society dried up and Johnson proved unable or unwilling to stop the escalation of the war in Vietnam, King became increasingly critical of the beleaguered president and his administration. He openly criticized Johnson's abandonment of the War on Poverty as well as the administration's policy toward Vietnam, calling once again for an end to the military campaign. "There may be others who want to go another way, but when I took up the cross, I recognized its meaning," King intoned. "The cross may mean the death of your popularity. It may mean the death of your bridge to the White House, but take up your cross and just bear it."[46] This public condemnation enraged Johnson, who felt that King had betrayed him.

While King's newly articulated commitment to urban economic justice and peace in Vietnam irritated and angered Johnson, both leaders were disheartened by the fragmentation of the Democratic base that had propelled the president into the White House in 1964. Working-class whites in the North withdrew some of their support of the party in retaliation for its fervent calls for civil rights. The ever-deteriorating relationship between Jews and blacks also hurt the party, as the two groups had played critical roles in its rise to power. Jewish champions of the civil rights movement were angered that black people from SNCC and other organizations supported the Palestinian struggle, and African Americans were critical of Jewish store owners in black communities who failed to hired blacks and charged what critics considered to be high prices for wares.

By the fall of 1967, King believed that significant plans should be made to bolster the dwindling white endorsement for the fight to end racism. At the annual meeting of the SCLC, he declared that nothing short of a complete "restructuring of American society" was in order. "The problem of racism, the problem of economic exploitation, and the problem of war are all tied together." Not long afterward, he announced his plans to lead a "Poor People's Campaign" to "dramatize the whole economic problem of the poor," and to mobilize a massive multiracial gathering in support of this new initiative in Washington DC. Although King was positive that "the time has come for a return to mass non-violent protest," he knew that his call for a fundamental restructuring of America's socioeconomic system would alienate many supporters of the status quo. Yet, he maintained, "We have, through massive nonviolent action, an opportunity to avoid a national disaster and create a new spirit of class and racial harmony."[47]

Early in 1968 King recruited participants from across the racial spectrum for his Poor People's Campaign, indicating that it "must not be just black people, it must be all poor people. We must include American Indians, Puerto Ricans, Mexicans, and even poor whites."[48] The SCLC asserted that the Poor People's Campaign would be the most massive, widespread campaign of civil disobedience yet undertaken by what King described as the "second phase" of the civil rights movement. He and other leaders endeavored to bring 1,500 activists to Washington to lobby Congress and governmental agencies for an "economic bill of rights." Campaign organizers called on the federal government to prepare a $30 billion antipoverty package that would include a commitment to full employment, a guaranteed living wage for every American, and increased construction of low-income housing. Event activities in the nation's capital were to be coordinated simultaneously with demonstrations throughout the rest of the nation. Despite division within the SCLC over the scope of the campaign and the ability of the organization to meet ability to meet its goals, King pushed the campaign forward, spoke relentlessly about the evils of poverty, and led "people-to-people tours" to recruit participants.

The war not only sapped Johnson of most of his political energies; it also consumed the budget surplus that the president had planned to use to fund his antipoverty Great Society programs, something about which he truly cared. LBJ was desperately afraid to "lose" the war, but he did not start it. He wanted to get out of Vietnam and he truly wanted to help the poor. Nevertheless, these circumstances angered King, who believed that Johnson had deliberately sacrificed justice at the altar of political pressure and had chosen white supremacy, elitism, imperialism, anticommunism, and war over the spiritual, social, and economic well-being of his fellow citizens.

In March 1968 King accepted an invitation to participate in a march in Memphis, Tennessee, where black sanitation workers were striking in an attempt to unionize and secure better hours and pay. Memphis mayor Henry Loeb refused to negotiate with the strikers, so the workers turned to King for support. He believed that his support of the 1,300 predominantly black sanitation workers would help generate positive press for his work on behalf of black people and the Poor People's Campaign.

King brought his leadership and experience to the protests in Memphis. He supported the workers' boycott of Memphis merchants, who supported the city's unwillingness to negotiate with the sanitation workers, and participated in the march on March 18 as promised. Yet he was saddened that the nonviolent march descended into chaos when several protestors broke ranks and began breaking windows in downtown Memphis shops. King was blamed for the unfortunate end to the march, and he assumed responsibility for it. Determined to see the boycott through to a successful end, he returned to Memphis to demonstrate that nonviolent methods could still yield positive results. He arrived on April 3, checking into the black-owned Lorraine Motel. His staff used this time to attempt to secure a permit to march and to persuade young gang members to refrain from disrupting the march. That evening, as final preparations for the march were being made, King delivered his final and arguably most prophetic speech:

> Like anybody, I would like to live a long life. Longevity has its place. But I'm not concerned about that now. I just want to do God's will. And He's allowed me to go up to the mountain. And I've looked over. And I've seen the promised land. I may not get there with you. But I want you to know tonight, that we, as a people, will get to the promised land. And I'm happy, tonight. I'm not worried about anything. I'm not fearing any man. Mine eyes have seen the glory of the coming of the Lord.[49]

The next day, on April 4, 1968, as he stood on the balcony of the Lorraine Motel, King was assassinated by a white supremacist named James Earl Ray. His murder brought forth a storm of fury and violence in black communities. More than 125 cities exploded in riots. By April 11, forty-six people had lost their lives, thirty-five thousand were wounded, and more than twenty thousand had been arrested as a result of the riots.

Within days of King's killing, Congress passed the Civil Rights Act of 1968, also known as the Open Housing Act, which outlawed racial discrimination in the sale and rental of houses and empowered the Justice Department to file suit against housing infractions. Johnson had proposed the measure two years earlier, but King's murder motivated Congress to act. King's assassination also increased support for the Poor People's Campaign, now led by Abernathy. The campaign was officially launched in May 1968, when more than two thousand protestors arrived in Washington DC and settled into a makeshift shantytown that organizers named Resurrection City. Every day for more than one month they marched from Resurrection City to the building of a federal agency, and they staged a major protest on June 19. The activists were expelled from Resurrection City on June 24, however, and the campaign came to an abrupt end. Without King's leadership, the SCLC soon declined in stature as well.

The civil rights movement brought about monumental changes in America. The federal government affirmed its support, albeit under intense pressure, for its citizens' most basic rights. Through legislation, rulings on behalf of activists, and the enforcement of the rule of law, two presidents and Congress used their political and military powers to aid the black freedom struggle. Black leaders, both young and old, instigated confrontations with white supremacists in order to secure media coverage, and to provoke the government to intervene on behalf of black people and racial justice. For more than a decade, black activists and their allies waged an unrelenting battle for racial integration and justice, cultural autonomy, and economic opportunity. The Civil Rights Act of 1964 and the Voting Rights Act of 1965 represented the zenith of the movement on the Southern front, while structural changes such as deindustrialization and suburbanization fostered crises in urban areas in the North and West. Militant black organizations and leaders emerged in these areas to call for black power, and to forge the Black Arts Movement to give their radicalism and cultural nationalism texture and expression. The white backlash to the militant demands of black people emerged out of a competitive environment in which African Americans threatened to make inroads into previously all-white spheres of influence.

As urban areas became increasingly black, they were described as ghettos. Yet it was within these communities that black artists and activists captured the trials, tribulations, beauty, and promise of modern black America. The black power era of the 1960s emerged as a provocative critique of the nonviolent movement for the civil rights of black people. Black power advocates, whether champions of its principles, its rites, or its chauvinist bravado, greatly influenced black Americans, and, ostensibly the entire nation. The assassination of Martin Luther King Jr., the nation's unsurpassed prophet of peace, reminded African Americans that the United States was still unsafe for those who understood and challenged its racist and classist dogmas, mechanisms, and structures. By 1968 it became clear once more that ultimately black people could depend on no one but themselves to defeat white supremacy. Black power freed the minds of African Americans, just as black liberation theology liberated their spirits. Black power served as a counternarrative of American culture by casting black people as naturally beautiful, the descendants of a noble past. It also emphasized the experiences of everyday black people who suffered under the yoke of racism and poverty. As the 1970s drew near, despite their many losses and setbacks, black people had accomplished much. They now looked to the future with a renewed sense of pride, group identity, a fierce sense of determination, and the power inherent in collective action.

4

"SO LET IT BE DONE," 1968–1980

> Now, then, in order to understand white supremacy we must
> dismiss the fallacious notion that white people can give anybody
> their freedom. In order for America to really live a new society
> must be born. Racism must die. The economic exploitation by this
> country of non-white peoples must also die.
>
> —STOKELY CARMICHAEL, "Black Power," delivered at the
> University of California, Berkley, October, 1966

King's murder unleashed a torrent of violence, as many African Americans, saddened and enraged at the same time, responded to the news by taking to the streets. The violence was quelled only when President Johnson sent 20,000 army troops and 24,000 National Guardsmen to urban areas to stop the violence and enforce curfews. By April 11, 46 people lay dead, 2,600 were injured, and more than 21,000 had been arrested, primarily on charges of looting. Property damage from the riots totaled $67 million. Radical black leaders called for retaliation for King's murder. Stokely Carmichael suggested staging a violent rebellion, while the NAACP's Roy Wilkins argued that King would have been disheartened by such reactionary behavior. Wilkins answered Carmichael's message with a call for a nationwide campaign against racial violence, stressing the importance of jobs and improved community relations.

Despite Wilkins's pleas, the Black Panther Party stepped up its rhetoric and activities, and the FBI became more aggressive in its efforts to undermine it. Undercover agents infiltrated the BPP, instigating violence and mayhem. No one disputes that certain members of the BPP were far from innocent. Huey P. Newton, for instance, possessed a long criminal record. He was imprisoned for murder in 1968, acquitted, released, and then charged again with murder and assault in 1974. After living in exile in Cuba until 1977, he returned to the United States and was acquitted again. He would be murdered in 1989 in an altercation over drugs in Oakland at the age of forty-two. Nevertheless, the FBI and its agents helped shape negative public opinions of the Panthers through a propaganda campaign. FBI agents and informants also wreaked havoc in black power organizations by provoking much of the violence associated with them. For example, police killed at least 28 Panthers and jailed 750 others. In arguably the most shocking incident, Chicago police officers killed Fred Hampton and Mark Clark, who were still sleeping, during a predawn raid on the Illinois BPP Headquarters on December 4, 1969. The police riddled the tenement offices with more than two hundred rounds of ammunition. A mere two shots were fired in self-defense from the apartment before the activists succumbed to the police gunfire.

Although black radicals were targeted for infiltration and destruction, black militancy did not end. The prison rights movement is perhaps the most illuminating reflection of this enduring radicalism. From its beginnings, the BPP called attention to the plight of black prisoners, who constituted more than half of the American prison population. Black activists, particularly Angela Davis, argued that these numbers reflected a conscious effort to suppress political dissent. They also denounced what they considered unjust sentencing and the deplorable conditions inside prisons.

At Attica, a maximum security prison in upstate New York, African American and Latino prisoners led a rebellion to protest their poor treatment. On September 9, 1971, 1,200 inmates took over most of the prison, made hostages of the prison guards, and demanded better treatment, facilities, and food. Four days after the revolt began, those prison guards not taken hostage, with the state police, retook control of the prison in a deadly assault. Tom Wicker, a columnist for the *New York Times*, reported on the clash:

A task force consisting of 211 state troopers and corrections officers retook Attica using tear gas, rifles, and shotguns. After the shooting was over, ten hostages and twenty-nine inmates lay dead or dying. At least 450 rounds of ammunition had been discharged. Four hostages and eighty-five inmates suffered gunshot wounds that they survived. After initial reports that several hostages had died at the hands of knife-wielding inmates, pathologists' reports reveal that hostages and inmates all died from gunshot wounds. No guns were found in the possession of inmates.[1]

The Attica rebellion demonstrated that black militancy and political consciousness had reached as far as incarcerated communities of African Americans. On the other hand, this rebellion and its ending also revealed the lengths to which white people were willing to go to squash black insurgency.

Black leaders, radical and moderate, were not alone in calling for collective action after King's assassination. President Johnson emphasized the need for unity. "We can achieve nothing by lawlessness and divisiveness among the American people,"[2] he proclaimed. Rather, he called for all Americans to mourn the loss of King. Millions responded to Johnson's call, and memorials and rallies were held throughout the nation immediately following King's death. Public schools, public libraries, museums, many seaports, thousands of businesses, and the stock exchanges observed the solemn occasion. Sporting events, Hollywood's Academy Awards ceremony, and the presidential nomination campaigns were all postponed. Despite Johnson's efforts to publicly mourn the loss of King and honor his legacy, he continued to sacrifice his support of black people, and to compromise the integrity of his War on Poverty, at the altar of military involvement and escalation in Vietnam.

Vietnam: A Black Man's Fight?

As much as Lyndon Baines Johnson hated the Vietnam War, it took up an increasing amount of his energies and the nation's dollars. A proponent of the domino theory, Johnson joined other "cold warriors" of the day who feared that, should one nation "fall" to communism, its neighboring nations would likely be the next to convert to communism as well. Consequently, Johnson's Cold War strategies rested on the theory of containment. A French colony from the 1860s until World War II, when Japan took the colony by force, Vietnam was soon controlled by communists led by Ho Chi Minh, who proclaimed independence. Aided financially by the United States, France recaptured Vietnam and controlled it from 1945 until Ho's forces defeated the European nation in 1954. Stunned and disappointed by France's defeat, the United States orchestrated a partition of Vietnam into a U.S.-backed South Vietnam (which contained a number of communist guerrilla fighters called "Viet Cong" by Americans) and a communist-led North Vietnam. Unwisely, the United States failed to calculate that as a sponsor of South Vietnam it would, as the French had done, incur the wrath of Vietnamese citizens who rejected white colonial rule and sought the reunification of their country.

For nearly a decade, under the leadership of Presidents Eisenhower and Kennedy, the United States government aided and bolstered the shady and inept South Vietnamese government based in Saigon. When Johnson gained the presidency, he was faced with the sobering reality that only a major escalation of U.S. involvement in the conflict, including extensive bombing of North Vietnam and the deployment of many U.S. troops into South Vietnam, would enable the South Vietnamese government to continue to stave off the forces of the North. Indeed, at the time of President Kennedy's assassination, sixteen thousand U.S. military "advisors" were already deployed to Vietnam.

Johnson was not enthusiastic about an escalation of America's involvement in the war, nor did he want the conflict to undercut his Great Society programs, which he considered to be the defining elements of his presidency. Johnson later revealed:

> I was bound to be crucified either way I moved. If I left the woman I really loved—the Great Society—in order to get involved with the bitch of a war on the other side of the world, then I would lose everything at home. All my programs. All my hopes to feed the hungry and shelter the homeless. All my dreams to provide education and medical care to the browns and the blacks and the lame and the poor. But if I left that war and let the Communists take over South Vietnam, then I would be seen as a coward and my nation would be seen as an appeaser and we would both find it impossible to accomplish anything for anybody anywhere on the entire globe.[3]

Johnson, therefore, was aware of the "quagmire" he entered via Vietnam. He stepped up America's intervention in the country slowly, substantially, and relentlessly. He increased the number of American advisors in the region, and stretched their responsibilities following the Gulf of Tonkin incident, in which a small band of North Vietnamese soldiers in a few relatively small boats reportedly attacked the destroyers uss *Maddox* and uss *C. Turner Joy*. Johnson used this incident to increase the power of the president in unofficially sanctioned acts of war. By securing congressional approval of escalation through passage of the Gulf of Tonkin Resolution,

Johnson expanded the powers of the President to make war, and thereafter the U.S. military presence in Southeast Asia increased dramatically. Some 550,000 American soldiers were deployed in Vietnam in 1968, but even this huge surge in troop numbers failed to turn the tide in the conflict, as an average of more than 1,000 U.S. troops died every month in Vietnam in 1967 and 1968. At the height of the war in 1969, 543,400 American military personnel were stationed in Vietnam.

The Vietnam War was particularly costly to African Americans. In the war's early years, African American men registered the highest casualty rate of all soldiers. As was the case in many other wars in American history, black people were divided in their views of the conflict. Black leaders, however, emerged as among the nation's most outspoken opponents of the war, reminding Americans that it was hypocritical to send African American soldiers abroad to fight for "freedom" while they were reviled and discriminated against at home. SNCC spoke out against the war and advocated draft evasion as early as 1966. One so-called "draft dodger," who sought refuge in Canada, agreed with SNCC when he argued, "I'm not a draft evader, I'm a runaway slave."[4] In Vietnam, black, white, Indigenous, and Latino soldiers killed and died together for a country that was loath to send them together to integrated schools. Further, the great majority of U.S. troops were poor and working class, as were those they fought against. Black leaders, especially the more militant ones, were not shy about reminding the American public of this reality.

The Vietnam War was the second war in which African American troops participated in a fully integrated U.S. military: the Korean War had been the first. Black men were overrepresented among the troops during Vietnam: while black people were eleven percent of the American population, thirteen percent of the 58,193 American troops who were killed in Vietnam in 1965 were black. Naturally, the black community and its leaders found this statistic deeply disturbing. Even though many African Americans called on the U.S. government to ameliorate this imbalance, little was done about it. The death rates of African American troops in the Vietnam War remained higher than those of their white counterparts throughout the conflict. Black men, who were less likely to be eligible for student and medical deferments such as those used by future white political leaders Dan Quayle, Bill Clinton, and George W. Bush, were drafted at higher rates than were white men. At the same time the National Guard, a fashionable sanctuary for whites who did not wish to go to Vietnam, refused to accept more than a small number of black volunteers. Furthermore, white men dominated the officer corps: 20 percent of all combat troops and 2 percent of officers were black. Even within the fully integrated military, the opportunities available to black men remained limited. Colin Powell, who would go on to become a four-star general, a member of the Joint Chiefs of Staff, and the first black Secretary of State, served two tours of duty in Vietnam. During these tours, he was as an advisor to the Army of the Republic of Vietnam in 1962, and a battalion executive officer in 1968. Powell had a distinguished military career and was awarded eleven medals, including a Bronze Star and a Purple Heart.

Just as black soldiers fought the Double V during World War II, African American soldiers in Vietnam waged war on multiple fronts. Identifying the enemy was not easy for these soldiers. Some of them viewed the Vietnamese as a colonized people of color who were victims of white American imperialism, while others simply saw them as an enemy to be defeated. In any event, while serving their country, black soldiers endured de facto segregation, white bigotry, racist graffiti, vile insults, the flying of the Confederate flag, and physical assaults during the late 1960s. While white troops were permitted to display Confederate flags and tag military installations with racist graffiti, including racist epithets, the armed forces frowned upon symbols of black culture and community, such as the Black Panther logo and clench-fisted black power salutes. Many black soldiers, therefore, considered racial conditions in Vietnam to be every bit as retrograde and racist as they were in the United States, where cities were consumed with racial conflict and violence.

In 1966 the U.S. Defense Department initiated Project 100,000 to offset the high rejection rate of blacks in the military. This project unintentionally changed the institution's racial balance of power. The initiative empowered recruiters to consider applicants who had criminal records or few, if any, skills. Of the 340,000 soldiers this program recruited, 136,000 were black. These increased numbers transformed the war into, as many black people saw it, "a white man's war but a black man's fight." Black Project 100,000 recruits were told that they would receive training and "rehabilitation" during their service, but instead they quickly became overrepresented in combat missions. This overrepresentation complicated African Americans' relationship to the military through the rest of the Vietnam War.

Prior to the withdrawal of U.S. troops from Vietnam in the mid-1970s, the radicalization of black soldiers led to racial conflicts within the military. Early in 1970 the U.S. armed services acknowledged that racial conflicts in their ranks constituted a serious problem, and they enacted firm policies to restrict symbols of black and white cultural nationalism. These officials also endeavored to educate white soldiers on issues that offended African Americans. The military also engaged in affirmative action by elevating qualified blacks to what was still a predominantly white officer corps. These changes marked a fundamental shift in the consciousness of white military leaders. In 1971 the newly established Congressional Black Caucus (CBC) held hearings on racism in the armed services, bringing further attention to the status of African Americans in the U.S. military. By 1975 Daniel "Chappie" James Jr., a Tuskegee airman, became the first African American to be made a four-star general. In 1979 Hazel Winifred Johnson became the first black woman to be promoted to brigadier general as head of the Army Nurse Corps.

The Black Arts Movement

By this time one could discern African Americans' newfound assertiveness not only in politics and protest, but also in the artistic contributions of people such as Imamu Amiri Baraka. Between 1965 and 1975 black people engaged in very intense dialogue about the cultural and political future of black America. The black power movement challenged African Americans to examine black politics in the post–civil rights era; this discussion frequently hinged upon the role black artists played in the cause of black freedom and progress. The Black Arts Movement (BAM) was a response to and celebration of this discussion. Launched, in part, by the work of Baraka, the BAM gave artistic expression to a new generation of black power advocates. It included artists of many talents whose writing, music, and comedy answered the call of black power leaders to produce art that would help inspire and advance the black freedom struggle. However, like their predecessors during the Harlem Renaissance, members of the BAM struggled with the matter of the political or aesthetic relevance of black art. Though some in the black community had difficulty placing the movement within a political context, the poetic torchbearers of the revolutionary BAM, for example, produced innovative writing and critiques of "the white aesthetic." In their work, these artists, including Sonia Sanchez, Nikki Giovanni, and Don L. Lee (later Haki R. Madhubuti), emphasized black pride and beauty. Giovanni distinguished herself with a radical screed entitled "The True Import of Present Dialogue, Black v.

Negro," which was published in her first collection of poems, *Black Feeling, Black Talk* (1967). She followed this offering with *We a BadddDDD People* in 1970. Giovanni and other artists were pulled into the umbrella of the BAM through Baraka's leadership in particular. Indeed, the advent of the BAM coincided with Baraka's creation of the Black Arts Repertory Theater. The principles of the BAM were articulated by Baraka himself, who explained, "The Black man must seek a Black politics, an ordering of the world that is beneficial to his culture, to his interiorization and judgment of the world. The Black Artist . . . is desperately needed to change the images his people identify with, by asserting Black feeling, Black mind, Black judgment."[5] In 1968, with Larry Neal, Baraka prepared a collection of essays entitled *Black Fire*, which shed light on many African Americans' growing rejection of integration and documented the ascendency of cultural nationalism among members of the BAM. For his part, Larry Neal also defined the goals of the movement:

> The Black Arts Movement is radically opposed to any concept of the artist that alienates him from his community. Black Art is the aesthetic and spiritual sister of the Black Power concept. As such, it envisions an art that speaks directly to the needs and aspirations of Black Americans. In order to perform this task, the Black Arts Movement proposes a radical reordering of the western cultural aesthetic. It proposes a separate symbolism, mythology, critique, and iconography. The Black Arts and Black Power concept both relate broadly to the Afro-American's desire for self-determination and nationhood. Both concepts are nationalistic. One is concerned with the relationship between art and politics; the other with the art of politics.[6]

The BAM faced many critics. Some objected to the movement's cultural nationalism, others denounced its homophobia, and some still others bemoaned its obsession with black masculinity. The BAM, however, did not comprise a homogeneous monolith. Maya Angelou, for example, published her autobiographical novel, entitled *I Know Why the Caged Bird Sings*, in 1970. Her writing gave expression to the suppression of black women within African American communities, and it also revealed her history of sexual abuse. During the 1970s more black women contributed to a centrist canon, even as they agreed with and supported many of the ideas and positions of BAM philosophies.

Some proponents of the BAM acknowledged the movement's place within a larger history of black arts. A number of writers, including Gwendolyn Brooks, Lorraine Hansberry, Langston Hughes, and James Baldwin, linked the BAM with the African American cultural revivals of the 1930s, 1940s, and 1950s. Brooks continued to underscore the artist's duty to give back to his or her community. She also stressed the responsibility of artists, suggesting that they should foster and maintain connections with their audience. Expanding on her longstanding commitment to grassroots art programs, Brooks "converted" to a black nationalist view during the 1960s and supported the ideals and work of young members of the BAM. While numerous artists, including Baraka; playwrights, including Ed Bullins and Ron Milner; and spoken-word artists, such as the Last Poets and Gil Scott-Heron, were inextricably linked to the BAM, local artists formed the backbone of working-class literary circles throughout the United States.

Perhaps the most widely read and celebrated author of the era was James Baldwin. Although quite critical of white America, Baldwin was also a proponent of integration. He balked at what he considered the simplistic and reactionary tenets of black power. "I think all theories are suspect," he wrote; "that the finest principles may have to be modified, or may even be pulverized by the demands of life, and that one must find, therefore, and move through the world hoping that center will guide one aright."[7] Yet in *The Fire Next Time* (1963), another of Baldwin's works, the author aligned himself with many in the BAM. The best seller examined the relevance of the Nation of Islam (NOI) and predicted that racial violence would consume the United States if whites did not come to view black Americans as equals. Baldwin's work made him a target of the FBI. Following the assassination of Martin Luther King Jr., he began to believe that violence was an unavoidable route to racial justice. He grew more optimistic about race relations in America by the time of his death in 1987, though he continued to criticize whites who failed to confront their deep-seated prejudices and racist notions about black people.

Poetry and publishing played important roles in the BAM, with Harlem, Chicago, Detroit, and San Francisco serving as the epicenters of the movement. Artists worked hard to make their creations available to the black community, with BAM poetry mostly disseminated through fledgling publishing houses and journals. *Black Dialogue* (1964), the California-based journal edited by Arthur A. Sheridan, Abdul Karim, Edward Spriggs, Aubrey Labrie, and Marvin Jackmon, and *Soulbook* (1964), edited by Mamadou Lumumba and Bobb Hamilton, published the poetry of some of America's cutting-edge artists. When *Black Dialogue* received unprecedented numbers of submissions, its editors established the *Journal of Black Poetry* to meet the demand for poetry. The journal featured the work of many black poets, including Ahmed Alhamisi, Don L. Lee (later Haki R. Madhubuti), Clarence Major, Larry Neal, Dudley Randall, Ed Spriggs, and Askia Touré. Internationalist in orientation, the *Journal* published the works of African, Caribbean, Asian, and other international revolutionary poets. In 1969, Nathan Hare and Robert Chrisman founded the *Black Scholar*, which they identified as "the first journal of black studies and research" in the United States.[8]

Other black publications were founded during the 1960s as well. The Chicago-based *Negro Digest/Black World* was created in 1961 by John Johnson, already the publisher of America's most popular black magazines, *Jet* and *Ebony*. The *Negro Digest* was edited by Hoyt Fuller, an intellectual with encyclopedic knowledge of black literature and an extensive network of friends and business associates. Modeled after the *Reader's Digest*, which targeted white readers, the *Negro Digest* targeted the avant-garde in the world of black literature and poetry. By 1970, the *Negro Digest* embraced the voices of militant black nationalist poets, and changed its name to the *Black World*. The *Black World* published annual poetry, drama, and fiction editions, sponsored contests, and handed out awards for poetry and literature. Johnson ceased publication of *Black World* in April 1976, though demand for the publication had not abated. Many argued that he did so to stop the loss of advertisement revenue from companies that objected to the publication's cultural nationalist, Marxist, pro-Palestinian disposition.[9]

The most widely read BAM presses, however, were poet Dudley Randall's Broadside Press in Detroit and Haki R. Madhubuti's Third World Press in Chicago. From a literary point of view, Broadside Press, which focused almost entirely on poetry, was the most influential. Founded in 1965, Broadside published the work of more than four hundred poets in more than one hundred books, and it was primarily responsible for introducing longstanding poets such as Brooks, Sterling A. Brown, and Margaret Walker to new audiences. The press also introduced emerging poets, including Giovanni, Madhubuti, Sanchez, and Etheridge Knight, who became pillars of the BAM. Plagued by financial difficulty and limited by staffing problems, Broadside descended into relative obscurity by the late 1970s.[10]

The decline of the BAM began in 1974, following the disruption and co-optation of the black power movement. Leaders of the BAM, like black power movement leaders, were hounded, co-opted, repressed, intimidated, threatened, and eliminated by government leaders and programs such as COINTELPRO. In turn, government institutions and academicians championed and supported artists whose political ideologies were unthreatening; the lack of support offered to artists of the BAM by government institutions and academicians was starkly apparent. The BAM movement, therefore, suffered from external interference as well as internal financial and structural instability. As major film, record, book, and magazine producers flocked to less threatening and more mainstream or "bankable" artists, the fragile independence of the BAM grew wounded and strained. The legacy of the BAM endures, however. As poet and essayist Robert Chrisman argued, "More so than the Harlem Renaissance, in which Black artists were always on the leash of white patrons and publishing houses, the Black Arts [M]ovement did it for itself. Black people going out nationally, in mass, saying we are an independent Black people and this is what we produce."[11]

Though the BAM declined, many of the artistic genres and forms it championed continued. Music was an important component of the movement. Cultural nationalists within the BAM venerated jazz artists, and held their music up as melodic and lyrical exemplars. Indeed, jazz and rhythm and blues, Baraka argued, constituted a unique idiom that artists created to give musical expression to the joy and pain within the black American experience. BAM participants believed that music could help mold and explain black identity, and foster the requisite pride needed to sustain the struggle for black progress. Moreover, jazz, with its extemporaneous sound, generated a hybrid alternative to Western rhythm, synchronization and pitch. Jazz musicians expressed themselves through music in unconventional ways. In a society that erected many barriers to black freedom and prosperity, jazz offered artists opportunities to interpret the environment anew, in ways suitable to each individual. For oppressed people, jazz provided a bastion of self-reflection, independence, space for political dialogue, and artistic freedom.

The famous novelist Ralph Ellison, a great aficionado of the genre, described jazz as "an art of individual assertion within and against the group." He continued, "Each true jazz moment springs from a contest in which each artist challenges all the rest; each solo flight, or improvisation, represents a definition of his identity: as individual, as member of the collectivity and as a link in the chain of tradition."[12] Some of the most celebrated jazz musicians of the era included Ornette Coleman, John Coltrane, Eric Dophy, Charlie Parker, Thelonious Monk, Pharoah Sanders, and Archie Shepp. The late Ronald Milner, a famous African American playwright, described Coltrane as "a man who through his saxophone before your eyes and ears completely annihilates every single western influence."[13] The remarkable trumpet player, Miles Davis, however, was arguably the most revered jazz performer. His trailblazing album *Kind of Blue* (1959), is hailed as one of the most innovative and popular jazz recordings of all time. Davis moved jazz to a new level of sophistication without sacrificing accessibility or mass appeal. Black cultural nationalists admired his unyielding self-determination and the ways in which he implemented tonal inflections and extemporaneous shifts in sound that are rooted in the African and African American lyrical and musical tradition, conventions that defined America's prevailing European musical customs; one observer even suggested that Davis could "dance underwater and not get wet."[14]

Despite its revolutionary appeal, however, jazz primarily attracted intellectuals. The majority of African Americans gravitated towards rhythm and blues, soul, funk, and gospel music, rather than to jazz. Black artists, who were also commercial acts who performed for the own personal reasons like any other artist, often took to the stage and performed their music to raise funds for the black freedom struggle and to affirm their pride and commitment to black America. Ray Charles (Robinson) and Aretha Ray Franklin, for example, connected their music to politics by permitting members of SNCC to attend their concerts free of charge. Just as freedom songs had done during the civil rights movement, the soul music of the late 1960s and 1970s brought black people together under the banner of black power and self-determination.

Charles succeeded by combining bawdy lyrics that revealed the underbelly of black life with a hybrid blues-jazz-gospel sound in "I Got a Woman" (1955), the sexually suffused "(Night Time Is) The Right Time" (1959), and the severe "Let's Go Get Stoned" (1966). Franklin, the "Queen of Soul" and daughter of prominent Detroit minister Reverend C. L. Franklin, recorded and released a cover of Otis Redding's "R.E.S.P.E.C.T." in 1967 ; it became a runaway hit and an anthem of black feminism. The rousing lyrics of "Say It Loud, I'm Black and I'm Proud" (1968), performed by James Brown, the "Godfather of Soul" (fig. 19), became a sacred song and a battle cry in black communities across America. It was a smash hit for Brown, and it became a highlight of his concerts, in which an arena filled with black people would sing the chorus, "I'm black and I'm proud!" in unison. In his 1986 autobiography, Brown wrote of the song:

[It] is obsolete now. But it was necessary to teach pride then, and I think the song did a lot of good for a lot of people. People called "Black and Proud" militant and angry—maybe because of the line about dying on your feet instead of living on your knees. But really, if you listen to it, it sounds like a children's song. That's why I had children in it, so children who heard it could grow up feeling pride. The song cost me a lot of my crossover audience. The racial makeup at my concerts was mostly black after that. I don't regret it, though, even if it was misunderstood.[15]

Other black musicians likewise communicated their experiences through their work. Nina Simone's "Young, Gifted, and Black" (1969) gave voice to and affirmed the dignity and potential among black youth. "Respect Yourself," released in 1971 by the Staple Singers, emphasized the importance of self-love in the black community. Marvin Gaye's "What's Going On" (1971) assessed violence, poverty, ignorance, and injustice in America. His "Inner City Blues" (1971) echoed the anger and despair associated with unemployment, inflation, police brutality, and hopelessness in the black community. Gaye sang, it "make me wanna holler, / And throw up both my hands!"

Black people within the music industry also supported political work. Berry Gordy, founder of Motown Records, which was one of the most important and successful black-owned record companies in U.S. history, donated large sums of money to the black freedom struggle. The music he produced helped to create examples of black artistic power and presence. Gordy also backed the Chicago campaign of Martin Luther King Jr. by engineering a fundraising performance by Stevie Wonder at the city's Soldier Field. Gordy bankrolled portions of the campaigns of political leaders, and he donated significant amounts of money to the NAACP and the NUL. Although Gordy subjected his artists to strict schedules and rules that governed their behavior and speech, he permitted them to push the envelope enough to express a new level of cultural autonomy and garner the support of a fair number of black militants. During the late 1960s and early 1970s the rhythmic and lyrical originality of Gaye, Wonder, and the

Temptations, a black male vocal group that achieved fame as one of the most successful acts to record for Motown, revealed the label's own politicization. In a speech delivered to the inaugural meeting of Jesse Jackson's People United to Save Humanity (PUSH) in 1971, Gordy proclaimed, "I have been fortunate to be able to provide opportunities for young people. The first obligation we (as black businessmen) have is to ourselves and our own employees, the second is to create opportunities for others."[16] Soul singer Curtis Mayfield, another celebrated artist of the era, said it more clearly. "Our purpose is to educate as well as to entertain," he declared. "Painless preaching is as good a term as any for what we do."[17]

While followers of King's message of reconciliation and integration still exerted tremendous influence, more radical musicians and recording artists believed that substantive change could only be brought about through revolution. Groups such as the Last Poets, using the spoken word and music, critiqued what they considered to be the ineffectual politics of nonviolence. In "Niggers Are Scared of Revolution" (1970), the Last Poets denounced apathy and black people's lack of aggressive or direct challenges to white supremacy. Gil Scott-Heron, a vocalist with similar views, spoke to black yearnings and despair, as well as to white supremacy and the need for black revolutionary action in the United States in albums such as *Small Talk at 125th & Lenox* (1970), *Pieces of a Man* (1971), *Free Will* (1972), and *Winter in America* (1974).

Some of the most influential soul and funk performers of the era came together in August 1972 to participate in the Watts Summer Festival, an event that commemorated the seventh anniversary of the Watts riots and the postriot advancement of African Americans. Sponsored by Stax Records and the Schlitz Brewing Company, the festival ended with a seven-hour concert at the Los Angeles Memorial Coliseum that was attended by one hundred thousand people, most of whom were black. The revenue generated by the concert was donated to the Sickle Cell Anemia Foundation and the new Martin Luther King Hospital in Watts. The concert, hosted by Reverend Jackson, included performances by Kim Weston, the Staple Singers, the Soul Children, Rufus Thomas, Carla Thomas, and Albert King. This concert was capped off by a highly anticipated performance by Isaac Hayes, who performed what was known as the period's black male anthem and the theme song from the black cult classic film, "Shaft" (1971), starring Richard Roundtree. Hayes also performed his hit "Soulsville" (1971), which addressed joblessness, alcoholism, drug use, and black male despondency in inner city America. In it Hayes sang, "Trying to ditch reality, by getting so high / . . . you can never reach the sky." The concert was filmed, and *Wattstax* was released as a motion picture and album. The concert and movie affirmed and enhanced the spirit of unity and pride that permeated the black community and inspired African Americans to seek a greater stake in American society.

The tone of black America was also reflected in the humor of some of its most visible comedians. Dick Gregory, the first black comedian to perform for black and white audiences, used his quick wit, acerbic humor, commitment to black progress, and passion for justice to educate many about the perils of racial and economic injustice during the 1960s and 1970s. By exposing white audiences to his hard-hitting satire, he lent a comedic voice to the civil rights and black power movements. Richard Pryor (1940–2005, see fig. 20), perhaps the most influential comedian in American history, became a legendary figure who attacked racial conventions and white supremacy, transcended racial barriers, and challenged America's consciousness with biting, derisive, irreverent humor. As cultural critic and author Mel Watkins of the *New York Times* noted:

> Mr. Pryor's brilliant comic imagination and creative use of the blunt cadences of street language were revelations to most Americans. He did not simply tell stories, he brought them to vivid life, revealing the entire range of black America's humor, from its folksy rural origins to its raunchier urban expressions. At the height of his career, in the late 1970's, Mr. Pryor prowled the stage like a restless cat, dispensing what critics regarded as the most poignant and penetrating comedic view of African-American life ever afforded the American public. He was volatile yet vulnerable, crass but sensitive, streetwise and cocky but somehow still diffident and anxious. . . . His monologues evoked the passions and foibles of all segments of black society, including working-class, church-going people and prostitutes, pimps and hustlers.[18]

Pryor, the only child of Leroy Pryor and Gertrude Thomas Pryor, grew up in Peoria, Illinois. His living arrangements were anything but pedestrian, as he recalled, "I lived among an assortment of relatives, neighbors, whores and winos . . . the people who inspired a lifetime of comedic material." His parents and grandmother were bar and bordello owners. Pryor, in order to survive, used his quick wit and belligerent humor to gain respect from the street gangs and bullies in his neighborhood. Although he was

FIG. 20. Comedian Richard Pryor. © Michael Ochs Archives/Corbis.

highly intelligent, his manic behavior led to his expulsion from school in the eighth grade. He went on to work as a truck driver, a field hand, and a factory worker before joining the Army in 1958, where he served in Germany until he was discharged for beating and stabbing a white U.S. soldier during a fight in 1960. Pryor believed that the white soldier "was a bit too amused" at the racially charged sections of Douglas Sirk's movie *Imitation of Life*.[19]

Pryor returned to Peoria, married, fathered a son named Richard Jr., and, motivated by the work of comedians Redd Foxx and Dick Gregory, two pioneering black comedians known for their fearless vulgarity and their commitment to speaking truth to the power and the nature of white supremacy respectfully, started performing in local nightclubs. Between 1962 and 1964 Pryor became an itinerant comedian on the "chitlin circuit" of small black nightclubs in cities such as Chicago, Cleveland, and St. Louis, and in clubs in New York City's Greenwich Village, including Cafe Wha?, The Living Room, Papa Hud's, and the Bitter End. He eventually performed at Harlem's hallowed Apollo Theatre, which has been the nation's most popular arena for emerging and established African Americans since 1914, and he made his television debut on widely viewed shows such as "The Ed Sullivan Show" and Johnny Carson's "Tonight Show" in 1964. After growing tired of performing what he considered uninspired, irrelevant, "lily-white" material that did not address the isolated, seedy, unequal, and persecuted nature of his youth, he yelled "What am I doing here? I'm not going to do this anymore!" and stormed off the stage of the Aladdin Hotel in Las Vegas in 1967. Pryor maintained, "There was a world of junkies and winos, pool hustlers and prostitutes, women and family screaming inside my head, trying to be heard. The longer I kept them bottled up, the harder they tried to escape. The pressure built till I went nuts."[20]

Though club owners, agents, and advisers urged him not to put more critical, racialized material in his routines, Pryor underwent a personal journey, drawing upon the real experiences of being black in America that he knew firsthand. Seeking authenticity, he began using the term "Nigga" in his material, a term he had long used among black people. His first comedy album, labeled *Richard Pryor* (1967), demonstrated his new focus with irreverent sketches and coarse yet sidesplitting routines that addressed various aspects of race and racism in America. *That Nigger's Crazy* (1974), Pryor's next album, shocked the record industry by appealing broadly to white and black audiences. Despite its X rating, vulgarity, and sexually charged subject matter, the album sold over half a million copies and won the Grammy for best comedy album of the year. He produced another album the next year, entitled . . . *Is It Something I Said?* (1975), which also went gold and garnered him another Grammy nod. He became the most sought-after guest host on "Saturday Night Live" in 1975, and in 1977 he produced, directed, and starred in a series of television specials for NBC. He distinguished himself as lead writer for Redd Foxx's highly rated television series "Sanford and Son," as well as for "The Flip Wilson Show" and the Lily Tomlin television specials of 1974, for which he won an Emmy Award for best comedy writing.[21]

Pryor's politics evolved just as his comedic career had reached stardom. Following a trip to Africa in 1979, he noted that he stopped using the word "Nigga" in his onstage materials. Affected by the newly acquired freedom, independence, and pride of African peoples while traveling on the continent, Pryor came to view black people in a new, more positive light. He also appeared in forty films during his career, including *Greased Lightning* (1972) and *Silver Streak* (1972), both with Gene Wilder. He reached the high point of his career in 1979 with his first concert film, shot during a live appearance in Long Beach, California. *Richard Pryor: Live in Concert* still stands as the standard by which most stand-up comedy films are judged. This film captured Pryor at the height of his creative genius. Through his material, he pondered the implications of his chaotic life, recalled a marital dispute during which he shot his wife's car, waxed whimsical about the death of his pet monkeys, and described a near-fatal heart attack, a bit that concluded with the following line: "I woke up in the ambulance, right? And there was nothin' but white people starin' at me. I say . . . I done died and wound up in the wrong heaven."[22]

Rebellious musicians and comedians like Pryor gave voice to disaffected, direct, and forceful blacks. In addition, a string of controversial television sitcoms featuring prominent African American characters undermined stereotypes of black people and challenged American racism during the 1970s. *Julia* (1968–71), starring Diahann Carroll, depicted a young, middle-class Vietnam War widow working as a nurse in the aerospace industry. The show was a smash hit. Many viewers were pleased to see a black character play a smart, refined, resilient woman who struggled alone against racism and sexism while raising her son, who played with a white kid: their exchanges exposed the silliness of racism through a child's simple logic. Although the program was well received and was viewed by millions of people on a regular basis, some criticized it, describing it as unrealistic and unrepresentative of the majority of black people and their lifestyle. The *Saturday Review*, for example, argued that the show was "a far, far cry from the bitter realities of Negro life in the urban ghetto."[23]

By 1970, Jewish television producers Norman Lear and Bud Yorkin began producing highly successful and provocative television sitcoms that helped change the history of the industry. Their programs attempted to avoid the simplistic and bland nature of *Julia* by offering more well-rounded and hard-hitting examinations of black culture and community. These programs set a new tone for prime-time television by exploring issues that had rarely been touched in the media. In the end, they proved that programs with African Americans in leading roles could indeed be significant and popular.[24]

Lear and Yorkin's *Good Times* (1974–79) was an instant hit. The sitcom followed the challenges and joys of the close-knit Evans family—patriarch James (John Amos), mother Florida (Esther Rolle), eldest son and accomplished amateur painter James "J.J." Evans Jr. (Jimmie Walker), brainy and beautiful daughter Thelma (Bern Nadette Stanis), and youngest son Michael (Ralph Carter), a political and social activist, who lived together in a high-rise housing project on the South Side of Chicago. Audiences had first met Florida as the no-nonsense maid on the series *Maude* (1972), another Lear and Yorkin production. In a television landscape populated almost exclusively by prosperous white characters living in idealized settings, wherein black marriages and families were nearly always presented as somehow broken or fractured, *Good Times* was the first prime-time series to feature a strong black man, albeit a poor and relatively powerless one, in a loving marriage at the head of a close-knit family. The show took an honest look at the harsh reality of urban America, tackling social and political issues concerning race, poverty, unemployment, inflation, crime, and addiction. Critics, however, were dismayed by J.J.'s often clown-like behavior, capped by his signature catchphrase "Dyn-o-mite!" and they dismissed his antics as buffoonish and antithetical to the spirit of the show. Despite these criticisms, *Good Times* was perhaps the first sitcom starring an all-black cast to offer unabashed critiques of America's racialized, socioeconomic underbelly.

On the heels of *Good Times'* success, *The Jeffersons* (1975) emerged as another extremely popular sitcom. It was a spin-off of one of television's most notable shows, *All in the Family* (1970), whose main character was the openly chauvinistic and racist working-class curmudgeon, Archie Bunker. In 1973, Lear cast Sherman Hemsley in the role of George Jefferson, Archie Bunker's cantankerous, militant, and upwardly mobile black neighbor in a dingy neighborhood in Queens New York. Jefferson proved so popular "with viewers that Hemsley was soon cast in its spin-off series. *The Jeffersons* focused on the lives of a nouveau-riche African American couple, George and Louise Jefferson (Isabel Sanford). George Jefferson was a successful businessman, millionaire, and owner of seven dry-cleaning stores. He lived with his wife in a ritzy penthouse apartment on Manhattan's fashionable and moneyed East Side. 'We're movin' on up!' intoned the musical theme of the show opener that featured George, Louise and a moving van in front of 'their deluxe apartment in the sky.'" *The Jeffersons* was the first television program to feature an interracial married couple, the Jefferson's upstairs neighbors in their tony apartment building, and it offered an uncommon, albeit comic, portrayal of a successful African American family. It was one of several programs of the period to rely heavily on confrontational humor, and, like *Good Times*, the sitcom tackled issues such as homelessness, racism, sexism, classism, and violence.[25]

The New Student Movement

The most intense manifestation of black militancy was found among African American college students. In general, they possessed greater dedication to revolutionary change than their older contemporaries. These more militant students ushered in major changes between 1968 and 1975, the period referred to by many as the "second phase of the civil rights movement," (following the first phase, identified as having been between 1960 and 1968). By 1968 the majority of the student groups that thrived during the height of the civil rights movement, including SNCC, had lost much of their institutional stability and influence. The black student movement underwent a fundamental shift, however, with the mass murder of African American students at South Carolina State College in Orangeburg on February 8, 1968.

Despite the enactment of the Civil Rights Act of 1964, and the desegregation of many places of public accommodation in South Carolina, Orangeburg's All Star bowling alley continued to refuse black people admission. During the evening of February 6, black students from South Carolina State College and Claflin College gathered in protest in front of the bowling alley. When they returned the following evening, they were greeted by the police, who immediately arrested fifteen of them. Nevertheless, the protest continued, and by February 8 tensions had reached a fever pitch. State officials deployed the highway patrol and the National Guard to Orangeburg. As the students moved their protest to the campus of South Carolina State, law enforcement officers and the National Guardsmen followed. Once on campus, students started a bonfire. As law enforcement officers tried to put the fire out, the students bombarded them with rocks, bottles, and bricks. One officer was hit with a large piece of wood. Without notice, a highway patrolman fired his gun into the air to calm the crowd. Rather than ending the chaos, however, the shot caused the other officers to open fire. In the hail of bullets, nine students lost their lives and twenty-seven others suffered injuries. The nine patrolmen involved in the incident were charged with using excessive force; all were acquitted. In the same incident, however, Cleveland Sellers, a black SNCC activist, was charged with and convicted of rioting and served almost one year in prison. He was eventually pardoned.

The rebellious acts of the students in Orangeburg set the stage for other forms of black student activism. Indeed, African American students began to cite the lack of a critical mass of African American students, faculty, and administrators on predominantly white campuses and the absence of curriculum that reflected African American history, life, and worldviews as not only narrow-minded, but antithetical to universal education, the very purpose of higher universities. This desire for more inclusive college campuses led to the creation of black studies. Known alternately as Africana studies, Afro-American studies, African American studies, Black Diaspora studies, and Pan-African studies, black studies emerged as early as 1968 as a legitimate field of academic and intellectual inquiry, thereby constituting the second phase of the black student movement. Indeed, the quest for civil rights, black power, and African American artistic expression created an unprecedented environment in which activist students and faculty members fought for revolutionary changes in traditional Eurocentric curricula. In search of relevance, black students and their supporters demanded curricula that addressed their unique history and life. Similarly, black students founded organizations for themselves that would support the development of race consciousness and black life. Black students knew that education was key to their empowerment and intellectual growth, but African Americans and their history and life were grossly underrepresented, even misrepresented, on most predominately white campuses, as opposed to the small number of all-black colleges. By 1970 African American students made up only 2 percent (or 95,000 of the 5,000,000) of the student body population at predominantly white colleges and universities. In 1960 a mere 227,000 African Americans were enrolled in all colleges and universities in the United States. By 1970 the number had doubled, and by 1977 1,100,000 black students were enrolled in college in the United States. Though they were a politically heterogeneous group, most of these black college students abhorred the isolation they felt as outsiders in largely all-white institutions. In fact, many black students found college campuses to be foreign, hostile places offering them little with which they could identify. Not surprisingly, many black students set out to change these circumstances.[26]

Creating black studies programs proved difficult at many colleges and universities. The first black studies units were established in response to student protests at San Francisco State College; Merritt College in Oakland, California; and Cornell University in Ithaca, New York. In 1968, with the support of San Francisco State College's Black Student Union (BSU), and the Third World Liberation Front (TWLF), a multiracial group of supporters, led by Jimmy Garrett and Jerry Varnado and supported and mentored by recently hired sociology professor Nathan Hare, pressured the administration to create the first black studies department in the United States.[27]

On Nov 5, the BSU and African, Asian, Latino, and Native American members of TWLF presented San Francisco State president Robert R. Smith with a combined list of fifteen nonnegotiable demands. The first and most important demand was for the college to immediately establish departments of Ethnic Studies for students from the "third world." Their demands were rejected and on November 16, the BSU and TWLF launched their boycott of classes, university services, and administrative mandates regarding student activities. The strike was marked by student expulsions, the firing of faculty who joined the student-led protest, violent confrontations between local police and strikers, and multiple closures of the entire college. The strike finally ended on March 22, when Smith and the college's administration acquiesced to the student's demands and Hare was charged with preparing and implementing a proposal that led to the creation of the Department of Black Studies at San Francisco State.

Similar events led to the establishment of an Afro-American Studies program at Yale University in 1968. One year later James E. Turner, a doctoral student, was installed as the head of the new African Studies and Research Center at Cornell University. Harvard University established an Afro-American Studies program in 1969. That year, the Institute of the Black World, "a community of black scholars, artists, teachers, and organizers" in Atlanta, oversaw a project that endeavored to define and frame the techniques and goals associated with black studies, offering training and guidance to directors of these programs. The field's first major textbook, entitled *Introduction to Black Studies*, was written by Maulana Karenga, an African American author, political activist, and college professor best known as the creator of Kwanzaa. By 1973, only five years after the creation of the first black studies program, there were nearly two hundred such programs in the United States.[28]

Black studies programs continued to attract attention, and soon expanded to graduate studies. By the late 1980s black studies programs at Cornell, Yale, and UCLA offered master's degrees in African American studies, and in 1988, Molefi Kete Asante, a black scholar, historian, philosopher, and professor of African American studies at Temple University, led a successful effort to establish a PhD program in African American studies at Temple University, the first of its kind. By 2002 Michigan State University became the sixth university to offer a doctorate in the field, and by 2006 Northwestern University offered its own PhD in African American studies. Although there was no explicit definition of precisely what black studies comprised, most of its practitioners agreed that they should strive to: 1) develop solutions to the many problems facing black people throughout the African Diaspora; 2) engage in critical analyses of black history and life that contest and supplant the existing Eurocentric ideal; 3) endorse social change and advances in higher education; and 4) institutionalize the study of black people within a field of inquiry with its own culture, theories, methods, philosophies, symbols, and language.[29]

While black studies opened new doors for black students, presaging a new era in black activism and intellectual life, major shifts in America's political culture challenged and aided in black upward mobility. The presidential campaign of 1968, in fact, was a watershed moment in American and African American history. It was also one of the most chaotic presidential campaigns in U.S. history. In November 1967, Senator Eugene McCarthy of Minnesota joined the race for the Democratic presidential nomination on an antiwar platform as an alternative to the incumbent Johnson. Few, however, gave McCarthy a realistic shot at winning. Also announcing his candidacy was Senator Robert F. Kennedy of New York, who soon emerged as a serious contender. When Johnson announced that he was withdrawing from the race in March 1968, Kennedy and McCarthy proceeded to battle it out in a series of primaries, joined by Vice President Hubert H. Humphrey, who inherited the support of many party regulars who still controlled the selection of a majority of the delegates. Kennedy, to whom many young people looked up because of his commitment to antipoverty programs, racial conciliation, and anticorruption, was assassinated in June 1968, bringing an end to his insurgent campaign. The anger and resentment generated by RFK's murder, the seemingly endless war in Vietnam, and nasty internal political and ideological rivalries boiled over at the Democratic National Convention in Chicago that August, making it the most contested and violent party nominating convention in modern U.S. history. Humphrey emerged as the party's nominee, but the impression of chaos, division, and violence left by the convention proved damaging to his prospects in the fall contest.

Due to the instability and infighting of the Democratic Party and Republican nominee Richard M. Nixon's commitment to "law and order," Nixon won the presidential election, squeezing out a slim victory over Humphrey. Nixon secured 43.1 percent of the popular vote to Humphrey's 42.7 percent, and 301 Electoral College votes to Humphrey's 191. George Wallace, the white supremacist governor of Alabama, won 13.5 percent of the popular vote and 46 electoral votes in his first presidential bid. Wallace ran as the American Independent Party candidate, and he garnered widespread support for his backlash opposition to gains minorities had made during the civil rights movement. He also called for the censorship of antiracist and antiwar activists, and he promised to root out communism at home and abroad.

Richard Nixon proved to be one of the most ideologically complicated presidents in American history. He was, by the conventions of the mid–twentieth century, considerably progressive in orientation. He helped establish the Environmental Protection Agency; championed the Equal Rights Amendment to the U.S. Constitution, which would have made discrimination on the basis of gender illegal; and approved more regulatory legislation aimed at America's financial industry than any other president before or since. Nixon was also a racist bigot who carefully recorded all of his conversations, tapes that, when they were later made public in connection with the Watergate scandal that ended his political career, revealed the nasty language that Nixon used behind closed doors, even as he sat in the White House. He complained, for example, that "most of them [blacks] are basically just out of the trees."[30] But despite his perfection of the "southern strategy," which reconfigured the Republican Party by engaging it in the duplicitous politics of white over black, and despite his personal bigotry as president, Nixon embraced a number of unconventional policies that sought to improve conditions for African Americans. Perhaps most significantly, Nixon appointed Daniel Patrick Moynihan, a highly respected expert on social policy, to serve as his national policy adviser.

An old veteran of government service, Moynihan, when he was assistant secretary of labor in 1965, had prepared a major document, one rife with organizational problems and sweeping generalizations, entitled the "The Negro Family: The Case for National Action." More popularly known as the "Moynihan Report," this internal memorandum supported Johnson's War on Poverty, asserting that a disturbing number of black families suffered from instability and breakdown, an instability that resulted in endless cycles of joblessness and poverty. The root of the problem was, according to the report, the social, psychological, and "pathological" damage wrought by slavery and Jim Crow. These forces, Moynihan argued, undermined the role of black men in African American families, thereby creating a disproportionate number of dysfunctional families headed by single black women. In arguably the most cited section of the report, Moynihan argued that the black community was dominated by

a matriarchal structure, [which] because it is so out of line with the rest of American society, seriously retards the progress of the group as a whole, and imposes a crushing burden on the Negro male. . . . Obviously, not every instance of social pathology afflicting the Negro community can be traced to the weakness of family structure . . . [but] once or twice removed, it will be found to be the principal source of most of the aberrant, inadequate, or anti-social behavior that did not establish, but now serves to perpetuate the cycle of poverty and deprivation.[31]

Soon after its issue, the report was leaked to the press, instantly becoming an object of intense controversy. Many believed that Moynihan had disparaged the black family, belittled black men, and stigmatized black women. Distinguished psychologist William Ryan, offered one response to the Moynihan report, penning a book entitled, *Blaming the Victim*

(1970), a phrase coined by the author himself. On the other hand, the Moynihan report was based in part on the work of black scholars such as E. Franklin Frazier and drew the support of prominent black leaders like Roy Wilkins, Whitney Young, and King, partly because it had at least identified the black family and community as a subject worthy of national study and attention Nixon, fascinated by Moynihan's work, asked the new Counselor to the President for Urban Affairs to develop a plan to aid poor families. Moynihan's work led to the creation of the Family Assistance Plan (FAP), which Nixon announced during the summer of 1969.

The FAP fundamentally modified programs that had been created during the New Deal for families in need. It called for the replacement of programs such as Aid to Families with Dependent Children (AFDC), food stamps, and Medicaid. In their place, the federal government provided direct cash payments to recipients, who now included the single-parent families who had traditionally qualified for AFDC, food stamps, and Medicaid, as well as the working poor. Under the new plan, all recipients, with the exception of mothers of preschool-age children, would be required to work or take job training. Critics, however, complained about the FAP. Many noted that the income level proposed by Nixon, only $1,600 per year for a family of four, was insufficient. Opponents of welfare programs, in contrast, opposed *any* guaranteed annual income for people without jobs. Organized labor rejected the FAP as a threat to the minimum wage. Even social workers avoided the FAP for fear of losing their jobs should families received direct cash payment from the government. Still others believed that the addition of the working poor to the welfare rolls would expand caseloads by the millions. Remaining determined in the face of his critics, Nixon presented the bill to Congress multiple times with slight variations, but it was finally killed in 1972 by the House of Representatives. Despite the rejection of this plan, Nixon won reelection by a landslide that same year. During his first term, he had redirected power away from the federal government, but he had also fought for and passed legislation that helped people of color and women.

Despite these efforts, Nixon's use of the southern strategy undermined his work on behalf of black people. It also raised the ire of the NAACP, which threw its support behind school busing to bring about school integration. One of the first major civil rights battles of the 1970s, in fact, involved the federal judiciary's refusal to act on desegregation laws by ordering the busing of students out of their home districts to try to achieve a racial balance in public schools. Nixon was determined to exploit the busing conflict to attract white voters all over the nation, but especially in the South. He pressured federal officials, including Robert Finch, a close friend who was then Secretary of Health, Education and Welfare (HEW), and Elliot Richardson, who replaced Finch in 1971, to "disavow" HEW's busing plan. In fact, Nixon asked Richardson and the HEW to cease busing entirely, even though this would halt the desegregation of schools. The president described integration as "counterproductive, and not in the interest of better race relations."[32] In the North, residential and school segregation went hand in hand; consequently, to integrate schools, some children had to be bused out of their neighborhood schools. In Boston, which showed some of the most contentious and violent resistance to busing in the nation, schools in predominantly black neighborhoods were given far fewer financial resources than those in white neighborhoods, even though schools in black neighborhoods were dilapidated, lacking in supplies and equipment, and severely overcrowded.

The courts eventually outweighed Nixon's pronouncements and the lower courts' silence on busing. In 1974 U.S. district judge W. Arthur Garrity ruled in favor of a consortium of African American parents who had filed a class-action lawsuit against the Boston School Committee. The judgment proclaimed that the school committee was in violation of the equal protection clause of the Fourteenth Amendment. To bring about racial balance in Boston schools, the judge ordered the busing of thousands of students between predominantly white schools in Hyde Park, South Boston, and Dorchester, and the overwhelmingly black Roxbury. The white backlash to the court decision on "forced busing" was swift and furious. Tensions spread throughout Boston like wildfire. White Bostonians organized antibusing "rallies" and boycotts, during which mobs of angry white brandished knives, bats, and guns, to stop their children from riding through, and attending schools in, black communities. They also sought to stop black children from attending all-white schools. During the first week of busing in Boston, white families, including women and children, protested with outpourings of anger outside South Boston High School. For weeks angry whites smashed windows, overturned cars, set trash bins ablaze, and engaged in physical confrontations with blacks and the police. Shops and bars were closed, and streets were cordoned off. Although the busing order remained in place, random violence continued to erupt for the next two years in the city.

Despite Nixon's appeasement of southern whites and the lack of support he offered African Americans on the busing issue, the president's policies assisted black people more than he is often given credit for. The president expanded affirmative action policies through the Philadelphia Plan, in which companies with federal construction contracts received mandates to create hiring goals that increased African American employment. In addition to supporting some issues of racial and economic justice, he also helped create laws to clean up the environment and provide funds and social capital for local race-based, class-based, and gender-based initiatives. His "New Federalism," however, withered on the vine as he fought in vain to win the Vietnam War and preserve his presidency during the Watergate scandal that led to his impeachment.

When Nixon entered the White House, he inherited a difficult, expensive war that was quickly losing the support of the American public. Seeking "peace with honor," Nixon attempted to reduce the number of U.S. troops deployed to the region. He transferred duties from U.S. troops to those in the South Vietnamese army in a process that he called "Vietnamization." South Vietnamese troops were not prepared to assume the full burden of the conflict with the North Vietnamese, however, so they continued to rely almost exclusively on the United States and the shadow government of South Vietnam for resources. The massive air bombing of North Vietnam by U.S. forces resumed under Nixon's direction, as did U.S. attacks on Cambodia and Laos, two nations that neighbor Vietnam. When these bombings began killing North Vietnamese refugees in Cambodia in early 1970, American citizens protested U.S. military actions. One such protest, held at Kent State University on May 4, 1970, ended in a flurry of state-imposed violence when Ohio National Guardsmen dispatched to the campus opened fire on approximately two thousand protesters and students, resulting in four deaths and nine injuries. This violent act perpetrated against a crowd of young persons marked a turning point, lowering national opinion of the war and of those who would go to any length to support it even more.

The United States and North Vietnam appeared to end the conflict in October 1972, following negotiations between National Security Advisor Henry Kissinger and North Vietnamese Prime Minister Le Duc Tho. The agreement was short-lived, in part because the South Vietnamese took issue to the settlement. In the wake of the failed armistice the United States carpet-bombed North Vietnam again, this time for eleven days straight, yet the warring nations conceived a new agreement in January 1973. This one called for the withdrawal of U.S. troops, a cease-fire, the release of any prisoners of war, and the creation of an international peacekeeping organization.

The Vietnam War strained the U.S. government as well as the American people, but so did the actions of President Nixon. The president had been elected for his promise to restore law and order, though he soon proved himself to be a criminal. A paranoid man, Nixon deeply distrusted all who disagreed with him. He increasingly assumed that his opponents were dangerous elements in need of exposure and punishment. During the 1972 presidential campaign, which Nixon won over the Democrat George McGovern, Nixon's top aides orchestrated a break-in at the Democratic Party headquarters, which were located in the building that also houses the Watergate Hotel. For a time the culprits were unknown, but journalists Bob Woodward and Carl Bernstein of the *Washington Post* proved through their own investigations that several of Nixon's aides had been involved. The president denied any involvement in or knowledge of the burglary. Further investigations, however, demonstrated Nixon's guilt. Critics soon called for his impeachment; the president, wishing to avoid being officially ousted from office, resigned on August 9, 1974.

Nixon's departure left no one with his level of influence or fluid approach to public policy at the highest levels of the Republican Party. His resignation left the party vulnerable to doctrinaire, ideological conservatives who demonstrated little if any substantive concern for African Americans. This shift was reflected in the difficulty that Nixon's successor, Gerald Ford, experienced when he sought the party's presidential nomination against California governor Ronald Reagan, the new star of the right. Reagan had little intention to engage African Americans or any other racial minority, let alone to address their needs.

The Ascendency of Black Political Power

Before the far right reemerged and coalesced behind Reagan during the 1980s, African American made significant gains in politics. Just as King pursued alternative strategies following the early successes of the civil rights movement, many of his activist peers marshaled the collective power of the reenfranchised body of African American voters. After the implementation of the Voting Rights Act of 1965, Vernon Jordan, the director of the Voter Education Project, orchestrated voter registration drives and seminars throughout the South, saying, "Too many of these people have been alienated from the political process for too long a time, and so we have to teach them what a local government is, how it operates, and try to relate their votes to the things they want."[33]

At the same time, black voters began to make their impact felt in the North. In 1974, 1,593 African American elected officials served their constituents in the North, a number that rose to 2,455 by 1980. Although northern blacks had not been barred from voting as had their southern counterparts in the aftermath of Reconstruction, they were nonetheless consigned to marginal status within larger white-dominated political machines for nearly a century. During that time, the Great Migration resulted in blacks flocking to northern cities, and by the 1960s they were an electoral force to be reckoned with.

The ascendency of black power and the impact of the Voting Rights Act signaled a radical departure from the past. Highly motivated to vote, black people were free from the debilitating fear they had known in the past when it came to voting. Their expanded exercise of the franchise translated into unprecedented political influence. For example, in 1967, Cleveland's significant black population, with the help of white business leaders, played a key role in electing Carl Stokes as the first African American major of a major U.S. city. Later that year attorney Richard G. Hatcher was elected mayor of Gary, Indiana, where the black population, like that of Cleveland, had expanded significantly since World War II. Though he received only 14 percent of the white vote, Hatcher garnered 96 percent of the black vote.

The unprecedented victories of Stokes and Hatcher led to the organization in 1972 of the National Black Political Convention in Gary, Indiana. Otherwise known as the "Gary Convention," this was arguably the most pivotal event of modern black political history. Cochaired by Congressman Charles Diggs of Detroit, Hatcher; Amiri Baraka, the Black Arts Movement progenitor and cultural nationalist; and political scientist Ronald Walters, convention attendees endeavored to assess and unify the many ideological factions that existed within the newly enfranchised black community. The convention was held between March 10 and March 12, 1972; the disparate group was comprised of elected officials, revolutionaries, integrationists, black nationalists, Christians, and Muslims. Even Coretta Scott King and Betty Shabazz, the widows of Martin Luther King Jr. and Malcolm X, respectively, were in attendance. Whites were excluded, and for that reason

Roy Wilkins of the NAACP denounced the gathering. Participants attended to experience new political possibilities, self-determination, and a desire to forge a united front against black marginality and despair.

Delegates to the Gary Convention created a National Black Political Agenda with specific goals. They called for the election of a proportionate number of black representatives to Congress, local board or community control of schools, national health insurance, and a moratorium on capital punishment. Naturally, the national media zeroed in on the most provocative components of the convention and agenda, including motions to recognize a Palestinian homeland, to endorse more widespread busing to integrate schools, to express opposition to integrated schools, and to reject white discriminatory unions in favor of all-black organized labor groups. The media was also transfixed by the stark differences between black nationalists such as Amiri Baraka and Maulana Karenga, persons who viewed black power as a movement to control their own communities and forge separate cultural institutions, and black elected officials including Stokes and Hatcher, who advocated integrationist approaches to black problems. Cochair Ronald Walters captured the tensions between these segments of black leadership when he noted, "It was this body of people who really were contending for the national leadership of the black community in the early seventies. And in the seventies this new group of black elected officials joined the civil rights leaders and became a new leadership class, but there was sort of a conflict in outlook between them and the more indigenous, social, grassroots-oriented nationalist movement."[34]

There was unity to be found in Gary, however. Hatcher noted the collective spirit of the convention when he observed, "People had come to Gary from communities all over the United States where they were politically impotent, but they went back home and rolled up their sleeves and dived into the political arena." When it was published, the agenda included a note addressing the idealism of the process: "At every critical moment of our struggle in America we have had to press relentlessly against the limits of the 'realistic' to create new realities for the life of our people. This is our challenge at Gary and beyond, for a new Black politics demands new vision, new hope and new definitions of the possible. Our time has come. These things are necessary. All things are possible."[35] Nearly eight thousand people attended the convention in Gary. In addition to creating the agenda for black empowerment, they harnessed black voting power, investigated the efficacy of coalitions, and explored the achievability of a viable third party to compete against the two major parties in state and federal elections. The convention also inspired an unprecedented number of African Americans to seek elected office at the local, state, and national levels.

The Gary Convention signaled a major shift from mass demonstrations and protests to using the electoral process as the primary strategy for black progress. Absolute unity was not achieved at later conventions, but delegates at the last National Black Convention, held in Little Rock, Arkansas in 1974, scuttled the idea of a black third political party. Major philosophical differences and organizational tensions prevented serious unification and cooperation between black nationalists and the ever-expanding number of black elected officials. Black nationalists supported more militant, Afrocentric solutions to community empowerment, and moderate black leaders were more interested in working within established institutions, multiracial networks, and modes of political advocacy that reflected Eurocentric aesthetics. Furthermore, the sexism that permeated each camp undermined black people's ability to provide much-needed support to Shirley Chisholm, the first African American to wage a legitimate campaign for the Democratic presidential nomination in 1972. Indeed, many white men and even "progressive" black males routinely failed to view women as equals, and most withheld their support from aspiring white and black female politicians.

Though the National Black Conventions showed only limited measurable success, African Americans benefitted from the hope and commitment to meaningful political gain articulated by these efforts, and it was expressly this newfound commitment that jump-started a renaissance in black political office-holding. At the time of the Gary convention in 1972, there were thirteen black members of Congress; by 1977, that number had more than tripled to forty. Further, in 1972, only 2,427 African Americans held elected office, but by 1992 this number had grown to 8,106. A 1975 amendment to the Voting Rights Act empowered racial minorities to challenge voting procedures that weakened the impact of bloc voting. This amendment also helped the numbers of black elected officials to expand. Indeed, race was now taken into account when drawing and redrawing electoral districts, something that greatly enhanced the ability of black people and others to elect African Americans to highly influential offices. These changes helped Virginia state Senator L. Douglas Wilder become the first African American lieutenant governor in the South since Reconstruction. In 1989 he was elected governor.

Between 1971 and 1975 the number of black mayors increased from 8 to 135, a dramatic expansion that prompted the creation of the National Conference of Black Mayors in 1974. Coleman Young in Detroit (1974) and Thomas Bradley in Los Angeles (1973) became the first black mayors of cities with more than a million residents. Bradley emerged victorious even though African Americans accounted for a mere 15 percent of the Los Angeles electorate, reflecting the developing mainstream appeal of black politicians. A decade later, in 1983, Harold Washington was elected the first African American mayor of Chicago, the same city that had marginalized blacks and tormented King less than twenty years earlier. Riding the waves of success and self-confidence forged from the fires of the civil rights and black power movements, African Americans cemented themselves as significant players in America's political culture.

But even as blacks made inroads in electoral politics during the 1970s, America's seemingly impenetrable wealth and power took a turn for the worse. Generations of Americans had seen their incomes rise, and the majority of their children expected to be more prosperous than their parents. Between World War II and the 1970s the median American family income doubled. The majority of Americans viewed themselves as citizens of the world's wealthiest nation, and they valued the comfort and status that accompanied this position. By 1973, however, the celebrated American standard of living began to decline as the foundations of postwar prosperity, including cheap energy, steadily rising wages, and low rates of inflation, began to crumble. The financial costs of the war in Vietnam, coupled with an oil embargo fueled by conflict in the Middle East, beset America with significant economic stresses that only added to the blow to many people's sense of national pride and identity that the Watergate scandal and Nixon's resignation delivered.

If many white people experienced this downturn as a setback, black people experienced it as a full-scale depression. Though the gap between the incomes of the top 20 percent of black people and their white counterparts had closed, the gap between African Americans and white people at the bottom of the economic barrel widened. Black professionals advanced, but those living in poverty descended even deeper into the financial abyss. In 1969 nearly 10 percent of white men and 25 percent of black men earned less than $10,000; by 1986, however, nearly 40 percent of African American men between the ages of twenty-five and fifty-five earned less than $10,000, in contrast to only 20 percent of white men of the same ages. In other words, between 1970 and 1986, the proportion of African American families with earnings less than $10,000 grew from 26.8 to 30.2 percent, even as the purchasing power of $10,000 decreased during this same time period due to inflation. Not all was bleak, however, as the black middle class expanded; 4.7 percent of black families earned more than $10,000 in 1970, and by 1986 that percentage had grown to 8.8 percent. In the end, despite areas of improvement, the general financial condition of African American earners remained the same or grew slightly worse.

Exacerbating African Americans' precarious economic condition were mounting assaults on the policies and programs designed to foster diversity and parity in employment and action. In 1978 the Supreme Court ruled, in *University of California Regents v. Bakke,* that affirmative action policies, which were purposely designed to reserve a number of seats for qualified black students, constituted "reverse discrimination" against white students. Failing to gain admission, Allan Bakke, a white student, sued to challenge the admissions process of the University of California, Davis School of Medicine. Portraying himself as a victim of reverse racial discrimination, he asserted that he was a better qualified candidate than those who benefitted from policies that set aside sixteen slots in the entering class of one hundred for "disadvantaged students."

Many white people across the nation, but especially those on the political right, loudly supported Bakke and began to rail against all affirmative action programs, citing so-called quotas as unfair. Many white women joined this denunciation of affirmative action, even though they, as a demographic group, were among the greatest beneficiaries of the policy, as the Civil Rights Act of 1964 banned workplace discrimination based upon gender as well as race. The high court upheld the constitutionality of the admissions policies that took race and racial disparities into account in the *Bakke* case, but in doing so it ruled against "quotas." Thurgood Marshall, who had been appointed to the Supreme Court by President Johnson in 1967, criticized the convoluted decision. "The experience of Negroes in America has been different in kind, not just in degree, from that of other ethnic groups," he wrote in his dissenting opinion. "The dream of America as the great melting pot has not been realized for the Negro; because of his skin color he never even made it into the pot." Though powerful, Marshall's dissenting opinion represented the minority, and affirmative action was redefined to exclude quotas. But even before the decision was handed down in *Bakke,* emerging assaults on blacks' relatively modest gains, a perceptible backlash by many whites, and the nation's economic downturn, inspired many African Americans to look to the federal government and their own devices once again for support and affirmation.

Much hope existed in the United States as the nation celebrated its bicentennial in 1976. That year, American flags flew everywhere, fire hydrants were painted red, white and blue, and virtually every city in America held parades honoring the nation's 200th birthday. For black people, 1976 was a critical year, as it marked the first time since 1964 that the candidate who received most African American votes won the election. Jimmy Carter, the former governor of Georgia, received 90 percent of the African American vote. A Southern Baptist with a calm demeanor and an established record of dealing earnestly with black people, he needed black people as much as they needed him. Most African Americans found it easy to vote for him, rather than the incumbent, Gerald Ford. For his part, Carter willingly acknowledged his debt to the black community by appointing a number of African Americans to plum positions in his administration. He installed Andrew Young, former congressman from Georgia and an old friend, as ambassador to the UN; Eleanor Holmes Norton as the first female chair of the Equal Employment Opportunity Commission (EEOC); Patricia Harris as the secretary of Housing and Urban Development; Clifford Alexander Jr. as the secretary of the army; Ernest Green, one of the Little Rock Nine, as assistant secretary of the Department of Labor; Wade McCree as solicitor general in the Justice Department; Drew Days III as assistant attorney general for civil rights; historian and former University of Colorado chancellor Mary Frances Berry as assistant secretary for education; and Louis Martin as his special assistant, the first African American to hold that position on the White House staff. These appointments were both symbolic and substantive for the black community. Carter appointed more black people to positions that influenced the lives of the average American than any other president in U.S. history. He also helped solidify advancements in civil rights by vetoing legislation that would have stopped school busing, by shoring up the authority of the Equal Employment Opportunity Commission (EEOC), and by pressuring the Justice Department to prosecute cases of discrimination in the housing market under the auspices of the Fair Housing Act.

However, the Carter administration's attention to the needs of black people fell short of their expectations. For example, the Public Works Employment Act called for 10 percent of public funds to be dispersed to racial minority contractors to create 585,000 jobs, but Carter did not use the power of his office to enforce the act. Congress did not ensure that the act was implemented: many black contractors who might have benefitted from the act did not. Carter did not aid congressional Democrats in passing full employment and universal health-care bills, and many blacks also criticized the president for eliminating welfare programs, including financial aid to black students and school lunch programs.

America's economy damaged Carter's image and undermined many of his goals, but it was the Iran hostage crisis of 1979 that doomed his presidency. African Americans, however, were less concerned with his poor handling of the hostage controversy than they were with his seemingly uninspired and politically stunted support for civil rights, and his inability to ease the economic woes of most Americans, let alone African Americans. The 1980 Republican nomination of former California governor Ronald Reagan, a conservative politician who opposed affirmative action, however, offered most black voters a far less attractive choice. In the 1980 election, 90 percent of African American voters cast their ballots for Carter, but their support was not enough to elect him a second time. Carter's failures had damaged the Democratic brand: the Republican Party exploited his failures and reemerged as a force in American politics. Indeed, Reagan, with rising support for his conservative agenda (an agenda that seemed designed to overturn the gains made by people of color since World War II), won the election and ushered in a new era in American politics. For the first time since 1954 the Republicans won control of both the White House and Congress and immediately refashioned the texture and tone of American social and economic policy.

"For many Americans, the economic, social and political trends of the previous two decades, ranging from crime and racial polarization in many urban centers to the economic downturn and inflation of the Carter years, engendered a mood of disillusionment." These trends also strengthened a renewed suspicion of government and of its ability to deal effectively with the country's deep-rooted social and political problems. Conservatives, long out of power at the national level, were well positioned to exploit this new mood. It was a time when many Americans were receptive to the conservative message of limited government, strong national defense, and the protection of traditional, middle-class, white American values against what were seen as the encroachments of a permissive and often chaotic modern society corrupted by liberals, unruly women, and militant minorities.[36]

5

"TO THE BREAK OF DAWN," 1980–2000

> I remember Marvin Gaye, he used to sing to me. He had me feeling
> like black was the thing to be. And suddenly the ghetto didn't seem
> so tough. And though we had it tough, we always had enough.
>
> —TUPAC SHAKUR, "Keep Ya Head Up," 1993

The Republican return to power during the 1980s swung America's political pendulum sharply to the right. This transition profoundly affected
black Americans, especially the poorest among them. When Reagan
became president, the office rescinded its tradition of support for civil
rights. Moreover, Reagan and the Republican Congress slashed welfare
programs and purged federal agencies of staff members who supported
affirmative action in order to replace them with individuals who rejected
it. The Republican Party became almost entirely white and was dominated
by powerful right-wing southerners who had long opposed the expansion
of civil rights and remedies for racial and gender inequality. When LBJ
signed the Civil Rights Act of 1964 into law, the once "solid" Democratic
South had begun to shift to the Republicans; by the time of Reagan's election the Democratic Party no longer held sway over the South. American political culture, therefore, underwent a major ideological realign-
ment during the 1980s and 1990s, as well as an entrenchment between
progressive Democrats on the one hand and conservative Republicans
on the other.

President Reagan, a former actor, used his charisma and remarkable
communication skills to offer the American people a vision of economic
and social redemption through conservative, even old-fashioned ideals.
Many embraced his message, and their support, coupled with his leadership, led to the triumph of the "New Right." The New Right, however,

was not simply a product of Reagan's celebrity and charm. A great many members of the New Right were dissatisfied with the progressive changes brought about during the 1960s and 1970s. These operatives established conservative groups and institutions that the Republican Party embraced. These groups tended to reject equal rights for women, abortion rights, the rights of the accused, and the illegality of obligatory prayer in public schools. The New Right comprised white southerners unhappy with the changes fostered by the civil rights movement, white northerners furious over school busing, all those who opposed affirmative action, and opponents of welfare programs; this coalition quickly reached a critical mass during and following the 1980 election.

The New Right, led between 1981 and 1993 by the Reagan administration and that of his Republican successor, George H. W. Bush, reduced federal aid to cities by half, thereby eliminating programs of critical importance to the socioeconomic status of thousands of African American families. While the government slashed funding designated for beleaguered urban communities and public housing, city budgets long used to federal subsidies saw revenues drop from 14.3 to 5 percent. Urban communities, in which 56 percent of indigent residents were black and poor, grew even more unstable during these twelve years. Reagan argued that the federal government was too large and was ill-suited to provide its citizens with the type of social and economic support that many in the civil rights and black power movements had come to expect and benefit from under earlier administrations. The new president believed in supply-side economics, otherwise known as economic "trickle-down theory," or, to its critics, "voodoo economics." In other words, Reagan believed that the economic strength and security of the nation's richest companies and citizens should be shored up through generous tax breaks that favored them. The expanding wealth of these corporations and individuals, Reagan's theories suggested, would reverberate down through the middle class, working class, and the poor. Trickle-down economics did indeed further enrich what was already a euphoric class of stunningly rich corporations and families, but their unprecedented wealth never translated into better economic conditions for poor people of any color. The average income of the top 1 percent of American wage earners, who were overwhelmingly white, grew from $312,206 in 1980 to $548,970 in December 1990. At the same time, the unemployment rate rose to 10.8 percent for black Americans, twice the rate experienced by their white counterparts.

Reagan and members of the New Right also alienated many black people and other marginalized groups through their lack of attention to, and callous dismal of, issues that disproportionately affected African Americans. After the emergence of the HIV/AIDS epidemic in 1981, the Reagan administration approached the developing crisis with a laissez-faire attitude rooted in a retrograde, right-wing, theological view of the disease. "Maybe the Lord brought down the plague," Reagan argued, "because illicit sex is against the Ten Commandments."[1] The president, who viewed the lesbian, gay, bisexual, transgender, and queer (LGBTQ) community with pity, if not contempt, viewed HIV/AIDS as a providential sign of God's abhorrence of "the gay lifestyle." African Americans soon accounted for more than half of new HIV/AIDS cases, and consequently were particularly affected by federal policies regarding the disease. Often viewed as inherently flawed and prone to violence, promiscuity, and disease, black people suffering with HIV/AIDS were denied proactive health education and treatment by members of the New Right. For his part, Reagan remained distant and unmoving, watching quietly as the number of HIV/AIDS diagnoses in the United States climbed to over sixty thousand and the death toll to over forty-one thousand before even bothering to address the issue in March 1987. Many on the far right believed that HIV/AIDS would simply disappear after decimating the LGBTQ community and black people. In 1986 conservative writer William F. Buckley Jr. suggested that HIV/AIDS could be tracked and regulated if people with the disease were tattooed with a signifying mark on their buttocks and forearms.

Reagan's disdain extended beyond disease, as he often blamed poor, disfranchised African Americans for their own subordinate status. He reserved some of his most racist remarks for indigent black women who received government aid, describing them in speeches as "welfare queens living in Cadillacs."[2] Moreover, Reagan attacked virtually every policy and program that the civil rights movement and black activism had engendered. He blocked busing efforts, cut funding for Head Start, slashed school lunch programs (arguing at one point that ketchup counted as a fresh vegetable), replaced vocational schools with prisons, and offered no financial assistance to needy college students. His disregard for African Americans was bold, even stunning. Reagan launched his presidential campaign by touting the virtues of "states' rights," the credo of the Jim Crow South ever since the Civil War, at the Neshoba County Fair in Mississippi, which was the site of the vicious murder of civil rights workers Michael Schwerner, Andrew Goodman, and James Chaney in 1964. Reagan's comments and choice of venue communicated his disrespect for African Americans to both white southern segregationists and black people. To predominantly white onlookers in Stone Mountain, Georgia, an infamous bastion of white supremacy, Reagan described Jefferson Davis, the president of the Confederacy, as one of his role models. Reagan also idolized John Wayne, the American movie legend known as "The Duke." Wayne, when asked to comment on black activism and racial equality, had declared, "[White people] can't all of a sudden get down on our knees and turn everything over to the leadership of the blacks. I believe in white supremacy until blacks are educated to the point of responsibility. I don't believe in giving authority and positions of leadership to irresponsible people."[3] Reagan was celebrated as an "All-American" optimist who revived the nation's hope for a brighter future, but his presidency and that of his successor, George H. W. Bush, dimmed the hope and dashed the dreams of many black Americans.

Reagan and Bush tried to conceal their efforts to undo progressive policies by appointing black conservatives to federal agencies that played key roles to assisting black people. Reagan replaced Eleanor Holmes Norton at the EEOC, for example, with William Bell, an inexperienced and little-known businessman who ran a one-man employment agency in Denver, Colorado. Black leaders protested Bell's installation, but Reagan merely replaced the appointee the next year with Clarence Thomas (fig. 21), an open opponent of affirmative action. Thomas immediately slashed the commission's staff, permitted the number of backlogged affirmative action cases to rise to forty-six thousand, and let the adjudication time for such cases stretch to as long as ten months. Reagan also moved against the U.S. Commission on Civil Rights (CCR). The tenacious character of Mary Frances Berry, the CCR's vice chair, however, provided the president with his staunchest resistance. Indeed, soon after Reagan took office, the CCR began to challenge his emerging record on civil rights. The president responded by replacing Arthur S. Flemming, the CCR's white progressive chair, with Clarence Pendleton, a black conservative Republican and former executive director of the San Diego Urban League. Berry, who was earlier appointed to her position by Jimmy Carter, called Pendleton's leadership into question, thereby prompting Reagan to dismiss her from the CCR. She sued successfully to keep her position, becoming known as "the

FIG. 21. Supreme Court justice Clarence Thomas, 2007. AP Photo/John Duricka
(911011050).

woman the president could not fire." Despite her efforts, the commission's
potency dwindled under Pendleton's leadership.

Bell, Thomas, and Pendleton were members of a prominent and growing cohort of prosperous and conservative black thinkers, professionals,
and politicians who thrived during the Reagan presidency. This cadre of
so-called black neoconservatives cultivated political relationships within
the Republican Party. They also found support in relatively small groups
and organizations that championed their ideas, subsidized their work, and
communicated their message. Unlike black Democrats, who played substantive and influential roles and represented a major constituency within
their party, black Republicans wielded little power in their party but were
expected to uphold the ideological and programmatic agenda established
by the Republican Party's overwhelmingly white power structure. They
were also well-rewarded for their compliance by becoming iconic.

Not all black conservatives proved to be completely at odds with other
black people, but many of them allied with white conservatives to blame
the black community for the social challenges it faced, arguing that the
problems of black people, and especially those experienced by the poor
and others locked in decaying inner cities, were of their own doing. Further, some members of the black conservative establishment sought to dis-

sociate themselves completely from what they perceived as fallen and corrupt black inner-city populations. Black neoconservatives such as Thomas Sowell, Shelby Steele, Walter Williams, Alan Keyes, Clarence Thomas, and Ward Connerly have suggested that flawed cultural traits and the existence of the American welfare system created many of the problems of poor urban black people. Thomas Sowell, a conservative black economist, social critic, and writer, for example, stated that African Americans in inner cities suffered from sloth and indecency, which only perpetuated their poverty and socioeconomic isolation. Rather than expand social programs to help impoverished people, however, Sowell argued for the termination of affirmative action and welfare programs, believing that they undermined middle-class values such as hard work and frugality. Black conservative leaders also suggested that the racism of the 1950s and 1960s no longer existed in the 1980s. As a result, they concluded, the problems experienced by masses of African Americans during the Reagan and first Bush administrations were not rooted in government policy or corporate capitalism. Rather, black people's problems stemmed from black folk themselves: their delinquent youth, welfare mothers, and deadbeat dads. Defining government assistance of any kind as the antithesis of personal responsibility, black conservatives seemed to have no problem with endorsing government subsidies to corporations and tax breaks to the wealthy.

The rise and relevance of black conservatism was underscored in 1991, when President Bush nominated Clarence Thomas (1948–) to a seat on the U.S. Supreme Court. Born and raised in rural Georgia, Thomas earned his undergraduate degree from Holy Cross College in Massachusetts and his JD from Yale University Law School. The president selected Thomas to replace the recently deceased Thurgood Marshall, a lifelong advocate for black people and arguably the greatest civil rights lawyer of the twentieth century. The personal and ideological differences between Thomas and Marshall could not have been starker; many African Americans believed that Thomas was unqualified professionally and ill-suited ideologically to fill the seat vacated by Marshall. Where Marshall was unapologetically liberal, a defender of civil rights, and a towering figure in the black freedom struggle, Thomas was an unremarkable attorney and judge and a black neoconservative with a dubious record on civil rights. Black and white progressives uniformly denounced his selection, noting also that his mere fifteen months as an appellate court judge by no means qualified him for a seat on the Supreme Court. Despite their alarm, however, most blacks were wary of criticizing Thomas publicly and reluctant to challenge even the cynical tokenism of the Bush administration, because they were fearful of losing the "black" seat on the high court, and because they did not want to be complicit in the demise of yet another African American on the national stage. Even so, some black leaders did speak out. The NUL proclaimed,

> We welcome the appointment of an African American jurist to fill the vacant seat left by Justice [Thurgood] Marshall. Obviously, Judge Thomas is no Justice Marshall. But if he were, this administration would not have appointed him. We are hopeful that Judge Thomas' background of poverty and minority status will lead him to greater identification with those in America who today are victimized by poverty and discrimination. And [we] expect the Senate, in the confirmation hearings, to explore whether he is indeed likely to do so.[4]

The Bush administration expected Thomas's confirmation process to be a swift one, but the matter soon turned complicated by the testimony offered by black law professor Anita Hill (1956–, see fig. 22). Hill, who, according to historians Darlene Clark Hine, William C. Hine, and Stanley Harrold, "had worked under Thomas during her stint at the EEOC, submitted a confidential statement to the Senate Judiciary Committee alleging that Thomas had sexually harassed her 10 years earlier, when they were both single."[5] According to CBS News, "the FBI had already investigated the charges and given the committee what was called an inconclusive report. The committee decided not to pursue the matter. But two days before the full Senate was expected to confirm Thomas, Hill's statement was leaked to reporters. Hill, under pressure from women's groups and Democrats in the Congress, was summoned before the Judiciary Committee, which heard testimony on Thomas' confirmation, to testify before live television cameras. More than twenty million households tuned in to watch the proceedings." Her comments ignited an explosion of controversy.[6]

Hill accused Thomas of having sexually harassed her at the EEOC. Her revelation intensified the already raucous protest of Thomas's candidacy, while also exposing deeply rooted gender divisions within African American communities. Hill had not intended to testify during Thomas's hearings, but she was compelled to speak honestly and directly about her ordeal when she was called to do so. Hill's testimony alleged that Thomas

FIG. 22. Anita Hill testifies before the Senate Judiciary Committee on the nomination of Clarence Thomas to the Supreme Court on Capitol Hill, October 11, 1991. Hill testified that she was "embarrassed and humiliated" by unwanted, sexually explicit comments made by Thomas a decade earlier. AP Photo/John Duricka, file (9110110187).

had subjected her to lewd, explicit, and unsolicited remarks in the workplace. "He spoke about acts that he had seen in pornographic films involving such matters as women having sex with animals and films showing group sex or rape scenes," Hill stated, noting that "on several occasions, Thomas told me graphically of his own sexual prowess." Also, during a meeting "he got up from the table at which we were working, went over to his desk to get the Coke, looked at the can and asked, 'Who has put pubic hair on my Coke?'" Hill told senators. Hill also stated that Thomas bragged about being "well-endowed" and having "experience in pleasing women intimately." She also testified that she became quite concerned about her work environment. "I began to feel severe stress on the job," Hill told the committee. "I began to be concerned that Clarence Thomas might take out his anger with me by degrading me or not giving me important assignments. I also thought that he might find an excuse for dismissing me." Moreover, "when it came time for Thomas to publicly respond to Hill's allegations," Hine, Hine, and Harrold argue, Thomas "turned the tables on his interrogators, exploited the history of violence against black men in American history, even though he had often criticized African Americans for having a 'victim's mentality,' and for all intents and purposes ended the debate." During the hearing, Thomas said, "This is a circus. It's a national disgrace. It is a high-tech lynching for uppity blacks who in any way deign to think for themselves and it is a message that unless you kowtow to an old order you will be lynched, destroyed, caricatured by a committee of the U.S. Senate rather than hung from a tree."[7]

Although many black people defended Thomas in the national media, others did not; progressive feminists, liberals of all races, and many African Americans supported Hill. Black feminists were enraged by the treatment Hill received from Thomas, the senators who questioned her, and members of the media. These activists were extremely vocal in their opposition to Thomas's political philosophy and nomination, and to the ridicule Hill was subjected to as an African American and a woman who dared to accuse a prominent black male of sexist and misogynistic behavior. Despite the breadth and tenor of the opposition to Thomas, the nominee was confirmed by a majority Senate vote of 52 to 48. As a Supreme Court justice, Thomas revealed himself to be one of the most conservative in U.S. history. His votes and opinions against progressive issues such as affirmative action have put him at odds with the majority of black Americans.

Thomas's political ideology mirrored that of Reagan and his successor George H. W. Bush. Indeed, the Reagan and Bush administrations differentiated between what some have described as the "old civil rights law," which Reagan and Bush purported to defend, and the "new civil rights law," which they rejected. Members of the New Right such as Reagan and Bush claimed to support the old civil rights, which banned deliberate racial discrimination such as that outlawed by the *Brown* ruling, the Civil Rights Act of 1964, and the Voting Rights Act of 1965. These leaders denounced new civil rights law, which they believed was preoccupied with inequitable results as opposed to premeditated prejudice. In other words, the New Right only fought prejudiced intentions; it did not concern itself with all instances of inequality. If an institutional structure disadvantaged black people, for example, the New Right would not interpret it as discriminatory. Conservatives repudiated the notion that one should assume discrimination was extant if, for instance, employees in a company were disproportionately white or male when the demographic makeup of the surrounding community was not. Similarly, the New Right did not challenge situations in which elected leaders of a racially diverse city or state were disproportionately white, or in which most white children attended all-white schools.

Affirmative Action

Since the Kennedy administration, legal correctives concerned with presumed discrimination and statistical disparities had been described by officials in the federal government, particularly in the executive branch and the Department of Labor, as affirmative action. These policies focused on developing mechanisms to increase the number of people from underrepresented groups, including black Americans, in the workplace, educational institutions, and political offices. Policy makers expected that redrawing electoral districts, for example, had the potential to raise the number of African American elected officials. Local governments and state legislatures, as well as colleges, universities, and businesses, often established methods and "guidelines" to achieve their goals of diversity and equality in learning and working environments. Many recalcitrant institutions, however, were mandated by court order to set goals and guidelines for diversification to comply with civil rights laws and court edicts.

Affirmative action, an example of the new civil rights law, was frequently contested during the administrations of Reagan and George H. W. Bush. Indeed, the backlash against affirmative action intensified greatly after the aforementioned *Bakke* decision of 1978. The ambiguity of this ruling, which outlawed inflexible "quota" systems but upheld the legality of affirmative action per se, angered the policy's supporters and infuriated its detractors as well. Fueled by "angry white men" as well as by white women, an all-out battle for the life of the policy emerged. For conservatives, the system was a zero-sum game that opened the door for jobs, promotions, or education to people of color while it shut the door on whites. In a nation that has celebrated the values of independence and "pulling oneself up by one's bootstraps," conservatives soon argued that "unqualified" racial minorities were getting a "free ride" in American schools and in the workplace as a result of affirmative action policies. They referred to affirmative action incorrectly and contemptuously as a system of "preferential treatment" and "quotas." Some even claimed that many people of color enjoyed playing the role of "professional victim" to exploit the policy for their own benefit.

Supporters of affirmative action argued that the policy corrected historical and continuing inequality. These supporters noted that the United

States offered fewer opportunities to people of color by virtue of its history of white supremacy, slavery, Jim Crow segregation, and lingering racism. Affirmative action, although imperfect, was nevertheless a practical means to redress forms of racism and inequality in education, housing, employment, and political districting. Conservatives, in contrast, urged African Americans to "get over" the legacies of slavery and Jim Crow, with many of them rejecting outright the notion that racism in America still erected major barriers to social, economic, and political equality. To defend the policy, progressives pointed out that, despite widespread fears that people of color were taking "white people's jobs," white men in particular still dominated the workforce by virtue of their positions, salaries, and prestige.

The conflict over affirmative action was also a result of its ambiguous and complex evolution. Many progressives, for instance, understood the injustices of the affirmative measures associated with *Wygant v. Jackson Board of Education* (1986), in which black employees retained their jobs while white employees with seniority were laid off. In addition, many conservatives struggled to offer a better alternative to the imposition of a strict quota system in *United States v. Paradise, et al.* (1987), in which the defiantly racist state officials of the Alabama Department of Public Safety refused to promote any African Americans above entry-level positions, even after they were mandated to do so by twelve years of court orders.

Continued debate over affirmative action soon focused on California, one of the most diverse states in the union. There the Republican governor, Pete Wilson (1991–99), convinced the University of California's Board of Regents to end the state's affirmative action policy regarding public colleges and universities. "At a moment when affirmative action is under attack across the country, and just one day after President Bill Clinton told Americans that it had been 'good for America,' the vote made California the first state to eliminate race preferences in college admissions and put the state at the forefront of eliminating them nationwide,"[8] declared *Time* contributor Margot Hornblower.

Although Wilson's actions were opposed by many national figures, including Rev. Jesse Jackson, the governor's stance was popular with many conservative California voters. In 1996 California residents approved Proposition 209, the Civil Rights Initiative, which barred state agencies from executing affirmative action policies. Ward Connerly, a black neoconservative businessman, spearheaded the campaign for the adoption of the proposal. Born in rural Louisiana in 1939, Connerly was himself the recipient of more than $140,000 in state contracts that had been "set aside" for businesses owned by persons of color. Despite having benefited from such programs, Connerly argued loudly and passionately that affirmative action enabled the perpetuations of black stereotypes and dependency. Furthermore, he and his followers maintained that affirmative action had failed to eradicate educational disparities, unemployment, or poverty in minority communities. Rather, they asserted, it undermined the ability of marginalized groups to succeed through self-reliance and hard work, and had instead advanced only middle-class people of color and white women.

After Proposition 209 passed with the support of 54 percent of California's voters, it quickly influenced the affirmative action policies of many other states. The Supreme Court backed the proposition, paving the way for other states to pass similar legislation or to rule in favor of related laws. Proposition 209 measurably limited the number of people of color admitted to the University of California school system, particularly to UC Berkeley, one of the state's most distinguished public universities. In California and in Texas, which also eliminated affirmative action in its higher education system after a major legal dispute, many advocates for affirmative action in public education moved to counteract the effects of the abolition of affirmative action by admitting every student in the top 10 percent of his or her high school class to the states' best universities.

Although Clarence Thomas regularly opposed affirmative action programs, the Supreme Court remained divided in its opinions concerning affirmative action cases. Most of them were examined only incrementally; the highest court in the land directed its attention to narrow facets of policy in order to avoid ruling on the entire legal concept. In *Bakke*, for instance, the Court had split 5–4. Though the justices' opinions were nuanced in this and other decisions, they often obscured the larger issues of affirmative action more than they clarified them. Sandra Day O'Connor, considered by many a centrist jurist, found both problems and potential in affirmative action policies. In 2003 the Supreme Court, with O'Connor playing the role of moderate, authoritatively upheld the right of affirmative action in higher education in two landmark cases involving the University of Michigan. *Gratz v. Bollinger* and *Grutter v. Bollinger*, which involved respectively the undergraduate program and the law school of the University of Michigan and were first tried in federal courts in 2000 and 2001. In a 5–4 decision, the Supreme Court upheld the University of Michigan Law School's guidelines, deciding that race can be one of many factors taken into account by colleges during the admissions process, as this approach furthers "a compelling interest in obtaining the educational benefits that flow from a diverse student body." The Court ruled 6–3, however, that the more rigidly fixed point system method used by the University of Michigan's undergraduate admissions office, which awarded additional points to people of color during its admissions process, violated the rights of white students. The University of Michigan undergraduate program lost its case in the Supreme Court because, unlike the institution's law school, the former failed to offer "individualized consideration" of applicants as ordered by previous Supreme Court decisions on affirmative action.

One can easily view the rulings in the University of Michigan cases as the result of a political maelstrom concerning affirmative action. They preserved the principle of promoting diversity while challenging the use of such policies to redress past inequities. In the wake of the rulings, businesses, labor unions, academicians, and the military, each touting the importance of racial diversity and parity, filed record numbers of briefs in support of affirmative action. Justice O'Connor demonstrated that the majority of the justices understood these concerns when she noted, "In order to cultivate a set of leaders with legitimacy in the eyes of the citizenry, it is necessary that the path to leadership be visibly open to talented and qualified individuals of every race and ethnicity."

Despite the attacks on affirmative action that continued long after the Reagan and first Bush administrations, African Americans continued to rise within the ranks of the Democratic Party and to secure positions and power previously denied to them. African American elected officials numbered a mere 103 in 1964, but by 1994 the number had grown to almost 8,500, and African Americans continued to acquire power within the federal government. Forty-three blacks served in Congress in 2007. Congressman William H. Gray of Pennsylvania became the first black American to reach the highest levels of Congressional leadership when he became the chair of the House Democratic caucus and majority whip of the House of Representatives in 1988. In February 1990 Ronald H. Brown became the first African American chosen to head a major political party when he was elected chair of the Democratic National Committee. Later that year David Dinkins was elected the first African American mayor of New York City, and Sharon Pratt Dixon (Kelly) was elected mayor of

Washington DC; Dixon became the first female and the first person from the District of Columbia to hold the office. By 1995 more than four hundred towns and cities across the nation had elected African American men and women to political office.

By no means, however, did black men and women operate in these political positions as a monolith. Most female legislators, and particularly black females, excelled in their leadership roles because of their ability to practice a more fluid style of leadership than exhibited by their male counterparts. Women's leadership style, in general, differed from male legislative leadership. In general, legislative leadership is viewed as "transactional," a kind of aggressive negotiating method that mediates specific interests in a predominantly male legislative political arena. When women led, however, they generally employed an integrative and inclusive leadership style different from the transactional method. Black female legislators, in particular, demonstrated that by encouraging collaboration, shared problem-solving, and consensus, leaders could build broad-based coalitions to address the specific needs of African Americans while also acknowledging some of the basic needs of people regardless of race, ethnicity, or gender.

Black female legislators, including those who went on to chair important committees, brought to the U.S. Congress distinct life experiences that drove their work and influenced their vision. Their motivation and strategies were shaped by their styles of leadership experiences as black women, and consequently their leadership differed in important ways from that of their male counterparts. Black in a racist society, female in a sexist society, and invariably connected to the poorer segments of a society that stigmatizes poverty, black women legislators were keenly aware of this nation's most pressing socioeconomic problems, and they were uniquely equipped by virtue of their background and constituencies to devise effective ways to solve them. Black women, like women in general, tended to see political leadership as something more than the act of satisfying particular interests. Many endeavored to alter the ways in which the legislative process works, because they believed that the process itself played a critical role in oppressing many of the people they represented.

Black congresswomen mobilized against the exploitation and discrimination related to the interwoven factors of race, class, and sex that they and their constituents faced in everything from employment to housing. Most black female legislators learned early on that to ensure the advancement of their constituents of all races, and especially of black people, they needed to champion a process that encouraged others to take responsibility for their own futures while simultaneously becoming agents of social, economic, and political change. Consequently, black female legislators became particularly effective. They included Representative Barbara Jordan of Texas (1973–79), Representative Cardiss Collins of Illinois (1973–97), Representative Shirley Chisholm of New York (1968–81), Representative Sheila Jackson-Lee of Texas (1995–), Representative Cynthia McKinney of Georgia (1993–2003), Delegate Eleanor Holmes Norton of the District of Columbia (1991–), and Representative Maxine Waters of California (1991–).

Barbara Jordan (1936–1996), in fact, was one of the most influential black female politicians in American history. She grew up in one of the poorest black communities in Houston, Texas, attending segregated public schools and the all-black Texas Southern University, where she graduated magna cum laude. An award-winning speaker and debater, she chose law as a career because she believed it would enable her to work effectively on behalf of racial justice. "She wanted to attend Harvard University Law School," writer Jone Johnson Lewis states, "but was advised that a black woman student from a Southern school would not be accepted." In the end, Jordan applied to and was accepted by Boston University Law School.[9]

After earning her law degree in 1959, she returned to Houston, where she started a law practice in her parents' home. During this time she also got involved in the 1960 presidential election as a volunteer for Lyndon B. Johnson, who became her political mentor. "After unsuccessful attempts at being elected to the Texas House of Representatives, in 1966," Lewis writes,

> she became the first African American since Reconstruction elected to the Texas Senate, and the first black woman to be elected to the Texas legislature. In 1972, Jordan ran for national office, becoming the first black woman elected to Congress from the South, and, with Andrew Young, one of the first two African Americans elected since Reconstruction to the U.S. Congress from the South. While in Congress, Jordan came to national attention with her strong presence on the committee holding Watergate hearings, calling for impeachment of President Nixon on July 25, 1974. She was also a strong supporter of the Equal Rights Amendment for women, worked for legislation against racial

discrimination, and helped establish voting rights for non-English-speaking citizens.[10]

In 1976 Jordan made history when she became the first black women to deliver a keynote address at the Democratic National Convention. Her stirring address, writer Jone Johnson Lewis suggests, made her a political sensation and an inspiration to millions of women and people of color. Not long after she gave this speech, she declared that she would not seek another Congressional term. She chose a career in the academy instead, becoming a professor of government at the University of Texas–Austin. She went on to serve on the U.S. Commission on Immigration Reform in 1994, and worked as political counsel to Ann Richards, the second female governor of Texas, from 1991 to 1995. Barbara Jordan battled leukemia and multiple sclerosis toward the end of her life, finally succumbing to them in 1996. She is survived by her partner, Nancy Earl.[11]

During the Reagan and Bush years, black women and men played key roles in government at the highest levels even as their newfound power and influence remained limited relative to that of their white counterparts. During each of these administrations, one or both chambers of Congress were controlled by Democrats, which gave black legislators and voters greater opportunity to influence legislation. During this time Congress passed the Voting Rights Act of 1982, the Civil Rights Restoration Act of 1988, and the Fair Housing Act of 1988, in large part due to the electoral influence of African Americans. The Civil Rights Act of 1982 amended the 1965 Voting Rights Act to remove confusing language surrounding the purpose and intent of section 2 of the earlier act; this revision sharpened prohibitions against the dilution of minority voting power through various tactics, such as extensive federal oversight of elections and the refusal to allow states to implement any change affecting voting without first obtaining the approval of the Department of Justice through a process known as "preclearance." The 1982 act also prevented municipalities from gerrymandering, or creating racially drawn congressional districts to give minorities an unfair chance to elect candidates of their choice. The Civil Rights Restoration Act of 1988 required recipients of federal funds to comply with all civil rights laws, not just the rules of the particular program or activity that received federal funding. The Fair Housing Act of 1988 enabled individuals as well as the Department of Housing and Urban Development to file housing discrimination complaints and empowered federal judges to investigate housing complaints, levy fines, issue injunctions, and award punitive damages. Such laws, along with the Civil Rights Act of 1991, which amended the Civil Rights Act of 1964 in an effort to strengthen federal civil rights laws and provide for damages in employment discrimination cases, were enacted to counteract the effects of Supreme Court rulings that had weakened the effectiveness of earlier civil rights legislation.

During the 1980s and 1990s, African Americans also sought symbolic affirmation of their advancement by breaking barriers in popular culture, through the struggle for freedom, and through their newly acquired ability to influence public policy at the highest levels of government in sustained and substantive ways. No one embodied this progress more than Michael Jackson (1958–2009).

Michael Joseph Jackson was born August 29, 1958 in Gary, Indiana, to Joseph "Jo" Jackson and Katherine Jackson. The Jacksons, a large, African American working-class family, were closely knit and extremely talented. Jo Jackson played the guitar semiprofessionally until he dispensed with his musical goals to support his family as a crane operator. Jo Jackson, recognizing his sons' musical and dancing prowess, worked them into a musical group during the early 1960s. In the beginning the performers in the Jackson family included Michael's older brothers Jackie, Jermaine, and Tito. Michael joined his brothers when he was five, and after he shocked his father and almost everyone else with his stunning singing and dancing talents, he quickly emerged as the group's lead vocalist and principal attraction. He demonstrated exemplary range and power for his age, astonishing crowds and industry professionals, including Smokey Robinson, with his ability to communicate adult, multifaceted emotions. When Marlon Jackson, who was a year older than Michael, eventually joined the band, they named themselves the Jackson 5.

In August 1969, the Jackson 5 was presented to the music world at an exclusive event in Los Angeles, and they soon secured the position of opening act for the Supremes. Their first album, Diana Ross Presents the Jackson 5, debuted on the charts in December of 1969. The group's first single on that album was "I Want You Back." It was a smash hit that topped the charts at number one on the Billboard Hot 100 in January of 1970. While the Jackson 5 had tremendous success, it quickly became evident that one member stood out. By the age of thirteen, Michael had established himself as the most talented, visible and adored member of the

FIG. 23. Michael Jackson and Quincy Jones, April 9, 1983. © Bill Nation/Sygma/Corbis.

group. He released his first solo album, *Got to Be There*, which scored the hit title-track single, "Got to Be There." His 1972 album, *Ben*, introduced the emotional and distinctive ballad about a young boy and his beloved pet rat. The song was lauded for its depth of feeling and for Michael's rousing vocals. It also became Jackson's first number-one single as a solo artist. This was just the beginning of what would be a legendary career.

Reaching even greater heights, Michael Jackson paired up with renowned producer, Quincy Jones (see fig. 23), to deliver his second solo album *Off the Wall* in 1979. *Off the Wall* astonished the record industry and the artistic world with its contagious and transcendent mix of R&B, funk, and pop. This remarkable album produced a string of hit singles, including the Grammy Award-winning "Don't Stop 'til You Get Enough," "Rock with You," and the title track, "Off the Wall." His pained and remorseful song "She's Out of My Life," was also a success, though it did not receive the same critical acclaim as the other, more popularly songs on the album.

The tremendously affirming response to *Off the Wall* helped sustain the Jacksons' career as well. *Triumph* (1980) sold in excess of one million copies, and the brothers went on a large-scale concert tour to buttress the album's success. Michael Jackson, however, began to place a higher premium on his solo career. He teamed up with rock legend Paul McCartney on a 1982 duet, "The Girl Is Mine," which almost reached number one on the pop charts. The song also appeared on Michael Jackson's next solo album, *Thriller* (1982), which spawned a staggering seven Top-10 hits. On a television special honoring Motown's twenty-fifth anniversary, Jackson performed "Billie Jean"—eventually a number one hit—and unveiled his now-celebrated dance move, the moonwalk. Jackson, a learned and skilled entertainer at this point, refined the fairly obscure sliding, reverse-walking movements that had been exhibited by crack tap, free style, and B-Boy dancers for decades, and added his own grace and unmatched style to it. He also cochoreographed the dance sequences for the video of his other number-one hit, "Beat It." Millions of Americans tuned in to the *Motown 25* show to see a seasoned, dynamic, and astounding Michael Jackson. The next day, millions of Americans, enthralled with the moonwalk, attempted to imitate the move in school yards, family rooms, and dance studios.

Jackson's most stunning video, however, was for "Thriller," the album's title track. Directed by John Landis, the video presented a macabre, horror-show motif, starring Jackson and model-turned-actress Ola Ray. Dynamic dance sequences, jaw-dropping special effects, and a voice-over done by actor and Jackson friend Vincent Price enhanced the video's appeal. The already successful album got an additional boost in sales after the release of the video, keeping the album on the charts for eighty weeks, thirty-seven of which were spent in the number-one spot. The charts were not the only place where the song and album's success were recognized. *Thriller* earned twelve Grammy Award nominations, and won in eight of the twelve categories, showcasing the diverse nature of Jackson's work. He won the Grammy Award for Best Rhythm and Blues Song for "Billie Jean," which highlighted his songwriting skills. He won Best Pop Vocal Performance, Male for "Thriller" and added a win under Best Rock Vocal Performance, Male for "Beat It." With coproducer Quincy Jones, he shared the highly coveted Grammy Award for Album of the Year.

Thriller was an unparalleled and unstoppable musical movement. Twenty-seven years after its release, *Thriller* still stands as the best-selling studio album in the United States, is certified twenty-eight times platinum, and has sold over 50 million copies internationally. Sales statistics alone cannot set the benchmark for the album's success, however. As Jackson moonwalked his way into music history, *Thriller* set a new standard for blockbusters that changed how the music business promoted and marketed superstar releases.[12]

The album and its video also changed Music Television (MTV), breaking down the cable network's racial barriers, with Jackson becoming the first black artist to break into the burgeoning music video scene on December 2, 1983. It significantly raised the bar for video quality and ingenuity. In 1985 Jackson joined what was then intended to be the final tour with the Jacksons promoting the album *Victory*. Jackson's duet with Mick Jagger, "State of Shock," was the major hit from the album, garnering much attention and fanfare. Later that year Jackson revealed his philanthropic yearnings with "We Are the World," a charity single for USA for Africa that he cowrote with Lionel Ritchie. A number of other notable stars also participated in this project, including Lionel Ritchie, Ray Charles, Bob Dylan, Willie Nelson, Bruce Springsteen, and Tina Turner. In 1987, a handful of years after the release of *Thriller*, Jackson released his follow-up, *Bad*. While the record placed him at the top of the charts again and included five number-one hits, it did not replicate the phenomenal sales of *Thriller*. "Man in the Mirror," "The Way You Make Me Feel," and the title track were major players on the album. Jackson promoted the album on the road for more than a year with numerous high-energy concerts and appearances.

While his onstage persona was anything but calm, Jackson was actually quite shy and a quiet person offstage. His religious upbringing as a Jehovah's Witness may have contributed to this demeanor. Although he received a lot of media attention, that was never Jackson's preference, as he seldom gave interviews. To escape many of the stresses brought on by his career and by events in his childhood, Jackson created his own personal whimsical sanctuary in the late 1980s at his Neverland Ranch in California. At Neverland he had exotic pets, including the now-famous chimpanzee, Bubbles. Jackson also had a number of his own amusement rides at the ranch, perhaps, as some maintain, to aid in an exploration of a second childhood. He did not keep Neverland to himself alone, however, as he would occasionally open up the ranch for children's events. Because of his reclusive nature, odd behaviors, and preference to avoid the media, rumors began to circulate. Three of the initial rumors involved his skin color, sleeping habits, and sexuality. Many say that he intentionally lightened his skin to appear white, although this was later dispelled by Jackson in a rare televised interview. His sleeping routine came under speculation when a rumor spread that he slept in a special chamber in order to increase his life span. In reality, Jackson suffered from a severe version of vilitigo, a skin disease, and his chamber sleeping was likely staged and overblown. Some also posited that Jackson was homosexual, but Jackson dismissed these claims.

In 1991 Jackson released *Dangerous*, his first album of the early 1990s, which featured the hit song "Black or White." In 1993 he performed at several important events, including the halftime show at Super Bowl XXVII. Later that year the first allegations of child molestation against Jackson emerged when a thirteen-year-old boy claimed that the music star had fondled him. While Jackson was known to have sleepovers with boys at his Neverland Ranch, prior to this accusation there had never been any known charges of wrongdoing. Jackson maintained his innocence at the onset and throughout all of the allegations. Police officers searched Neverland Ranch, but never found any evidence to support the molestation claim. In 1994 Jackson settled out of court with the accuser's family.

Around the mid- to late 1990s, Jackson's musical career began to lose steam in many populations, particularly America's younger white community. His 1995 album, *HIStory: Past, Present, and Future, Book I*, was expected to do incredibly well on the sales charts, but fell short of expectations. The album featured both well-known earlier hits and new material. Although the record as a whole did not sell as expected, two individual tracks achieved the status that the album as a whole did not. "You Are Not Alone" reached number one on the pop and R&B charts, and his duet with sister Janet Jackson, "Scream," reached the Top 10 on the same charts and became wildly popular. "Scream," in fact, earned Michael and Janet the Grammy Award for Best Music Video, Short Form that year.

According to one of the most popular fan website of the time, "by the release of 2001's *Invincible*, Jackson was better known in many circles, primarily white, and young, as an eccentric whose quirks were reported in the tabloids, than as a performer. The album sold well, but stories of his odd behavior started to overshadow his talent. He often appeared in public wearing a surgical mask, and he hid his children's faces under veils." Moreover, "Jackson faced more legal woes in 2004 when he was arrested on charges related to incidents with a thirteen-year-old boy the previous year. Facing ten counts in all, he was charged with lewd conduct with a minor, attempted lewd conduct, administering alcohol to facilitate molestation, and conspiracy to commit child abduction, false imprisonment, and extortion. The resulting 2005 trial was a media circus with fans, detractors, and camera crews surrounding the courthouse." On June 14, 2005,

Jackson was acquitted of all charges, and many speculated that the star was merely the victim of false accusations and carefully executed extortion attempts. "He stayed at Neverland for only a short time after the trial and then moved to Bahrain," Michael Jackson BlogSpot reported, and "Jackson sold his Neverland Ranch in 2008. Around this same time, the largely reclusive Jackson announced that he would be performing a series of concerts in London as his 'final curtain call.' There had been some speculation regarding whether the often fragile-appearing singer would be able to handle the rigors of fifty concerts. However, despite all of the allegations and stories of odd behavior, Jackson remained a figure of great interest, as demonstrated by the strong response to his concert plans."[13]

"Set to appear at the 02 Arena beginning July 8, 2009," the highly respected Michael Jackson Blogspot announced, industry watchers "saw the tickets to these shows sell out in only four hours. Michael Jackson, one of the most popular artists of all time, died suddenly of cardiac arrest on June 25, 2009, in Los Angeles just before the concert series. He was 50 years old."[14] His death stunned millions and prompted many to reflect upon his impact upon the entertainment industry and popular culture. In addition to being the record-breaking "King of Pop," Michael Jackson was one of the most generous entertainers of all time. Many argue that he paved the way for the current surge in celebrity philanthropy, supporting dozens of charities during his life, including USA for Africa, the Make-a-Wish Foundation, and the Elizabeth Taylor AIDS Foundation. Michael Jackson's death marked not only the death of a man, but the end of a movement. His music comforted his fans. His success buoyed them and his altruism, activism, and philanthropy uplifted them. Even in the midst of scandal and of his often eccentric and inexplicable behavior, much of the music he produced and many of the performances he rendered were nearly flawless. His impact on the music industry is mind-boggling, and he single-handedly changed the music video industry and perceptions of what is possible for people of African descent.[15]

Just as many blacks appreciated and supported the material and symbolic success of Michael Jackson, they also called for the establishment to celebrate the other titans of black history and life. To this end, millions of African Americans supported the effort to make Martin Luther King Jr.'s birthday a federal holiday, which would lift him to the celebrated status of George Washington and Abraham Lincoln, whose birthdays were already recognized with federal holidays. Reagan, supported by powerful political leaders including Senator John McCain of Arizona, rejected the movement to honor King and his values, but under pressure from African Americans and their allies, the president capitulated, and on January 20, 1985, the United States observed the first Martin Luther King Jr. Day, the only federal holiday to recognize the life and legacy of a black American.[16]

African American activism and electoral clout also played a key role in elevating Jesse Jackson (1941–, fig, 24). Jackson was born on October 8, 1941, in Greensville, South Carolina. He adopted the name of his step-father, Charles Jackson, at the age of fifteen. Jackson was a very good high school student and leader, having been elected class president. He would later secure an athletic scholarship to play football at the University of Illinois (1959–60). He transferred soon after to the predominantly black Agricultural and Technical College of North Carolina in Greensboro and earned a BA in sociology in 1964. He relocated to Chicago in 1966, completed graduate studies at Chicago Theological Seminary, and was ordained a Baptist minister in 1968.

The *Arena* states that "while an undergraduate, Jackson became involved in the civil rights movement." Indeed,

In 1965 he went to Selma, Alabama, to march with Martin Luther King Jr. and became a worker in King's Southern Christian Leadership Conference (SCLC). Jackson helped found the Chicago branch of Operation Breadbasket, the economic arm of the SCLC, in 1966 and served as the organization's national director from 1967 to 1971. He was in Memphis, Tennessee with King when the civil rights leader was assassinated on April 4, 1968, though his exact location at the moment King was shot has long been a matter of controversy. Accused of using the SCLC for personal gain, Jackson was suspended by the organization, whereupon he formally resigned in 1971 and founded Operation PUSH (People United to Save Humanity), a Chicago-based organization in which he advocated black self-help and achieved a broad audience for his liberal views.[17]

In 1983, in response to Reagan's efforts to "roll back the clock" on civil rights and social welfare programs, Jackson and PUSH initiated a major voter-registration drive to mobilize African Americans in opposition to conservative policies that undermined the social and economic stability of the black community.

FIG. 24. Jesse Jackson. Library of Congress.

"In 1984," the *Arena* notes, "Jackson established the National Rainbow Coalition, which sought equal rights for people of color, women, working class whites, and members of the gay and lesbian communities. These two organizations merged in 1996 to form the Rainbow/PUSH Coalition. Jackson began traveling widely in the late 1970s to mediate or spotlight international problems and disputes. In 1979 he visited South Africa, where he spoke out against apartheid, and he later journeyed to the strife-ridden Middle East and campaigned to give Palestinians their own state. While some observers and government officials frowned on his diplomatic missions as meddlesome and self-aggrandizing,"[18] Jackson still garnered a great deal of support for negotiating the release of U.S. soldiers and civilians around the world, including a trip to in Syria in 1983, where he made a dramatic personal appeal to President Hafez al-Assad to secure the release of Navy Lt. Robert Goodman, a captured American pilot who had been shot down over Lebanon; in Havana in 1984, when he met with Cuban President Fidel Castro to negotiate successfully the release of twenty-two Americans who were held by Cuba's government; and in Iraq in 1990, where he secured the release of several British citizens and twenty Americans on the eve of the Persian Gulf War.[19]

By the early 1980s Jackson had cultivated an international reputation as an advocate for racial, social, and economic justice, as well as for peace. In 1984, on the heels of the success of his Syrian and Cuban missions, Jackson launched the second major effort by an African American to gain the Democratic nomination for President of the United States. His supporters formed a board coalition of the working poor, gays, and lesbians, white progressives, and people of color, which Jackson described as his "rainbow coalition." He hoped that this widespread and diverse base of support would catapult him to the nomination and the White House.[20]

Despite his antisemitic and highly controversial reference to New York as "Hymietown," Jackson ran an astonishingly competitive campaign, winning primaries in five states, including Michigan. Ultimately, Jackson garnered 21 percent of the primary vote but gained only 8 percent of the party's delegates, and consequently lost the nomination to former Vice President Walter Mondale. Jackson mounted another presidential campaign in 1988. During this one he won more than 7 million primary votes. After winning the South Carolina primary, finishing second in the Illinois primary, and winning the Democratic caucus in Michigan, Jackson became the Democratic frontrunner. Massachusetts governor Michael

Dukakis recaptured the lead, however, with wins in the Colorado and Wisconsin primaries. Having lost his momentum and early lead, Jackson decided, for the sake of party unity, to drop out of the race.[21]

Jackson has not run for president again, but since 1992 he has functioned as a power broker within the Democratic Party. In 1990 he won the largely symbolic position of the District of Columbia's senator, a platform from which he lobbied for statehood for the nation's capital. In 1997 he founded the Wall Street Project, which has endeavored to increase African American influence on the behaviors and cultural competency of corporate America. Jackson returned to the international stage in 1999, this time traveling to Belgrade during the war in Kosovo to meet with Slobodan Milosevic, who was the Yugoslav president at the time. Jackson skillfully obtained the release of three U.S. prisoners of war. Later that year he helped broker a cease-fire in war-ravaged Sierra Leone.[22]

Jesse Jackson has been characterized as bold, defiant, and controversial by supporters and critics alike, and he has elicited praise for inspiring the black masses and the poor with acute rhetorical skills and addresses interspersed by slogans such as, "I am somebody" and "Keep hope alive." Critics, however, denounced him as bullish, self-aggrandizing, hypocritical, and an instigator of racial conflict. Jackson's reputation was sullied by a revelation in 2001 that, though he was married, he had fathered a child out of wedlock with Rainbow Coalition staffer Karin Stanford. His public image as a moral leader, which still suffered from his infamous antisemitic comments in 1988, deteriorated. Jackson, however, remained a highly sought-after public figure and wielded a tremendous amount of power within and beyond African American communities.[23]

Even as Jackson was becoming a household name by championing the poor, progressives, and people of color, in 1984 black people everywhere challenged Reagan's stance on human rights at home and abroad. African Americans were particularly disappointed with their president's policy of "constructive engagement" with apartheid, the sweeping social, political, and economic oppression of black people by the white minority in South Africa. Not only did Reagan and his administration offer very little criticism of the African nation's white supremacist and segregationist policies, but the United States continued to do business with South Africa, which African Americans and other opponents of apartheid believed was both a cop-out and an indirect reward for the South Africans. In addition, the United States remained reluctant to enforce economic sanctions against the nation's racist regime in defiance of a UN resolution. The U.S. Congressional Black Caucus routinely called for sanctions, but Reagan would not be moved. Instead, the president denounced the notion of the United States pressuring South Africa, a Cold War ally, into altering any of its policies, even its deplorable treatment of its black citizens.

Refusing to let the matter drop, black U.S. Congressional leaders and other activists continued to challenge apartheid, and they organized what became a global boycott and critique of South African apartheid.

In response to Reagan's unwillingness to act, black leaders sought to aid their fellow members of the Black Diaspora. Eleanor Holmes Norton, the former EEOC chief and Georgetown University law professor, who was a congresswoman from the District of Columbia at the time, took the lead. Most Americans had first heard of Norton when Reagan fired her as head of the EEOC for her unyielding criticism of his record on civil rights. "We had to do something," Norton remarked outside the South African embassy in Washington DC just weeks after the 1984 election. "The Reagan policy of 'constructive engagement'" amounted to "little more than letting the South African government go and do what it feels like doing."[24] Norton announced that she and other black leaders would enter the South African embassy, where they planned to protest until the South African government released its political prisoners, including Nelson Mandela, the leader of the African National Congress; ended apartheid; and afforded civil and human rights to black South Africans. She was joined at the embassy protest by Mary Frances Berry, whom Reagan was unable to fire from the Civil Rights Commission, and Walter Fauntroy, the former head of the SCLC and a Washington DC congressman. The protest was organized by Randall Robinson, the leader of Trans-Africa, an antiapartheid association. Robinson and Trans-Africa were already mobilizing U.S. support for the black freedom struggle in South Africa; the efforts of leaders such as Norton helped publicize their political aims. When Norton, Berry, Fauntroy, and Robinson entered the embassy, made their intentions clear, and announced their demands, the South African ambassador stormed out, leaving his assistant to ask, "Is there anything we can do to work this out?" Berry replied, "You can comply with the demands."[25]

The protest against apartheid was quickly dispersed by the police. The three leaders were arrested, charged with a misdemeanor for unlawful entry of an embassy, jailed, and promptly released on bail. They immediately held a press conference to announce the formation of the Free South Africa Movement. Throughout the remainder of 1984 they held daily protests, including massive rallies outside the South African embassy. Scores of black activists and proponents of racial justice came to the embassy to support the protest and to be arrested in solidarity. Rosa Parks, Coretta Scott King, and Stevie Wonder joined a total of six thousand people who were arrested at the embassy and at South African consulates throughout the United States. Archbishop Desmond Tutu, the leader of the Anglican Church of Southern Africa and the winner of the 1984 Nobel Peace Prize, infused the campaign with additional moral authority when he delivered a series of stirring antiapartheid addresses across the United States. Due to widespread protests on America's college and university campuses, including Columbia and Stanford, many schools adopted policies that barred the investment of endowment funds in businesses that operated in South Africa. Cities, states, and retirement funds soon followed suit, calling on companies to retire their investments in South Africa.

The antiapartheid movement was the first major effort organized by African Americans to use nonviolent civil disobedience to challenge systematic racial injustice since the civil rights movement. These efforts were buoyed by dramatic and often violent black resistance within South Africa. The campaign in America sought sanctions against the white supremacist regime, which leaders hoped would create an economic hardship in South Africa that would compel its government to change its racist policies. In 1986 Representative Ronald Dellums, a Democrat from Oakland, California, introduced the Comprehensive Anti-Apartheid Act, which promised to level stiff economic sanctions against the South African government. Few believed that the act would pass, as similar bills had already failed. The antiapartheid movement and unrest in South Africa, however, persuaded a number of Democratic and Republican congressional leaders to endorse Dellums's legislation. The House and Senate passed the bill, but Reagan vetoed it. In September 1986, however, the House and Senate overrode the veto. Robinson proclaimed, "We had won. We had turned the course of the most powerful country on earth."[26] South Africa soon caved under pressure from global sanctions and boycotts against it as well as from intense protests within its borders. Apartheid was abandoned in 1990, and Nelson Mandela (1918–, fig. 25), who had been charged and convicted of "sabotage," was released from prison after twenty-seven years of incarceration. Mandela became South Africa's first black president in 1994.

FIG. 25. Nelson Mandela toasts his supporters shortly after becoming South Africa's first black president, May 2, 1994. AP Photo/David Brauchli (9405020166).

Despite Jackson's rise and the success of the antiapartheid movement, the election of Bush, Reagan's vice president, to the presidency in 1988 reminded black Americans that race and racism were still serious problems within the United States. Bush ran on a platform calling for "a kinder, gentler America," but his campaign benefited immensely from a racially polarizing television ad highlighting Willie Horton, a black convict who raped a white woman during a furlough from a Massachusetts prison. Horton's furlough was issued as part of a program endorsed by Democratic presidential nominee Michael Dukakis, who was then governor of Massachusetts, and by a preceding Republican governor of the state. Black leaders denounced the ad as a deliberate appeal to the racist fears of whites. Bush, however, would not repudiate it.

The general perception among many whites that African American men were inherently criminal only intensified after Bush's victory. Even as the Democratic Party gained some political traction during the early 1990s with the election of Bill Clinton as President in 1992, the notion that young black people were inherently violent remained a bedrock principle within American political culture. Presumptions of black criminality led to an increase in racial profiling, police brutality, and a disproportionately high number of black men being arrested, convicted, sentenced, and incarcerated. By the mid-1990s the black community was confronted with the adverse ramifications of the jailing of large numbers of black people. A number of states strip convicted felons of their right to vote, leading to the disfranchisement of a large portion of the black male population.

Of the 4.7 million felons in the United States by 1999, 1.8 million of them were African American. African American men were incarcerated in shockingly high numbers. The increasing incarceration rates affected the black community in ways other than voting power. This gender imbalance in incarceration rates removed black men from the home and exacerbated the socioeconomic vulnerability of the black family. As of 1999 one in every seven black men was in prison or jail. In addition, 10 percent of black men in their later twenties were incarcerated in 1999, and over 30 percent of black men who dropped out of high school were incarcerated at some point in their lives, often for drug-related crimes.

Activists, including Angela Davis, argued that the vicious condition of U.S prisons and the institutions' high incidence of violence and rape begged for the attention of U.S. elected officials and the courts. Political leaders and judges, however, were loath to address the brutality commonplace in American prisons. Indeed, in 1994 Supreme Court Justice Thomas voted to dismiss claims that prisons failed to protect inmates, arguing, "Prisons are necessarily dangerous places, they house society's most antisocial and violent people in close proximity with one another. Regrettably, some level of brutality and sexual aggression among [prisoners] is inevitable no matter what the guards do unless all prisoners are locked in their cells twenty-four hours a day and sedated."[27] In short, the federal government remained unwilling to address its incarceration crisis or the racial implications of that crisis.

The disproportionate number of African Americans in the U.S. criminal justice system was attributable in part to the policing of black communities in America by law enforcement agents, some of whom viewed blacks as problems or as altogether subhuman. "In March 1991," Williby's Court Justice reported, "while driving down the 210 freeway in Los Angeles with two friends, Rodney King was detected speeding by the California Highway Patrol. Fearing that his probation for a robbery offense would be revoked because of the traffic violation, King led the highway patrol on a high-speed chase, eventually hitting 115 miles per hour. . . . By the time he was caught and ordered to exit his vehicle, several Los Angeles

Police Department (LAPD) squad cars had arrived on the scene. A struggle ensued, and some of the officers quickly decided that King was resisting arrest. Sergeant Stacey Koon fired two shots into King with a Taser gun, and after that failed to subdue him, the officers, including Laurence Powell, beat him mercilessly with their batons."[28] "The incident was videotaped by a man named George Holliday," TIME *Magazine* reported, "who lived nearby, and it didn't take long for the tape to send shockwaves around the world and enrage already frustrated African American communities in Los Angeles, which felt that racial profiling and abuse by the police had long gone unchecked."[29]

A jury of eleven white Americans and one Latino American eventually acquitted the four police officers charged in the beating of King. Following the verdict, South Central Los Angeles, not far from the epicenter of the Watts Riots of 1965, erupted in the worst single episode of urban unrest in American history. Believing that the verdict demonstrated the perpetuation of American racial injustice, black rioters looted and set fire to buildings, targeting especially Korean- and other Asian-owned stores that had treated black customers shabbily. In one case a crowd pulled a white truck driver, Reginald Denny, who was stuck at an intersection, from his car and beat him. By the time the violence died down, thousands of people had been injured, four thousand had been arrested, fifty-three lay dead, and upward of five hundred million dollars in property was damaged or decimated.

The Rodney King affair and the ensuing riots reverberated throughout the nation. In Phoenix, Arizona, black activist Lincoln Ragsdale cited local police brutality and a retreat from civil rights as two elements that thwarted the cultivation of constructive race relations. For instance, he and other black leaders characterized the "overwhelmingly" white Phoenix police department as "insensitive to blacks." Their comments rang true, for in March 1998 a jury awarded a $45 million judgment to the family of Edward Mallet, a twenty-five-year-old black man and double amputee who died at the hands of Phoenix police officers in 1994. Wrongly suspected of gang activity because of, among other things, his "physical appearance," Mallet was stopped, doused with pepper spray, and put in a neck hold by police officers. The neck hold cut off Mallet's flow of oxygen and suffocated him to death. The police supported their actions by arguing that Mallet had resisted arrest. Despite Mallet's status as a double amputee, police officers claimed that he was a large man who displayed superior strength, which, they argued, gave them reason to apply the life-ending neck hold to Mallet. In the wake of the Rodney King debacle, no one was buying their story. Following the verdict, the city began paying the Mallet family the $45 million judgment in $5 million installments.[30]

Police brutality against African Americans continued into the twenty-first century. In another high-profile case, Abner Louima, a Haitian immigrant, was beaten and sodomized with the handle of a toilet plunger while in custody at a Brooklyn police station in 1997. In 1999, New York City police shot Amadou Diallo, a West African immigrant, forty-one times after he reached for his wallet to retrieve his identification for them; in Albany, a jury acquitted the four police officers charged in the Diallo killing. Also in 1999, Patrick Dorismond, another Haitian immigrant, was gunned down following an argument with undercover police officers when he refused to purchase drugs from them. On July 27, 2000, a grand jury declined to indict Officer Anthony Vasquez in the death of Dorismond, announcing that they had found the shooting to be accidental.

In 2006, New York police officers killed an unarmed twenty-three-year-old, Sean Bell, the night before his wedding to the mother of his two children. Ensnared in an undercover sting operation, Bell was riddled with bullets as officers fired more than fifty times into his car. Every time an incident of police brutality gripped the black community, African Americans protested the racial profiling that placed black people in harm's way as well as the violent tactics that typically accompany profiling. Leaders such as the Reverend Al Sharpton, an outspoken and controversial advocate for civil rights and black Americans, denounced racial profiling as unjust and racist. Sharpton urged black people to unify in their opposition of such tactics. "We cannot allow this to continue to happen," he announced. "We've got to understand that all of us were in that car."[31]

The most explosive event involving race in America during this period was the murder trial of O. J. Simpson, the African American collegiate and professional football star, actor, and commentator for ABC's popular *Monday Night Football*. In June of 1994 Simpson was charged with the murder of his white ex-wife, Nicole Brown Simpson, and an acquaintance of hers, Ronald Goldman, in Los Angeles. The televised trial that followed dragged on for eight months, garnering some 150 million viewers. Most Americans developed emotional positions on the presumed innocence or guilt of Simpson. Ultimately a jury of nine blacks, two whites, and one Latino acquitted Simpson, positing that the state did not prove its case, which had moved in Simpson's favor when his team of attorneys, led by maverick black attorney Johnnie Cochran, revealed that one of the white police officers had manufactured evidence and covered up his own racist views and behavior in an effort to help convict Simpson. This is one reason Simpson was acquitted, but far from the only one. The LAPD and the DA's office were also ineffective and negligent, and the handling of evidence was questionable.

In Simpson's civil trial, which ended in February 1997, a jury of nine whites, one Latino, one Asian, and a person of African American and Asian lineage found him liable for the wrongful deaths of Ronald Goldman and Nicole Simpson, and ordered him to pay $35 million to the families of the murder victims. The verdict in both cases exposed the degree to which conflicting views of race and racism caused racial tensions to endure in America. The standards of guilt were different in the two cases, but still there was widespread speculation that race was an important factor in the two outcomes. Many African Americans were seen rejoicing in the streets following the verdict in the criminal case, some holding signs that read "Don't squeeze the Juice," a reference to Simpson's nickname. On the other hand, television cameras captured crowds of white people responding to the decision by lashing out verbally in disgust and anger. On October 3, 1996, a CNN/USA Today/Gallup Poll showed that after the criminal trial only 20 percent of whites thought that the jury was right to acquit Simpson, while 62 percent of African Americans agreed with the decision.

Many leaders have argued that the aforementioned incidents were not merely evidence of white supremacy. These leaders urged interested parties both within the United States and abroad to view racial profiling, police brutality, and crime within the black community as complex issues not always attributable to racism. Police officers, for example, are routinely subjected to stressful and violent circumstances, primarily because American society is itself violent. Citizens' easy access to weapons also places police officers on the defensive. Some argue that skewed perspectives, the erosion of one's moral compass, and errors in judgment, as tragic as they may be, should be anticipated. Moreover, critics note that crime is so intense in many black neighborhoods that police must present more force. Indeed, these critics note that the black community sorely needs a greater police presence. The murder rate in black America in 1997 was seven times that of whites, and black victims represented 49 percent of all murders, even though black people comprised only 12 percent of the population. Well over 90 percent of all incidents of assault, rape, and murder involving African Americans were committed by black people. Further, the murder rate for African American men between fourteen and seventeen years old tripled between 1976 and 1993. While these numbers receded during the late 1990s, as did all violent crime in the United States, black people still suffered from disproportionately high crime rates.

High crime rates severely undermined the stability of the black community and forced business costs in black neighborhoods to balloon, which repelled job growth and critical investment capital in areas that needed it the most. Between 1969 and the late 1990s, black gang activity emerged from and intensified poor socioeconomic conditions in black neighborhoods. While the United States waged war in Vietnam and fought the war on poverty at home, lack of funds, ineffective plans to confront inner-city poverty, and heightened police and military violence against African Americans contributed to conditions which gave rise to African American gangs throughout America, including the infamous Crips, founded in 1969, and Bloods, organized in 1972 in Los Angeles, California. As these gangs fought over turf and illicit yet lucrative drug trafficking, the violence associated with their activities spread across the whole of many black communities.

The fear of being a victim of violent crime prompted many inner-city dwellers to fortify their homes and literally lock themselves inside. Once-bustling communities were transformed into veritable war zones. Even Rosa Parks, the chief heroine of the civil rights movement, fell victim to the violence that plagued the black community. In 1994, she was beaten and robbed in her Detroit apartment by a twenty-eight-year-old unemployed African American man who attacked her even though he recognized the revered activist.

Since African Americans have been disproportionately victimized by crime, most have called on law enforcement to assist them in alleviating their suffering. Due in large part to their enhanced political influence, black people made modest inroads in helping the police become more responsive to crime, as well as more consistent and fair in law enforcement. The black community, for instance, lobbied successfully to have blacks appointed as police chiefs in hopes that they might be able to improve the conduct of other police officers and foster better relationships with black citizens.

Many black leaders argued that the social and economic policies of the Reagan and Bush administrations, the hopelessness they provoked in inner city Americans, and the proliferation of crack cocaine and guns in America's urban areas during the 1980s and early 1990s exacerbated crime and socioeconomic dislocations in black neighborhoods. In fact, much of the aid to black people that was eliminated by Reagan and Bush between 1981 and 1993 had been the only resources that stood between stability and abject poverty for millions of African Americans. The unemployment rate for black Americans increased to 20 percent in 1982, twice that of white Americans at that time. Salaries for American CEOs skyrocketed by 514 percent between 1980 and 1993, while the wages of American workers rose by only 68 percent, an increase that lagged well behind inflation. In 1992 the average CEO earned 157 times as much as the average factory worker. In addition, as a result of changes in tax code, average workers paid a higher proportion of their salaries to the federal government, while CEOs and the companies they headed paid far less. Corporate profits reached record highs, while "downsizing" and capital flight left millions unemployed; this was particularly harmful to African Americans.

Reeling from the neoconservative dismantling of the Great Society agenda and the cuts in government and private support of local programs that once supplied job training, health care, and family planning, the inner city became home to concentrated poverty, health crises, unstable families, and gang violence. As jobs, better educational opportunities, and social support networks continued to flow out of cities and into suburbs, the socially and economically segregated and subordinated inner-city minorities became trapped in a vicious cycle of joblessness and hopelessness that sociologist Harold M. Baron labeled "the web of urban racism."[32]

The Clinton Years

It was no wonder, then, that African Americans welcomed the presidential candidacy of Democratic Arkansas governor William Jefferson "Bill" Clinton in 1992. Comfortable around black people, Clinton promised to commit himself to fighting for racial, gender, and economic equality, endearing himself to black grassroots organizers and civil rights leaders. He visited black churches, schools, organizations, and homes, where he delivered rousing, emotional speeches that touted the need for diplomacy, innovation, service, and equal opportunity. The vast majority of black Americans eagerly supported his bid against that of the incumbent

Republican, George H. W. Bush, whose relationship with African Americans was virtually nonexistent, and third party phenomenon H. Ross Perot, a Texas businessman.

White Americans were also disillusioned with Bush. Though his support among whites spiked after the American military success in expelling Iraqi forces from Kuwait in the first Gulf War in 1991, this support was short-lived. Early in 1992 Bush's national approval rating dropped significantly due to the nation's mounting economic problems. Even so, few people believed that Clinton had a legitimate chance to win the election. The Democrat presented himself as a centrist, however, and cunningly distanced himself from the left wing of the Democratic Party and from so-called black interest groups embodied by Jackson and the Rainbow Coalition. When Clinton did speak at the annual meeting of the Rainbow Coalition, he seized the moment to rebuke rapper Sister Souljah, who had suggested that "blacks take a week and kill white people"[33] in retaliation for racist attacks by whites. Though he promised to create an administration that would "look like America," Clinton was quick to reassure Americans that he rejected "quotas." Furthermore, his youth, good looks, sharp mind, quick wit, and mesmerizing charisma enabled him to dodge accusations of draft evasion, marijuana smoking, and womanizing. He effectively criticized Bush's record and convinced millions of Americans that he would take the United States in new, more positive directions.

Clinton's message of hope, reconciliation, and economic opportunity resonated with the voting public. He was elected in November 1992 with only 43 percent of the popular vote to Bush's 38 percent and Perot's 19 percent. Clinton garnered 78 percent of the black vote and 39 percent of the white vote in "battleground states" such as California, Illinois, Michigan, New Jersey, and New York. Although Clinton won, he did so by a slim margin, and even as Democrats maintained control of the House of Representatives, they lost ground in the Senate. Without a clear mandate and in the face of intense Republican efforts to undermine his leadership, the Clinton administration ushered in some notable changes in American and African American life and leadership.

The majority of black people viewed Bill Clinton as the most sympathetic president on matters of race and the needs and desires of black people since Lyndon Johnson. Writer Toni Morrison even referred to Clinton, in jest, as America's first black president. Others jokingly described him as the first female president because of his steadfast support for equal

FIG. 26. Colin Powell and Condoleezza Rice meet with President George W. Bush, September 19, 2001. National Archives and Records Administration.

rights for women. Clinton made history by appointing more women and African Americans to influential federal posts than any of his predecessors. He appointed four black Americans to his first cabinet: Ronald H. Brown, the former chair of the Democratic National Committee, as secretary of commerce; Hazel O'Leary, a Minnesota energy mogul, as secretary of energy; Jesse Brown, executive director of the Disabled American Veterans, as secretary of veterans' affairs; and Mississippi Congressman Mike Espy as secretary of agriculture. Moreover, Clinton retained General Colin Powell as the first black chairman of the Joint Chiefs of Staff.

While Clinton endeared himself to many blacks with such high-profile appointments, he raised their ire with respect to Lani Guinier and Jocelyn Elders. Clinton nominated Guinier, his longtime friend and fellow Yale Law School graduate, to serve as assistant attorney general for civil rights, but withdrew her nomination when conservatives condemned her for being "too liberal." In 1993 he was complicit in the shameful treatment of Elders, another of his closest friends. He had appointed Elders to the post of surgeon general, the first African American and the second woman to hold the position. She was an outspoken and uncompromising supporter of health care, especially for those who were unable to gain regular access to medical attention. As surgeon general, Elders quickly established herself as a controversial figure. She entertained proposals for the legalization of some recreational drugs for medicinal purposes; to combat teen pregnancy and the spread of stds, she endorsed the distribution of contraceptives in schools. It was during her address to the UN conference on AIDS in 1994, however, that she rendered her most provocative opinion. When asked whether it would be appropriate to promote masturbation as a means to prevent young people from engaging in dangerous forms of sexual activity, she responded by saying, "I think that it is part of human sexuality, and perhaps it should be taught."[34] This remark stirred up a hornet's nest of controversy, and Clinton settled the issue and saved face by firing Elders.

Although Clinton's handling of black political appointments was far from perfect, he revealed himself as the closest thing to a friend in the White House that African Americans had ever seen. As a candidate he had toured riot-ravaged South Central Los Angeles in 1991, worshipped in black churches, and played the saxophone on the extremely popular late-night *Arsenio Hall* television show. His closest friends and members of his transition team included attorney and former NUL head Vernon Jordan,

Barbara Jordan, William Gray III, and Marian Wright Edelman, the inaugural president of the Children's Defense Fund. Clinton also gave Eleanor Holmes Norton, as delegate to Congress from Washington DC, the authority to select U.S. marshals, U.S. attorneys, and U.S. district court judges for the District of Columbia; this prerogative is usually only exercised by U.S. Senators. Clinton also signed the 1994 King Holiday and Service Act, which was cosponsored by Atlanta congressman and former CORE activist John Lewis to make the King Holiday a national day for public service. In 1997, Clinton appointed John Hope Franklin, the distinguished historian, to chair the president's Commission on Race. Finally, reflecting his interest and appreciation for black Americans and their historic and contemporary links to Africa, Clinton became the first American president to visit sub-Saharan Africa in 1998.

Despite Clinton's symbolic appeal and substantive efforts to make racial progress, myriad socioeconomic problems continued to dog black Americans. Indeed, for every sign of racial progress, alternative signs indicated that racism remained a potent force in American society. Affirmative action remained hotly contested and under attack, and major racial discrimination lawsuits against Denny's restaurants and Texaco during the Clinton years served as painful reminders of the staying power of white supremacy and de facto segregation. Poor and working-class blacks were not the only people to feel the sting of American racism. In *The Rage of a Privileged Class* (1993), black journalist Ellis Cose shed light on the racism and associated frustrations and trauma that middle- and upper-class blacks faced even as they took advantage of new job opportunities in areas long blocked to them. In addition, Cornel West, a scholar at Princeton University, published a bestselling collection of essays entitled *Race Matters* (1993), which lamented the "widespread mistreatment of black people, especially black men, by law enforcement agencies." West also indicated that his "blood began to boil" when he, a Harvard-educated Ivy League professor, was passed over in favor of a white woman as he attempted to hail a taxi in New York. He recognized that the incidents of discrimination that middle-class blacks endured were "dwarfed by those like Rodney King's beating or the abuse of black targets of the FBI's COINTELPRO efforts of the 1960s and 1970s," but he reminded readers that "the memories cut like a merciless knife at my soul as I waited on that godforsaken corner."[35]

In addition to lingering racism, the persistence of poverty among black Americans inspired many to wonder why civil rights reforms had helped improve the lives of some African Americans and not others. In 1993, in fact, 33 percent of black Americans still lived in poverty. As Clinton worked to reform the nation's welfare system, old debates about the causes of black poverty were resuscitated. Warring factions attributed black indigence to racial inequalities, and especially to limited educational and employment options, on one hand, or to inherent personal shortcomings in moral fiber, intelligence, and work ethic on the other. Despite these protests, little was done to assist impoverished African Americans. By the end of Clinton's first term, the president appeared to be less interested in combating poverty and defending the quality and integrity of life for the masses of black people and more concerned about ending deficit spending.

Clinton's shift in attention was informed by several obstacles in both terms of his presidency and by the competing agendas he brought to the White House. His efforts to pass health care reform, which were led by First Lady Hillary Clinton, utterly failed. Further, the 1994 midterm elections put conservative Republicans in control of both houses of Congress. Finally, a sex scandal involving Bill Clinton and Monica Lewinsky, a twenty-two-year-old White House intern, resulted in an investigation that raised questions about whether Clinton had committed perjury or obstructed justice; this led to his impeachment by the U.S. House of Representatives in 1998, though the president managed to stay in office. As president, Clinton wanted to demonstrate to the Republican Congressional majority and to American voters, who were dissatisfied with the Democratic "brand," that his party was as socially and fiscally responsible as the Republicans. Moreover, he planned to deliver on his campaign promise to "end welfare as we know it." After turning his attention to eliminating deficit spending, however, Clinton failed to create any new antipoverty programs. Instead, he withdrew significant support for programs vital to the stability of the black community.

After routinely vetoing sweeping Republican welfare reform bills during the first years of his first term, Clinton succeeded in facilitating the passage of the Personal Responsibility and Work Opportunity Reconciliation Act in 1996. This comprehensive welfare reform legislation required states to reconstitute their programs. The new bill mandated that all those who received aid must secure work within two years and eliminate their need for assistance within five years, even if they were unable to remain employed. Critics of the legislation indicated that the reform did little to prepare welfare recipients for employment, and it did nothing to provide child care for poor single mothers as they prepared for and secured jobs. Leaders such as Edelman warned that Clinton's reforms, coupled with the failure of his health plan, would throw poor people, and especially struggling black people, into a downward spiral of socioeconomic despair. Clinton, however, gained a great deal of political capital from the passage of this legislation, as Republicans could no longer criticize him for unchecked welfare spending.

The results of Clinton's welfare reform were not as cataclysmic as his critics warned, nor were they as far-reaching as he had hoped. Many former welfare recipients found work, not because the federal government had prepared them for a job but because the job market improved during the late 1990s. During Clinton's presidency, in fact, the economy grew significantly, unemployment dipped from 7.2 to 5.5 percent, a 1993 tax increase in combination with a reduction in federal spending slashed the deficit by 50 percent, and American businesses created ten million new jobs. Furthermore, during his second term, Clinton ameliorated the more hard-hitting facets of his legislation by rewriting the sections that denied disability benefits to illegal immigrants. He also offered health care coverage for poor children, and he instituted an earned income tax credit to provide wage enhancement to many of the working poor.

Clinton was criticized by African Americans for seeming to abandon Guinier and Elders, and for his efforts to court the right and curtail welfare assistance, but he remained extremely popular among black Americans. His unprecedented number of black political appointments, and his symbolic support and affection for African Americans, signaled a watershed moment in American history. Still, as one observer noted:

> The hypnotic racial dance of cultural authenticity that Bill Clinton performed in office lulled many blacks into perceptual fog. Clinton actively cultivated a unique and intense relationship with black voters. He relished this bond and often acknowledged his honorary blackness. It is important to remember that the description of Clinton as black was prompted by his experience of personal, public humiliation at the hands of his political foes. It is not a claim about his racial heritage, but instead a reaction to his experience with and use of cultural markers that often stand for the denigrated elements of black life in America. As Clinton performed blackness, real black people got poorer. The poorest African-Americans experienced an absolute decline in income, and they

also became poorer relative to the poorest whites. The richest African-Americans saw an increase in income, but even the highest-earning blacks still considerably lagged their white counterparts. Furthermore, the '90s witnessed the continued growth of the significant gap between black and white median wealth.[36]

Congressional Republicans and radical right-wing conservatives revealed a visceral hatred of Clinton and his presidency, announcing their intention to "take back the White House" well before he left office. During the Clinton administration, right-wingers spearheaded massive fundraising drives and political rallies to make the Republican Party as visible and competitive as possible. Democrats, on the other hand, seemed dispirited by the Republican onslaught, and they failed to mobilize their massive black support as Clinton had during the height of his power. Democratic stagnation and submissiveness, coupled with Republican energy, creativity, and determination, had helped Republicans take control of both houses of Congress in 1994. Following their resounding victory that year, Republicans implemented their conservative agenda, which included fighting affirmative action and environmental protections such as green energy technologies and solar, wind and geothermal energy, efficiency requirements on automobiles, and clean nuclear energy; the prohibition of offshore drilling in the most ecologically sensitive areas. They also favored reducing taxes for the wealthy, slashing benefits for the elderly, privileging Christianity over other religions in their discourse, enabling white supremacist rhetoric and activities by routinely referring to "states' rights," supporting legislation that withholds much needed social and economic capital from black communities, and not consistently and aggressively speaking out against and punishing racist behavior and hate crimes.

Awakened by the 1994 conservative "revolution," many blacks and other progressives responded with a renewed sense of purpose. Jesse Jackson Jr. was elected to Congress in 1994, representing a South Side Chicago district. Once in office, the young Jackson called for a new, comprehensive agenda for black America that prescribed heath care, full employment, quality public education, affordable housing, unobstructed access to the ballot, gender equality, and environmental protections. Democrats also came to understand that race was not merely a black and white issue. Asian/Pacific Island Americans, Arab Americans, Indigenous people, and Latino Americans made their voices heard and their needs known, and

Democrats began to lay the groundwork to tap into these reservoirs of political power. Immigrants, many of whom were from Mexico, formed political organizations and labor unions to fight for their immigrant and human rights. Democrats, however, proved unable to bring these seemingly disparate groups together, and nothing concrete came of these desires. Indeed, hopes for legislation that acknowledged racial difference and assisted all people with universal concerns, such as quality education, employment opportunity, a living wage, affordable housing, universal health care, and comprehensive immigration reform, were unrealized.

Ironically, even Clinton's most passionate black critics were quieted by the election of George W. Bush, the son of George H. W. Bush, to the presidency in 2000. With the younger Bush in office, they soon realized that Clinton's relatively modest challenges to poor blacks and seeming indifference to other marginalized people paled in comparison to the social and economic policies of Bush. Running against Vice President Albert Gore Jr., Bush gained support from the mobilization and organization of primarily white Christian conservatives. Although Gore garnered support from a diverse group of Americans, he ran a lackluster campaign. The election of 2000 was exceedingly close, and the result in Florida was contested through December 2000. Ballots in many districts in Florida were disputed, as were recount efforts. The issue reached the Supreme Court, whose 5–4 ruling (falling precisely along the party lines of the justices) in *Bush v. Gore* (2000) was that Bush had won the state. The decision also halted a recount of the Florida ballots, which the Court considered a violation of the Fourteenth Amendment due to the Florida state Supreme Court's mishandling of the process. The win in Florida also meant that Bush had won the national presidential election.

The *Bush v. Gore* decision remained a contested issue for many Americans. Clinton called it "an appalling decision," comparing it to other decisions regarded as heinous by modern Americans, including *Dred Scott* and *Plessy v. Ferguson*. Clinton's decision to link *Bush v. Gore* to other rulings regarding African Americans was not coincidental. Many African Americans in Florida had reported that they were unable to vote in the 2000 federal election. Indeed, many voting irregularities in the state occurred in districts with large African American populations. One lawsuit alleged that votes were inappropriately discounted as "undervotes" or "overvotes" in Jacksonville, for example, and that this practice was particularly prevalent in the districts of the city with the highest black populations. As many as twenty-six thousand ballots were allegedly not counted in Duval County, and many black voters arrived at voting sites only to be told that they been (illegally) placed on "felony" rolls. These districts included many African American voters and also polled overwhelmingly for the Democratic candidate in the race. Ultimately, the U.S. Civil Rights Commission determined the state disfranchised tens of thousands of black voters, noting in a draft of one of its reports, "African American voting districts were disproportionately hindered by antiquated and error-prone equipment like the punch card ballot system."[37] In other words, those voters who were more likely to vote for Gore rather than Bush, whose brother was then governor of Florida, were unable to successfully do so; the votes that were discounted were disproportionately cast by African Americans and the state's poor. Mary Frances Berry later noted,

> The United States Supreme Court helped undermine the pursuit of equal opportunity by African Americans for most of our history. *Bush v. Gore* was so striking, in part, because the 5–4 majority has been assiduous about deference to state courts and state's rights in general. What the Court has done is to remind us that judges have social and political views that are reflected in their decisions. Each side has used the equal protection clause of the Fourteenth Amendment to convey its policy preference. But, unlike the majority, in cases involving African American voting and the outcome of the 2000 election, the justices in dissent have remained consistent.[38]

Notwithstanding the Supreme Court's ruling, such racialized voting irregularities, coupled with the already large number of black men who were disfranchised due to incarceration, helped George W. Bush win. Studies have shown, in fact, that the 2000 presidential election would have been reversed if felons in a single state (Florida) had had the right to vote. In addition to gaining the presidency, Republicans also maintained majorities in Congress in 2000; they now had control over both the executive and legislative branches of government for the first time since 1954. African Americans braced themselves for additional rollbacks in social programs and expanded attacks on race-conscious remedies for lingering issues in education, employment, housing, and health care.

6

"THE AUDACITY OF HOPE," 2000–2008

There is not a liberal America and a conservative America—there is the United States of America. There is not a black America and a white America and Latino America and Asian America—there's the United States of America.

—BARACK H. OBAMA, keynote speech, Democratic National Convention, July 2004

In his most famous work, The Souls of Black Folk, the black intellectual W. E. B. Du Bois (1868–1963) offered his readers a vision of the United States in which people of African descent could embrace both their African heritage and their American identity, a "double consciousness," and share the richness of their hybrid status with all their fellow Americans. Black people were given little chance to integrate their "double consciousness" during Du Bois's lifetime, but African Americans made substantive progress toward making his dream of a unified America a reality soon after his death with the successes of the civil rights and black power movements. Due in large part to Du Bois's vision and the hard work of subsequent generations of everyday black folk and those who boldly rose to lead them, black Americans helped make the nation and the world anew. The ascendency of African Americans to the highest levels of government service, the sports world, the professions, the military, academia, entertainment, and business, and the "soul," or new race consciousness offered them by Du Bois, Malcolm X, Stokely Carmichael, Amiri Baraka, James Brown, and others, gave black people both pride and strength, moving them from the demonized margins of American civilization to its celebrated center. Indeed, by the first decade of the twenty-first century, African Americans, though still wrestling with discrimination, were also honored for their unsurpassed contributions to American music, dance, language, fine arts, sports, ideas, and ideals.

The effects of the modern civil rights movement still reverberate in the United States. This movement shifted America from a society characterized by naked racism and unconstrained racial brutality to one governed by the rule of law, de jure racial integration, access to the ballot, and more equal economic opportunity. These major advancements enabled millions of African Americans to rise from the abyss of abject poverty and political disfranchisement. Like their white, Indigenous, Latino, and Asian American counterparts, large numbers of black Americans began acquiring high school and college educations and living healthier and longer lives as well. However, white Americans continued to earn more money and live longer lives.

Despite such substantial progress, the acute poverty, dismal educational options, and violent crime that continued to destabilize and demoralize millions of black people would leave Du Bois frustrated and befuddled if he were here today. Moreover, the continued isolation of so many black people from America's formal and informal pipelines of social and economic opportunity would surely lead him to question the efficacy of legal desegregation and the symbolic advancements of African Americans' societal standing. Sadly, he would probably not be shocked by the staying power of racism or the stereotypes that continue to tax the minds and ensnare the hearts of millions of Americans. Du Bois, like many black Americans, would recognize that the African Americans of today are linked not merely by a shared heritage, culture, and success, but by a sense of distinctiveness and external menace.

Du Bois's double consciousness, therefore, continues to endure more than a century after he first penned the words, but his theory became harder to apply in the face of recent advancements made by black Americans at home and abroad. In other words, black people made inroads into previously inaccessible areas of society, making them more "American" than ever before. But they continued to be viewed as foreign in their own country. Double consciousness, therefore, is not something that Du Bois wanted African Americans to achieve and celebrate, nor is it something that he wanted black people to shed in a fully integrated society. It is simply an enduring reality, as African Americans continue to be seen as being in America, but not of America, in an ongoing experiment in democracy.

African Americans had always been forced to negotiate their racial selves with the many other characteristics that form their identities. But even as America edged closer to understanding Du Bois's double consciousness, new voices arose to force American society to consider and ultimately accept other identities associated with immigration status, religious affiliation, political philosophy, and sexual orientation. In negotiating a complex consciousness that, if anything, had grown even more so, black Americans grappled with their racial identities, an effort sometimes made more difficult by the social and economic fault lines within black communities. In short, this negotiation has emerged as the signature challenge of modern black America.

The Best and the Brightest

At the dawn of the twenty-first century, African Americans took major steps toward assimilating multiple identities, but not without struggling to reconcile them. The steady rise of influential blacks, the establishment of the black middle class, African American solidarity, domestic crises, immigration, and renewed commitment among black people to help themselves during this period reflected the increasing diversity of the African American experience.

Despite his conservative agenda, which was designed to scale back the gains for which most African Americans and other marginalized groups had fought, President George W. Bush appointed black people to high-ranking positions, and, in some cases, to major posts that no other black American had ever filled. While critics argued that these appointments amounted to pandering to African American communities, no one could deny that the appointees were of high caliber.

George W. Bush made history by appointing General Colin L. Powell (1937–) as secretary of state, making him the first African American to serve in this position, and, at that point, the highest-ranking black person in the history of American government. Born in the Bronx, New York, to Jamaican-immigrant parents, Powell attended primary and secondary school in the Hunts Point neighborhood of the South Bronx. He graduated from City University of New York with a BA in geology, and he was commissioned as a second lieutenant after four years in the Reserve Officer Training Corps (ROTC). Powell's first military post was in West Germany: it was there that he realized that racial integration in the U.S. army, which outpaced that of civilian society, afforded him opportunities for advancement that one could scarcely find outside the armed services. In light of this revelation, he decided to forge a career in the military.

Powell took advantage of the Army's college education–funding programs to earn an MBA from George Washington University in 1971. During his tenure at George Washington, he was awarded a highly competitive White House fellowship that allowed him to work as an aid to high-ranking members of the Nixon administration. "In 1972," historian Gerry Butler writes,

> Powell was appointed a battalion commander of the elite 101st Airborne in South Korea; by 1979, he was a Brigadier General and Deputy Commander at Fort Leavenworth in Kansas. As a lieutenant general, Powell commanded the Fifth Corps, U.S. Army, in Frankfort, Germany, from 1983 to 1986. In 1987, at 49 years of age, Powell was named National Security Advisor in the Reagan administration. While serving in this capacity, Powell became the first black American elevated to the rank of general. In 1989, George H. W. Bush appointed him Chair of the Joint Chiefs of Staff, from which post he directed U.S. military actions in Panama, the Philippines, and Operation Desert Storm (1991). In the final of these engagements, he established the "Powell Doctrine," a new approach to military engagement that maximized the likelihood of success and minimized casualties through the application of overwhelming force, particularly airpower. As chair, Powell was not only the first black American but also the youngest person to hold this position.[1]

Powell's career continued beyond the administration of George H. W. Bush. As an officer, he was lauded for his loyalty and pragmatism. His talents, honesty, integrity, and accessibility made him a highly sought-after figure among American political leaders for political appointments, advice, and support. Despite the fact that Powell was a Republican, many Democrats respected his moderate positions on military matters. Likewise, many Republicans viewed him as independent and wise in the areas of strategy and national security. He next served in the Clinton administration until his retirement from the military after thirty-five years of service in 1993. As a registered Republican, Powell campaigned for his party following his military retirement. He was even touted as a possible opponent to Clinton in the 1996 presidential election. Citing a desire to shield his family from the intense media scrutiny a presidential candidate must endure, Powell declined to run, choosing instead to devote much of his time to writing and public speaking.

Powell returned to politics in 2001, however, when he became George W. Bush's secretary of state, a position from which he resigned in 2005. Despite ongoing requests from the Democratic and Republican parties to rejoin the political world and run for office, Powell has chosen to remain in the private sector since his resignation. He joined the Board of Trustees at Howard University, the Board of Directors of the United Negro College Fund, and the Board of Directors of the Boys and Girls Club, and he became chairman of the Eisenhower Fellowship Program. During a speech at Howard University, Powell articulated the degree to which he relished his function as ambassador of America's diversity:

> It's just terrific to be able to walk into a room somewhere in Africa, Russia, Asia, and Europe, and you know they're looking at you. . . . They're looking at you and they recognize your position and who you are, and they also recognize that you're black. And it's always a source of inspiration and joy to see people look at me and through me see my country and see what promise my country offers to all people to come to these shores for a better life.[2]

Another distinguished African American Bush appointee was Condoleezza Rice (1954–), who became the national security advisor in 2001. Rice was the first African American and the first woman to be selected for this position. Following Powell's resignation as secretary of state in January 2005, Bush appointed Rice to replace him, making Rice the first black woman to serve in this post.

A former provost and professor of political science at Stanford University, Rice specialized in international affairs; she rose to these positions from her native Deep South. Born to John Wesley Rice Jr. and Angelena (Rary) Rice, she grew up in the black middle-class Titusville area of Birmingham, Alabama. Denise McNair, one of the four young girls killed in the bombing of the 16th St. Baptist Church in September 1963, had been one of her childhood friends. Despite the trauma, Condoleezza proved to be an excellent student, entering the University of Denver at the age of fifteen. Enthralled with Russian politics, she graduated with a bachelor's degree in political science at nineteen. By the age of twenty she had earned a master's degree in political science from the University of Notre

Dame, and at twenty-six she earned a PhD in political science from the Graduate School of International Studies at the University of Denver.

Upon completing her education, Rice launched her professional career. She became a professor of political science at Stanford University and a fellow at the university's prestigious Hoover Institute. Her expertise in Russian politics, as well as her conservative views, led Reagan to make her the special assistant to the Joint Chiefs of Staff in 1986. George H. W. Bush appointed her to the office of director of Soviet and Eastern European Affairs for the National Security Council in 1989. In 1991 Rice returned to Stanford to serve as provost of the university, the first female, the first African American, and the youngest (at the age of thirty-six) person to hold this title. In just three years as provost, she helped convert the university's $20 million annual deficit into a $14 million surplus. As national security advisor, and later secretary of state, to the administration of George W. Bush, Rice became a principal architect of the Bush administration's foreign policy. The president and Rice forged a close working relationship, which gave her a tremendous amount of power within his cabinet. As a result, Rice has become one of the most powerful women, as well as one of the most influential African Americans, in the United States.

African Americans paid particular attention to Bush's educational policies. Throughout his 2000 campaign, Bush promised to make sweeping changes in the American educational system so that it would better meet the needs of students. Black Americans continued to call attention to de facto segregation and inequality in American schools, especially in urban areas. They were hopeful that Bush would act upon his pledge to improve the system. His appointment of black Texan Rod Paige as secretary of education gave blacks reason to believe that Bush would indeed alter the U.S. educational system. Paige introduced a massive piece of legislation entitled the No Child Left Behind Act, which Bush wholeheartedly supported. To the utter dismay and consternation of most African Americans and their allies, and to the disappointment of the majority of teachers, No Child Left Behind reflected the concerns of the people least affected by racial and economic inequality in the nation's schools: white working- and middle-class Americans. The act, which was passed in 2003, focused on student and teacher aptitude through continuous standards testing in math, reading, and science to evaluate both student and teacher performance. Some wondered whether the constant testing took valuable classroom time.

The new legislation required states to make test results public and penalize "failing" schools that didn't make the grade by cutting matching federal dollars and replacing administrators at failing schools. The legislation failed to address the effect of racial and economic disparities on student performance, nor did it acknowledge that, even within "high-performing" schools, a disproportionate number of black students lagged significantly behind their white peers, or that the legislation made it more difficult to teach children with special needs. Moreover, No Child Left Behind abandoned racial integration as a signature educational policy goal, undermined compulsory busing, and championed a voucher system that would, at least in theory, have enabled parents to send their children to charter and private schools of their choice at public expense. Some black Americans, such as Mayor Anthony Williams, of Washington DC, endorsed vouchers, declaring that "underperforming" schools (often located in poor neighborhoods) would improve if administrators were compelled to compete with high-performing schools (often located affluent neighborhoods). In contrast, Reginald Weaver, the African American president of the National Educational Association, rejected vouchers and proclaimed that such programs failed to provide aid or viable options to the majority of students in impoverished schools. Indeed, the No Child Left Behind Act, Weaver argued, was "a bill that gives $13 million to 2,000 kids who are going to voucher schools, and $14 million to 167,000 other kids. I think it is political, not educational."[3] The extremely controversial act soon drew fire from across the political spectrum. Liberals and conservatives denounced the legislation for establishing unattainable goals for students and schools that did not possess the human or financial capital to compete in a new environment characterized by much higher standards.

The HIV/AIDS Crisis

While black Americans continued to focus on politics, many also turned their attention to HIV/AIDS, which had become one of African Americans' most devastating problems. As the HIV/AIDS pandemic gripped the globe during the 1980s and 1990s, it wreaked particular havoc on African Americans. Black leaders such as Ervin "Magic" Johnson played key roles in raising awareness of HIV/AIDS. A six-foot-nine, five-time world championship professional basketball player with the Los Angeles Lakers, three-time playoff MVP, twelve-time All-Star, Olympic gold medal winner, entrepreneur, philanthropist, and sports commentator, Johnson learned that he was "HIV positive," a carrier of the HIV virus that causes AIDS, in November 1991. Although Johnson admitted that his lifestyle as a sports celebrity included many sexual encounters, he had never suspected that he might contract HIV, which he, like many Americans at the time, thought was spread only among gay men.

After doctors advised Johnson to quit basketball immediately in order to protect his health, he became a voice for AIDS awareness. "I want [kids] to understand that safe sex is the way to go," Johnson told *People* magazine. "Sometimes we think only gay people can get it [HIV], or that it's not going to happen to me. Here I am. And I'm saying it can happen to anybody, even Magic Johnson."[4] Johnson was appointed to the National Commission on AIDS by President George H. W. Bush, but he resigned from the commission to protest what he considered the president's lack of support for HIV/AIDS research and education. As recently as May 2013, Johnson has remained free of AIDS symptoms. Physicians credit Johnson's exercise habits and ability to use the newest and most powerful drugs to ward off the full-blown disease. He has also continued to speak about HIV/AIDS and raise money for research.

Black leaders such as Jesse Jackson and Rodney Hood, the former president of the National Medical Association, have also called on African Americans to educate themselves about HIV/AIDS, depicting the illness as a political as well as a health crisis. Jackson placed the impact of HIV/AIDS on black people in a transnational context within the African Diaspora:

> As it is in Africa, AIDS is now the leading cause of death for African Americans between twenty-five and forty-four in the United States. Almost two-thirds (63 percent) of all women reported with AIDS are African American; 62 percent of all reported pediatric cases are African American children; 1 in 50 African-American men and 1 in 160 African American women are estimated to be HIV infected. Like Africans, many African Americans do not know their HIV status; like Africans, many African Americans cannot access care or afford adequate treatment. Like Africans, many African Americans are in poverty, and many of their communities lack the infrastructure needed to meet the needs of those infected and afflicted by AIDS. Simply speaking, as we begin to understand our commonalities, our difference will no longer be a continent away.[5]

Hood shared Jackson's concerns, arguing, "Racism exists in medicine, especially if you are a person of color. It's very real and it's killing us."[6] Indeed, in 2008 black Americans had the highest rates of HIV and AIDS infection of any racial group in the United States; the disease ranked thirteenth among the fifteen leading causes of death among all groups in the nation. In 2008 African Americans accounted for more HIV and AIDS cases, people estimated to be living with AIDS, and HIV-related deaths than any other racial group in the United States. Although black Americans comprised about 12 percent of the U.S. population, they accounted for 50 percent of all new AIDS cases. Despite medical advances which have significantly reduced HIV-related death rates, these rates are still much higher for blacks than for any other group in America. This is primarily due to the fact that for black men and black women, unprotected sex with a man is more common than among members of other racial groups. Black women are hugely, and disproportionately, affected by AIDS, with the most likely transmission route being heterosexual sex. Some 85 percent of African American women living with HIV were infected this way and account for nearly half of the country's entire female epidemic. Moreover, most cannot afford the expensive but life-saving drugs needed to avoid developing full-blown AIDS.[7]

Reparations

Some black Americans also pushed for monetary reparations, a controversial proposal that would, in theory, help alleviate racial tensions and solve some of the socioeconomic problems that continue to confront black people. Individuals like Jackson and Hood cited American racism for fostering egregious disparities in health care between people of color and whites. These, and other socioeconomic disparities, they argued, were inextricably linked to the vestiges of slavery and Jim Crow segregation. In an effort to close the gap between whites and blacks and push the U.S. government to atone for its role in nurturing and abetting slavery and Jim Crow, the topic of reparations began to receive serious attention in the last decades of the twentieth century. In his 1969 "Black Manifesto," civil rights leader and writer James Forman asked America's religious institutions to raise $500 million as "a beginning of the reparations due to us as a people who have been exploited and degraded, brutalized, killed, and persecuted."[8] White churches and other major predominantly white institutions, however, failed to answer his call. In 1973 Boris Bittker, a professor at Yale Law School, raised the topic again and posited in *The Case for Black Reparations* that slavery and the longevity of government-backed racism warranted recompense and damages to African Americans. Beginning in 1993 John Conyers, a black Democratic Congressman from Detroit, sponsored legislation in each congressional session to create a federal commission to examine the history of slavery and its socioeconomic legacy. The bill has been killed routinely in subcommittees and has yet to reach the House floor for a vote.

In 2000 the matter of reparations for American slavery intensified and garnered national attention. That year Randall Robinson, a graduate of Virginia Union University and Harvard University Law School and founder and president of TransAfrica, published *The Debt: What America Owes to Blacks*. In it, Robinson argued that "only by reclaiming their lost past and proud heritage can blacks lay the foundation for a viable future." According to him, "white Americans can make reparations for slavery and the century of de jure racial discrimination that followed with monetary restitution, educational programs, and the kinds of equal opportunities that will ensure the social and economic success of all citizens." Robinson noted precedent for reparations to African Americans; since Jews and Japanese Americans were remunerated for the dreadful experiences they endured during World War II, Robinson argued, black Americans are also owed monetary recompense for slavery, which "for 246 years [was an] enterprise murderous both of a people and their culture." The author bluntly told his readers that "white America owes blacks"[9] for the free labor they rendered and the state-sanctioned suffering they experienced, which to this day continues to relegate some black people to poverty, insufficient health care, substandard housing, and unequal educational opportunities.

Other leaders added their voices to the call for reparations. Molefi Asante, an "Afro-centrist" and professor at Temple University, supported Robinson's stance, but Asante insisted that the federal government should issue long-term financial aid packages, including "educational, health care, land or property grants, and a combination of such grants" as targeted compensation for slavery and Jim Crow. He explained, "What I have argued for is the establishment of some type of organization that would evaluate how reparations would be determined and distributed: the National Commission of African Americans would be the overarching national organization to serve as the clearinghouse for reparations."[10]

A number of prominent conservative black journalists, however, completely rejected the notion of reparations as an unrealistic solution to the legacy of slavery and white supremacy in America. William Raspberry of the *Washington Post*, Juan Williams of Fox News, and John McWhorter, a linguist and cultural critic, repudiated the concept outright. Raspberry supported increased appropriations for education in black communities, "not because of debts owed to or incurred by our ancestors, but because America needs its citizens to be educated and productive." Williams proclaimed that "the suffering of long-dead ancestors is not a claim check for a bag full of cash. I don't want any money that belongs to any slave. That is obscene. The struggle of African-Americans for civil rights is not about selling out for a check."[11]

Though the federal government has not taken steps to address reparations, other institutions and individuals continued to pursue the issue. In 2004 Ruth Simmons, president of Brown University and the first black American to lead an Ivy League school, created a committee to investigate Brown's historic connection to profits secured from the slave trade and to ascertain the possibility that the university might pay reparations. Mary Frances Berry, in her 2005 book, *My Face Is Black Is True*, chronicled the life of Callie House, a formerly enslaved woman, washerwoman, mother of six, and cofounder of the Mutual Relief, Bounty, and Pension Association, who had called for reparations for American slavery back in 1899. "If the Government had the right to free us," House argued, "she had a right to make some provision for us and since she did not make it soon after Emancipation she ought to make it now."[12] The fight for reparations endures as many black Americans lobby Congress and corporations for a systemic acknowledgement of the legacy of slavery and white supremacy and the need for restitution and resolution.

9/11 and Its Aftermath

Even as black people continued their long march toward equality and unfettered acceptance at the turn of the new millennium, the complacency of all Americans came to a painful and abrupt end. The nation was staggered and horrified when, on September 11, 2001, Islamic extremist terrorists hijacked four commercial airplanes and crashed two of them into the World Trade Center towers in New York, one into the Pentagon in Washington DC, and one into a field in rural Pennsylvania. At least three hundred black Americans were among the more than three thousand people killed in the devastation of that day. Americans experienced many emotions following the September 11 attacks; among the diverse human fabric that is America, African Americans constituted one community that understood very well the adversity and intense emotions that visit victims of terrorism. They had, after all, endured 246 years of enslavement only to survive another hundred years of Jim Crow segregation, lynchings, mass murder, and the destruction of black towns and business districts across the United States. Moreover, in recent decades, the rolling back of certain civil rights laws, the ongoing incarceration of masses of young black people, racial profiling, and police brutality continued to torment African Americans. While mainstream America searched its collective soul for answers to the problem of terrorism, a problem that some considered new, many black people asked themselves, "Since when has America been free of terror?" Some even feared that the new rounds of laws called for by President Bush and passed by Congress in the wake of September 11 to "keep America safe" would target people of the Islamic faith and/or people of Middle Eastern descent unjustly.

Racial stereotyping and profiling, many black people believed, subjected people of Middle Eastern descent to humiliating and unlawful treatment by the new Department of Homeland Security (DHS) as primary targets for surveillance, detention, deportation, and prosecution. Black Americans paid particular attention to these events, for as political science professor Sylvia Hill suggested, such legislation "may be an abuse of the rights of people who look Middle Eastern, but it will sooner or later come back to any group."[13] This legislation, in other words, could be used to further the aims of those engaged in enemy-making, and black Americans remembered all too well the tactics of former FBI director J. Edgar Hoover, which had included the illegal surveillance of Dr. Martin Luther King Jr., Malcolm X, and other civil rights activists of the 1960s and 1970s.

Black people debated the meaning of the terrorist attacks and the response of the U.S. government. On October 16, 2001, more than two hundred people crowded the moot court at Howard University's School of Law for a "black community national dialogue" on terrorism, war, and peace. The participants said much about the 9/11 attacks, terrorism, and the subsequent U.S. military invasion of Afghanistan, ordered by Bush in order to root out and destroy the al-Qaeda terrorist cells that orchestrated the attacks. The opinions expressed that night echoed those that could be heard throughout black communities following 9/11. These opinions spoke to one common theme: although most opinion polls indicated that the overwhelming majority of Americans of all races and ethnicities stood with the president as he moved to wage war with those who had attacked the United States, more blacks than whites questioned America's commitment to combating terrorism on all fronts, foreign and domestic. The views of many African Americans were influenced by racial, economic and political injustice, and by a history fraught with treacheries that can be neither casually discarded nor formally buried. Moreover, patriotism was a sophisticated notion that resonated differently among blacks, whose ancestors did not enjoy the same freedoms or privileges as did past generations of whites. As writer Ron Walters argued, "White patriotism is patriotism of ownership of the state. Black patriotism is one of ambivalence; it is patriotism that has suffered."[14]

Despite such trepidation and internal conflict, most black people joined other American citizens in repudiating the violence that befell their nation. Leonard Pitts Jr., an award-winning black syndicated columnist, captured the emotions of most Americans when he penned a passionate pro-American manifesto addressed to a mysterious enemy:

> Did you want to tear us apart? You just brought us together. Let me tell you about my people. We are a vast and quarrelsome family, a family rent by racial, cultural, political and class division, but a family nonetheless. We're frivolous, yes, capable of expending tremendous emotional energy on pop cultural minutiae, a singer's revealing dress, a ball team's misfortune, a cartoon mouse.... Some people—you, perhaps—think that any or all of this makes us weak. You're mistaken. We are not weak. Indeed, we are strong in ways that cannot be measured by arsenals.[15]

Perhaps more than anything else in recent history, 9/11 inspired black and white Americans to focus on what they had in common, but this sense of national solidarity was fleeting. When the Bush administration went ahead with its plans for an invasion of Iraq in a desperate and ill-advised attempt to capture or destroy the forces it claimed were linked to the 9/11 attack, black people were among the first to boldly question the motivation and justification for the invasion. Historian and activist Manning Marable commented on what he learned about the United States following the 9/11 attacks: "No political ideology, no crusade, no belief in a virtuous cause, can justify the moral bankruptcy of terror. Yet, because of the military actions of our own government, any claims to moral superiority have now disintegrated, in the minds of much of the black and brown world."[16]

Indeed, African Americans were among the many Americans disappointed by the U.S. government's foreign policy following the 9/11 attacks. Like all Americans, black people wanted Bush to capture Osama bin Laden and dismantle the al-Qaeda network, which were responsible for 9/11. In addition, African Americans expected the Bush administration to direct the military to chase the Taliban from Afghanistan and to eliminate the organization completely. None of these expectations were fully realized by 2008, however. Mullah Omar, the leader of the Taliban, fled capture even though thousands of U.S. troops searched for him and other members of the organization in Afghanistan. Nonetheless, Bush argued almost immediately that military actions in Afghanistan were successful. Following the president's declarations of success, as of 2013, the Taliban has increased its fighting in Afghanistan and warlords and insurgents continue to run much of the country. Other leaders have criticized Bush's actions following 9/11. Richard A. Clarke, who served as chief counterterrorism advisor to Clinton and Bush, argued that President Bush and National Security Advisor Rice had ignored clear warnings of a possible terrorist attack prior to 9/11. He also suggested that Bush had intended to use 9/11 as a reason to enter Iraq and attack its president, Saddam Hussein.

In any event, the Bush administration geared up to battle Iraq beginning in early 2002, even as massive opposition to a preemptive, U.S.-led war in Iraq grew domestically and internationally. Citizens protested in the United States, and the UN refused to support American plans to begin the war. Colin Powell, then secretary of state, lobbied the UN on behalf of the Bush administration. In February 2003 Powell provided evidence to the UN Security Council that Saddam Hussein in Iraq possessed weapons of mass destruction and connections to al-Qaeda. This evidence later proved to be false and misleading. Powell's testimony notwithstanding, the UN Security Council voted against authorizing the invasion. Undeterred, the United States pursued the war in Iraq without support from the UN and invaded the country on March 19, 2003. The only member of the international community to support the U.S. war effort substantially was Great Britain.

Shortly after U.S. forces had invaded Iraq, Bush declared the war a success. Indeed, just a few weeks after the initial invasion, U.S. troops entered and occupied Baghdad. On May 1, 2003, Bush donned a flight suit and, after landing on the deck of a U.S. Navy aircraft carrier, proudly announced the end of major combat operations in Iraq under a banner that read "Mission Accomplished." Though a dictator had been overthrown, the hearts and minds of Iraqis had hardly been won. Fighting within the country continued and the nation soon fell into chaos as warring factions competed for control of disputed land and for political power. Iraqi insurgents attacked U.S. troops and those Iraqi civilians who supported the occupation. This upset quickly demonstrated that U.S. military leaders had not been prepared for the realities of war, but had instead assumed that Iraqi civilians would welcome a U.S. invasion. Critics were quick to argue that U.S. actions in Iraq were strengthening rather than combating terrorism. The Bush administration's inability to find weapons of mass destruction (WMDs) in occupied Iraq (which their "intelligence" had guaranteed the American people were there) or to prove any connection between Hussein and al-Qaeda, or between Hussein and those behind the attacks of 9/11, greatly harmed the Bush administration (including Powell)and the reputation of the United States in the eyes of the international community.

By the beginning of the 2004 presidential campaign the ongoing war in Iraq was an extremely polarizing issue in the United States; abortion rights and the legality of gay marriage also divided Americans. Republican incumbent Bush and Dick Cheney, his vice president, squared off against John F. Kerry, a Democratic senator from Massachusetts, and his running mate, John Edwards of North Carolina. As a voting bloc, African Americans remained among the Democratic party's most loyal constituents. No longer considered representatives of minor "special interest" groups, by 2004 black leaders stood at the vanguard of a more diverse Democratic Party, and they demanded that their treatment reflect their status. Two African Americans in particular vied for the Democratic nomination that year: Carol Moseley Braun, former U.S. Senator from Illinois, and Reverend Al Sharpton of New York. Braun and Sharpton campaigned long and hard to win the party's nomination before ultimately withdrawing from the race and supporting Kerry.

Despite their withdrawals, Braun and Sharpton, along with Jesse Jackson, continued to push Democrats to acknowledge and address the unique needs of black Americans. Each delivered passionate speeches at the Democratic National Convention in Boston. But even as they paid tribute to Kerry and denounced the "failed policies of Bush," which included his invasion and ongoing occupation of Iraq, they also reminded delegates of the desolation and despair, the lack of adequate health-care insurance, the high unemployment rates, and the horrible shape of public schools in black communities. Though Braun, Sharpton, and Jackson inspired their audiences, the brightest and most inspiring African American speaker at the convention proved to be a relatively obscure forty-two-year-old state senator from Illinois. Barack Hussein Obama (1961–, fig. 27), who was at the time campaigning for a seat in the U.S. Senate, electrified the convention with his youth, good looks, polished rhetorical skills, charisma, and message, one that emphasized his belief in the oneness of the American people and the ability of the government to lead the nation to new levels of freedom and prosperity. He became an overnight celebrity and the new face of black progress.

Obama's background, in addition to his poise and dignified manner, made him unique. He was born in 1961 in Honolulu, Hawaii to Barack Obama Sr., a black African born in the Nyanza Province of Kenya, and Ann Dunham, a white American who grew up in Wichita, Kansas. Obama's maternal grandfather, Stanley Dunham, worked on oil rigs during the Great Depression. Following the Japanese attack on Pearl Harbor, he enlisted in the army of General George S. Patton, and fought in Europe while his wife, Madelyn Dunham, worked on the home front on a bomber assembly line. When the conflict was over, she and her husband attended college on the GI Bill, moved to Hawaii, and bought their first home with assistance from the Federal Housing Program. Obama's parents met at the University of Hawaii at Manoa, fell in love, conceived their son, married, separated when Obama was only two years old, and eventually divorced. Obama's father later earned a PhD at Harvard before returning to Kenya. The young child only saw his father once following his parents' divorce, during a visit in 1971. His mother married Lolo Soetoro, a man from Indonesia, in 1967, and the family moved to Jakarta, where Obama's half-sister, Maya Soetoro-Ng, was born. Obama attended schools in Jakarta, and he quickly learned the Indonesian language.

When Obama, known as "Barry" throughout his youth, was ten years old, he returned to Hawaii, where he lived with his maternal grandparents and later with his mother, who died of ovarian cancer in 1995. Obama was enrolled in the prestigious Punahou Academy in Hawaii, where he completed high school and graduated with honors in 1979. It was at Punahou, as one of only three black students, that Obama first experienced racism

FIG. 27. With a backdrop of Chagall stained glass, President Barack Obama pauses after laying a wreath for United Nations staff members killed in the line of duty at the United Nations, September 23, 2009. © Charles Dharapak/AP/Corbis 42-30046113.

and the difficulties associated with being African American in the United States. In his autobiography, *Dreams from My Father: A Story of Race and Inheritance* (1995), which became both a number-one best seller and won a Grammy Award for the audio version, Obama revealed how he struggled to cope with the ways in which society perceived, and often ridiculed, his multiracial heritage. After graduating from high school, Obama studied at Occidental College in Los Angeles for two years and then transferred to Columbia University in New York City, graduating in 1983 with a bachelor's degree in political science.

After two years working in business in New York, Obama moved to Chicago to become a community organizer for poor, predominantly black residents on the city's South Side. It was his work on behalf of these needy people that taught him "that meaningful change always begins at the grass-roots, and that engaged citizens working together can accomplish extraordinary things." It was also during this time when Obama, who "was not raised in a religious household," joined the Trinity United Church of Christ and visited his paternal relatives in Kenya, where his father and grandfather were buried. After serving the residents of the South Side for three years, Obama enrolled in Harvard University Law School in 1988. He was elected the first black editor of the *Harvard Law Review* and graduated magna cum laude in 1991.[17]

Obama returned to Chicago to work as a civil rights attorney for the firm of Miner, Barnhill, and Galland while teaching part-time at the University of Chicago Law School. He continued to volunteer on the South Side by registering voters during Clinton's 1992 presidential campaign. He also pursued a relationship with Michelle LaVaughn Robinson, whom he had met and begun to date in 1988 when he was a summer associate at the Chicago law firm of Sidley & Austin. After they married in October 1992, the couple moved into a home in the South Side neighborhood of Kenwood. Obama's work as a community activist fired his interest in politics and inspired him to make a successful run as a Democrat for a seat in the Illinois state senate in 1996. In 2000 he made an unsuccessful bid for a seat in the U.S. House of Representatives.

Early in his political career, Obama established himself as a leader of national significance. Following the attacks of 9/11, he was not afraid to speak out as an early opponent of Bush's plans to invade Iraq. Obama, who was then still a state senator, denounced the Congressional resolution that authorized the use of force against Iraq during a rally at Chicago's Federal Plaza in October 2002. "I am not opposed to all wars," he declared. "I'm opposed to dumb wars." He continued,

> What I am opposed to is the cynical attempt by Richard Perle [chair of the Defense Policy Advisory Committee in the Bush administration] and Paul Wolfowitz [deputy secretary of defense under Bush] and other arm-chair, weekend warriors in this administration to shove their own ideological agendas down our throats, irrespective of the costs in lives lost and in hardships borne.[18]

Obama's opposition to the war did not mean that he approved of Saddam Hussein. While commenting on the dictator of Iraq, Obama noted, "He's a bad guy," explaining,

> The world, and the Iraqi people, would be better off without him. But I also know that Saddam poses no imminent and direct threat to the United States, or to his neighbors, that the Iraqi economy is in shambles, that the Iraqi military a fraction of its former strength, and that in concert with the international community he can be contained until, in the way of all petty dictators, he falls away into the dustbin of his-

tory. . . . I know that even a successful war against Iraq will require a U.S. occupation of undetermined length, at undetermined cost, with undetermined consequences. I know that an invasion of Iraq without a clear rationale and without strong international support will only fan the flames of the Middle East, and encourage the worst, rather than best, impulses of the Arab world, and strengthen the recruitment arm of al-Qaeda.[19]

When the American invasion of Iraq began in 2003, Obama announced his decision to run for the U.S. Senate. Winning 52 percent of the vote in the 2004 Democratic primary, he defeated multimillionaire businessman Blair Hull and Illinois comptroller Daniel Hynes. That summer he was invited to deliver the keynote address at the 2004 Democratic National Convention. In his mesmerizing speech, Obama critiqued the Bush administration's "diversionary use of wedge issues":

> We worship an awesome God in the blue states, and we don't like federal agents poking around our libraries in the red states. We coach Little League in the blue states, and yes, we've got some gay friends in the red states. There are patriots who opposed the war in Iraq, and there are patriots who supported the war in Iraq. We are one people, all of us pledging allegiance to the Stars and Stripes, all of us defending the United States of America.[20]

In November 2004 Obama won his bid for the U.S. Senate in a landslide victory against Alan Keyes, his neoconservative black Republican opponent, whom Republicans had convinced to move from Maryland to Illinois, thinking the black neoconservative Keyes had a real chance against a Democratic challenger who was considered a young upstart.

Hurricane Katrina: The Politics of Indifference

President Bush's response to Hurricane Katrina's human toll damaged his popularity as much as his foreign policy had, and helped pave the way for a major shift in political leadership in the United States. Hurricane Katrina was one of the deadliest and most costly hurricanes in U.S. history. It was the sixth strongest Atlantic hurricane ever recorded and the third strongest on record to reach the continental United States. Forming during the Atlantic hurricane season, Katrina devastated much of the north-central Gulf Coast of the United States. The most severe loss of life and property

FIG. 28. New Orleans, Louisiana, September 4, 2005. Messages on rooftops conveyed information about the occupants of homes devastated by a levee break following Hurricane Katrina. National Archives and Records Administration.

damage occurred in New Orleans, Louisiana, which was largely covered by floodwaters after the levee system suffered a calamitous failure. The storm caused destruction not only in New Orleans, but across the entire Mississippi coast and into Alabama (as far as a hundred miles from the storm's center), uncovering weaknesses, prejudices, and inequalities throughout the Gulf Coast and within the whole of American society.[21]

More than one million Gulf Coast residents were displaced by Katrina, relocating in cities in all fifty states. Many of Katrina's so-called refugees were living well below the poverty line before the storm struck, which made them extremely vulnerable to the storm's wrath and to the many human failures that followed. At least 1,836 people were killed by Hurricane Katrina and its aftermath, making it the deadliest storm in the United States since the Okeechobee Hurricane in 1928. Katrina also caused property damage estimated at $81 million, making it the costliest natural disaster in U.S. history.

Criticism of the federal, state, and local governments' reaction to the storm was widespread and resulted in an investigation by the U.S. Congress and the resignation of the Federal Emergency Management Agency (FEMA) director, Michael Brown, a friend of the President and

Bush appointee. The storm also prompted congressional review of the U.S. Army Corps of Engineers, which designed and was charged with maintaining the nation's levee protection system. The federal government's response to the human suffering and endangerment wrought by Hurricane Katrina revealed as much about American society and the inextricable link between race, class, gender, and age in our nation as it did about nature's fury. It unearthed the devastating penalty for structural racism and classism. As the world watched the televised coverage of Hurricane Katrina during the storm and in the days and weeks after it in horror, America's racial inequality and shocking levels of poverty, vulnerability, and dislocation, particularly among African Americans, lay naked for the world to see.

After Katrina, the hurricane's survivors faced the same racial, economic, and political injustices that had marginalized their existence before the storm. The same discrimination that had placed them squarely in harm's way during the hurricane undermined their ability to rebuild their often shattered and scattered lives after it. The most enduring and jarring stories associated with Hurricane Katrina, however, were of the abject poverty and racism that had marked the region for generations. Television cameras from around the world captured indelible images of people walking, floating, and sometimes drowning in contaminated water. Once the flood water receded, the same cameras captured frightening images of bloated corpses lying on deserted streets, crowds of people dying slowly of hunger and dehydration, and people fainting and thrashing about in pain for want of desperately needed medical treatment for both recent injuries and chronic illness. As Michael Eric Dyson, a black public intellectual, observed:

> Photo snaps and film shots captured legions of men and women huddling in groups or hugging corners, crying in wild-eyed desperation for help, for any help, from somebody, anybody, who would listen to their unanswered pleas. The filth and squalor of their confinement, defecating where they stood or sat, or, more likely, dropped, bathed in a brutal wash of dredge and sickening pollutants that choked the air with ungodly stench grieved the camera lenses that recorded their plight.[22]

Scores of people took to the streets dotted by deserted shops and restaurants, scavenging for food, water, and clothing. The hordes were multiracial, but the overwhelming majority of the displaced and disinherited were black. At first glance, many people would have assumed that the sight they were seeing was taking place in some other corner of the so-called "third world" such as Liberia, Rwanda, or Sierra Leone. Many people asked: could this really be happening in the United States of America? Could the wealthiest and most powerful nation in the world abandon some of its poorest citizens when they needed their government the most? As the renowned black philosopher and public intellectual, Cornel West, argued,

> What we saw unfold in the days after the hurricane was the most naked manifestation of social policy towards the poor, where the message for decades has been: "You are on your own." Well, they really were on their own for five days in that Superdome, and it was Darwinism in action, the survival of the fittest. People said: "It looks like something out of the Third World." Well, New Orleans was Third World long before the hurricane.[23]

The federal government eventually poured more than $115 billion in aid into the Gulf Coast after the storm, but it could not offset the failure of the Bush administration to respond swiftly and effectively to the crisis. President Bush was on an extended stay away from the White House while Katrina flattened much of the Gulf Coast and left New Orleans engulfed by floodwater. His hiatus proved to be a defining moment of his presidency. The image of a president who critics accused of being aloof from details and too eager to delegate was driven home when he ordered Air Force One to fly low over the stricken region two full days after the storm hit, the levees collapsed, and New Orleans was flooded, so he could get a bird's-eye view of the destruction as he returned to Washington. "It's devastating, it's got to be doubly devastating on the ground,"[24] Bush said as he flew over the area—and flew away, never landing to see the devastation up close. "The impact of Katrina was profound," said former White House press secretary Ari Fleischer. "It caught a tired White House staff off guard and turned out to be one of the most damaging events of his presidency."[25]

Many African Americans wondered why President Bush did not descend to the devastated city, as he did when he visited lower Manhattan in the wake of 9/11. Many wondered aloud if Bush was indifferent to their suffering. In a September 3, 2005, televised interview with CNN correspondent Anderson Cooper, Jesse Jackson reminded viewers that America, particularly its leaders, "have great tolerance for black suffering and black marginalization."[26] Celebrated and notorious black recording artist Kanye West ignited a firestorm of controversy when he criticized President Bush directly. On September 2, 2005, during a benefit concert for Hurricane Katrina relief on NBC, "A Concert for Hurricane Relief," West was a featured speaker. He deviated from the prepared script and proclaimed: "George Bush doesn't care about black people."[27] The emotional, impromptu critique was seen by millions of people around the world, and while many white Americans dismissed West's remarks as the baseless rants of a militant black rapper, millions of African Americans, others left behind in New Orleans, and many more who experienced betrayal and isolation, identified with West's feelings.

The scope of the catastrophe in the Gulf Coast can be measured in various ways. Statistics offered a bleak glimpse: in addition to the dead, more than 250,000 homes and businesses destroyed; property damage exceeding $70 billion; more than 250,000 residents having left the state never to return; and nearly two hundred square miles of coastal wetlands destroyed or severely damaged. The human tragedy, however, was even more disturbing. More than five years after Katrina hit, hundreds of thousands of people still had no idea of their future. Their homes and places of employment were destroyed, and many still awaited financial assistance from the federal government years after the hurricane.

Those who chose to wait out the storm in the Superdome in New Orleans, in addition to thousands who assembled there after the flooding, were bused to the Ernest N. Morial Convention Center, where they endured insufferable conditions for days, forced to live in a facility without electricity or running water, to endure the constant fear and intimidation from small gangs of thugs who terrorized them and looted surrounding businesses, and to face the seemingly heartless response from federal, state, and local officials to their pleas.

In addition to President Bush and FEMA director Michael Brown, accusations of neglect were directed at Governor Kathleen Blanco, who was blamed by many for not making sure that local and state governments were prepared and for being slow to deploy state resources to the scene while she awaited federal aid, and at New Orleans mayor, Ray Nagin, who was criticized for not developing and implementing a disaster plan, for waiting until twenty hours before the storm hit to order an evacuation, and for behaving as if he was overwhelmed by the disaster. Leaders at the federal, state, and local levels, especially FEMA, failed to provide transportation to evacuate the victims or to transport the necessary supplies to those in need. Moreover, FEMA suffered from an almost complete breakdown in communication. Brown would later claim that he didn't know about the seriousness of the flooding until the day after the storm. FEMA also failed to coordinate relief efforts with the Red Cross, Salvation Army, and countless other organizations that were ready to assist if called on to do so. Although there were individuals in FEMA who rendered heroic service to those in need, FEMA as a whole failed miserably.

The apathy reflected in the slow, lackluster response to Katrina's carnage by President Bush's administration, as well as by state and local government, can still be seen. Many sections of New Orleans remain in ruins or dirty and rundown as of 2013, and entire communities have vanished. Once a large metropolitan area, New Orleans has lost half of its pre-Katrina population. The majority of the displaced residents who have not returned, or who cannot return, are African American. A city that boasted a black majority for hundreds of years, the "Big Easy," may no longer be able to do so. Poverty, homelessness, and crime have skyrocketed in the city, and many experts believe that New Orleans will never be the same. Due in large part to the staggering ineptitude of the federal government, one of the largest and most storied cities in the United States, one that once possessed distinct, vibrant, and historic African American communities, may have been consumed by the unnatural disaster that followed Hurricane Katrina.

African American Life and Culture in the New Millennium

The human catastrophe that played out in the aftermath of Hurricane Katrina was a sharp reminder to black Americans that despite signs of progress and change, their hold on expanding influence and upward mobility remained tenuous. Indeed, for millions of poor African Americans, the vulnerability, poverty, and maltreatment associated with racism, sexism, and classism continued to lock them into a vicious cycle of dislocation and want.

The salience of African American poverty and the problems it engendered ignited a fiercely contested and highly publicized debate within black America. In 2004, on the fiftieth anniversary of the *Brown* decision, at a televised celebration at Constitution Hall in Washington DC, Bill Cosby, the celebrated black comedian, actor, and philanthropist, repudiated "irresponsible black poor parents and their delinquent children," positing that middle-class blacks should take "personal responsibility" to act as good role models for indigent black people. Indeed, Cosby complained, poor African Americans removed themselves from middle-of-the-road America so that they could emulate street life and "gangsta" culture.[28]

Some African American leaders were quick to denounce Cosby's angry rant, describing it as an assault on one of the most beleaguered groups in American society and an ill-advised act of "airing the black community's dirty laundry." In response to Cosby's comments, Michael Eric Dyson wrote *Is Bill Cosby Right? Or Has the Black Middle Class Lost Its Mind?*. Dyson suggested that Cosby's position was mean-spirited and devoid of nuance, and failed to speak to the intricacies of class stratification. He also argued that Cosby did not understand how class divisions influenced personal conduct, particularly among young black people in America. As he argued,

> There are many black middle-classes: the one barely a paycheck or two from poverty; the one a notch above, with jobs in the service economy; the one more solidly in the middle, with low-level professional jobs; and one in the upper stratum, with high level professional employment and the esteem such labor yields. Moreover, in strictly literal economic terms; the black definition of class embraces style and behavior as well.[29]

Indeed, during the first decade of the twenty-first century, the schism between poor and prosperous African Americans widened as never before, illuminated not only by acute poverty in black communities but by the historic power and wealth that many highly visible blacks came to enjoy. Influential black political leaders, including Powell, Rice, and Obama, as well as public intellectuals such Johnetta B. Cole, Dyson, John Hope Franklin, Henry Louis Gates, Cornel West, and Darlene Clark Hine climbed to the acme of their disciplines, while also educating popular audiences about the nature and relevance of race, class, and gender in American history and life.

Although whites dominated the ranks of the megarich, the number of black Americans in their midst expanded greatly. Entertainers, including Bill Cosby; Michael Jackson, the former Motown child star turned 1980s music icon; Oprah Winfrey; Will Smith; and Tyler Perry, who became the first African American to establish and head a black-owned major motion picture studio in 2008, amassed mammoth fortunes. Athletes such as Michael Jordan and Eldrick "Tiger" Woods attained superrich status as well. These leaders, both through their sheer existence and their works, benefited the black community.

Oprah Winfrey (1954–, fig. 29), born in Kosciusko, Mississippi, became one of America's leading television personalities and media barons during the late twentieth and early twenty-first centuries. Born in a rural town to a poor teenage single mother, and later reared in inner-city Milwaukee, Winfrey was raped at the age of nine. At fourteen, she gave birth to a son who perished in infancy. Winfrey was then sent to live with the man she identified as her father in Tennessee, where she landed a job in radio while still in high school. Before graduating from Tennessee State University, Winfrey was hired as a reporter and anchor by the WTVF television station in Nashville. Not long thereafter, her passionate, extemporaneous communication style helped her secure work in daytime talk-show television. After boosting a local Chicago talk show to first place in the ratings, she launched her own production company, Harpo Studios in Chicago, and her show became internationally syndicated.

In the late 1980s and early 1990s, Winfrey won multiple Emmy Awards for the *Oprah Winfrey Show*, played a leading role in Steven Spielberg's critically acclaimed *The Color Purple* (1985), was nominated for an Academy Award, and became the youngest person ever to win the "Broadcaster of the Year" award. One of the world's most influential philanthropists, she has been very active in efforts to prevent child abuse and combat HIV/AIDS. In 2003 *Forbes* magazine listed Winfrey as the first black woman to achieve billionaire status, and in 2007 she invested $40 million of her own money to establish the Oprah Winfrey Leadership Academy for Girls near Johannesburg, South Africa.

Michael Jordan (1963–, fig. 30) also reached the ranks of wealthy, powerful Americans at the end of the twentieth century. Born in Brooklyn, New York, and raised in North Carolina, young Michael's first love was baseball, but he also played football and basketball. By the time he entered Laney High School in Wilmington, North Carolina, he was fully committed to basketball as his primary sport. Jordan was cut from the varsity basketball team during his sophomore year because he stood 5'9" tall at that time. Rather than deterring him, his dismissal drove him to work even harder on his basketball skills. As Jordan grew physically to 6'1" by his junior year of high school, his game improved dramatically, earning him an athletic scholarship to the University of North Carolina at Chapel Hill. There, under the tutelage of the legendary coach Dean Smith,

FIG. 29. Oprah Winfrey, February 29, 2004. © Kurt Krieger/Corbis.

FIG. 30. Michael Jordan wears a handful of championship rings on a billboard on E. 125th Street in Harlem, May 2000. © Lee Snider/Photo Images/Corbis.

Jordan was named the Atlantic Coast Conference Freshman of the Year, and made the game-winning three-point shot during the final seconds of the national championship game against Georgetown University. Jordan was named the College Player of the Year twice, and he was awarded the coveted Naismith and Wooden awards for basketball excellence during his junior year. Jordan's distinguished college career led to his selection as the third overall pick in the 1984 National Basketball Association draft by the Chicago Bulls.

Jordan, standing at 6'6" at the start of his professional career, took the NBA by storm during his rookie season. He stunned crowds with his speed, agility, phenomenal leaping ability, and high-octane offensive skills. A broken bone in his left foot kept Jordan on the bench throughout most of his second pro season, but he returned to the court late that season to score an NBA playoff record of sixty-three points in a first-round game against the storied Boston Celtics. Between 1990 and 1993 the Chicago Bulls won three championships with Jordan leading the way. Following the death of his father in 1993, Jordan retired from basketball. In 1994 he fulfilled his childhood dream of playing professional baseball, which he did with the Birmingham Barons, a minor league baseball team owned by the Chicago White Sox.

Jordan came out of retirement and returned to the NBA for the 1995–96 season. He signed a $30,000,000 one-year contract with the Bulls, which made him the highest-paid athlete in the history of team sports. He quickly recaptured his status as the world's best basketball player. Between 1996 and 1998 the Jordan-led Chicago Bulls won three more championships for a total of six won during his career. By now Michael was one of the most famous people in the world and one of the wealthiest black men in American history. Citing a lack of competitive desire in basketball, Jordan retired again in 1999. In 2000 he became a minority owner and general manager of NBA's Washington Wizards. Frustrated over the team's performance, he came back out of retirement, donned a uniform, and played for the team during the 2001–2 season, thereby making the first person to serve simultaneously as an owner, general manager, and player in NBA history. Despite his age, Jordan averaged over twenty points per game, and even scored forty points in one game shortly after he turned forty. He retired from basketball again, this time for good, in 2003.

During his tenure as a player, Jordan won the NBA Finals Most Valuable Player Award in each series in which he played, as well as league regular season MVP honors in 1988, 1991, 1992, 1996, and 1998. He averaged more than thirty points per game during his fifteen-year professional career, was a ten-time All-NBA First Team selection (1987–1993, 1996–1998), a nine-time selection to the NBA All-Defensive First Team (1988–1993, 1996–1998), and won the Defensive Player of the Year award in 1988. In 1996 he was named one of the fifty greatest players in NBA history.

Jordan remains an icon for athletic excellence and popular culture. His book, entitled *Driven from Within* (2005), sold over one hundred thousand copies in its first year. In 2006 *Forbes* magazine ranked him among the top thirty sports endorsers in the United States. Moreover, due to the popularity of Nike's Air Jordan apparel, which netted the company $500 million in annual sales, Jordan earned over $32 million in endorsements in 2006 alone. That same year, he became part-owner of the NBA's Charlotte Bobcats. Today Michael Jordan remains one of the most powerful African Americans on earth.

Joining Winfrey and Jordan at the pinnacle of influence and financial success are a relatively small, but no less influential cadre of black elites: Robert L. Johnson, founder of Black Entertainment Television (BET), the first black American billionaire and the first black American to become the majority owner of a professional basketball team following his purchase of the Charlotte Hornets; Russell Simmons, who forged a music and fashion empire; Richard Parsons, chair of the board of Time Warner; Kenneth I. Chenault, CEO of American Express; E. Stanley O'Neal, CEO of Merrill Lynch; and Alphonse Fletcher Jr., a Wall Street financier. The financial success of these individuals, and of other members of the black elite, is remarkable by any measure.

Yet what is perhaps most notable is the degree to which black Americans have made gains across the board in employment, income, and assets since the dawn of the civil rights era. Hard work, laws that prohibited racial discrimination in employment, and affirmative action enabled millions of African Americans to access higher-paying jobs in government, education, law, medicine, and the private sector. A mere 5.2 percent of black men and 6.4 percent of black women labored in white-collar jobs in 1940, but those percentages leaped to 35.3 percent and 62.3 percent respectively by 2000. This advance in upward mobility bore fruit in the number of economically stable, if not prosperous, African American families. Further, the disparity in income between two-parent black households and two-parent white ones also decreased between 1960 and 1998, as 61 percent of African American families came to earn as much as their white counterparts. By 1998 black families earned 87 percent as much as white families, and African American women earned 94 percent as much as their white counterparts.

Though real progress had been made, much work remained to be done to close the earning gap between black and white families. African Americans still lagged far behind their white counterparts in income and assets. This disparity was largely due to the legacy of slavery and racial discrimination and the entrenched poverty that legacy generated. For centuries, black people were unable to acquire property or other resources that could be passed on to their progeny.

One resource traditionally passed down in families is property, and the wealth of most Americans lies in their homes; but low-wage jobs, restrictive covenants that barred black people from predominantly white and generally more prosperous neighborhoods, racist lending practices, and white supremacist terrorist activity systematically undermined black people's ability to generate and maintain intergenerational asset accumulation and wealth. In 1950 only 35 percent of black families owned their homes; by 2005, 46.8% did so, but this figure lags far behind that of their white counterparts. In 2005, 70.7 percent of whites owned their own home and whites held many more assets than their black counterparts. Clearly these statistics still indicate a substantial disparity between white and black wealth, one that has implications for future generations of Americans who will stand to inherit from current homeowners.

Although many black Americans enjoyed more economic freedom and security during the first decade of the twenty-first century, others continued to be oppressed by acute poverty, while many continued to struggle to stay afloat, much less accumulate wealth. For example, in 2006, 30 percent of blacks in Illinois lived in poverty, compared with only 8 percent of whites. Nearly one million black children in the United States lived in extreme poverty that year. The national unemployment rate stood at 4.4 percent, while the rate for blacks hit 10 percent. Unemployment rates do not reveal the complete picture, however, because they fail to consider underemployed workers or those who have simply given up looking for work altogether.

Though African Americans earned more at the start of the twenty-first century than they ever had before, the wealth gap between blacks and whites expanded. By 2006 black net worth declined to $5,998 per household, while the net worth for white households grew by 17 percent to $88,651 during the same year. Twenty percent of black median net worth lay in cash at roughly $1,200, while the remainder of black median net worth was invested in home equity. The housing foreclosure crisis that grew in the beginning of the twenty-first century, however, wiped out between $72 billion and $93 billion of black America's wealth in home equity.

The financial crisis of the first decade of the twenty-first century did not immediately improve for anyone, but African Americans were particularly slow to recover. According to sociologist Thomas Shapiro, "black families lost 25 percent of their wealth during the jobless recovery from the recent recession" of 2007–08. Indeed, by 2008 many African Americans struggled with basic living conditions, including job acquisition, paying rent or a mortgage, utilities, insurance, health care costs, and grocery bills. Shapiro also indicated that only "26 percent of black families could survive more than three months after a major income interruption. The other 74 percent would be forced to seek government assistance, dip deep into savings, sell off assets, relocate with a friend or relative, file bankruptcy or become homeless."[30]

Black poverty, coupled with a discriminatory criminal justice system, contributed to an increase in the percentage of black Americans in prisons during the late twentieth and early twenty-first centuries. The number of black male inmates increased more than 500 percent to over 2 million between 1972 and 2005. Of this large number of inmates, 600,000 were black men between the ages of twenty and thirty-nine. By 2004, 818,000 black men were incarcerated, on parole, or otherwise involved in the prison system, in contrast to only 630,700 white men. These numbers indicate that no less than 12 percent of black men in their twenties and early thirties were in jail or prison in 2005. Though many members of the black community continue to organize to combat these incarceration rates and the structural elements that cause them, much work remains.

A dearth of educational opportunities also limited the opportunity to rise for a great many African Americans. Education is a primary factor that separates black people who find economic stability from those who do not. Black people in the beginning of the twenty-first century graduate from high school at the highest rates in African American history. Though just 3.7 percent of African Americans between twenty-five and twenty-nine years of age were high school graduates in 1960, this number skyrocketed to 86.8 percent by 2000. This increase closely matched the high school graduation rate of white students, which was 94 percent in 2000. In addition, more black students enrolled in college at the turn of the century than ever before. Only 136,000 black students attended college in 1960, but 1,548,000 did so in 2000. White students still attended college in greater proportion than their black peers, but African American enrollment rates put this demographic among the best-educated communities in the world. Indeed, African American students enjoyed better high school graduate rates than did all students in Canada, Britain, Italy, and France. African American students were also more likely to graduate from college than were students in those developed nations.

Black students who wished to gain a higher education, however, still faced many hurdles in doing so. Students living in inner-city and rural areas experienced particular difficulty obtaining quality high school educations and gaining admission to college; these areas continued to offer fewer resources to students than did suburban and wealthier urban areas. White flight by the wealthier to the suburbs, coupled with regressive tax policies, left many urban public schools underfunded. Furthermore, affirmative action policies that helped qualified black people of an earlier generation to enter college were completely eliminated in California and Texas and limited in many other parts of the United States. The repeal of these policies prevented many black students from gaining admittance to elite colleges and universities. Poor schools and increasingly shrinking opportunities left thousands of black students with fewer reasons to succeed in or complete school.

Another problem African Americans still faced in the new millennium was that of limited access to resources such as quality health care. "As the poorest group in America," Princeton University scholar Nell Irvin Painter argued, "black Americans have always suffered disproportionately from diseases associated with want, stress, and limited access to healthcare."[31] Racial discrimination, poverty, poor living conditions, and limited access to health education and care left black people especially susceptible to diseases such as cancer, diabetes, HIV/AIDS, and hypertension, which ravaged African American communities. According to *The Covenant with Black America*, an anthology of essays written by scholars and activists that was published in 2006, "African Americans are 13 percent of the nation's population and account for 56 percent annually of new HIV infections. A quarter of these infections are among people under 25 years of age."[32] Of the individuals newly diagnosed with HIV/AIDS, 63 percent of them were black women. About 70 percent of black Americans with HIV/AIDS contracted the virus through intravenous drug use and unprotected sex. Despite the many gains made by the black community, HIV/AIDS continued to limit African Americans' opportunities to live healthy lives.

Identity issues surrounding sexual orientation, conventions of masculinity and femininity, and relationships between black men and women stimulated intense dialogue and debate among African Americans when a 2003 report challenged popular conceptions of sexual practice and infection rates of HIV/AIDS. The report demonstrated that not only did black women register more new cases of HIV/AIDS and seek testing and treatment more often than men, but many black men lived in denial of their HIV/AIDS status and shunned the testing and treatment that could extend their lives. In addition, the report led some community members to question the sexual activities of black men; as a result, some African American men were revealed to be engaged in the "Down Low." These men, while leading what appeared to be the "straight" lives of heterosexuals, were secretly engaging in unprotected sex with men. As a result of these practices, they transmitted the HIV virus that causes AIDS to unsuspecting female partners.

The phenomenon of the Down Low was covered widely by news media, prompting intense dialogue about the nuances of black male sexuality. J. L. King, an HIV/AIDS activist and author of *On the Down Low: A Journey into the Lives of "Straight" Black Men Who Sleep with Men*, emerged as a leading voice in the timely dialogue:

> Many bisexual men choose not to reveal their sexual orientation because they dread the negative fallout that such a disclosure would likely cause. Homophobia is real. We all witness the harsh words and ridicule to which the gay/lesbian community is subjected. Also, there's tremendous normative pressure to keep closeted about any behavior that exists outside the prevailing social and religious norms. Being judged and ostracized isn't something most folks would sign up for, especially not a DL man whose sense of self is intricately linked to his ability to express masculinity and fulfill the traditional gender expectation assigned to men.[33]

The African American HIV/AIDS crisis reflected just one aspect, albeit a disastrous one, of black America's heightened vulnerability to disease and premature death. Studies continue to indicate that even when researchers control for income and access to health education and care, African Americans became sick and died at a higher rate and at an earlier age than did nonblacks. Interestingly, this disparity was not caused by a vulnerability to all diseases, as black Americans were less likely than whites to develop alcohol addiction or commit suicide. Nevertheless, the overall health of African Americans suggested that the future of black America will be determined not simply by political or economic progress for a modest number of middle-class and affluent blacks, but by African Americans' collective ability to acknowledge, understand, and address critically important health issues that affect black Americans across the political and economic spectrum.

7

CONTEMPORARY BLACK AMERICA

Understanding American race relations and using its lessons can help us break out of the contemporary cycle of racial polarization and fragmentation and move into a cycle of racial understanding and unity.

—RICHARD W. THOMAS, *Understanding Interracial Unity*, 1996

Throughout the history of modern black America, African Americans continued to advance socially, economically, and politically, despite the many problems they faced. Although significant advances were made by 2000, many black Americans still faced serious problems related to disproportionate levels of joblessness, poverty, broken families, substandard housing and homelessness, poor educational opportunities, delinquency, and crime. Thus, the criminal justice system and the prison-industrial complex played an unsurpassed role in the lives of millions of African Americans, and especially of black men. Even the most "successful" African Americans, who benefited from the advantages that the civil rights and black power movements wrought, struggled with the uncertainty and stress related to isolated acts of racial violence, subtle displays of prejudice and racial profiling, and restricted prospects for socioeconomic progress as they endeavored to ascend to the apex of their fields and occupations.

Leaders in Arts and Culture

Several African Americans at the beginning of the new millennium proved particularly successful in artistic and cultural endeavors. Venus and Serena Williams, for example, excelled in the world of professional tennis; Serena made her mark in the fashion world with her own line of clothing. Their successes allowed them to join other sports figures such as NBA greats Charles Barkley, Magic Johnson, Shaquille O'Neal, and Michael Jordan, as well as golf great Tiger Woods, as icons of American sports. Spike Lee broke barriers in Hollywood by writing, directing, and producing films with predominantly black casts concerning provocative issues that stand at the intersection of race, class, gender, and sexuality in American history and life. His most notable films include *Do the Right Thing* (1989), starring Ruby Dee and Ozzie Davis; *Malcolm X* (1992), starring Denzel Washington; and *4 Little Girls* (1997), a chilling documentary of the infamous racial terrorist bombing of the 16th Street Baptist Church in Birmingham during the height of the civil rights movement. Actors and actresses also broke new barriers in their careers. Denzel Washington and Halle Berry were lauded for their artistry when they won Academy Awards for Best Actor and Best Actress in 2002; they were only the second black man and the first black woman to win an Oscar in those categories. Comedian-turned-actor Jamie Foxx became the third African American man to win an Academy Award for Best Actor in 2004 for his portrayal of Ray Charles, the famous blues artist. That same year, Morgan Freeman won an Oscar for Best Performance by an Actor in a Supporting Role for his role in *Million Dollar Baby*.

Will Smith (1968–), who began his entertainment career as half of the hip-hop duo known as DJ Jazzy Jeff and the Fresh Prince, crossed over from the music world to the motion picture industry, becoming the highest-paid actor in Hollywood by 2008. Born Willard Christopher Smith Jr. in Philadelphia, Pennsylvania, Smith attended Overbrook High School in Winfield, Pennsylvania, where he soon became known as "The Prince" for his charm and quick wit. At the early age of twelve, he began rapping and developing his own style under the influence of hip-hop legend Grandmaster Flash. Just four years later, at only sixteen, Smith met Jeff Townes, also known as DJ Jazzy Jeff, with whom he eventually collaborated with under the title Fresh Prince. The two artists produced a number of songs, including the worldwide hits "Girls Ain't Nothin' But Trouble" (1989) and "Parents Just Don't Understand" (1989), which won a Grammy award for Best Rap Performance. Eventually Smith ventured out on his own and became a solo artist in 1997 with his debut album, entitled *Big Willie Style*.

Even before he released his first album, Smith had already branched out into acting. In 1990 he was cast in *The Fresh Prince of Bel-Air*, a hit television sitcom. His acting breakthough soon led to opportunities to work in the movies. He starred in the critically acclaimed and Oscar-nominated *Six Degrees of Separation* (1993), as well as in box-office hits *Bad Boys* (1993), *Independence Day* (1996), *Men in Black* (1997), *I, Robot* (2004), *I Am Legend* (2007), and *Hancock* (2008). Smith's films garnered him Academy Award nominations for Best Actor for his role in *Ali* (2001) and *The Pursuit of Happiness* (2006). He became a major Hollywood producer in his own right. With the assistance of James Lassiter, his partner, Smith founded Overbrook Entertainment, an artist management and film and television production company.

Black people found success in other artistic and scientific fields as well. African American playwrights distinguished themselves during the post-1980 cultural eruption and helped resuscitate theater in the United States. August Wilson, one of the greatest black playwrights of the era, won the Pulitzer Prize for his Broadway plays *Fences* (1987) and *The Piano Lesson* (1990). In addition, in 1993 Toni Morrison won the Nobel Prize for Literature and Rita Dove became the U.S. Poet Laureate. Mae Jemison became the first black woman astronaut in 1993, following Guion S. Bluford Jr., who had become the first African American male astronaut in 1983.

Toni Morrison (1931–, fig. 31) was born Chloe Anthony Wofford in Lorain, Ohio and reared in a working-class family. She earned a BA degree in English from Howard University and an MA degree in English from Cornell University. She taught at Howard University, Texas Southern University, Yale University, Bard College, Rutgers University, the State University of New York at Albany, and Princeton University, where she continues to hold the Robert F. Goheen Professorship in the Humanities. Now an internationally known writer and the recipient of many awards, Morrison is the author of eight novels, including *The Bluest Eye* (1973), the story of a black girl's quest for identity and acceptance in a world of white privilege; *Sula* (1973), which explored the complexity of friendship and black womanhood; *Song of Solomon* (1977), which followed Milkman Dead, the narrative's male protagonist, on his search for heritage and identity; and *Tar Baby* (1981), which explored a love affair between a couple from distinct socioeconomic backgrounds. Morrison's fifth novel, entitled *Beloved* (1987), was a chilling story about the horrors of slavery and an enslaved mother's desperate effort to shield her children (through infanticide) from the dehumanizing effect of bondage. *Beloved* won the Pulitzer Prize and paved the way for Morrison to receive the Nobel Prize for Literature in 2003. In 2006 *Beloved*, which was earlier made into a major motion picture starring Oprah Winfrey, was identified as the greatest

FIG. 31. Toni Morrison, 2003. © Dana Lixenberg/Corbis.

work of American fiction in the past twenty-five years by *The New York Times Book Review*.

Other black artists not only produced stunning works but also created institutions to support themselves and their peers. In 1980 Toni Cade Bambara won the American Book Award for *The Salt Eaters*. Shortly thereafter, in 1981, the Kitchen Table: Woman of Color Press was launched by writer Barbara Smith to provide a publishing outlet to black women writers who had long struggled to publish their works due to the reticence of the major publishing houses, which were predominantly white-owned. One year later Alice Walker won the Pulitzer Prize and the American Book Award for *The Color Purple*, which was later adapted for the big screen by acclaimed director Steven Spielberg. Whoopi Goldberg, another comedian who became a highly successful actor, starred in the film, and Winfrey and veteran actor Danny Glover were cast in supporting roles. Winfrey received an Academy Award nomination for her portrayal of the spirited, assertive, and often seemingly impervious Sophia.

Popular audiences as well as critics responded well to African American artists, making them household names in the process. In 1992 Morrison, Walker, and Terry McMillan, who wrote the widely read *Waiting to Exhale* and *How Stella Got Her Groove Back*, appeared on the *New York Times* best-seller list simultaneously, reflecting a growing fan base and multiracial admiration of African American literature. During the first decade of the twenty-first century, black entertainers continued to receive unprecedented accolades for their work on stage and in film. In 2005 Oprah Winfrey launched the Broadway production of *The Color Purple*, which drew over one million people to the play in New York before it closed its doors to relocate to Chicago in 2007. That year, Forrest Whitaker won the Academy Award for Best Actor for his portrayal of Ugandan dictator Idi Amin in *The Last King of Scotland*, while Jennifer Hudson won an Oscar for Best Supporting Actress for her role in *Dreamgirls*.

Like Richard Pryor and Eddie Murphy, comedians Chris Rock and Dave Chappelle used quick wit, sharp minds, and a mixture of slapstick and derisive humor to offer blistering critiques of racism, sexual politics, and economic exploitation. David Khari Webber Chappelle (1973–) proved a particularly important figure after the turn of the century. Born in Yellow Springs, Ohio, Chappelle was raised in Washington DC where he studied acting at the Duke Ellington School of the Arts. He developed and polished his skills as an easygoing yet socially conscious comic in the area's clubs. After making his film debut as one of the "merry men" in Mel Brooks's *Robin Hood: Men in Tights* (1993), Chappelle returned to the club circuit and focused on stand-up comedy while making guest appearances on late-night and cable television. He returned to film, making scene-stealing appearances in Eddie Murphy's *The Nutty Professor* (1996) and *Con Air* (1997). In 1998, Chappelle made a career breakthrough when he cowrote and costarred in the "prison/pothead caper" *Half Baked* (1998). He made several other films between 1998 and 2002, but his role in the blaxploitation (the exploitative and/or satirical depiction of African Americans in movies featuring or intending to appeal to, but not exclusively, black people), spoof *Undercover Brother* (2002), in particular, garnered him a great deal of attention.[1]

Chappelle's slashing humor, however, cemented his status as one of the nation's most creative comedians when he began working with cable channel Comedy Central. In 2002 he voiced a prank caller to *Crank Yankers*, the network's vulgar puppet show. His character proved so popular that the network offered him his own series the following year. *Chappelle's Show* proved to be one of the network's most successful shows, as well as one of the most controversial half-hour shows in U.S. television history. It offered burning social commentary, particularly on matters of race, while regularly pushing the boundaries of good taste and Federal Communications Commission regulations. The show's sketch comedy routines included a depiction of Clayton Bigsby, a blind black white supremacist who, unaware of his race due to his blindness, rallied the Ku Klux Klan in support of "White Power"; the "Racial Draft," a satirical yet controversial allocation system developed to settle debates about who belonged to various racial communities; a hypothetical scenario that explored what would happen if black people in America were given $1 trillion in reparation money; and a fictional "True Life Story" of Rick James in which Chappelle mixed analyses of class, color consciousness, male sexuality, and sexism with farcical commentaries on the personal lives of celebrities. Pryor, one of Chappelle's role models, enjoyed *Chappelle's Show* and was quoted as saying that he had "passed the torch" to Chappelle.

Chappelle's Show was nominated for two Emmy awards, and home DVD sales of the television show made it the highest-grossing of its genre in American history. Following the show's second season, Viacom, which owns Comedy Central, allegedly offered Chappelle a $55 million contract, which included a large percentage of revenue generated by DVD distribution, to remain with the show for two more years. In a move that shocked admirers as well as detractors, Chappelle left during production of the show's third season in May 2005. He stated that he was displeased with the direction his show had taken, citing in particular one sketch in which he believed that racial satire had given way to racial mockery. He departed the for South Africa, where he told *Time* magazine's South African bureau chief that he left the United States to reflect on his life, religion, and career:

> I don't normally talk about my religion publicly because I don't want people to associate me and my flaws with this beautiful thing. And I believe [Islam] is a beautiful religion if you learn it the right way. It's a lifelong effort. Your religion is your standard. Coming here I don't

have the distractions of fame. It quiets the ego down. I'm interested in the kind of person I've got to become. I want to be well rounded and the industry is a place of extremes. I want to be well balanced. I've got to check my intentions, man.[2]

Late in 2005 Chappelle returned to the United States and to stand-up comedy. He made a surprise appearance on *Def Poetry*, a show on the HBO network. He also participated in a highly anticipated interview with Michael Schimmel on *Inside the Actors Studio* on December 18, 2005, for an episode aired on February 12, 2006. During this interview he explained, "I would go to work on the show and I felt awful every day. I felt like some kind of prostitute or something. If I feel so bad, why keep on showing up to this place? I'm going to Africa." He also explained that he had come to believe that some of his sequences were "socially irresponsible." One of these was the "pixie sketch," in which "pixies appeared to people and encouraged them to reinforce racial stereotypes. Chappelle donned blackface for this sketch and was outfitted like a minstrel. During the filming of it, he recalled, a white crew member giggled in a manner that elicited uneasy feeling in Chappelle, "It was the first time I felt that someone was not laughing with me but laughing at me."[3]

In 2006 he released *Dave Chappelle's Block Party*, a documentary film inspired by *Wattstax*. Written and hosted by Chappelle, the film followed him during the summer of 2004 as he organized a major block party on the corner of Quincy and Downing Streets in the Clinton Hill area of Brooklyn, New York. Though the film was released after his trip to South Africa, it was produced before Chappelle's highly publicized break with his hit television show. In addition to treating the large crowd who attended the party to comedic monologues and sketches, Chappelle hosted a number of alternative hip-hop and neo-soul artists including Kanye West, Mos Def, Jill Scott, Erykah Badu, The Roots, and the Fugees (with lead singer Lauryn Hill).

Chappelle's choice of performers for the block party reflected the commercial success and international popularity of hip-hop during the early twenty-first century. Indeed, from its origins in the early 1970s, hip-hop was emblematic of the post–civil rights and post–black power generations of black America. By 2008 it had grown into a constantly evolving lifestyle with its own language, style of dress, music, and mindset. Hip-hop consists of four elements: DJing, emceeing, B-boying (breakdancing), and graffiti art(or tagging). In some circles, hip hop heads (enthusiasts) will identify a fifth element, identified as either knowledge, fashion, or beat-boxing (producing drumming and other rhythmic sounds with one's mouth). Although DJs emerged as the most visible participants in the early world of hip-hop, emcees, or rappers, later garnered the most attention.

At its core, rap is a form of rhythmic speaking that emphasizes rhyming. With origins in African culture and the African American oral tradition, rap music is extremely diverse and serves as hip-hop's highest form of expression. Historian Robin D. G. Kelley found much of value in hip-hop culture, and explained the meanings that rap music holds for black people:

> In America there has always been verbal acrobatics or jousting involving rhymes within the Black community. Signifying, testifying, the Dozens, school yard rhymes, and double Dutch jump rope rhymes are some of the names and ways that various forms of rap have manifested. This signifying often took on a playful tone, but it became a way of communicating serious objections to racial oppression, police brutality, political isolation, elitism, educational inequalities, war and more. Rap emerged as a window into, and critique of, the criminalization, socioeconomic isolation, and negative perceptions of black youth, and has evolved into a multi-racial, multi-generational critique of rigid structures, classism, and representative authority.[4]

At the beginning of the twenty-first century, rap music was already thirty years old. The genre emerged in 1973 in the South Bronx as a way to settle disputes between warring young gang members. Rap pioneer Clive Campbell, otherwise known as DJ Kool Herc, began using rap samples to accompany a mixture of beats played on two separate turn tables, and he encouraged local inner-city youth to settle their conflicts through nonviolent, extemporaneous rapping and dance competitions. During Herc's break beats, B-boys, and sometimes B-girls, took center stage and danced in such a way as to simulate "popping" and "locking" movements to the base and snare-drum beats. In addition, Herc's rhymes were inspired by the work of Gil Scott-Heron and the Last Poets, who were well known in New York in the late 1960s and early 1970s. Heron, a black poet, musician, and author, distinguished himself during the late 1970s as a spoken word performer. He also fused jazz, blues, and soul music with lyrical content concerning social and political issues of the time, delivered in both rapping and melismatic (multiple notes sung on one syllable) vocal styles. The Last Poets, a group of militant black poets and musicians, emerged from the civil rights and black power movements of the late 1960s. Music critic Jason Ankeny argues that "with their politically charged raps, taut rhythms, and dedication to raising African American consciousness, the Last Poets almost single-handedly laid the groundwork for the emergence of Hip Hop."[5]

As DJ Kool Herc forged an underground movement of positive rapping and dancing competitions, Afrika "Bam" Bambaataa engineered a highly politicized style of rap that combined black nationalist philosophies from the Nation of Islam with the cultural nationalism of the Black Panthers. Bambaataa, who grew up in the South Bronx, was instrumental in the early years of hip-hop. He was one of the originators of break beat deejaying (playing the same record on two turntables and playing the break repeatedly by alternating between the two records, letting one play while spinning the second record back to the beginning of the break). Bambaataa is also known for co-opting the street gang, the Black Spades, of which he had been a member, into the music- and culture-oriented recording group the Universal Zulu Nation, which went on to spread hip-hop throughout the world.[6]

Bambaataa's Zulu Nation hosted rapping and break-dancing competitions, supported the work of local graffiti artists, and promoted rap throughout New York City's black and Latino communities. Joining Herc and Bambaata during the early days of hip-hop was emcee Joseph Saddler, otherwise known as Grandmaster Flash. Together, this new cadre of grassroots artistic leaders divided New York City into territories and "battled" each other on a regular basis. The battles were of course nonviolent affairs in which dancers competed without touching. Victory was determined through the verbal affirmation of local youth who gathered around battles to judge contestants on rhythm, creativity, precision, and fluidity of motion. Like B-boys battling each other, graffiti artists also attempted to best one another in separate competitions to see who could write their name or "tag" more often and in the most aesthetically pleasing ways.[7]

Rap soon found some measure of crossover legitimacy. The genre's first commercial hit was "Rapper's Delight" (1979) by the Sugar Hill Gang. It was this song that popularized the term hip-hop. Grandmaster Flash and the Furious Five produced a new commercial success in album entitled

The Message (1982), a searing exposition of urban poverty, drug culture, and despair: "Don't push me, cause I'm close to the edge. / I'm trying not to lose my head."[8]

The Message fused 1970s funk, rap vocals, and scratching, in which a DJ manipulates a record album back and forth under a record player needle to produce screeching yet rhythmic sounds that form a single autonomous melody.

Young black people who felt largely abandoned and forgotten by mainstream society found a home in the burgeoning hip-hop scene; for some, hip-hop became the defining movement of their lives. It was an artistic realm in which African American youth could discuss and negotiate issues of deep concern to them, in particular racism and economic oppression. During the Reagan era most members of middle-class America rarely acknowledged the existence of inner-city dwellers or urban corrosion. Meanwhile, conditions worsened steadily during this period for young black people as urban America came under assault by gang violence and dislocation wrought by an influx of guns and crack cocaine. In the midst of this cauldron of anguish, the "keep it real" lifestyle of hip hop heads helped foster a sense of community and purpose among a generation who otherwise felt sequestered and forgotten.[9]

Over time, however, the message of hip-hop changed. The earliest rap songs were primarily positive in tone, even as they explored and exposed the stark conditions of inner-city life. By the late 1980s and 1990s this style had largely been eclipsed by "gangsta" rap, the work of West Coast artists, including Ice-T and Niggaz wit Attitude (NWA), that told explicit stories of life in blighted urban America, typically ones punctuated by joblessness, poverty, drugs, gang violence, broken families, and homelessness. Gangsta rap artists freely used blistering language, misogynistic lyrics, and intense bravado, with many listeners particularly offended by the relentless objectification and dehumanization of women in "hard-core" rap music, videos, and eventually Hollywood films.[10]

Indeed, rap artists' seemingly persistent use of the misogynist terms *bitch* and *ho* to describe black women revealed deep gender divisions within the black community at large. Rap's depiction of black women as things or goods that men could control, buy, and sell came to bear a striking resemblance to white supremacist portrayals of black women during the eras of slavery and Jim Crow. One of the lasting legacies of hip-hop is its treatment of women, an issue addressed in emerging research and intellectual work on the genre. Indeed, hip hop studies became an academic field examining both the history and societal impact of the phenomenon. New research has examined hip-hop's relationship to commercial rap music, demonstrating, for example, that most of what popular audiences consume is actually a very narrow subset of the rap music produced by contemporary artists. Scholars such as T. Denean Sharpley-Whiting and Mark Anthony Neal have explicitly examined hip-hop's treatment of black women, the relationships between black men and women as revealed by the genre, and the homophobia prevalent in the movement. Their research challenges hip-hop artists and audiences. Sharpley-Whiting asked, for example, "How have hip-hop's lyrics and visual riffs on the acrimonious and sexually charged nature of male-female relationships encouraged the sexual abuse of young black women?"[11] These questions remain open, and must be addressed by old and new generations of hip hop heads.[12]

In 2007 the use of sexist lyrics in hip-hop became a national controversy when Don Imus, a white radio talk show host, referred to the black members of the Rutgers University women's basketball team as a bunch of "nappy-headed hos," an on-air comment that saw millions of black people erupt in anger. Jesse Jackson and Al Sharpton led a protest that ended in the firing of Imus. Many who defended the talk show host said that he had simply spoken in ways reflective of rap music, and that those who repudiated him and his remarks should be equally critical of rappers. Other commentators maintained that Imus's racist comments, and the use of similar language in rap music, emerged from the same retrograde notions of black womanhood that are fixtures in American culture, insisting that these expressions are repugnant and unacceptable in any context.[13]

To the consternation of many Americans, and especially to the disappointment of those who exist outside the hip-hop community, gangsta rap endures as one of the most popular subgenres of rap music. The violence associated with gangsta rap reached a fever pitch with the violent murders of two of the most successful and creative rappers in American history, Tupac (2Pac) Shakur and The Notorious B.I.G. (Biggie Smalls).

Shakur was born in New York City on June 16, 1971. His mother, Afeni Shakur, was a Black Panther activist who was pregnant with Tupac while being held in jail by the FBI on federal bombing charges. It is now believed the defendants were victims of a nationwide FBI-led attempt to neutralize the Black Panther Party. Although Afeni Shakur has never publicly revealed who Tupac's biological father is, it is suspected by many that his father was Billy Garland, a truck driver and former member of the Black Panther Party. Tupac enjoyed acting as a child and joined a theater company based in Harlem called "The 127th Street Ensemble." As a young adult he lived in Baltimore, and attended the Baltimore (High) School for the Arts, where he took acting and dance classes, including jazz, modern, and ballet. It was during this time he discovered rap and began traveling to New York City to perform as an MC. Shakur moved with his family to Oakland, California in the late 1980s, and there he became a member of the group Digital Underground, which had enjoyed early fame with the song "The Humpty Dance."[14]

Shakur's true calling as a solo artist became evident early on in his career. In 1991 he reinvented himself, taking the name 2Pac, and releasing his debut solo album, "2Pacalypse Now." One track from that album, "Brenda's Got a Baby," reached number three on the Billboard Hot Rap Singles chart. His second album, "Strictly 4 My N.I.G.G.A.Z.," demonstrated 2Pac's ability to cross over to the pop charts with singles like "I Get Around" and "Keep Ya Head Up." Shakur's appeal to the mainstream pop market boosted the album to platinum status when it sold more than one million copies. Shakur's interest in acting never waned, and he also appeared in several films in the early 1990s, including *Poetic Justice* (1993) opposite Janet Jackson. 2Pac gained both notoriety for the violence central to his art and acclaim for the truth and power behind his lyrics. In addition to poverty, discrimination, and police brutality, Shakur addressed the violence that plagued urban America, "thug life," and sex. Like a number of other young hip-hop artists, a number of arrests for violent crimes confirmed that Shakur lived the gangsta life that he rapped about in his music. In 1994 he was convicted of two assaults, one of which was sexual assault, and spent several days in jail after he physically attacked director Allen Hughes. The violence that he rapped about caught up with him when he was shot five times during a robbery in the lobby of a recording studio. After Shakur recovered from his injuries, he began to serve a sentence of four and a half years for the sexual assault conviction.[15]

During this time his next album, "Me Against the World" (1995), debuted at number one on the charts. Music critics praised tracks like "Dear Mama" for "keeping it real" and diving into more profound and deeper material. Shakur served eight months in prison; his time served was rumored to have been cut short thanks to a $1.4 million bond paid by Death Row Records CEO Marion "Suge" Knight. He quickly released another album, "All Eyez on Me" (1996). The album's most popular track, "California Love," returned Shakur to the image of the LA gangsta and featured a collaboration with the famous rapper-producer Dr. Dre. The album produced several additional smash hits, including "How Do You Want It," which also climbed to the top of the pop charts. Shakur seemed to be on top of the world.[16]

While Shakur was enjoying his tremendous success, he had also become caught up in a battle between East and West Coast rappers. His primary nemesis was Biggie Smalls. In an April, 1995 interview in *Vibe*, Shakur, then in prison after having been convicted of sexual assault, accused Uptown Records founder Andre Harrell, Sean Combs, and Smalls of having prior knowledge of the robbery that left him beaten and shot five times in November 1994.[17] Wallace was present in the same recording studio at the time of the occurrence, but denied the accusation. Writer Jennifer Berube recalls that "in June 1996, Shakur released "Hit 'Em Up," a song in which he explicitly claimed to have had sex with Wallace's wife, singer Faith Evans, and accused Wallace of copying his style and image." On the night of September 7, 1996, Shakur and his entourage left a professional boxing match in Las Vegas that had featured one-time heavyweight champion Mike Tyson, and headed for Club 662, a known hangout of the Bloods street gang. "Shakur sat in the passenger seat of a black BMW 750, with Suge Knight in the driver's seat," Berube writes. "Just after 11 p.m., Knight stopped at a red light, and Shakur began flirting with a car full of girls who had pulled up to his left. At the same time, a white Cadillac with four black men inside pulled up on his right. By the time Shakur noticed the car full of gunmen to his right it was too late. He was shot four times at point blank range before Knight could flee the scene. Shakur was rushed to hospital, where he had several surgeries. They did not save his life. The damage to his body was too extensive in the end, and he died six days later on September 13, 1996."[18]

Six months after Shakur's murder, Smalls was in Los Angeles for the eleventh annual Soul Train Music Awards. After the ceremony, he and his entourage, including Sean Combs, piled into their SUVs to go to an afterparty. With Combs leading the way in his black Suburban, the caravan drove to the intersection of Fairfax Avenue and Wilshire Boulevard, where they were stopped for a red light. While stopped behind Combs in a green Suburban, Smalls, in the driver's seat, heard what he thought was a fan yelling at him from the street. He rolled down his window to discover a Chevrolet Impala pulling up right beside him. The driver, a black man dressed in a suit and bowtie, pulled out a gun and shot Smalls several times in the chest. Wallace was rushed to hospital, where he was pronounced dead at 1:15 a.m. on March 9, 1997.[19]

The murders were never solved, but many followers of hip-hop and the feud between the two rappers believe that each one of them was in some way involved in the other's death. Since their murders, their record labels have released many posthumous albums featuring previously unreleased work. The albums have sold millions of copies: their legend as irreverent critics of entrenched authority, poverty, police brutality, racism, and urban life still inspires millions around the world. Observers continue to debate whether gangsta rap exacerbates or merely reflects the rising tide of gang violence in American life, but the deaths of Shakur and Smalls still dominate that conversation.

As hip-hop scholars have noted, control over the genre of hip-hop remains a point of contention. Black critics have charged that the violent and misogynist lyrics of gangsta rap are encouraged primarily by white male executives in the music industry. African American entrepreneurs, however, have seized control of an increasing portion of the production, dissemination, and profits of hip-hop. This control may yield greater responsibility in hip-hop lyrics and message. Russell Simmons (1956–), for example, founded his own business to produce and market hip-hop. He became a concert promoter in the mid-1970s and pushed rap artists to remain true to the styles of dress and language that created hip-hop. He collaborated with others in 1984 to create Def Jam Records, which promoted artists including Run-DMC, Public Enemy, and LL Cool J. The record label remains extremely popular, and has sold millions of albums. Simmons also created the clothing label Phat Pharm to sell hip-hop clothing, and he began to promote poetry and comedy through venues such as the HBO *Def Poetry* cable television show. Simmons shifted his entrepreneurial efforts in 2000 by selling his share of Def Jam for more than $100 million. Currently he is worth more than $350 million.

Other black entrepreneurs also found opportunities in hip-hop. Diddy, otherwise known as Sean "Puff Daddy" Combs (1969–), grew up in New York City, and in 1990 he dropped out of Howard University to launch his career in the hip-hop industry. He began working for Uptown Records,

FIG. 32. Russell Simmons and Sean "Diddy" Combs attend the Jackie Robinson Foundation awards gala at the Waldorf-Astoria on March 7, 2011, in New York City. © Reuters/Corbis.

but he soon used his knowledge of hip-hop and his talent for identifying hit music to form his own company, Bad Boy Records. His enterprise became successful quickly, and he extended his operation to Sean Jean, a clothing line, and a fragrance called Unforgivable. In 2008 Diddy was worth an estimated $340 million.

Hip-hop quickly expanded from its originators in the South Bronx to the rest of the nation. Run-DMC was particularly popular. In the mid-1980s the group was featured on (then) new cable music channel Music Television (MTV), which introduced it to a wider audience, including white teenagers throughout the United States that previously had only limited contact with hip-hop. As a result of attention from MTV and other outlets, the genre spread throughout the nation, reaching black people living outside of New York as well as white people who had no or limited contact with African Americans. Each urban area created its own version of hip-hop, including beliefs about the hip-hop lifestyle. Hip-hop fashion soon developed to include sagging, baggy jeans, which clothing companies quickly assimilated into their products. These companies mass-produced the new products, even selling them at high prices back to the very inner-city residents who first gave birth to the style. Ironically, the majority of the consumers of hip-hop were, and continue to be, white youth.

As with other musical genres in the twentieth century, hip-hop exhibits a tension between black creativity and white profits. Given the political purposes of hip-hop, this tension has fueled new debate. Gregg Tate, a black journalist, longtime *Village Voice* writer, and author of *Everything But the Burden: What White People Are Taking from Black Culture*, declared, "Our music, our fashion, our hairstyles, our dances, our anatomical traits, our bodies, our souls continue to be considered ever ripe for the picking and biting by the same crafty devils who brought you the African slave trade and the Middle Passage."[20]

Despite these fights for control, rap music did and continues to include many artists who consciously reject gratuitous cursing, sexism, and violence. Queen Latifah, born Dana Elaine Owens (1970–), has, like Will Smith, crossed over from music to become a critically acclaimed film star. Latifah has also, however, routinely championed the education and empowerment of black men and women. Nominated for an Academy Award for Best Supporting Actress for her performance as prison matron Mama Morton in the Hollywood adaption of the hit Broadway play *Chicago*, she continues to serve as a member of the figurative hip-hop royalty. In this capacity, she promotes positive messages of hope and renewal. Other artists have joined Latifah in the pantheon of black female rappers, including The Real Roxanne, MC Lyte, TLC, The Lady of Rage, Foxy Brown, Trina, Lil' Kim, and Missy Elliot. Whereas Latifah's lyrics promote enlightenment and unity, the work of Brown, Trina, and Kim gained notoriety for their bawdy, highly sexualized lyrics and videos. In contrast, artists such as Public Enemy, KRS-1, The Roots, Mos Def, Common, Dead Prez, Immortal Technique, and Talib Kweli used their rhetorical "skillz" to raise awareness of issues of critical importance to black people. These artists also critiqued rigid structures, classism, and representative authority.[21]

The impact of those artists who gave rise to hip-hop, and the artists and executives who have kept it alive, made the lifestyle of hip-hop and its associated art and business a global force that prompted some observes to refer to the Earth as a "Hip Hop Planet." Indeed, hip-hop has influenced music throughout the world. Rap music's ability to merge with alternative music genres to forge unique musical fusions, and the worldwide spread of American popular culture, will likely ensure a long life for hip-hop as it evolves and continues to blossom.[22]

As in previous generations, black intellectuals in the early twenty-first century served as sources of knowledge and often as advocates for Americans, especially African Americans, grappling with problems. For the first time in American history, large numbers of black scholars, thinkers, and critics established themselves as highly sought-after public intellectuals who transcended traditional life in the "ivory tower," long the bastion of white males, to play major roles in the public and political spheres. The academy itself is no longer the exclusive province of white men. Scholars and writers such as Du Bois, E. Franklin Frazier, James Baldwin, Richard Wright, Ralph Ellison, and John Hope Franklin (fig. 33) distinguished themselves in the academic world before 1970. Since 1970, black scholars in large numbers have continued to pushed past barriers to become some of the most highly honored and influential intellectuals in the United States. These scholars include Cornel West, Henry Louis Gates, William Julius Wilson, Shelby Steele, Michele Wallace, Michael Eric Dyson, Nell Irvin Painter, Adolph Reed, John Edgar Wideman, Robin D. G. Kelley, Anthony Appiah, and Darlene Clark Hine. Their work and philosophies were as diverse as their backgrounds; members of this group of scholars embraced both liberal and conservative views. All of them, however, endeavored to explore and understand black culture and consciousness, in addition to the relevance of race, class, and gender in America. Darlene Clark Hine (1947–), in particular, helped transform African American studies, and especially black history, from a field of inquiry that fixated entirely on men to one that acknowledged and examined the unique history and life of black women. She is the author of *Hinesight: Black Women and the Reconstruction of American History* (1994) and *A Shining Thread of Hope: A History of Black Women in America* (1998), and the editor of a three-volume, award-winning encyclopedia, the first of its kind, on black women's history, *Black Women in America* (2005). Hine strives not only to explore African American history, but also to redefine the discipline of history itself. She has argued, "To me the historical profession is still too caught up with the wealthy and the influential in political, social, and cultural arenas, who actually number only a very small minority of the human population . . . Because so few of the new social historians have included black women, who remained at the very bottom of the ladder in the United States, we continue to lose much understanding and wisdom."[23]

FIG. 33. Renowned Harvard University historian John Hope Franklin is interviewed on the publication of his autobiography *Mirror to America* at Barnes & Noble's Union Square store in New York. Author of the groundbreaking bestseller *From Slavery to Freedom* (1947), Dr. Franklin was awarded the Presidential Medal of Freedom by President Bill Clinton in 1995. One of the intellectual patriarchs of the Civil Rights Movement, Dr. Franklin's landmark appearance at Barnes & Noble highlights the bookstore's celebration of Black History Month 2006. © Marc Brasz/Corbis.

Hine was inspired by the work of other black women historians who worked to carve out a place for the study of black women's experiences in overwhelmingly masculinist environments. Rosalyn Terborg-Penn and Eleanor Smith founded the Association of Black Women Historians in 1979. Under the auspices of this organization, they promoted historical and literary works about black women that were consumed by popular audiences and academics alike. As the numbers of black women in colleges and universities grew, courses such as "Black Women Writers" and "Black Women's History" were incorporated into black studies and women's studies curricula. These changes led black women's history to become a field of inquiry in its own right. Conferences, exhibits, scholarly books, reference works, and anthologies underscored the many contributions that African American women made to black history and life, and to the whole of American culture.

Many black scholars of the early twenty-first century can attribute their rise to the black studies programs established during the late 1960s and early 1970s. Once isolated and grossly underfunded on a relatively small number of college and university campuses, such programs now have a permanent place at virtually every major college and university. At Northwestern University, for example, Hine led the way in creating a doctoral degree program in the Department of African American Studies. Northwestern is joined by Temple University, the University of Massachusetts at Amherst, Harvard University, Yale University, Michigan State University, and the University of California at Berkeley in awarding PhD degrees in African American Studies or a variation thereof. Black scholars explore a variety of topics as they seek to understand black history and life, but most subscribe to one of four primary modes of analysis: Afrocentrist, integrationist, Diasporic, and intersectionalist, in the last of which a scholar examines the inextricable links between race, class, and gender.

Afrocentrists remain among the most prominent and controversial members of the black intellectual community. One can trace Afrocentricity and its theories and methodologies back to the political movement that gave rise to black studies. Molefi Kete Asante, a professor at Temple University, became synonymous with Afrocentricism. Born Arthur Lee Smith in Valdosta, Georgia, in 1942, Asante graduated cum laude with a bachelor's degree from Oklahoma Christian College in 1964, with a master's degree from Pepperdine College in 1965, and with a doctorate from UCLA in 1968. During his tenure at Southwestern Christian College, Smith met Essien Essien, a Nigerian scholar, who encouraged him to learn more about Africa. Smith followed Essien's advice, studied African languages and literature, visited Africa often, and eventually served as director of the English-language journalism curriculum at the Zimbabwe Institute of Mass Communications.

Smith, who had changed his name to Molefi Kete Asante in 1973, assumed a professorship at Temple University in Philadelphia in 1980, the same year he published his most influential and controversial book, *Afrocentricity: The Theory of Social Change*, one of the first major theoretical examinations of Afrocentricity since the black power movement. In an interview with the editors of *Contemporary Black Biography*, Asante proclaimed that he had founded the "Afrocentric Movement" to "examine why it was that we African-Americans as a people were so disoriented." He concluded that slavery, Jim Crow, and their legacies led black people to identify almost entirely with European traditions and the trappings of the Western world. In doing so, Asante argued, black people learned little about their African heritage or about non-Western ways of thinking and problem solving. Afrocentricity, he reasoned, was part of the solution. This mode of consciousness "attempts to repair the damage of hundreds of years of mistreatment that Africans have endured at the hands of a Eurocentric society," while demonstrating how African Americans "can get back to a center where we begin to [learn] from our own history."[24]

Asante revised and enhanced his exploration of these ideas in *The Afrocentric Idea* (1987). In this work, Asante stated that Afrocentricity is "not only a new perspective but a different framework for understanding human behavior."[25] He maintained that an African-centered perspective was necessary to redirect African Americans from the margins of Eurocentric intellectual inquiry and an American society dominated by whites. Black people, he believed, should put themselves at the center of their worldview. In its boldest form, then, Afrocentricism affirmed that African civilization, especially ancient Egypt, gave birth to European civilization. Adherents of Afrocentricism also emphasize the existence of highly advanced societies in other regions of Africa to disprove notions of African (and ostensibly African American) inferiority. Afrocentrists reject the idea of an American "melting pot," believing that assimilation constitutes the repudiation of black people's African roots and complicity in the Western world's cruelty toward and subjugation of African peoples. Even as other black scholars began to challenge his views, Asante continued to defend Afrocentrism, arguing that it "is a terribly maligned concept. Afrocentricity is the idea that African people and interests must be viewed as actors and agents in human history, rather than as marginal to the European historical experience—which has been institutionalized as universal."[26]

Many scholars, however, including a large number of black intellectuals, denounced Afrocentricity as simplistic, counterproductive, and conducive to self-segregation. African American writer Earl Ofari Hutchinson, for instance, argued, "In their zeal to counter the heavy handed 'Eurocentric imbalance of history,' some have crossed the line between historic fact and fantasy. They've constructed groundless theories in which Europeans are 'Ice People,' 'suffer genetic defects,' or are obsessed with 'color phobias.' They've replaced the shallow European 'great man' theory of history with a feel-good interpretation of history."[27] White historian Arthur Schlesinger Jr. claimed that Afrocentrism isolated both African scholarship and people of African descent from the rest of humanity. He accused Asante and other Afrocentricists of "saying, essentially that Africa is the source of all good and Europe is the source of all evil." Hutchinson, Schlesinger, and other critics believed that Afrocentrists' tendency to manufacture "a glorious past" for African Americans effectively called the intellectual integrity of African and African American studies into question.[28]

As Afrocentrists battled Eurocentrism and fought to revitalize black America's knowledge of and appreciation for its history and worth, other forces in African America attempted to revitalize and inspire the community through grassroots movements. When longtime NOI leader Elijah Muhammad died in 1975, Wallace D. Muhammad, Elijah's son, seized control of the organization. The new leader rejected many of his father's teachings. In addition, he attempted to move the NOI toward orthodox Islamic traditions. Louis Farrakhan, once the protégé and later the enemy of Malcolm X, and other NOI followers repudiated the organization's new direction and leader. In 1978 these dissidents reestablished the NOI under Farrakhan's leadership and once again began to promulgate the teachings of Elijah Muhammad. Farrakhan first became nationally known in 1984, when he broke with the NOI's policy of abstention from politics, supported Jesse Jackson's 1984 bid for the Democratic party's presidential nomination, and stirred up a hornet's nest worth of controversy in the process. When many Jewish Americans took offense at Jackson's infamous "Hymietown" remark, Farrakhan, whose FOI provided security for the Jackson camp, defended the candidate's remarks. In doing so, however, Farrakhan only exacerbated Jackson's problem. Appearing on the CBS *Evening News* on February 24, 1984, Farrakhan declared, "I say to the Jewish people, who may not like our brother. It is not Jesse Jackson you are attacking. When you attack him, you are attacking the millions who are lining up with him. You're attacking all of us. Why dislike us? Why attack our champion? Why hurl stones at him? It's our champion. If you harm this brother, what do you think we should do about it?"[29]

Farrakhan's ranting about Jewish people proved relentless. He directed a torrent of criticisms and insults at them throughout 1984, describing them as the primary enemy of black Americans. Antisemitic groups throughout the nation supported Farrakhan's barrage, while Jewish groups and the Anti-Defamation League denounced his rhetoric as divisive, hateful, and reminiscent of that of Hitler. Farrakhan blamed Jews for many of black America's problems, despite Jewish Americans' history of working arm-in-arm with African American activists during the civil rights movement. Although Jackson's presidential bid suffered from Farrakhan's controversial remarks, Farrakhan himself grew in stature as a result of the media attention his comments attracted. Privately, many African Americans were inspired by Farrakhan's comments, not for the antisemitic nature of some of them, but by his ability to convey their disappointment and anger.

The NOI remained in the national news through the end of the twentieth century. In a shocking turn of events, Qubilah Bahiyah Shabazz, one of Malcolm X's daughters, was implicated in a plot to murder Farrakhan in 1995. Farrakhan, whose involvement in Malcolm X's assassination had long been suspected, denied any involvement in the plot. Just prior to Malcolm X's murder, however, Farrakhan was infamously quoted as saying, "Only those who wish to be led to hell, or to their doom, will follow Malcolm. The die is set, and Malcolm shall not escape. Such a man as Malcolm is worthy of death." When a journalist queried Farrakhan on Malcolm X's assassination thirty years later, the leader of the NOI was more ambiguous, saying, "I can't say I approved, and I really didn't disapprove."[30]

Farrakhan retooled his image in the mid-1990s, suppressing his more provocative opinions in an attempt to reach a larger, more diverse group of African Americans. In 1995, as part of this larger recruitment effort, he called for a Million [black] Man March in Washington DC. The purpose of the march was to engage in a "Holy day of Atonement and Reconciliation to reconcile our spiritual inner beings and to redirect our focus to developing our communities, strengthening our families, working to uphold and protect our civil and human rights, and empowering ourselves through the Spirit of God, more effective use of our dollars, and through the power of the vote."[31]

While people continue to debate the success of the Million Man March, few can doubt the significance of the event for the estimated crowd of four hundred thousand who gathered in the nation's capital on October 16, 1995. The march attracted international media attention, and it inspired many black men to recommit themselves to their communities and to the cause of antiracism. The conservative values of the NOI, which included community responsibility, the importance of the family, religion, self-respect, and capitalism, reached the attendees of the event and black people throughout the United States. Marchers later noted that even if they did not support the NOI, they found strength in the peaceful solidarity of the event.

This sense of solidarity ended just three months after the Million Man March, however, when Farrakhan traveled internationally. During his World Friendship Tour in Africa and the Middle East, Farrakhan met with General Sani Abacha, the leader of Nigeria and a particularly repressive military regime. This event, combined with Farrakhan's inability to create a long-term plan for African Americans, prevented him from creating substantial or long-lasting change in the United States. Other black intellectuals publicly disagreed with Farrakhan's values and plans, which were undoubtedly conservative. Adolph Reed, one of the nation's most famous writers and culture critics, for example, noted that Farrakhan "weds a radical oppositional style to a program that proposed private and individual responses to social problems; he endorses moral repressiveness; he asserts racial essentialism; he affirms male authority; and he lauds bootstrap capitalism. His focus on self-help and moral revitalization is profoundly reactionary and meshes perfectly with the victim-blaming orthodoxy of the Reagan/Bush era."[32]

Despite the controversy associated with Farrakhan's leadership, women organized a march to match the Million Man March. Philadelphia residents Phile Chionesu, a small business owner, and Asia Coney, a public housing activist, organized the event for October 25, 1997 in Philadelphia. That day, approximately three hundred thousand black women gathered in a celebration of their power and a call to action on issues important to them, which included domestic violence, health care, and education. The attendees listened to Maxine Waters, then president of the Congressional Black Caucus and a congresswoman from California; Sister Souljah, a rap artist; and Winnie Mandela, the South African activist. The Million Woman March did not attract the same level of international media attention as the Million Man March had two years earlier. The march itself, as well as the dearth of attention it received, highlighted the struggles that black women continued to face in the United States, as well as their resilience. Like the Million Man March, this event did not articulate specific solutions to the problems it addressed, but instead provided black women with the opportunity to engage with one another and find meaning in community.

Hip-hop, the rise of black intellectuals and African American studies, and massive grassroots movements educated, inspired, advanced, and unified black Americans in the late twentieth and early twenty-first centuries. Despite these systemic and individual acts of solidarity, however, black people remained incredibly diverse. Americans of African, American Indian, and European descent have initiated interracial relationships and formed families, both consensually and nonconsensually, since the seventeenth century. As a result, black Americans have always been multiracial in character, as evidenced by the multitudes of skin colors (which vary from very dark to extremely fair) that one can see in African America. Per U.S. law and federal judicial decisions, "one drop" of African lineage made a person black in the United States from the dawn of the republic until the late 1960s. Indeed, European ancestry among African Americans came to be represented primarily through Irish, British, and French surnames, even in cases in which the black person in question possessed alabaster skin, blue eyes, and blonde hair. The numbers of consensual interracial relationships and marriages, interracial children, and people identifying as biracial or multiracial have grown exponentially since the civil rights movement, which shattered most of the old barriers to interracial relationships and marriage. Such relationships became even more prevalent beginning in the late 1960s, when the U.S. Supreme Court ruled against antimiscegenation laws that still remained on the books in its landmark *Loving v. Virginia* case in 1967.

Changing demographics even evoked response from the federal government. In 2000, for the first time in American history, the U.S. Census acknowledged that its citizens could be of multiple races, though scholars continue to identify "race" as socially constructed. Of the 36,419,434 Americans who identified themselves as black or African American, 34,658,190 described themselves as nothing else. Yet 1,761,244, or 4.8 percent of these respondents, classified themselves as black *and* something else. Interestingly, a disproportionate number of these respondents were young and lived in the West. The issue of multiracial identification remains complex and controversial. Indeed, two percent of the population that identified themselves singularly as black also identified as Latino. Further, 18.5 percent of African Americans who declared themselves to be multiracial described themselves as Latino. This means that individuals who share African American and Latino heritage identify themselves differently, or understand their racial heritage in varied ways.

Apparently the Census Bureau could not process this information, as it abandoned reporting on people identifying as multiracial after the 2000 census. By 2001 the Census Bureau declared that America's largest racial minority group was Latinos, whose numbers reached 37 million, surpassing the 36 million black Americans. These numbers were deceiving, however, because Latinos, in U.S. Census information, could actually belong to any race. Black Americans numbered nearly 38 million when people who identified as multiracial, including Latino, were taken into consideration.

Black Americans have always comprised an ethnically diverse community. By the first decade of the twenty-first century, this ethnic diversity was displayed in striking detail. Black Americans spoke many different languages, lived in every region of the nation, and hailed from regions across the globe. In 2000, 2.2 million people, or 6.3 percent of America's black population, were "foreign born." This percentage reflected an increase from 4.9 percent in 1990. Most foreign-born blacks came from the West Indies and Africa. Immigrant status does not always easily reveal socioeconomic information, however. In 1999 immigrants from Africa tended to be better educated than "native-born" Americans of all races. Despite that fact that Africans were the best-educated immigrants in the United States, they earned less than immigrants from Europe and blacks born in America. It must be noted, however, that the nearly 1 million African immigrants in the United States in 2000 who relocated of their own accord reflect a significant percentage of "African Americans" and could quite literally claim the term *African American* as their own. By 2002 Nigeria (8,129), Ethiopia (7,574), Egypt (4,875), Somalia (4,537), and Ghana (4,256) dispatched the largest numbers of African immigrants to the United States.

Not unlike other immigrants to America, Africans send a good portion of their earnings to struggling family members in their homeland. In total, Africans send approximately $1 billion to the continent annually. They also routinely embrace negative stereotypes of American-born blacks, whom they often consider lazy and prone to "bellyaching," even as so-called native-born black Americans routinely ridicule black immigrants as inferior, smug, and ungrateful for the opportunities that they enjoy as beneficiaries of the black American freedom struggle. Such stereotypes, combined with competition for jobs, economic resources, housing, and educational opportunities, create tensions within America's heterogeneous African American communities. African immigration promises to alter the nation's longstanding definition of what constitutes an African American. Such immigrants embody and underscore the salience and relevance of ethnicity and culture among African Americans.

Black Feminism and Gay and Lesbian Rights

Like African and Caribbean immigrants, the black feminist movement and the gay rights movement have contested conventional notions of racial identity during the close of the twentieth and the beginning of the twenty-first centuries. Both movements sprang forth from the civil rights movement, but, in addition to race, each emphasizes distinct facets of a person's identity, namely their gender and sexual orientation.

A new wave of feminism emerged on the American political landscape in the 1960s and 1970s, transforming gender relations in the United States. The 1964 Civil Rights Act outlawed sexual as well as racial discrimination in employment, but the elimination of sexual discrimination was not an explicit goal of the civil rights movement at the time; in fact, congressional leaders who opposed the Civil Rights Act included mention of sexual discrimination in an effort to reduce the law's chances of passage. Nevertheless, the inclusion of gender-specific language helped broaden discussions of civil rights to include the gender discrimination that had oppressed women for generations. Many white female activists in SNCC and other civil rights groups assumed leading roles in the emerging feminist movement, often employing the same strategies and tactics that had worked in the struggle against white supremacy.

The so-called second wave of feminism, which occurred during the 1960s and 1970s, achieved many important changes during the height of its influence. Whereas first-wave feminism strived to overturn legal barriers to gender equality, second-wave feminism also attacked unofficial gender inequality. The National Organization for Women, cofounded in 1966 by black activist Pauli Murray, fought employment discrimination; advocated for safe, effective, and legal forms of birth control; lobbied for federal- and state-supported child care; and promoted women's privacy and abortion rights. One of the movement's most important early victories was Title IX of the Educational Amendments of 1972, which required colleges and universities to ensure equal access for women. The movement also hailed the Supreme Court's ruling in *Roe v. Wade*, which legalized abortion, as one of its victories.

While the feminist movement went far toward liberating American women from the clutches of male domination in the social, legal, political, and, to a lesser extent, economic spheres, it had its critics. Conservative men and women had bitterly opposed the ultimately unsuccessful Equal Rights Amendment to the Constitution, which sought to guarantee equal rights under the law for Americans regardless of sex, and to promote equality of the sexes. Further, tension and conflict developed between second-wave feminists and the third-wave feminists who succeeded them after 1980. The latter generation criticized their second-wave predecessors for their unwillingness to acknowledge the differences among women due to race, ethnicity, class, nationality, and sexual orientation. Moreover, disagreement between feminists and their conservative detractors endures. Black feminists helped give life to modern feminism, yet, unlike their white counterparts, they also called attention to the inextricable link between patriarchy, racism, and economic oppression.

To the chagrin of most black women, leading white feminists routinely ignored racism as a legitimate and urgent problem, and black male leaders proved to be hesitant at best on matters of gender equality. Elaine Brown, a former Black Panther leader, revealed, "A woman in the black power movement was considered at best irrelevant. A woman asserting herself was a pariah."[33] Most white feminists regarded sexism as their leading nemesis, while most black men believed that racism was African Americans' chief adversary. These attitudes failed to acknowledge, or to respond accordingly to, the dual nature of black women's oppression. Some black men, in their zeal and haste to affirm their own manhood and self-worth, even argued that black feminists, as they fought for their rights and dignity, were complicit in the emasculation of black men. "It is true that our husbands, fathers, brothers and sons have been emasculated, lynched, and brutalized," black feminist Frances Beale has responded. "They have suffered from the cruelest assault on mankind that the world has ever known. However, it is a gross distortion fact to state that black women oppressed black men."[34] Black feminist scholars, writers, entertainers, and activists fought within and outside the civil rights, black power, and feminist movements to fight the sexism and racism prevalent in each one.

Black feminists continued their organizing throughout the late twentieth and early twenty-first centuries. The National Black Feminist Organization (NBFO), founded in 1973, advocated on behalf of black women and confronted a range of issues, including the sexual harassment and violation of black women; intraracial conflict over skin tone, facial features, and hair texture; interracial dating and marriage between black men and white women; and economic inequalities between black and white women. The NBFO also rejected the myth of the black matriarchy, as well as condemning racist and sexist depictions of black women in popular culture. The organization had a brief life span, dissolving by 1975. Nevertheless, it played a key role in promoting spirited dialogue and activism among black feminists. Thanks to the activism and organizing efforts of their predecessors, black feminists today speak widely about racism, sexism, domestic violence, sexual harassment, and rape, and also about political representation and economic empowerment. They continue to educate those who will listen, explaining that, as UCLA law professor Kimberlé Crenshaw argued, "When feminism does not explicitly oppose racism, and when antiracism does not incorporate opposition to patriarchy, race and gender politics often end up being antagonistic to each other and both interests lose."[35]

In addition to feminism, the civil rights movement also motivated gays and lesbians to emerge from the margins of American society to combat homophobia as well as the suffering and violence it generated. Gay and lesbian people had been persecuted and had lived in seclusion throughout U.S. history; the gay and lesbian movement exploded in New York's Greenwich Village on June 28, 1969, when a multiracial gathering of gays and lesbians at Stonewall Inn, a local hotel turned nightclub, defended themselves physically against local police officers' longstanding efforts to exploit and terrorize them. By 1980 the movement that grew out of the Stonewall riots had pushed cities and states throughout America to pass legislation that decriminalized homosexual activity and forbade discrimination on the basis of sexual orientation in places of public accommodation and employment. Though tensions existed between gay men and lesbians within the movement, these activists were largely effective at working jointly to fight for recognition and equal treatment, even in the face of staunch conservative opposition, which was particularly fostered by the conservative Christian right.

Black members of the lesbian, gay, bisexual, transgendered, and queer (LGBTQ) community, however, were often marginalized and discriminated against by white members of this demonized population, as well as by heterosexual Americans. As within the feminist movement, the gay and lesbian movement was dominated by members of the white middle class. Although virulently racist members of the gay and lesbian communities existed, the movement itself did not embrace the prevailing racism of the era. Rather, white members of the gay and lesbian movement tended to subordinate antiracism, or to ignore race altogether, in their overall fight for gay and lesbian rights. In other words, black gays and lesbians found themselves forgotten in the struggle against homophobia. To address this problem, grassroots organizers Billy Jones and Delores Berry formed the National Coalition of Black Gays (NCBG) in 1978. The NCBG gave rise to local organizations in Washington DC and Baltimore, Maryland. In 1979 the NCBG was the leading organizer of the first March on Washington for gay rights. In the 1980s the NCBG added *Lesbian* to its name to become the National Coalition of Black Lesbians and Gays (NCBLG).

Many African American leaders and organizations, including John Lewis, Jesse Jackson, Eleanor Holmes Norton, and executives of the NAACP, championed the NCLBG's goals and efforts. These leaders, like many black people, believed that the rights of gay and lesbians were fundamentally linked to the rights of everyone, and, therefore, rallied to their cause. Those within the gay and lesbian movement, as well as more mainstream civil rights activists, called for an end to employment discrimination, education, health care, housing, and places of public accommodation for any reason, including sexual orientation. In 2002 Coretta Scott King, in a speech before the National Gay and Lesbian Task Force, argued that the fate of black gays and lesbians, feminists and nationalists, and all who hunger for a nation and world free from discrimination and persecution, were bound in a single garment of destiny: "I believe very strongly that all forms of bigotry and discrimination are equally wrong and should be opposed by right-thinking Americans everywhere. Freedom from discrimination based on sexual orientation is surely a fundamental human right in any great democracy, as much as freedom from racial, religious, gender, or ethnic discrimination."[36]

King's speech on behalf of all Americans dramatized the progress that black Americans had made by the twenty-first century, and the many changes that lay ahead. By 2008 many African Americans celebrated the fruits of their long struggle for freedom and equality in the United States, the fulfillment of aspects of Martin Luther King's dream. A great deal had changed since Du Bois first spoke of black people's double consciousness at the dawn of the twentieth century. When Du Bois put forth this notion, most Africans suffered under the yoke of European colonialism, and African Americans, who had recently emerged from the brutality of bondage, found themselves again oppressed under the cruelty of Jim Crow. But thanks to the dogged determination of those African Americans who refused to accept their second-class citizenship, 143 years after the ratification of the Thirteenth Amendment to the Constitution of the United States, black Americans held the power to sway political elections and influence the formation of U.S. foreign policy to Africa, their ancestral homeland. The black middle class continued to grow, and a relatively small yet critical mass of rich and powerful African Americans influenced public policy, big business, and popular all facets of culture.

Even as unprecedented gains were made, however, many black Americans struggled to overcome the problems associated with disproportionate levels of joblessness, poverty, broken families, substandard housing and homelessness, poor educational opportunities, delinquency, and crime. The criminal justice system and the prison-industrial complex, therefore, increasingly controlled the lives of millions of black people, and especially of African American men. Even many so-called successful blacks, who benefited from the gains of the civil rights and black power movements, battled angst and anxiety associated with knowledge of isolated acts of racist terrorism, subtle manifestations of bigotry and racial profiling, and limits in the opportunities available to break the "glass ceiling" as they sought to rise to the pinnacle of their occupations and professions.

As black Americans liberated themselves from the shackles of historic oppression, they were challenged by new transformations in American society and beyond. The Million Man and Million Woman Marches reflected a renewed sense of collectivism and common purpose among black Americans even as increasingly diverse African American communities ushered in new attitudes and divisions. The introduction of Africans to America, and the crucible in which they fought for survival and carved out a future, transformed African people in America into African Americans, a distinct people who remained fundamentally linked to their African past and their counterparts in the African Diaspora. The circumstances that influence black America today may very well transform the community, and its identity, yet again into something that will lead America and the world to new levels of inclusion and development.[37]

8

HOPE AND CHANGE

The New Millennium and Freedom's Promise

> This union may never be perfect, but generation after generation
> has shown that it can always be perfected.
>
> —BARACK OBAMA, "A More Perfect Union," March 18, 2008

On February 10, 2007, Barack Obama announced his candidacy for President of the United States in front of the state capitol building in Springfield, Illinois. The announcement site was extremely meaningful because it was also where Abraham Lincoln, in 1858, had delivered his historic "House Divided" speech. Obama's campaign promised progressive change and a fundamental shift in America's political culture. He pledged to bring all Americans of all persuasions together in common cause for freedom and democracy, end U.S. participation in the war in Iraq, increase the nation's energy independence, and provide universal health care.[1]

Obama's campaign stunned political pundits and experts with its broad-based appeal and fundraising acumen. He took in a record $58 million during the first half of 2007, and he set another fundraising record in January 2008 with $36 million. The latter was the most ever raised by a presidential candidate in one month during a Democratic primary. Obama's principal opponent during the primaries was a formidable senator from New York and former first lady, Hillary Rodham Clinton. The two candidates waged an epic battle for the Democratic nomination, fighting to be either the first African American or the first woman nominated for president by a major political party.

Obama, a relative unknown outside the circle of involved Democrats and the residents of Illinois, proved to be a serious contender early in the primary season. He tied Clinton for delegates in key primaries, including New Hampshire, and secured more delegates than she did in the Iowa, Nevada, and South Carolina primary elections and caucuses. On February's "Super Tuesday," the day that hosts the largest number of elections during the primary campaign, Obama won twenty more delegates than Clinton. After Super Tuesday, he won the eleven primaries and caucuses scheduled for the remainder of February. He and Clinton split delegates and states equally in the March 4 contests of Vermont, Texas, Ohio, and Rhode Island. Obama ended March with victories in Wyoming and Mississippi.[2]

As Obama ascended and revealed himself to be the leading contender for the Democratic nomination, his blackness and American race relations became explicit issues on the campaign trail. Despite his early attempts to present himself as a candidate for a new era who would transcend race, he and his staff were forced to address his racial identity and its meaning for a campaign and a society in which race taxed the mind and ensnared the heart. Indeed, even though people of color and many whites had made tremendous gains since the era of Jim Crow, race and racism still mattered. Race, as Pauli Murray argued, is "the atmosphere one breathes from day to day, the pervasive irritant, the chronic allergy, the vague apprehension which makes one uncomfortable and jumpy. We know that the race problem is like a deadly snake coiled and ready to strike, and one avoids its dangers only by never-ending watchfulness."[3] Obama did not want his race to define his bid, but America's racist fixation on his heritage and associations forced him to discuss the relevance of race in the 2008 election, something he did with honesty and insight.

Early in the primary, African Americans found themselves divided in their support for Obama. Most blacks had long supported the Clintons for their symbolic and strategic support of African Americans. Other black people scrutinized Obama's racial identity, questioned his "authenticity" as a black man, and withheld support as a result. Black-oriented radio shows, National Public Radio, scholarly forums, Sunday morning news shows, and religious leaders weighed in on his racial legitimacy. Obama's biracial heritage, and his immigrant Kenyan father, gave many so-called native blacks pause, as his heritage did not parallel that of most people of African descent born in the United States. Some African Americans argued that only a black candidate whose ancestors had been enslaved in America, or one who had experienced firsthand the pain associated with this nation's racial past, could genuinely understand what it means to be black in America and to represent the political interests of African Americans.[4]

Other blacks, however, believed that this notion was narrow-minded and divisive. They argued that, at a time when black Americans, whether by birth or by choice, were moving to channel their collective political capital into a formidable voting bloc, they could ill afford to squander time arguing about who was "really" black. Nevertheless, a number of black scholars, religious leaders, and critics dissected Obama's every move. Charles Ogletree, a Harvard law professor, and Michael Mitchell, an Arizona State University political science professor, came to Obama's defense by noting that his record, particularly as it related to civil rights, was consistent with the voting patterns of the majority of African Americans. It was Obama himself, however, who succeeded in convincing the majority of black Americans to support his campaign. He proved himself to be a legitimate candidate, and he delivered a direct and rhetorically remarkable speech on race relations in America, entitled "A More Perfect Union," (appendix 7, page 323) on March 18, 2008. In the address, Obama spoke directly and candidly about who he was and where he came from:

> I am the son of a black man from Kenya and a white woman from Kansas. I was raised with the help of a white grandfather who survived a Depression to serve in Patton's Army during World War II and a white grandmother who worked on a bomber assembly line at Fort Leavenworth while he was overseas. I've gone to some of the best schools in America and lived in one of the world's poorest nations. I am married to a black American who carries within her the blood of slaves and slaveowners—an inheritance we pass on to our two precious daughters. I have brothers, sisters, nieces, nephews, uncles and cousins, of every race and every hue, scattered across three continents, and for as long as I live, I will never forget that in no other country on Earth is my story even possible.[5]

Many black Americans decided to endorse Obama's candidacy following public statements made by Bill and Hillary Clinton that angered them and exacerbated white racial fears. After Obama's victory in the South Carolina Democratic primary, Bill Clinton reminded observers that "Jesse Jackson won South Carolina in '84 and '88,"[6] though he ultimately failed to secure the Democratic nomination. Many black people believed that Clinton's implicit message was that the African American vote was insufficient to propel Jackson, Obama, or any other black presidential candidate to the Democratic nomination, and was therefore insignificant. Large numbers of blacks also believed that Clinton's message was meant to imply to white voters that their ballots would be wasted on Obama, who did not, as conventional wisdom held, have a realistic chance of winning. On the eve of the 2008 West Virginia primary, Hillary Clinton further angered many black people when she appealed to working-class white voters by labeling Obama an "elitist." Most African Americans viewed this as a duplicitous code word that disparaged Obama as "uppity": a black person who does not know his or her "place."

Even as Obama gained increasing momentum and prepared to clinch the Democratic nomination, America played host to a flurry of racist comments, editorials, and actions directed against the candidate, his family, and all African Americans. T-shirts depicting Obama as Curious George, the cartoon monkey, were printed and sold in the South; conservative talk-show host Bill O'Reilly referenced "a lynching party"[7] in comments he made about Michelle Obama; conservative pundit Ed Hill characterized the fist bump that Michelle Obama shared with Barack after a campaign speech as a "terrorist fist jab"[8]; the Fox News network ran a caption under televised video footage of Michelle Obama that identified her as "Obama's Baby Mama"; and an "art" exhibit in New York City explicitly disparaged the candidate's children, the artist displaying a giant photograph of the Obama couple's young daughters, Sasha and Malia, under a caption reading "Nappy Headed Hos."[9] Though many campaign offices have been vandalized in the course of a campaign, Obama's campaign offices were defaced with racist epithets.

Obama revealed little if any anger or bitterness over these acts as he continued to vie for the nomination. In April, May, and June, he won the North Carolina, Oregon, and Montana primaries, established a sizeable lead in the number of pledged delegates and super delegate endorsements, and on June 3, passed the threshold to become the presumptive Democratic nominee. That day, he delivered a passionate victory speech amid thunderous applause in St. Paul, Minnesota. Clinton reluctantly suspended her campaign and endorsed her opponent on June 7, calling on her fellow Democrats to "declare together with one voice right here, right now, that Barack Obama is our candidate and he will be our president."[10] Assaults upon Obama's character and values continued beyond the primary season. On September 4 Republican Representative Lynn Westmoreland of Georgia dispensed with white supremacist subterfuge, stating clearly and unapologetically that Michelle and Barack Obama were "uppity."[11]

Nevertheless, on Thursday, August 28, 2008, a date marking the forty-fifth anniversary of Martin Luther King Jr.'s "I Have a Dream" speech, Barack Obama took the stage at Invesco Field at Mile High Stadium in Denver, Colorado, alongside his running mate, Senator Joe Biden of Delaware, and accepted the Democratic Party's nomination for president. In doing so, he became the first African American to lead a major party ticket. That night at the Democratic National Convention, Obama addressed an estimated eighty-four thousand people, many of whom cheered, embraced, and even cried as they affirmed Obama's nomination and celebrated the transcendent moment as one of the most historic and electric nights in U.S. history. His speech was viewed on television and the Internet by more than thirty-eight million people; even Republican observers hailed the achievement. For his part, former president Bill Clinton described Obama's accomplishment as "a 21st-century incarnation of the old-fashioned American dream. His achievements are proof of our continuing progress toward the more perfect union of our founders' dreams. Barack Obama will lead us away from the division and fear of the last eight years back to unity and hope."[12]

After accepting the Democratic presidential nomination, Obama immediately turned his attention to Senator John McCain of Arizona, the Republican nominee for president, and McCain's running mate, Governor Sarah Palin of Alaska, whose candidacies were announced just days later. The contrasts between the two candidates went beyond the political to the personal. McCain was an extremely wealthy, surly, seventy-one-year-old white former Navy pilot and Vietnam prisoner of war. Obama, in contrast, was a young, charismatic, seemingly unflappable black man from a broken home and humble beginnings who rose from poverty and dislocation to graduate from Harvard Law School and become a professor and community organizer in Chicago. Obama and McCain waged a closely contested battle between August and November 2008. Obama criticized McCain as out of touch and in league with George W. Bush's failed economic and foreign policy. McCain attacked Obama as inexperienced, too liberal, and dangerous by virtue of his extremely limited associations with William "Bill" Ayers, a 1960s radical turned university professor who engaged in acts of domestic terrorism when Obama was eight years old, and his relationship with the minister of the church the Obamas attended in Chicago, the militant Reverend Jeremiah Wright.

In the end, McCain could not withstand Obama's momentum, message of redemption, and ability to tap into the American people's disappointment and yearning for a new direction. On November 4, 2008, Barack Obama won the presidential election by a wide margin in the popular vote and with a slim edge in the Electoral College, becoming the forty-fourth president of the United States of America. In the process, Obama also became the first African American to serve in the nation's highest office. Several factors led to Obama's victory. The election transpired amid a severe economic crisis, U.S.-waged wars in Iraq and Afghanistan, the eroding prestige of America in international affairs, and an increasing polarization that fostered narrow cynicism about the nation's prospects for a brighter future. Try as he did, McCain could not separate himself from the failed economic and foreign policies of the Bush administration and its extremely unpopular head (by the time George W. Bush left office, his presidential performance approval ratings were at an all-time low). In addition, nearly all African Americans who voted chose to cast their ballots for Obama. The senator from Illinois also garnered the majority of young voters, organized labor, teachers, urbanites, women, liberal and moderate whites, and other people of color. His message of change resonated, and the diversity he embodied gave faith to many that his election would reaffirm the American dream in ways that the election of McCain never could have.[13]

Perhaps more significant, however, was that McCain's Republican base was divided and in some cases in disarray. Long perceived as a firebrand Republican spoiler, McCain undermined party unity in the pursuit of his own often unpredictable and centrist brand of conservatism. His selection of the largely unknown, inexperienced, and highly ideological Sarah Palin merely alienated more of his Republican peers, particularly "intellectual Republicans" who bristled at Palin's unimpressive pedigree, naïveté, and lack of "ideas." The consequence of these perceptions and actions was the defection of moderate and intellectual Republicans and right-leaning Independents toward the Democratic ticket. Unlike McCain, Obama united his party behind his candidacy. Despite the testy 2008 primary and consequent internal divisions, virtually all wings of the Democratic Party threw their support behind Obama, even if they felt reservations about the candidate. To garner the support of moderate Republicans and

FIG. 34. With his family by his side, Barack Obama is sworn in as the forty-fourth president of the United States by Chief Justice John Roberts, January 20, 2009. Department of Defense photo by M.Sgt. Cecilio Ricardo, U.S. Air Force/Released (090120-F-MJ260-919).

conservative Democrats, Obama touted personal responsibility, calling attention to the problems associated with single-parent households and "deadbeat dads" in black America and beyond. Furthermore, he handled each potential problem in his campaign proactively and gracefully.

"We are in the midst of a crisis, our nation is at war, our economy is badly weakened, our health care is too costly, our schools fail too many, [and] the ways we use energy strengthen our adversaries and threaten our planet." President Obama spoke these words after being sworn into office on Tuesday, January 20, 2009, on the west front of the U.S. Capitol, in front of a record 1.8 million people (fig. 34). During his address, Obama also indicated that "less measurable but no less profound is a sapping of confidence across our land, a nagging fear that America's decline is inevitable, and that the next generation must lower its sights."

Then, Obama switched gears, adding a positive light to the address. "The challenges we face are real. They are serious and they are many. They will not be met easily or in a short span of time. But know this, America, they will be met." The new president reminded listeners that America's history of overcoming adversity is rich and instructive. He recalled the immigrants who built the nation and those who "fought and died in places like Concord and Gettysburg; Normandy and Khe Sanh. They saw America as bigger than the sum of our individual ambitions; greater than all the differences of birth or wealth or faction."[14]

As historian Peniel Joseph has argued, perhaps the most arresting aspect of the inauguration was the remarkable symbolism of the nation beholding a black man take the oath of office and deliver an inaugural address. "Both ordinary Americans along with celebrities and entertainers stood on the National Mall to take in what the *Wall Street Journal* described as a 'Glimpse of History.' Obama's racial biography in effect presented the nation with a democratic moment once considered unimaginable." As he stood tall high upon the western face of the Capitol building, every word Obama spoke and every gesture he made held enormous symbolic importance. Indeed, as Joseph argues, "Juxtaposed against Washington's still predominantly white cast of political power brokers and economic and social bureaucrats, Obama's physical presence offered both a refreshingly jarring portrait of change as well as a stark reminder of how rigid and enduring America's racial boundaries remain."[15]

President Obama's historic campaign, election, and moving inaugural address led many people to wonder whether he would sustain that same level of passion and success throughout his presidency. Moreover, the likelihood of racial progress, resolution, and even the elimination of race as a social construct altogether loomed over Obama's first two years in office. Transcending the racial symbolism of America's first African American president were numerous political crises, including wars in Iraq and Afghanistan, a lurking financial recession that proved to be the worst economic disaster since the Great Depression, and a cornucopia of global emergencies from Middle East conflicts to African genocide. Despite these problems, race continued to play a role in shaping the administration's first two years.

Obama's first twenty-four months in office were remarkable by any standard; increasingly intense and organized opposition from the far right and resistance from members of his own party did not halt progress. Obama and his Democratic allies in Congress appeared to deliver on many of the President's promises early on, compiling a substantial record of achievement, especially in regard to public policy. Still, two controversies, in particular, offer stunning glances of a nation struggling with the reality of electing its first black president outside the jubilation of inauguration-day revelry.

Obama's American Recovery and Reinvestment Act, passed on February 13, 2009, appropriated $260 billion in relief for American families reeling from the economic downturn, including a popular tax relief payment of $400 for individuals and $800 for families. Overall, the Recovery and Reinvestment Act contained many of the key points promoted by Obama during his campaign, and it brought the financial system back from the brink of collapse. On February 18, however, a *New York Post* cartoon depicting two police officers shooting a chimpanzee incited yet another national debate over Obama and race. "They'll have to find someone else to write the next stimulus bill," one of the cartoon officers declared. At its most nonthreatening, the cartoon commentary satirized the recent passage of President Obama's stimulus bill along with tales of a crazed chimpanzee from Connecticut who had mauled an innocent victim. Critics alleged that the chimp signified a caricature of the president and exploited festering anxiety that his huge personal triumph would eventually end in violence.

Leading black political and cultural activists, such as Spike Lee and Al Sharpton, called for a boycott of the *New York Post*. Their denunciation of the newspaper led to a partial editorial retraction that apologized "to those who were offended by the cartoon" though they unwaveringly maintained that "sometimes a cartoon is just a cartoon, even as the opportunists seek to make it something else." Obama chose not to insert himself into this uproar. He believed that it was more prudent to deliver another "race speech" when it was truly warranted. In the meantime, the *Post*'s "apology" cagily drew distinctions between Americans who could be understandably insulted by the cartoon and racial opportunists.

The controversy over the *New York Post* cartoon underscored the evolving yet static nature of race relations in the Obama age.[16] Expectations that his election would lead to a new era of "postracial" American politics crashed into a national history bursting with racial suspicions, anxieties, and fear. For African Americans, Peniel Joseph argues,

> The implicit equation of the nation's first black president with a chimp evoked painful memories of a not-too-distant past where blacks, regardless of their social standing, were compared to animals. During Reconstruction and continuing onto the long period of Jim Crow, blacks were

FIG. 35. Hundreds of demonstrators gathered outside *New York Post* headquarters to protest a controversial chimpanzee cartoon in the newspaper, February 19, 2009. Protestors said the cartoon in the tabloid was racist and linked President Obama with a violent chimpanzee that was shot dead by police. Photo by Mario Tama/ Getty Images 84927677.

caricaturized as brutes, beasts, and savages who were unworthy of citizenship. Far from being cultural artifacts from a buried racial past, such depictions of black Americans persisted well into the twentieth century, when civil rights activists such as Martin Luther King Jr. were characterized as coons and the NAACP were referred to as "planet of the apes." More than simply painful reminders of the past, these dehumanizing portrayals of blacks remain part of the nation's racial imagination.[17]

The same day that the *New York Post*'s alleged depiction of Obama as a chimp was published, Joseph points out, Attorney General Eric Holder gave a passionate keynote address at the Department of Justice in commemoration of Black History Month. Holder, America's first black attorney general, suggested that "to get to the heart of this country one must examine its racial soul," and then proceeded to attempt to make such an earnest assessment himself. Despite America's multicultural composition, its citizens remained "a nation of cowards" with regard to race, too afraid of the penalties associated with racial directness. Holder spoke of the racial milestones made by the United States since the 1954 *Brown* Supreme Court decision, but nevertheless acknowledged that America "has still not come to grips with its racial past," and that this reticence reflected a historic averseness to deal directly with race matters.[18]

Black History Month should be used to inspire a national dialogue about race, Holder maintained, particularly since de facto segregation continues to be a mainstay of American society. Through a comprehensive exploration of the ways in which slavery, Jim Crow, and civil rights protests reconditioned democracy in America, the Attorney General posited that black history offered a framework to reconceptualize America's racial limits as it advanced in the direction of a more inclusive future.

Joseph asserts that Holder's bluntness echoed Obama's celebrated "race speech" of 2008, but the response was much more divisive. Liberals applauded his comments as courageous and necessary for the advancement of race relations in America. Many went so far as to suggest that his more piercing references to slavery and racism made his homily more potent than Obama's. Conservative critics, however, attacked the speech as biased, inflammatory, and jaded. These detractors drew attention to Holder's interpretation of America as a "nation of cowards" concerning race relations as especially distasteful.

The controversy surrounding the *Post* cartoon and Holder's speech, Joseph argues, illuminates persisting limitations on the national conversation about race. If the age of Obama assured a more progressive, multifaceted, and refined dialogue about American race relations, the promise has not been kept. Instead, Americans have recoiled back to a post–civil rights era impasse. The lofty symbolism of Obama's election only momentarily confined the politics of racial hostility and xenophobia that have sullied America's electoral process since the dawn of the republic. As president, Obama has been less impervious to racism's more routine manifestations. This includes a national inability and unwillingness to discuss not only America's past racial misfortunes but also the nation's evolving racial drama.[19]

Indeed, when Republican South Carolina congressman Joe Wilson shouted, "You lie!" during President Obama's health care speech to Congress on September 9, 2009, "members of both major parties condemned the heckling. After the speech, Wilson issued a statement apologizing for his outburst. 'This evening, I let my emotions get the best of me when listening to the president's remarks regarding the coverage of illegal immigrants in the health care bill,'" Wilson stated. "While I disagree with the president's statements, my comments were inappropriate and regrettable. I extend sincere apologies to the president for this lack of civility."[20] Obama remained relatively silent on this issue and stayed above the fray, but the episode left many Americans, particularly black people, beside themselves with anger and indignation. Few could remember a president who had been subjected to such blatant and visceral contempt during nationally televised address to the nation, especially by a seated member of the U.S. Congress. In the eyes of African Americans, Wilson's rant was inspired by racism, even as the congressman cloaked his "lack of civility" in his seemingly legitimate opposition to Obama's health care proposal. To those who claimed that Wilson was simply a partisan politician who lost his temper, many African American activists pointed out that Wilson earned notoriety in his home state of South Carolina in the late 1990s when, as a state legislator, he was one of the staunchest defenders of the practice of flying the Confederate battle flag over the state capitol. Wilson, however, did more than vote to keep the Confederate flag. He went so far as to appear to defend the Confederacy, declaring in November of 1999 that "the Confederate heritage is very honorable."[21]

Obama's relative silence and Wilson's belligerence reflect America's narrative of race, as told by politicians, as a benign or triumphant story of redemption that stresses universal themes of citizenship, democracy, national unity, and honor. Holder's forthright speech, however, avoided themes of victorious self-felicitations in favor of condemning racism's contemporary face. The fact that Holder's speech engendered an assortment of responses is not unexpected, especially when one considers Obama's reluctance to address race and racism directly and with the same level of candor.

Still, Obama's first two years in office provided several opportunities for the president to remind Americans of how far the nation and African Americans had come, even if these occasions were not deliberate. April 29, 2009 marked the one hundredth day of the Obama administration. It was also the anniversary of a somber episode in U.S. history. Seventeen years earlier, in the wake of a not-guilty verdict of police officers charged with thrashing a defenseless Rodney King, Los Angeles had erupted in racially inspired violence that surpassed anything American had seen since the height of the Civil Rights Movement. "During the spring of 1992," Joseph recalls, "smoldering fires and black plumes of smoke dotted parts of the city's landscape. This formed a portrait of urban decay and racial tensions that echoed the worst aspects of the 1960s."[22] During and immediately after the riots, few could have envisioned that two decades later America's first African American president would hold a press conference observing his first one hundred days as commander and chief.

Despite these symbolic measures of racial progress and Obama's substantive achievements, the president continued to incur the wrath of an emboldened and resentful right and to face the frustrations of the left, whose hopes for progressive change exceeded Obama's capacity to deliver. During the spring of 2009, for instance, Obama convinced Congress to provide a $50 million subsidy designed to rescue the Big Three American automakers—Ford, General Motors, and Chrysler—from complete collapse, although in the end Ford did not accept the assistance while GM and Chrysler went through bankruptcy proceedings. That summer, Congress passed Obama's sweeping universal health care package, the Patient Protection and Affordable Care Act, the first of its kind in U.S. history, and Obama oversaw reform of the nation's federal student loan programs, making it possible for more Americans to attend college.

Despite these achievements, Obama continued to be subjected to some of the most intense and racially charged criticism of a sitting president in recent history. School districts in predominantly white communities across the United States required parental permission for students to watch and listen to Obama's speeches. Due to his African heritage, conservative activists, politicians, and pundits continued to demand evidence of the president's American citizenship, and many white Americans continue to believe, despite evidence to the contrary, that Obama is Muslim and that Michelle Obama is a "black power radical."

During 2010 President Obama's popularity began to slip. This slippage could be seen through two indicators. The first indicator was the gubernatorial elections that took place in November. The Democratic Party lost the governors' races in ten states where Democrats previously held the office. The second indicator was that Democrats also lost control of the House of Representatives. William A. Galston, a senior fellow of the Brookings Institution, attributes the decline in the popularity of the president and his Democratic allies to unrealistic expectations, on the one hand, and bigotry, on the other.[23] First, mainstream liberals, Obama's most loyal supporters, drew attention to the historic number and nature of problems that Obama inherited upon taking the oath of office. One of the most prominent issues Obama's administration faced was an acute economic crisis. The administration faced a greater challenge because, unlike a typical cyclical recession, this economic downturn was brought on by a financial crisis. This meant that recovery from the recession would take longer to achieve, as measures to upturn the economy unfolded gradually, leaving lingering high employment rates. This economic disaster decimated the nation's wealth. Obama and the federal government took controversial and expensive measures to avoid a complete collapse of the financial system, ballooning deficits, and increased debt in ways that most Americans found confusing and distressing. This distress and confusion yielded negative perceptions about the Obama administration, although others would argue that these harsh criticisms are not an accurate reflection of the administration's effectiveness. As the Brookings Institution's Thomas Mann argued:

> The simple fact is that no leader or governing party thrives politically in difficult economic times. Citizens today are understandably scared, sour, and deeply pessimistic about our economic future. The well-documented successes of the financial stabilization and stimulus initiatives are invisible to a public reacting to the here and now, not to the counterfactual of how much worse it might have been. The painfully slow recovery from the global financial crisis and Great Recession have led most Americans to believe these programs have failed and as a consequence they judge the president and Congress harshly.[24]

Advocates of this line of argument maintain that Obama and the Democrats were primarily the victims of forces not of their doing and beyond their control. Indeed, as Galston stated:

> Although they did everything in their power to restart the engine of growth, the economic clock is running more slowly than is the political clock, generating widespread discontent and a huge voter backlash. There is a political as well as an economic dimension to this thesis. A large part of Obama's appeal to independents and moderates was his promise to reduce the level of partisanship in Washington. Unfortunately for him, he couldn't deliver bipartisanship on his own, and (so runs the argument), the Republicans' decision to oppose his every initiative, starting on Day One, made it impossible for him to redeem his pledge.[25]

Republicans believed that because Obama and the Democrats controlled the executive and legislative branches of government, voters would hold them accountable for sustaining partisan power struggles. They were right. Even though the political gridlock was not Obama's fault, many Americans directed their discontent and partisan animosity toward him and the Democratic leadership.

It was obvious from the moment that Barack Obama was elected that he would be under a microscope held by the Republican Party. Despite his promises to be the president of all of the citizens of the United States of America, and wanting to unify "red America," and "blue America," he had an uphill battle on his hands. Barack Obama, who had always been able to inspire with his words, may have underestimated the opposition to his presidency and the desire of many to see him fail at all costs. Perhaps he underestimated the chasm that existed between the two major political parties.

Barack Obama ran his campaign based upon his desire for "change." The ability to change distinguishes the two political parties. The Democratic Party, which is generally considered more liberal than the Republican Party, is seen by most as more amenable to change. The divide between red states (Republican) and blue states (Democratic) proved to be more pronounced than the new administration anticipated. Indeed, the administration's efforts to move the nation in a different direction proved to be more contentious than they could have foreseen. President Obama had difficulty in designing, marketing, and implementing policy that would be palatable to both parties, and in achieving the changes that he wanted. The Democratic Party, though supportive of most of his policy proposals and quest for change, was often outmaneuvered and stymied by Republicans and the nascent Tea Party, an amalgamation of ultraconservative political activists and operatives, who made obstructing Obama's agenda their number one priority.

Another reason for Obama's decline can be traced directly to his own party. The extremely liberal side of the Democratic Party was critical of his presidency because they viewed him as too methodical and indecisive. They felt that he was too willing to compromise with Republicans; therefore ideas and substantial change were foiled in the stimulus bill, as well as in health care reform. He was even criticized by a once very famous former supporter, actor Matt Damon. Many believe that he misjudged the willingness of Republicans to compromise with him, and that precious time was wasted on concepts upon which the two sides would never agree. Many also believe that too much time was wasted on debate over universal health care, while topics such as climate change and immigration reform were put on a back burner. Finally, many were disappointed that Obama did not move swiftly to abolish the "don't ask, don't tell" policy; its removal would have ended the ability of the military to remove openly gay and lesbian military personnel. Obama eventually repealed the "don't ask, don't tell" policy on Friday, July 22, 2011. However, these issues, along with lingering economic woes, led to criticism from some members of the Democratic Party early in Obama's presidency.

Another reason Obama's detractors gave for his declining popularity was that they believed he proved to be more liberal and uncompromising than he had advertised himself to be as a candidate. Some believe that his initial efforts to include Republicans resembled a classic bait and switch. Republicans used this argument to help pressure, if not to scare, the American people into rejecting Obama's agenda and to embrace their ideas and proposed remedies for the nation's ills instead. These included the president's ideas on tort reform, health care, and the ability to purchase insurance coverage that traverses state lines. The 9.8 percent rate of unemployment and the continuing high rate of mortgage foreclosures were also detrimental to the president's popularity.

As Barack Obama's presidency moved further away from the pageantry reflected in his inauguration, the Republican Party ceased its kinder, gentler stance and reverted back to its hard-line conservative ideals with virtually no desire to compromise. Many Republicans were increasingly influenced by the Tea Party, a populist, ultraconservative, grassroots movement that grew out of protests over the economy and quickly consolidated its power over, and control of, many Republican candidates after 2009. Many saw the Tea Party Movement as an overtly racist collection of middle-class to wealthy older white men that had no desire to compromise with Barack Obama.

Great Expectations

Barack Obama entered into the presidency with tremendous fanfare and anticipation. His administration was an administration of firsts in many ways. Much was made of the symbolism of his and his family's every move. His promises of change and hope were open-ended promises, without perimeters. They sky was the limit. Many people who were unfamiliar with how government works were inspired to get involved in politics for the first time. Many expected change to come immediately. These individuals generally had little knowledge of how long change could, and often does, take, especially when political parties are mired in adversarial relationships that are antithetical to cooperation. Change can be excruciatingly slow when interested parties do not agree on what change should be, or when the lenses through which warring parties see are radically divergent. Barack Obama needed the cooperation of the House of Representatives and the Senate to bring about the change that he promised, and the Republican members of these bodies were largely resolute in their often visceral opposition to Obama and his agenda. When change did not come as promised, hope began to wane.

President Obama understood that his campaign rhetoric was ambiguous. After beating Hillary Clinton in the Democratic primary race, the nominee Obama did an interview with the *New York Times*. "I am like a Rorshach test," he said. "Even if people find me disappointing ultimately, they might gain something."[26] The people who voted for Barack Obama raised their expectations so high that the fall that resulted when change was obstructed was a long one. The Obama campaign was comprised of many different groups. Many of these constituents had felt disenfranchised in the past. Each group felt that Obama could deliver the change that they so feverishly desired. The old adage that one "can't please all of the people all of the time," truly reflected the sober reality that characterized the first two years of the Obama administration. The president could not please all of the people who had supported him during the election, and his failure to communicate and to fight uncompromisingly for the issues that they held most dear confused and disappointed many of them. This resulted in Obama's precipitous decline in the polls.

There were additional difficulties, which reflected contemporary political culture more than a reaction to Obama's political agenda. During the "age of Obama," American's belief in their government and in its ability to work for them was at an all-time low. While many admired the president and his goals, they had doubts about the dysfunctional, bureaucratic nature of government and its ability to be responsive to the needs of the people. The president seemed to feel that his charisma and sincerity would offset the distrust that the public held for government.

Economic Challenges

When Barack Obama became president of the United States, the economy was in crisis and the job market, especially for African Americans, was on brink of disaster. The Obama administration acted quickly to enact the American Recovery and Reinvestment Act of 2009. This "stimulus package" extended unemployment benefits, cut taxes for small businesses and working families, underwrote some jobs in public education, and saved many positions in public safety. However, after a short period of time, the bill's effectiveness leveled off. While struggling in an anemic economy, many Americans were also writhing with angst because of their inability to pay their mortgages. The rash of foreclosures that began under the Bush administration, escalated just as Obama entered office. The Obama administration did establish efforts to help with the mortgage crisis, but it underestimated malfeasance among mortgage lenders, and fund that were earmarked for homeowners in crisis never reached those in need. When funds did reach struggling homeowners, they were often insufficient to stave off foreclosure and eviction.

Leadership Style and Lessons Learned

When Barack Obama became president, he entered the office as a perceived and long-awaited instrument of change. Many Americans, tired of the same old cycle of divisiveness in Washington, looked forward to a new era of executive leadership and bipartisanship in the nation's capital. Barack Obama entered the office with an ambitious and sanguine agenda, buttressed by what he believed to be an effective team and strategy that would bring about the societal transformation so many desired. What Obama and his supporters seemed to overlook, however, was the fact that he would have to work with people who did not share the same vision. Not only did they not share his dream for a new and improved America, their agenda could not have been more opposed to the new president's. Barack Obama and his followers could not have foreseen that so many Republicans would do anything in their power to see him fail. Many simply wanted the public to believe that Obama was a fraud: not the great compromiser that he claimed to be, but the "same old tax-and-spend Democrat" that they had known in the past. Indeed, one Obama advisor argued that "it's not what people felt they sent Barack Obama to Washington to do, to be legislator in chief. David Plouffe, the former head of the president's campaign and one of his closest political advisors," supported this sentiment when he admitted, "I do think he's paid a political price for having to be tied to Congress." Many argued that things could not have unfolded in any other way. Another senior aide to the president said, "Here's a guy who ran as an outsider to change Washington who all of a sudden realized that just to deal with these issues, we were going to have to work with Washington."[27] It was extremely difficult for Barack Obama to get legislation passed. He needed the cooperation of both houses of Congress, which seemed like a virtual impossibility. His exemplary oratorical skills, which were first and foremost responsible for his election, were not a free pass to get legislation passed in a political atmosphere defined by opposing ideologies and seemingly gut-level opposition to Obama's very existence.

President Obama, on the other hand, appeared to have allowed himself to fall into the vacuum of legislative minutiae even as the country appeared stuck in a level of economic recession that had not been experienced for a generation. Most Americans reacted to the conditions with a combination of confusion and fear, and the president did little to allay these negative feelings. During his first years of being commander-in-chief, Barack Obama, who had only been known nationally and internationally since the Democratic National Convention of 2004 for his ability to inspire and unite people, was basically ineffectual when dealing with the Congress.

The Obama administration had a difficult time communicating goals and objectives, and its early failures to sway Congress on issues such as health care created intense disappointment among many who had voted for Obama and among those who had previously viewed Obama with an open mind. The argument over health care was disturbingly long, frustrating the president, Congress, and the public. This alarmingly long dispute alienated millions and eroded their hope for positive change. Many who had seen President Obama as a Washington outsider were disappointed by the behind-the-scenes deals he struck to get some aspects of his legislative agenda passed. This, to many members of his base, represented too much compromise. Democrats viewed his compromise on universal health care as anathema and felt it undermined the very concept of universal health care. Republicans fought as hard as they could to prevent the passage of anything that resembled true universal health care. The American public became weary of all the wrangling, which became less about what citizens needed and more about opposing political parties wanted. Instead of the compromise that had been promised, the public received a health care debate that became conflict-ridden and anticlimactic. The only policy change that the Obama administration and Congress could agree upon was financial regulatory reform.

While most Americans disagreed with the auto industry bailout, many believed that allowing the industry to fail would have plunged the country into a full-fledged depression. The Obama administration, while aware of public sentiment, forged ahead with the bailout. In an interview with the *New York Times*, in fact, President Obama recalled that "we probably spent much more time trying to get the policy right than trying to get the politics right. There was probably a perverse pride in my administration, and I take responsibility for this, that we were going to do the right thing, even if short-term it was unpopular." Perhaps President Obama had decided to modify his leadership style: "Anybody who's occupied this office has to remember that success is determined by an intersection in policy and politics and that you can't be neglect[ful] of marketing and P.R. and public opinion."[28]

Moving Forward

Because of the changes that occurred in Congress during the midterm elections of 2010, President Obama had to alter his leadership style and agenda. He was compelled to seek and secure support outside of the Democratic Party. He had to court centrist Republicans and independents to get any of his agenda passed. Although this was a political necessity for him, it was not easy to accomplish. Galston points out, using a survey conducted days before the November 2010 midterm elections, that the possibility of a different path did exist:

> While the electorate clearly wanted a change of course, it rejected key elements of the Republican agenda, including a freeze on all government spending except national security and a permanent extension of the Bush tax cuts for upper-income Americans. President Obama enjoyed a higher approval rating (47 percent) than either Ronald Reagan or Bill Clinton after their party's mid-term defeats, and polls showed that the American people were more favorably inclined toward his bid for reelection than they were for either Reagan or Clinton at comparable points in their presidencies.[29]

Still, Obama alienated his political base with too much compromise and failed to convert his adversaries. "There wasn't enough leadership early enough," argues Clarissa Martinez, director of immigration for the National Council of La Raza, America's leading Latino advocacy group. "There certainly is disappointment on that." Indeed, Robert Borosage, codirector of the left-leaning activist organization Campaign for America's Future, believed that Obama's supporters "went from hope to heartbreak". "He didn't meet our dreams," said Borosage, but "in comparison to the alternative, he's rising in our esteem."[30]

What is certain, however, is that Barack Obama, like so many African Americans before him, inherited an extremely dysfunctional system and overwhelming challenges. Despite the many obstacles that he faced, he accomplished a great deal in a relatively short period of time. Obama slowed down the recession and put the nation on the path to economic recovery; saved the U.S. automobile industry; shifted the focus of the war from Iraq to Afghanistan, while emphasizing the reduction of terrorism; and ameliorated anti-American tensions around the world.

President Obama also attempted, but ultimately failed, to close the torture and detention camps at Guantanamo Bay, a detainment facility operated by the United States in Cuba that was established in 2002 by the Bush administration to hold detainees (many of them without legal representation or trial) from the war in Iraq and Afghanistan. He made protecting the environment a national priority and a primary source for job creation; passed universal health care; appointed Sonia Marie Sotomayor to the Supreme Court, making her the first Latina to sit on the high court; appointed Eric Holder (fig. 36) to the post of U.S. attorney general, making him the first African American to hold the position; and restored faith in the American presidency. Moreover, his efforts at dialogue to solve complex domestic and global problems associated with racism, global warming, and war earned him the Nobel Peace Prize in 2009.

Despite his missteps, Obama impressed many with his leadership near the end of his first two years in office. When Arizona congresswoman Gabrielle Giffords was shot in the head and nineteen others were killed or wounded by Jared Lee Loughner in a suburb of Tucson, Arizona, on January 8, 2011, Obama impressed many with his handling of this shocking act of violence. In the face of tragedy, political leaders are expected to set the proper moral tone, console, and demonstrate authority and leadership. President Obama rose to the occasion amidst sagging poll numbers, and

FIG. 36. U.S. attorney general Eric Holder, 2009. United States Department of Justice.

moved swiftly and firmly to address the calamity and the atmosphere of intolerance that engendered it, following perceptions that he had reacted slowly in the "underwear bomber" case on Christmas Day 2009 and to the Orwellian BP oil spill during the summer of 2010.

Obama made an in-person statement on the Tucson shooting and sent FBI director Robert Mueller to Tucson to oversee the federal investigation. On January 9 he called for a national moment of silence at 11 a.m. on

Monday, January 10, which he and the White House staff observed from the South Lawn. The president also signed a proclamation ordering that flags be flown at half-staff and postponed a Tuesday trip to Schenectady, New York. The White House released photos portraying a president in charge, one showing him leading a meeting in the Situation Room (including his new chief of staff, William Daley), and another of him talking on the phone with the Republican governor of Arizona, Jan Brewer.

Despite Obama's efforts to unify the nation in the face of such violence, a bevy of accusations and counteraccusations by members of Congress and political activists over what led to this tragedy captured the attention of the nation. Many argued that that the gunman was inspired by volatile rhetoric—some of it from Tea Partiers—that encouraged violence. Although many on the right attempted to classify Jared Loughner as a mentally ill individual who espoused a "confused antigovernment ideology," many of the left viewed him as the embodiment of the kind of bigotry and intolerance that had reemerged and intensified during the age of Obama. Indeed, the conservative yet populist Tea Party movement and one of their heroes, Sarah Palin, using her political action committee (PAC), had targeted Giffords for defeat in November of 2010 with the graphic use of a bulls-eye in PAC materials; their use of images of rifle crosshairs on congressional districts and of slogans such as "don't retreat, reload," ramped up political speech-making and iconography with war-like rhetoric and imagery. President Obama, however, used the tragedy in Tucson to take the high road while other Democrats argued that many Republicans were using rhetoric that led to conflict and violence. Obama's approach, however, was not unique. "It is of course commonplace for presidents to use surrogates to take the low road, especially when they don't want to soil their skirts with that level of discourse,"[31] argued Bruce Buchanan, a presidential scholar at the University of Texas, Austin.

Obama continued to befuddle his detractors during his second year as president by handling volatile issues with the same aplomb with which he handled the tragedy in Tucson. When billionaire entrepreneur Donald Trump announced his intent to run as a Republican candidate for president in early 2012, he capitalized on the popularity of the birther movement, a coordinated effort to prove that Barack Obama is not an American citizen and is thus ineligible for the presidency, to draw attention to himself and cast Obama as being *in* America but not *of* America: a perpetual outsider to be distrusted, if not feared.

FIG. 37. In this January 25, 2011, photo, President Barack Obama makes a point during his State of the Union address on Capitol Hill in Washington. Photo/Pablo Martinez Monsivais, Pool (110125183308).

Obama handled this controversy with remarkable dexterity and panache. He exercised his reprisal on April 30, after weeks of attacks from his would-be Republican challenger Donald Trump, joking that Trump could bring change to the White House, transforming it from a "stately mansion into a tacky casino with a whirlpool in the garden."[32] Obama successfully utilized the White House Correspondents' Association annual dinner to diss Trump's presidential ambitions. The president, drawing from Trump's shameless reality TV career, said Trump, who was in attendance, "has shown the acumen of a future president, from firing Gary Busey on a recent episode of 'Celebrity Apprentice' to devoting endless energy to promoting conspiracy theories about [Obama's] birthplace." Obama had just released his long-form Hawaii birth certificate, and he cleverly asserted that "Trump could now focus on the serious issues, from whether the moon landing actually happened to 'where are Biggie and Tupac?'" "No one is prouder to put this birth certificate matter to rest than 'the Donald,'" Obama proclaimed, referring to Trump's bizarre claims that he was responsible for solving the mystery. Trump gave an effort to smile bemusedly at some of the earlier jokes, but quickly ended the façade when comedian Seth Meyers continued what Obama had started. "Donald Trump often talks about running as a Republican, which is surprising," said the Saturday Night Live actor, who acted as the Master of Ceremonies for the evening. "I just assumed he was running as a joke." The birth certificate was clearly the key punch line for the evening, which typically provides the president an opportunity to showcase his sense of humor in a city and nation consumed by politics and partisanship; this time in particular, it revealed the constant underlying issues of race that plague the nation.[33]

What was truly amazing about Obama's performance, however, was his ability to silence critics and bring levity to an atmosphere of angst and division, all while orchestrating one of the most risky, bold, calculated, well-coordinated, courageous, and timely convert military operations in modern American history. During the White House Correspondent Association's Dinner, Seth Meyers joked that "Osama bin Laden was hiding in plain sight by hosting an obscure C-SPAN show that no one ever watched." Journalists Peter Nicholas and Christi Parsons reported that "one person at the White House Correspondents' Association's dinner who clearly enjoyed the joke was President Obama. . . . Obama, dressed in a tuxedo, smiled broadly on Saturday night, in possession of a closely guarded secret. He knew where Bin Laden was living and he had already signed his death warrant, ordering a risky raid that would kill the world's most wanted terrorist the following day."[34]

Throughout the evening, Obama was receiving a steady stream of private briefings on the military mission. Nothing leaked. On Sunday night, May 1, 2011, Obama announced the successful outcome of the raid in a nationally televised East Room address. Bin Laden's killing represents Obama's biggest triumph in a position that he was not quick to embrace; that of commander in chief. The war in Afghanistan was deeply unpopular, while the one in Libya lingered on. Whatever else happens, though, history will remember Obama as the president who killed Bin Laden. Nicholas and Parsons provide a description of how the president continued to act as usual after giving National Security Advisor Tom Donilon the okay to move forward with the attempt to assassinate Osama Bin Laden:

> The operation was set in motion at 8:20 a.m. Friday, April 29, in the Diplomatic Room, when Obama told his national security advisor, Tom Donilon, that he wanted to proceed with the raid on the compound north of Islamabad, Pakistan. He then flew south, where he walked through a neighborhood in Tuscaloosa, Alabama, that was

nearly flattened by a tornado two days before. He told an aide he was overwhelmed by the destruction. Nothing could have been done for the many that were killed, the president said. "They're alongside God at this point," he said. From there he flew to Florida, speaking to graduating students in Miami and meeting with the crew of the space shuttle Endeavour. At 9:45 a.m. Sunday, Obama's motorcade left for Andrews Air Force Base for a round of golf. He played nine holes and spent a little time on the driving range. By 2 p.m., he was back at the White House for a meeting with senior officials to discuss what one aide called "final preparations." Every day, the White House announces a "lid," which means the president is no longer expected to leave the grounds or make any more public appearances. On Sunday, the lid was announced around 2:30 p.m. But seven hours later, an announcement came from the White House: Obama would soon make a statement. Standing alone before the cameras in the East Room at 11:35 p.m., the president delivered the news that Osama bin Laden was dead.[35]

Barack Obama overcame tremendous odds to become president during one of the most difficult periods in the nation's history. His leadership of the mission that killed Osama bin Laden, a signature event in recent U.S. history, and his devotion to a citizenry that often questioned his humanity and citizenship, reflected the complexities of his African American life in the twenty-first century.

After a contentious 2012 presidential race, Barack Obama was reelected on November 6. He defeated the Republican candidate, Mitt Romney, in part by cultivating a diverse constituency of people of color, women, labor, educators, and members of the LGBTQ community. In fact, *Time* magazine selected President Barack Obama as its person of the year in January of 2013, the second time it had chosen him. As Richard Stengel posited in his editorial prelude, "We are in the midst of historic cultural and demographic changes, and Obama is both the symbol and in some ways the architect of this new America." Obama was the person of the year, he declared, "for finding and forging a new majority, for turning weakness into opportunity and for seeking, amid great adversity, to create a more perfect union."[36] In addition, "blackness, as personified by the Obama family, embodies the type of hybridity that defines all Americans. African Americans are a fusion of humanity , but Obama's ascendancy has helped educate millions about just how diverse" black people are. Thanks to Obama, "we see that blackness, and a diverse racial lineage, are not antithetical. In fact, multiraciality is what helps to make African-Americans" who they are.[37]

Obama, like other highly successful blacks, acquired significant wealth and wielded unprecedented power. Despite such progress, however, prosperous and less fortunate African Americans alike still lagged behind whites in nearly every major statistical analysis. Moreover, black Americans continued to be viewed by many as being *in* the United States and not *of* the United States; perpetual outsiders whose legitimacy and loyalties were often called into question. How Obama, and other African Americans, would fare during the remainder of his presidency was yet to be seen. What was certain, however, was that the United States was a different nation in 2013 than it was in 1865, 1900, 2000, and 2008. Chattel slavery was abolished in 1865, de jure segregation was outlawed in 1954, black Americans' citizenship and voting rights were affirmed in 1965, and white supremacy, though still alive and malignant, is usually denounced publicly and looked upon by many as antiquated and utterly reprehensible.

The ability and eagerness of Americans of all backgrounds to embrace each other as fellow human beings and citizens exists in the twenty-first century in ways that were unimaginable only one generation ago. Despite the many challenges he faced, the election and reelection of Obama as President of the United States was a substantive measure of this seismic shift in American life, and his very person is the embodiment of America's promise. His rise to power, however, is not the final chapter in African American history, nor does it eradicate the many problems that confront modern black America. The African American struggle endures, and the fight to fulfill and maintain America's promise for freedom and justice for *all* continues.

APPENDIX 1

Excerpts from the U.S. Constitution (1787)

These clauses from the original constitution concern the status of African Americans. Article one, section two, paragraph three has since been voided by the Fourteenth Amendment, while section nine, paragraph one of the same article addresses the slave trade. Article IV, section 2, paragraph 1 is superseded by the Thirteenth Amendment.

We the People of the United States, in Order to form a more perfect Union, establish Justice, insure domestic Tranquility, provide for the common defence, promote the general Welfare, and secure the Blessings of Liberty to ourselves and our Posterity, do ordain and establish this Constitution for the United States of America.

Article. I.

SEC. 2.

Representatives and direct Taxes shall be apportioned among the several States which may be included within this Union, according to their respective Numbers, which shall be determined by adding to the whole Number of free Persons, including those bound to Service for a Term of Years, and excluding Indians not taxed, three fifths of all other Persons. . . .

SEC. 9.

The Migration or Importation of such Persons as any of the States now existing shall think proper to admit, shall not be prohibited by the Congress prior to the Year one thousand eight hundred and eight, but a Tax or duty may be imposed on such Importation, not exceeding ten dollars for each Person. . . .

Article. IV.

No Person held to Service or Labour in one State, under the Laws thereof, escaping into another, shall, in Consequence of any Law or Regulation therein, be discharged from such Service or Labour, but shall be delivered up on Claim of the Party to whom such Service or Labour may be due. . . .

APPENDIX 2

Executive Order #8802 (1941)

In response to the threat of a march on Washington DC, President Franklin D. Roosevelt banned discrimination in federal agency employment, as well as in war-related industries and unions, and established the Fair Employment Practices Commission to enforce this new policy.

Reaffirming Policy of Full Participation in the Defense Program by All Persons, Regardless Of Race, Creed, Color, or National Origin, and Directing Certain Action in Furtherance of Said Policy

Whereas it is the policy of the United States to encourage full participation in the national defense program by all citizens of the United States, regardless of race, creed, color, or national origin, in the firm belief that the democratic way of life within the Nation can be defended successfully only with the help and support of all groups within its borders; and

Whereas there is evidence that available and needed workers have been barred from employment in industries engaged in defense production solely because of considerations of race, creed, color, or national origin, to the detriment of workers' morale and of national unity:

Now, therefore, by virtue of the authority vested in me by the Constitution and the statutes, and as a prerequisite to the successful conduct of our national defense production effort, I do hereby reaffirm the policy of the United States that there shall be no discrimination in the employment of workers in defense industries or government because of race, creed, color, or national origin, and I do hereby declare that it is the duty of employers and of labor organizations, in furtherance of said policy and of this order, to provide for the full and equitable participation of all workers in defense industries, without discrimination because of race, creed, color, or national origin;

And it is hereby ordered as follows:

1. All departments and agencies of the Government of the United States concerned with vocational and training programs for defense production shall take special measures appropriate to assure that such programs are administered without discrimination because of race, creed, color, or national origin;

2. All contracting agencies of the Government of the United States shall include in all defense contracts hereafter negotiated by them a provision obligating the contractor not to discriminate against any worker because of race, creed, color, or national origin;

3. There is established in the Office of Production Management a Committee on Fair Employment Practice, which shall consist of a chairman and four other members to be appointed by the President. The Chairman and members of the Committee shall serve as such without compensation but shall be entitled to actual and necessary transportation, subsistence and other expenses incidental to performance of their duties. The Committee shall receive and investigate complaints of discrimination in violation of the provisions of this order and shall take appropriate steps to redress grievances which it finds to be valid. The Committee shall also recommend to the several departments and agencies of the Government of the United States and to the President all measures which may be deemed by it necessary or proper to effectuate the provisions of this order.

Franklin D. Roosevelt
The White House,
June 25, 1941.

APPENDIX 3

Brown v. Board of Education of Topeka (1954)

*After a succession of NAACP lawsuits concerning racial segregation in public
education, the U.S. Supreme Court denied the constitutionality of segregation in
public schools and facilities, overturning the doctrine of "separate but equal." Mr.
Chief Justice Warren delivered the opinion of the Court.*

These cases come to us from the States of Kansas, South Carolina, Virginia, and
Delaware. They are premised on different facts and different local conditions,
but a common legal question justifies their consideration together in this consolidated opinion. . . .

Today, education is perhaps the most important function of state and local
governments. Compulsory school attendance laws and the great expenditures
for education both demonstrate our recognition of the importance of education
to our democratic society. It is required in the performance of our most basic
public responsibilities, even service in the armed forces. It is the very foundation of good citizenship. Today it is a principal instrument in awakening the
child to cultural values, in preparing him for later professional training, and in
helping him to adjust normally to his environment. In these days, it is doubtful
that any child may reasonably be expected to succeed in life if he is denied the
opportunity of an education. Such an opportunity, where the state has undertaken to provide it, is a right which must be made available to all on equal terms.

We come then to the question presented: does segregation of children in
public schools solely on the basis of race, even though the physical facilities
and other "tangible" factors may be equal, deprive the children of the minority
group of equal educational opportunities? We believe that it does. . . .

We conclude that, in the field of public education, the doctrine of "separate but
equal" has no place. Separate educational facilities are inherently unequal. Therefore, we hold that the plaintiffs and others similarly situated for whom the actions
have been brought are, by reason of the segregation complained of, deprived of
the equal protection of the laws guaranteed by the Fourteenth Amendment. . . .

APPENDIX 4

The Civil Rights Act of 1964

The Civil Rights Act of 1964 prohibited discrimination in employment, public facilities, public schools, and federally funded programs in an attempt to fulfill the promises of Reconstruction.

An act to enforce the constitutional right to vote, to confer jurisdiction upon the district courts of the United States to provide injunctive relief against discrimination in public accommodations, to authorize the Attorney General to institute suits to protect constitutional rights in public facilities and public education, to extend the Commission on Civil Rights, to prevent discrimination in federally assisted programs, to establish a Commission on Equal Employment Opportunity, and for other purposes.

Be it enacted by the Senate and House of Representatives of the United States of America in Congress assembled, That this Act may be cited as the "Civil Rights Act of 1964."

Title I—Voting Rights . . .

SEC. 101. . . . (2) No person acting under color of law shall—

(A) in determining whether any individual is qualified under State law or laws to vote in any Federal election, apply any standard, practice, or procedure different from the standards, practices, or procedures applied under such law or laws to other individuals within the same county, parish, or similar political subdivision who have been found by State officials to be qualified to vote; . . .

Title II—Injunctive Relief Against Discrimination in Places of Public Accommodation

SEC. 201. (a) All persons shall be entitled to the full and equal enjoyment of the goods, services, facilities, and privileges, advantages, and accommodations of any place of public accommodation, as defined in this section, without discrimination or segregation on the ground of race, color, religion, or national origin. . . .

Title III—Desegregation of Public Facilities

SEC. 301. (a) Whenever the Attorney General receives a complaint in writing signed by an individual to the effect that he is being deprived of or threatened with the loss of his right to the equal protection of the laws, on account of his race, color, religion, or national origin, by being denied equal utilization of any public facility which is owned, operated, or managed by or on behalf of any State or subdivision thereof, other than a public school or public college as defined in section 401 of title IV hereof, . . . the Attorney General is authorized to institute for or in the name of the United States a civil action in any appropriate district court of the United States against such parties and for such relief as may be appropriate, and such court shall have and shall exercise jurisdiction of proceedings instituted pursuant to this section. The Attorney General may implead as defendants such additional parties as are or become necessary to the grant of effective relief hereunder. . . .

Title IV—Desegregation of Public Education

DEFINITIONS

SEC. 401. As used in this title—

(a) "Commissioner" means the Commissioner of Education.

(b) "Desegregation" means the assignment of students to public schools and within such schools without regard to their race, color, religion, or national origin, but "desegregation" shall not mean the assignment of students to public schools in order to overcome racial imbalance.

(c) "Public school" means any elementary or secondary educational institution, and "public college" means any institution of higher education or any technical or vocational school above the secondary school level, provided that such public school or public college is operated by a State, subdivision of a State, or governmental agency within a State, or operated wholly or predominantly from or through the use of governmental funds or property, or funds or property derived from a governmental source.

(d) "School board" means any agency or agencies which administer a system of one or more public schools and any other agency which is responsible for the assignment of students to or within such system. . . .

Title V—Commission on Civil Rights

SEC. 104. (a) The Commission shall—

(1) investigate allegations in writing under oath or affirmation that certain citizens of the United States are being deprived of their right to vote and have that vote counted by reason of their color, race, religion, or national origin; which writing, under oath or affirmation, shall set forth the facts upon which such belief or beliefs are based;

(2) study and collect information concerning legal developments constituting a denial of equal protection of the laws under the Constitution because of race, color, religion or national origin or in the administration of justice;

(3) appraise the laws and policies of the Federal Government with respect to denials of equal protection of the laws under the Constitution because of race, color, religion or national origin or in the administration of justice;

(4) serve as a national clearinghouse for information in respect to denials of equal protection of the laws because of race, color, religion or national origin, including but not limited to the fields of voting, education, housing, employment, the use of public facilities, and transportation, or in the administration of justice;

(5) investigate allegations, made in writing and under oath or affirmation, that citizens of the United States are unlawfully being accorded or denied the right to vote, or to have their votes properly counted, in any election of presidential electors, Members of the United States Senate, or of the House of Representatives, as a result of any patterns or practice of fraud or discrimination in the conduct of such election; . . .

Title VI—Nondiscrimination in Federally Assisted Programs

SEC. 601. No person in the United States shall, on the ground of race, color, or national origin, be excluded from participation in, be denied the benefits of, or be subjected to discrimination under any program or activity receiving Federal financial assistance. . . .

Title VII—Equal Employment Opportunity

DISCRIMINATION BECAUSE OF RACE, COLOR, RELIGION, SEX, OR NATIONAL ORIGIN

SEC. 703. (a) It shall be an unlawful employment practice for an employer—

(1) to fail or refuse to hire or to discharge any individual, or otherwise to discriminate against any individual with respect to his compensation, terms, conditions, or privileges of employment, because of such individual's race, color, religion, sex, or national origin; or

(2) to limit, segregate, or classify his employees in any way which would deprive or tend to deprive any individual of employment opportunities or otherwise adversely affect his status as an employee, because of such individual's race, color, religion, sex, or national origin. . . .

EQUAL EMPLOYMENT OPPORTUNITY COMMISSION

SEC. 705. (a) There is hereby created a Commission to be known as the Equal Employment Opportunity Commission, which shall be composed of five members, not more than three of whom shall be members of the same political party, who shall be appointed by the President by and with the advice and consent of the Senate. . . .

(g) The Commission shall have power—

(1) to cooperate with and, with their consent, utilize regional, State, local, and other agencies, both public and private, and individuals;

(2) to pay to witnesses whose depositions are taken or who are summoned before the Commission or any of its agents the same witness and mileage fees as are paid to witnesses in the courts of the United States;

(3) to furnish to persons subject to this title such technical assistance as they may request to further their compliance with this title or an order issued thereunder;

(4) upon the request of (i) any employer, whose employees or some of them, or (ii) any labor organization, whose members or some of them, refuse or threaten to refuse to cooperate in effectuating the provisions of this title, to assist in such effectuation by conciliation or such other remedial action as is provided by this title;

(5) to make such technical studies as are appropriate to effectuate the purposes and policies of this title and to make the results of such studies available to the public;

(6) to refer matters to the Attorney General with recommendations for intervention in a civil action brought by an aggrieved party under section 706, or for the institution of a civil action by the Attorney General under section 707, and to advise, consult, and assist the Attorney General on such matters. . . .

APPENDIX 5

The Voting Rights Act of 1965

Passed in 1965 and subsequently modified as well as extended in 1970, 1975, 1982, and 2006, the Voting Rights Act provided clarification and enforcement of the Fifteenth Amendment.

An act to enforce the fifteenth amendment to the Constitution of the United States, and for other purposes.

Be it enacted by the Senate and House of Representatives of the United States of America in Congress assembled, that this act shall be known as the "Voting Rights Act of 1965."

SEC. 2. No voting qualification or prerequisite to voting, or standard, practice, or procedure shall be imposed or applied by any State or political subdivision to deny or abridge the right of any citizen of the United States to vote on account of race or color.

SEC. 3. (a) Whenever the Attorney General institutes a proceeding under any statute to enforce the guarantees of the fifteenth amendment in any State or political subdivision the court shall authorize the appointment of Federal examiners by the United States Civil Service Commission in accordance with section 6 to serve for such period of time and for such political subdivisions as the court shall determine is appropriate to enforce the guarantees of the fifteenth amendment. . . .

(b) If in a proceeding instituted by the Attorney General under any statute to enforce the guarantees of the fifteenth amendment in any State or political subdivision the court finds that a test or device has been used for the purpose or with the effect of denying or abridging the right of any citizen of the United States to vote on account of race or color, it shall suspend the use of tests and devices in such State or political subdivisions as the court shall determine is appropriate and for such period as it deems necessary.

(c) If in any proceeding instituted by the Attorney General under any statute to enforce the guarantees of the fifteenth amendment in any State or political subdivision the court finds that violations of the fifteenth amendment justifying equitable relief have occurred within the territory of such State or political subdivision, the court, in addition to such relief as it may grant, shall retain jurisdiction for such period as it may deem appropriate and during such period no voting qualification or prerequisite to voting, or standard, practice, or procedure with respect to voting different from that in force or effect at the time the proceeding was commenced shall be enforced unless and until the court finds that such qualification, prerequisite, standard, practice, or procedure does not have the purpose and will not have the effect of denying or abridging the right to vote on account of race or color: . . .

SEC. 4. (a) To assure that the right of citizens of the United States to vote is not denied or abridged on account of race or color, no citizen shall be denied the right to vote in any Federal, State, or local election because of his failure to comply with any test or device in any State with respect to which the determinations have been made under subsection. . . .

(c) The phrase "test or device" shall mean any requirement that a person as a prerequisite for voting or registration for voting (1) demonstrate the ability to read, write, understand, or interpret any matter, (2) demonstrate any educational achievement or his knowledge of any particular subject, (3) possess good moral character, or (4) prove his qualifications by the voucher of registered voters or members of any other class. . . .

(e) (1) Congress hereby declares that to secure the rights under the fourteenth amendment of persons educated in American-flag schools in which the predominant classroom language was other than English, it is necessary to prohibit the States from conditioning the right to vote of such persons on ability to read, write, understand, or interpret any matter in the English language.

(2) No person who demonstrates that he has successfully completed the sixth primary grade in a public school in, or a private school accredited by, any State or territory, the District of Columbia, or the Commonwealth of Puerto Rico in which the predominant classroom language was other than English, shall be denied the right to vote in any Federal, State, or local election because of his inability to read, write, understand, or interpret any matter in the English language, except that, in States in which State law provides that a different level of education is presumptive of literacy, he shall demonstrate that he has successfully completed an equivalent level of education in a public school in, or a private school accredited by, any State or territory, the District of Columbia, or the Commonwealth

of Puerto Rico in which the predominant classroom language was other than English. . . . SEC. 6. Whenever (a) a court has authorized the appointment of examiners pursuant to the provisions of section 3(a), or (b) unless a declaratory judgment has been rendered under section 4(a), the Attorney General certifies with respect to any political subdivision named in, or included within the scope of, determinations made under section 4(b) that (1) he has received complaints in writing from twenty or more residents of such political subdivision alleging that they have been denied the right to vote under color of law on account of race or color, and that he believes such complaints to be meritorious, or (2) that, in his judgment (considering, among other factors, whether the ratio of nonwhite persons to white persons registered to vote within such subdivision appears to him to be reasonably attributable to violations of the fifteenth amendment or whether substantial evidence exists that bona fide efforts are being made within such subdivision to comply with the fifteenth amendment), the appointment of examiners is otherwise necessary to enforce the guarantees of the fifteenth amendment, the Civil Service Commission shall appoint as many examiners for such subdivision as it may deem appropriate to prepare and maintain lists of persons eligible to vote in Federal, State, and local elections. . . .

SEC. 10. (a) The Congress finds that the requirement of the payment of a poll tax as a precondition to voting (i) precludes persons of limited means from voting or imposes unreasonable financial hardship upon such persons as a precondition to their exercise of the franchise, (ii) does not bear a reasonable relationship to any legitimate State interest in the conduct of elections, and (iii) in some areas has the purpose or effect of denying persons the right to vote because of race or color. Upon the basis of these findings, Congress declares that the constitutional right of citizens to vote is denied or abridged in some areas by the requirement of the payment of a poll tax as a precondition to voting. . . .

SEC. 11. (a) No person acting under color of law shall fail or refuse to permit any person to vote who is entitled to vote under any provision of this Act or is otherwise qualified to vote, or willfully fail or refuse to tabulate, count, and report such person's vote.

(b) No person, whether acting under color of law or otherwise, shall intimidate, threaten, or coerce, or attempt to intimidate, threaten, or coerce any person for voting or attempting to vote, or intimidate, threaten, or coerce, or attempt to intimidate, threaten, or coerce any person for urging or aiding any person to vote or attempt to vote, or intimidate, threaten, or coerce any person for exercising any powers or duties under section 3(a), 6, 8, 9, 10, or 12(e). . . .

SEC. 13. . . . (c) (1) The terms "vote" or "voting" shall include all action necessary to make a vote effective in any primary, special, or general election, including, but not limited to, registration, listing pursuant to this Act, or other action required by law prerequisite to voting, casting a ballot, and having such ballot counted properly and included in the appropriate totals of votes cast with respect to candidates for public or party office and propositions for which votes are received in an election. . . .

SEC. 17. Nothing in this Act shall be construed to deny, impair, or otherwise adversely affect the right to vote of any person registered to vote under the law of any State or political subdivision. . . .

APPENDIX 6

Fair Housing Act (1968)

Title VIII of the Civil Rights Act of 1968, otherwise known as the Fair Housing Act, outlaws discrimination on the basis of race, color, religion or national origin in the financing, sale, and rental of housing. Congress has since expanded the protections and enforcement of this law with respect to sex, disability, and family status through subsequent legislation.

An act to prescribe penalties for certain acts of violence or intimidation, and for other purposes.

Be it enacted by the Senate and House of Representatives of the United States of America Congress assembled, . . .

Title VIII—Fair Housing

POLICY

SEC. 801. It is the policy of the United States to provide, within constitutional limitations, for fair housing throughout the United States. . . .

DISCRIMINATION IN THE SALE OR RENTAL OF HOUSING

SEC. 804. As made applicable by section 803 of this title and except as exempted by sections 803(b) and 807 of this title, it shall be unlawful—

(a) To refuse to sell or rent after the making of a bona fide offer, or to refuse to negotiate for the sale or rental of, or otherwise make unavailable or deny, a dwelling to any person because of race, color, religion, or national origin.

(b) To discriminate against any person in the terms, conditions, or privileges of sale or rental of a dwelling, or in the provision of services or facilities in connection therewith, because of race, color, religion, or national origin.

(c) To make, print, or publish, or cause to be made, printed, or published any notice, statement, or advertisement, with respect to the sale or rental of a dwelling that indicates any preference, limitation, or discrimination based on race, color, religion, or national origin, or an intention to make any such preference, limitation, or discrimination.

(d) To represent to any person because of race, color, religion, or national origin that any dwelling is not available for inspection, sale, or rental when such dwelling is in fact so available.

(e) For profit, to induce or attempt to induce any person to sell or rent any dwelling by representations regarding the entry or prospective entry into the neighborhood of a person or persons of a particular race, color, religion, or national origin.

DISCRIMINATION IN THE FINANCING OF HOUSING

SEC. 805. After December 31, 1968, it shall be unlawful for any bank, building and loan association, insurance company or other corporation, association, firm or enterprise whose business consists in whole or in part in the making of commercial real estate loans, to deny a loan or other financial assistance to a person applying therefore the purpose of purchasing, constructing, improving, repairing, or maintaining a dwelling, or to discriminate against him in the fixing of the amount, interest rate, duration, or other terms and conditions of such loan or other financial assistance, because of the race, color, religion, or national origin of such person or of any person associated with him in connection with such loan or other financial assistance. . . .

DISCRIMINATION IN PROVISION OF BROKERAGE SERVICES

SEC. 806. After December 31, 1968, it shall be unlawful to deny any person access to or membership or participation in any multiple-listing service, real estate brokers' organization or other service, organization, or facility relating to the business of selling or renting dwellings, or to discriminate against him in the terms or conditions of such access, membership, or participation, on account of race, color, religion, or national origin. . . .

INTERFERENCE, COERCION, OR INTIMIDATION

SEC. 817. It shall be unlawful to coerce, intimidate, threaten, or interfere with any person in the exercise or enjoyment of, or on account of his having exercised or enjoyed, or on account of his having aided or encouraged any other person in the exercise or enjoyment of, any right granted or protected by section 803, 804, 805, or 806. This section may be enforced by appropriate civil action.

APPENDIX 7

"A More Perfect Union"

Barack Obama's speech on race in America, Constitution Center, Philadelphia, Pennsylvania, March 18, 2008

"We the people, in order to form a more perfect union . . ." Two hundred twenty-one years ago, in a hall that still stands across the street, a group of men gathered and, with these simple words, launched America's improbable experiment in democracy. Farmers and scholars, statesmen and patriots who had traveled across an ocean to escape tyranny and persecution finally made real their declaration of independence at a Philadelphia convention that lasted through the spring of 1787. The document they produced was eventually signed but ultimately unfinished. It was stained by this nation's original sin of slavery, a question that divided the colonies and brought the convention to a stalemate until the founders chose to allow the slave trade to continue for at least twenty more years, and to leave any final resolution to future generations.

Of course, the answer to the slavery question was already embedded within our Constitution—a Constitution that had at its very core the ideal of equal citizenship under the law; a Constitution that promised its people liberty and justice and a union that could be and should be perfected over time. And yet words on a parchment would not be enough to deliver slaves from bondage, or provide men and women of every color and creed their full rights and obligations as citizens of the United States. What would be needed were Americans in successive generations who were willing to do their part—through protests and struggles, on the streets and in the courts, through a civil war and civil disobedience, and always at great risk—to narrow that gap between the promise of our ideals and the reality of their time.

This was one of the tasks we set forth at the beginning of this presidential campaign—to continue the long march of those who came before us, a march for a more just, more equal, more free, more caring, and more prosperous America. I chose to run for president at this moment in history because I believe deeply that we cannot solve the challenges of our time unless we solve them together, unless we perfect our union by understanding that we may have different stories, but we hold common hopes; that we may not look the same and we may not have come from the same place, but we all want to move in the same direction—toward a better future for our children and our grandchildren.

This belief comes from my unyielding faith in the decency and generosity of the American people. But it also comes from my own story. I am the son of a black man from Kenya and a white woman from Kansas. I was raised with the help of a white grandfather who survived a Depression to serve in Patton's Army during World War II and a white grandmother who worked on a bomber assembly line at Fort Leavenworth while he was overseas. I've gone to some of the best schools in America and lived in one of the world's poorest nations. I am married to a black American who carries within her the blood of slaves and slave owners—an inheritance we pass on to our two precious daughters. I have brothers, sisters, nieces, nephews, uncles and cousins of every race and every hue, scattered across three continents, and for as long as I live, I will never forget that in no other country on Earth is my story even possible.

It's a story that hasn't made me the most conventional of candidates. But it is a story that has seared into my genetic makeup the idea that this nation is more than the sum of its parts—that out of many, we are truly one. Throughout the first year of this campaign, against all predictions to the contrary, we saw how hungry the American people were for this message of unity. Despite the temptation to view my candidacy through a purely racial lens, we won commanding victories in states with some of the whitest populations in the country. In South Carolina, where the Confederate flag still flies, we built a powerful coalition of African Americans and white Americans. This is not to say that race has not been an issue in this campaign. At various stages in the campaign, some commentators have deemed me either "too black" or "not black enough." We saw racial tensions bubble to the surface during the week before the South Carolina primary. The press has scoured every single exit poll for the latest evidence of racial polarization, not just in terms of white and black, but black and brown as well. And yet, it has only been in the last couple of weeks that the discussion of race in this campaign has taken a particularly divisive turn.

On one end of the spectrum, we've heard the implication that my candidacy is somehow an exercise in affirmative action; that it's based solely on the desire of wide-eyed liberals to purchase racial reconciliation on the cheap. On the other end, we've heard my former pastor, Jeremiah Wright, use incendiary language to express views that have the potential not only to widen the racial divide, but views that denigrate both the greatness and the goodness of our nation, and that rightly offend white and black alike. I have already condemned, in unequivocal terms, the statements of Reverend Wright that have caused such controversy and, in some cases, pain. For some, nagging questions remain. Did I know him to be an occasionally fierce critic of American domestic and foreign policy? Of course. Did I ever hear him make remarks that could be considered controversial while I sat in the church? Yes. Did I strongly disagree with many of his political views? Absolutely—just as I'm sure many of you have heard remarks from your pastors, priests, or rabbis with which you strongly disagreed.

But the remarks that have caused this recent firestorm weren't simply controversial. They weren't simply a religious leader's efforts to speak out against perceived injustice. Instead, they expressed a profoundly distorted view of this country—a view that sees white racism as endemic, and that elevates what is wrong with America above all that we know is right with America; a view that sees the conflicts in the Middle East as rooted primarily in the actions of stalwart allies like Israel, instead of emanating from the perverse and hateful ideologies of radical Islam. As such, Reverend Wright's comments were not only wrong but divisive, divisive at a time when we need unity; racially charged at a time when we need to come together to solve a set of monumental problems— two wars, a terrorist threat, a falling economy, a chronic health care crisis and potentially devastating climate change—problems that are neither black or white or Latino or Asian, but rather problems that confront us all.

Given my background, my politics, and my professed values and ideals, there will no doubt be those for whom my statements of condemnation are not enough. Why associate myself with Reverend Wright in the first place, they may ask? Why not join another church? And I confess that if all that I knew of Reverend Wright were the snippets of those sermons that have run in an endless loop on the television sets and YouTube, or if Trinity United Church of Christ conformed to the caricatures being peddled by some commentators, there is no doubt that I would react in much the same way. But the truth is, that isn't all that I know of the man. The man I met more than twenty years ago is a man who helped introduce me to my Christian faith, a man who spoke to me about our obligations to love one another, to care for the sick and lift up the poor. He is a man who served his country as a United States Marine; who has studied and lectured at some of the finest universities and seminaries in the country, and who for over thirty years has led a church that serves the community by doing God's work here on Earth—by housing the homeless, ministering to the needy, providing day care services and scholarships and prison ministries, and reaching out to those suffering from HIV/AIDS.

In my first book, *Dreams From My Father*, I describe the experience of my first service at Trinity: "People began to shout, to rise from their seats and clap and cry out, a forceful wind carrying the reverend's voice up into the rafters.

And in that single note—hope!—I heard something else: At the foot of that cross, inside the thousands of churches across the city, I imagined the stories of ordinary black people merging with the stories of David and Goliath, Moses and Pharaoh, the Christians in the lion's den, Ezekiel's field of dry bones. Those stories—of survival and freedom and hope—became our stories, my story. The blood that spilled was our blood, the tears our tears, until this black church, on this bright day, seemed once more a vessel carrying the story of a people into future generations and into a larger world. Our trials and triumphs became at once unique and universal, black and more than black. In chronicling our journey, the stories and songs gave us a meaning to reclaim memories that we didn't need to feel shame about—memories that all people might study and cherish, and with which we could start to rebuild."

That has been my experience at Trinity. Like other predominantly black churches across the country, Trinity embodies the black community in its entirety—the doctor and the welfare mom, the model student and the former gang-banger. Like other black churches, Trinity's services are full of raucous laughter and sometimes bawdy humor. They are full of dancing and clapping and screaming and shouting that may seem jarring to the untrained ear. The church contains in full the kindness and cruelty, the fierce intelligence and the shocking ignorance, the struggles and successes, the love and, yes, the bitterness and biases that make up the black experience in America. And this helps explain, perhaps, my relationship with Reverend Wright. As imperfect as he may be, he has been like family to me. He strengthened my faith, officiated my wedding, and baptized my children. Not once in my conversations with him have I heard him talk about any ethnic group in derogatory terms, or treat whites with whom he interacted with anything but courtesy and respect. He contains within him the contradictions—the good and the bad—of the community that he has served diligently for so many years.

I can no more disown him than I can disown the black community. I can no more disown him than I can disown my white grandmother—a woman who helped raise me, a woman who sacrificed again and again for me, a woman who loves me as much as she loves anything in this world, but a woman who once confessed her fear of black men who passed her by on the street, and who on more than one occasion has uttered racial or ethnic stereotypes that made me cringe. These people are a part of me. And they are part of America, this country that I love. Some will see this as an attempt to justify or excuse comments that are simply inexcusable. I can assure you it is not. I suppose the politically safe thing to do would be to move on from this episode and just hope that it fades into the woodwork. We can dismiss Reverend Wright as a crank or a demagogue, just as some have dismissed Geraldine Ferraro, in the aftermath of her recent statements, as harboring some deep-seated bias.

But race is an issue that I believe this nation cannot afford to ignore right now. We would be making the same mistake that Reverend Wright made in his offending sermons about America—to simplify and stereotype and amplify the negative to the point that it distorts reality. The fact is that the comments that have been made and the issues that have surfaced over the last few weeks reflect the complexities of race in this country that we've never really worked through—a part of our union that we have not yet made perfect. And if we walk away now, if we simply retreat into our respective corners, we will never be able to come together and solve challenges like health care or education or the need to find good jobs for every American. Understanding this reality requires a reminder of how we arrived at this point. As William Faulkner once wrote, "The past isn't dead and buried. In fact, it isn't even past." We do not need to recite here the history of racial injustice in this country. But we do need to remind ourselves that so many of the disparities that exist between the African American community and the larger American community today can be traced directly to inequalities passed on from an earlier generation that suffered under the brutal legacy of slavery and Jim Crow.

Segregated schools were and are inferior schools; we still haven't fixed them, fifty years after *Brown v. Board of Education*. And the inferior education they provided, then and now, helps explain the pervasive achievement gap between today's black and white students. Legalized discrimination—where blacks were prevented, often through violence, from owning property, or loans were not granted to African American business owners, or black homeowners could not access FHA mortgages, or blacks were excluded from unions or the police force or the fire department—meant that black families could not amass any meaningful wealth to bequeath to future generations. That history helps explain the wealth and income gap between blacks and whites, and the concentrated pockets of poverty that persist in so many of today's urban and rural communities.

A lack of economic opportunity among black men, and the shame and frustration that came from not being able to provide for one's family contributed to the erosion of black families—a problem that welfare policies for many years may have worsened. And the lack of basic services in so many urban black neighborhoods—parks for kids to play in, police walking the beat, regular garbage pickup, building code enforcement—all helped create a cycle of violence, blight and neglect that continues to haunt us. This is the reality in which Reverend Wright and other African Americans of his generation grew up. They came of age in the late '50s and early '60s, a time when segregation was still the law of the land and opportunity was systematically constricted. What's remarkable is not how many failed in the face of discrimination, but how many men and women overcame the odds; how many were able to make a way out of no way, for those like me who would come after them.

For all those who scratched and clawed their way to get a piece of the American Dream, there were many who didn't make it—those who were ultimately defeated, in one way or another, by discrimination. That legacy of defeat was passed on to future generations—those young men and, increasingly, young women who we see standing on street corners or languishing in our prisons, without hope or prospects for the future. Even for those blacks who did make it, questions of race and racism continue to define their worldview in fundamental ways. For the men and women of Reverend Wright's generation, the memories of humiliation and doubt and fear have not gone away; nor has the anger and the bitterness of those years. That anger may not get expressed in public, in front of white coworkers or white friends. But it does find voice in the barbershop or the beauty shop or around the kitchen table. At times, that anger is exploited by politicians, to gin up votes along racial lines, or to make up for a politician's own failings.

And occasionally it finds voice in the church on Sunday morning, in the pulpit and in the pews. The fact that so many people are surprised to hear that anger in some of Reverend Wright's sermons simply reminds us of the old truism that the most segregated hour of American life occurs on Sunday morning. That anger is not always productive; indeed, all too often it distracts attention from solving real problems; it keeps us from squarely facing our own complicity within the African American community in our condition, and prevents the African American community from forging the alliances it needs to bring about real change. But the anger is real; it is powerful. And to simply wish it away, to condemn it without understanding its roots, only serves to widen the chasm of misunderstanding that exists between the races.

In fact, a similar anger exists within segments of the white community. Most working- and middle-class white Americans don't feel that they have been particularly privileged by their race. Their experience is the immigrant experience—as far as they're concerned, no one handed them anything. They built it from scratch. They've worked hard all their lives, many times only to see their jobs shipped overseas or their pensions dumped after a lifetime of labor. They are anxious about their futures, and they feel their dreams slipping away. And in an era of stagnant wages and global competition, opportunity comes to be seen as a zero-sum game, in which your dreams come at my expense. So when they are told to bus their children to a school across town; when they hear an African American is getting an advantage in landing a good job or a spot in a good college because of an injustice that they themselves never committed; when they're told that their fears about crime in urban neighborhoods are somehow prejudiced, resentment builds over time.

Like the anger within the black community, these resentments aren't always expressed in polite company. But they have helped shape the political landscape for at least a generation. Anger over welfare and affirmative action helped forge the Reagan Coalition. Politicians routinely exploited fears of crime for their own electoral ends. Talk show hosts and conservative commentators built entire careers unmasking bogus claims of racism while dismissing legitimate discussions of racial injustice and inequality as mere political correctness or reverse racism.

Just as black anger often proved counterproductive, so have these white resentments distracted attention from the real culprits of the middle class squeeze—a corporate culture rife with inside dealing, questionable accounting practices and short-term greed; a Washington dominated by lobbyists and special interests; economic policies that favor the few over the many. And yet, to wish away the resentments of white Americans, to label them as misguided or even racist, without recognizing they are grounded in legitimate concerns— this too widens the racial divide and blocks the path to understanding. This is where we are right now. It's a racial stalemate we've been stuck in for years. Contrary to the claims of some of my critics, black and white, I have never been so naïve as to believe that we can get beyond our racial divisions in a single election cycle, or with a single candidacy—particularly a candidacy as imperfect as my own.

But I have asserted a firm conviction—a conviction rooted in my faith in God and my faith in the American people—that, working together, we can move beyond some of our old racial wounds, and that in fact we have no choice if we are to continue on the path of a more perfect union. For the African American community, that path means embracing the burdens of our past without becoming victims of our past. It means continuing to insist on a full measure of justice in every aspect of American life. But it also means binding our particular grievances—for better health care and better schools and better jobs— to the larger aspirations of all Americans: the white woman struggling to break the glass ceiling, the white man who has been laid off, the immigrant trying to feed his family. And it means taking full responsibility for our own lives—by demanding more from our fathers, and spending more time with our children, and reading to them, and teaching them that while they may face challenges and discrimination in their own lives, they must never succumb to despair or cynicism; they must always believe that they can write their own destiny. Ironically, this quintessentially American—and yes, conservative—notion of self-help found frequent expression in Reverend Wright's sermons. But what my former pastor too often failed to understand is that embarking on a program of self-help also requires a belief that society can change.

The profound mistake of Reverend Wright's sermons is not that he spoke about racism in our society. It's that he spoke as if our society was static; as if no progress had been made; as if this country—a country that has made it possible for one of his own members to run for the highest office in the land and build a coalition of white and black, Latino and Asian, rich and poor, young and old—is still irrevocably bound to a tragic past. But what we know—what we have seen—is that America can change. That is the true genius of this nation. What we have already achieved gives us hope—the audacity to hope—for what we can and must achieve tomorrow.

In the white community, the path to a more perfect union means acknowledging that what ails the African American community does not just exist in the minds of black people; that the legacy of discrimination—and current incidents of discrimination, while less overt than in the past—are real and must be addressed, not just with words, but with deeds, by investing in our schools and our communities; by enforcing our civil rights laws and ensuring fairness in our criminal justice system; by providing this generation with ladders of opportunity that were unavailable for previous generations. It requires all Americans to realize that your dreams do not have to come at the expense of my dreams; that investing in the health, welfare and education of black and brown and white children will ultimately help all of America prosper.

In the end, then, what is called for is nothing more and nothing less than what all the world's great religions demand—that we do unto others as we would have them do unto us. Let us be our brother's keeper, scripture tells us. Let us be our sister's keeper. Let us find that common stake we all have in one another, and let our politics reflect that spirit as well. For we have a choice in this country. We can accept a politics that breeds division and conflict and cynicism. We can tackle race only as spectacle—as we did in the O.J. trial—or in the wake of tragedy—as we did in the aftermath of Katrina—or as fodder for the nightly news. We can play Reverend Wright's sermons on every channel, every day and talk about them from now until the election, and make the only question in this campaign whether or not the American people think that I somehow believe or sympathize with his most offensive words. We can pounce on some gaffe by a Hillary supporter as evidence that she's playing the race card, or we can speculate on whether white men will all flock to John McCain in the general election regardless of his policies.

We can do that. But if we do, I can tell you that in the next election, we'll be talking about some other distraction. And then another one. And then another one. And nothing will change. That is one option. Or, at this moment, in this election, we can come together and say, "Not this time." This time, we want to talk about the crumbling schools that are stealing the future of black children and white children and Asian children and Hispanic children and Native American children. This time, we want to reject the cynicism that tells us that these kids can't learn; that those kids who don't look like us are somebody else's problem. The children of America are not those kids, they are our kids, and we will not let them fall behind in a twenty-first-century economy. Not this time. This time we want to talk about how the lines in the emergency room are filled with whites and blacks and Hispanics who do not have health care, who don't have the power on their own to overcome the special interests in Washington, but who can take them on if we do it together.

This time, we want to talk about the shuttered mills that once provided a decent life for men and women of every race, and the homes for sale that once belonged to Americans from every religion, every region, every walk of life. This time, we want to talk about the fact that the real problem is not that someone who doesn't look like you might take your job; it's that the corporation you work for will ship it overseas for nothing more than a profit. This time, we want to talk about the men and women of every color and creed who serve together and fight together and bleed together under the same proud flag. We want to talk about how to bring them home from a war that should have never been authorized and should have never been waged. And we want to talk about how we'll show our patriotism by caring for them and their families, and giving them the benefits that they have earned. I would not be running for President if I didn't believe with all my heart that this is what the vast majority of Americans want for this country. This union may never be perfect, but generation after generation has shown that it can always be perfected. And today, whenever I find myself feeling doubtful or cynical about this possibility, what gives me the most hope is the next generation—the young people whose attitudes and beliefs and openness to change have already made history in this election.

There is one story in particularly that I'd like to leave you with today—a story I told when I had the great honor of speaking on Dr. King's birthday at his home church, Ebenezer Baptist, in Atlanta. There is a young, twenty-three-year-old white woman named Ashley Baia who organized for our campaign in Florence, South Carolina. She had been working to organize a mostly African American community since the beginning of this campaign, and one day she was at a roundtable discussion where everyone went around telling their story and why they were there. And Ashley said that when she was nine years old, her mother got cancer. And because she had to miss days of work, she was let go and lost her health care. They had to file for bankruptcy, and that's when Ashley decided that she had to do something to help her mom. She knew that food was one of their most expensive costs, and so Ashley convinced her mother that what she really liked and really wanted to eat more than anything else was mustard and relish sandwiches—because that was the cheapest way to eat. That's the mind of a nine-year-old.

She did this for a year until her mom got better. So she told everyone at the roundtable that the reason she joined our campaign was so that she could help the millions of other children in the country who want and need to help their parents, too. Now, Ashley might have made a different choice. Perhaps somebody told her along the way that the source of her mother's problems were blacks who were on welfare and too lazy to work, or Hispanics who were coming into the country illegally. But she didn't. She sought out allies in her fight against injustice. Anyway, Ashley finishes her story and then goes around the room and asks everyone else why they're supporting the campaign. They all have different stories and different reasons. Many bring up a specific issue. And finally they come to this elderly black man who's been sitting there quietly the entire time. And Ashley asks him why he's there. And he does not bring up a specific issue. He does not say health care or the economy. He does not say education or the war. He does not say that he was there because of Barack Obama. He simply says to everyone in the room, "I am here because of Ashley."

"I'm here because of Ashley." By itself, that single moment of recognition between that young white girl and that old black man is not enough. It is not enough to give health care to the sick, or jobs to the jobless, or education to our children. But it is where we start. It is where our union grows stronger. And as so many generations have come to realize over the course of the 221 years since a band of patriots signed that document right here in Philadelphia, that is where the perfection begins.

APPENDIX 8

African American Population as a Percentage of the Total Population, 1870–2008

Year	Total population	Black population	% black
1870[1]	39,818,449	5,392,172	13.5
1880	50,155,783	6,580,793	13.1
1890	62,947,714	7,488,676	11.9
1900	75,994,575	8,833,994	11.6
1910	91,972,266	9,827,763	10.7
1920	105,710,620	10,463,131	9.9
1930	122,775,046	11,891,143	9.7
1940	131,669,275	12,865,518	9.8
1950	150,697,361	15,042,286	9.9
1960[2]	179,323,175	18,871,831	10.5
1970	203,211,926	22,580,289	11.1
1980	226,545,805	26,495,025	11.7
1990	248,709,873	29,986,060	12.1
2000[3]	281,421,906	36,419,434	12.9
2007 (est.)	301,621,157	40,744,132	13.5
2010 (est.)	308,936,000	40,454,000	13.1

1. Adjusted to account for underenumeration in southern states.
2. First year census includes Alaska and Hawaii.
3. First year census allows multiracial identification. Totals include African American identification alone or in combination with one or more other races.

Sources: Kenneth Estell, ed., *The African American Almanac*, 6th ed. (Detroit MI: Gale Research, 1994), 635, 632, 634; Joe William Trotter Jr., *The African American Experience* (New York: Houghton Mifflin, 2001), A-30–A-31. Estimates for 2007 are taken from U.S. Bureau of the Census, "Censes of Populations for 2007. Characteristics of the Population" (Washington DC: Government Printing Office, 2008).

APPENDIX 9

Distribution of the African American Population by Region, 1870–2008

	PERCENTAGE OF AFRICAN AMERICANS LIVING IN:			
Year	Northeast	Midwest	South	West
1870	3.7	5.6	90.6	0.1
1880	3.5	5.9	90.5	0.2
1890	3.6	5.8	90.3	0.4
1900	4.4	5.6	89.7	0.3
1910	4.9	5.5	89.0	0.5
1920	6.5	7.6	85.2	0.8
1930	9.6	10.6	78.7	1.0
1940	10.6	11.0	77.0	1.3
1950	13.4	14.8	68.0	3.8
1960	16.0	18.3	59.9	5.8
1970	19.2	20.2	50.0	7.5
1980	18.3	20.1	50.0	8.5
1990	18.7	19.1	52.8	9.4
2000[1]	18.0	18.8	53.6	9.6
2007[2]	17.8	18.0	54.1	10.1

1. Totals include African American alone or in combination with one or more other races.
2. Estimate of the U. S. Census Bureau for July 1, 2007, released May 1, 2008.

Sources: Kenneth Estell, ed., *The African American Almanac*, 6th ed. (Detroit MI: Gale Research, 1994), 635, 632, 634; Joe William Trotter Jr., *The African American Experience* (New York: Houghton Mifflin, 2001), A-30–A-31. Estimates for 2007 are taken from U.S. Bureau of the Census, "Censes of Populations for 2007. Characteristics of the Population" (Washington DC: Government Printing Office, 2008).

APPENDIX 10

Black Population in the Twenty Largest U.S. Cities, 2008

City	Black population	Total population	% black of total population
New York	2,152,001	8,214,426	26.2
Los Angeles	388,505	3,773,846	10.3
Chicago	984,347	2,749,283	35.8
Houston	521,861	2,074,828	25.2
Phoenix	90,268	1,429,637	6.3
Philadelphia	656,100	1,448,394	45.3
San Antonio	91,276	1,273,374	7.2
San Diego	99,050	1,261,251	7.9
Dallas	294,831	1,192,538	24.7
San Jose	31,002	916,220	3.4
Detroit	702,115	834,116	84.2
Jacksonville	252,303	799,875	31.5
Indianapolis	219,732	789,306	27.8
San Francisco	55,014	744,041	7.4
Columbus	207,200	718,477	28.0
Austin	64,091	717,100	8.9
Memphis	412,801	643,122	64.2
Fort Worth	116,012	637,178	18.2
Baltimore	412,681	631,366	65.4
Charlotte	230,874	648,387	35.6

Source: U.S. Census Bureau, "American Community Survey, 2008. Ranked according to population estimates, released June, 2009" (Washington DC: Government Printing Office, 2009).

NOTES

Introduction

1. Painter, *Creating Black Americans*, iv–x; Whitaker, "A Nation within a Nation," unpaginated.
2. Painter, *Creating Black Americans*, iv–x; Whitaker, "A Nation within a Nation," unpaginated.
3. Whitaker, *Race Work*, 63.
4. Whitaker, *Race Work*, 63–64.
5. Whitaker, *Race Work*, 64; Whitaker, "A Nation within a Nation," unpaginated.
6. Whitaker, *Race Work*, 64; Whitaker, "A Nation within a Nation," unpaginated.
7. Whitaker, *Race Work*, 64; Whitaker, "A Nation within a Nation," unpaginated.
8. Whitaker, "A Nation within a Nation," unpaginated.
9. Whitaker, "A Nation within a Nation," unpaginated.
10. Whitaker, "A Nation within a Nation," unpaginated.

1. "Make Way for Democracy"

1. The title of this chapter is taken from DuBois, "Returning Soldiers," 13. Quotations in this paragraph are from DeGraaf, "Significant Steps," 25–26. Portions of this chapter have been influenced by and culled from my book, *Race Work*, pp. 63-87. This material is reprinted here with permission from the University of Nebraska Press.
2. Anderson, *A. Philip Randolph*, 256.
3. Franklin and Moss, *Slavery to Freedom*, 619.
4. Rawn, *The Double V*, 130.
5. Baker, "Lincoln Ragsdale," 96–99.
6. Hine, Hine, and Harrold, *African American Odyssey*, 485.
7. Johnson, *Negro Digest* 6 (1945): 87.
8. This section on black resistance on or near military installations in Arizona is influenced by real-time coverage by the *Arizona Republic* on November 27–28, 1942; November 30, 1942; February 26, 1943; January 15, 22, June 7, 24, August 11, 16, 1941; and by Luckingham's groundbreaking *Minorities in Phoenix*, 156–57.
9. Luckingham, *Minorities in Phoenix*, 156–57.

10. Savoy, "Stone's Throw," unpaginated.

11. Painter, *Creating Black Americans*, 222.

12. Painter, *Creating Black Americans*, 222.

13. Lewis, *Du Bois: Biography*, 363.

14. Lewis, *Du Bois: Fight*, 470.

15. "First Ladies of Color," *Crisis*, 287.

16. Hine, *Hine Sight*, 178.

17. Drake and Cayton, *Black Metropolis*, 754.

18. Herb Whitney, quoted in "Shooting Down Racism." This *Arizona Republic* article was obtained from the personal papers of Lincoln Ragsdale. It was in poor condition and listed no publication date. A copy of the piece is currently in the author's possession.

19. Taylor, *Racial Frontier*, 256–57.

20. Carson, Lapsansky-Werner, and Nash, *African American Lives*, 411.

21. Carson, Lapsansky-Werner, and Nash, *African American Lives*, 411.

22. CORE, "Making Equality a Reality," unpaginated.

23. Skinner, "Afro-Americans, Africa, and America," 145.

24. Bunche, "Negro's Stake in the World Crisis," unpaginated.

25. Robeson, *Undiscovered Paul Robeson*, 143.

26. Hine, Hine, and Harrold, *African Americans*, 576.

2. "Let Your Motto Be Resistance"

1. Lewis and Lewis, *Race, Politics, and Memory*, 24.

2. Hine, Hine, and Harrold, *African American Odyssey*, 515.

3. Oates, *Trumpet Sound*, 18.

4. King, *Testament of Hope*, 422.

5. Hardin, Kelley, and Lewis, *We Changed the World*, 39.

6. Garrow, *Bearing the Cross*, 15.

7. Phibbs, *Montgomery Bus Boycott*, 15.

8. Abdul-Jabbar and Steinberg, *Black Profiles in Courage*, 236.

9. Levine, *Freedom's Children*, 18.

10. Williams, *Eyes on the Prize*, 53.

11. King, *Autobiography*, 60–61.

12. Burns, ed., *Daybreak of Freedom*, 165.

13. King, *Papers 4*, 483.

14. King, *Papers 3*, 430.

15. King, *Papers 3*, 460.

16. King, *Papers 4*, 103–104.

17. Garrow, *Bearing the Cross*, 91.

18. National Park Service, "Little Rock Nine," unpaginated.

19. National Park Service, "Little Rock Nine," unpaginated.

20. National Park Service, "Little Rock Nine," unpaginated.

21. National Park Service, "Little Rock Nine," unpaginated.
22. King, "Letter from Birmingham Jail," unpaginated.
23. Kelley, *Yo' Mama's Disfunktional!*, 85.
24. Simba, "Malcolm X (1925–1965)," unpaginated.
25. Simba, "Malcolm X (1925–1965)," unpaginated.
26. Dwayne Mack, "Freedom Rides (1961)," unpaginated.
27. Williams, *Negroes with Guns*, 76.
28. Mack, "Freedom Rides (1961)," unpaginated.

3. *"Deep Rumbling of Discontent"*

1. Formwalt, "Albany Movement," unpaginated.
2. "Albany Movement," *The King Encyclopedia*, http://mlk-kppol.stanford.edu/kingweb/about_king/encyclopedia/albany_movement.htm.
3. Jackson, *Civil Rights to Human Rights*, 149.
4. Eskew, *But for Birmingham*, 44.
5. Hine, *Concise History*, 529.
6. King, *Autobiography*, 344.
7. Young, *Easy Burden*, 193.
8. Oates, *Trumpet Sound*, 219–20.
9. King, "Letter from Birmingham Jail," unpaginated.
10. Branch, *Parting the Waters*, 824.
11. King, "I Have A Dream," *Ebony*, 42.
12. Greenhaw, *Fighting the Devil*, 138.
13. Gold, *Civil Rights Act of 1964*, 112.
14. McKenzie, *All God's Children*, 8.
15. Garrow, *Bearing the Cross*, 408–9.
16. King, *Autobiography*, 230.
17. Hine, Hine, and Harrold, *African American Odyssey*, 545.
18. Strickland, *Malcolm X*, 213.
19. Kindred, *Sound and Fury*, 84.
20. Carson, *In Struggle*, 209.
21. Salter, "Stokely Carmichael (Kwame Ture) (1941–1998)," unpaginated.
22. Dyson, *I May Not Get There*, 207.
23. Lewis, *King*, 326.
24. Hine, Hine, and Harrold, *African American Odyssey*, 546.
25. Emerson, *People of the Dream*, 19.
26. James, *Talented Tenth*, 31–32.
27. Kindred, *Sound and Fury*, 58.
28. Roberts and Olson, *Winning Is the Only Thing*, 171.
29. Bingham and Wallace, *Ali's Greatest Fight*, 119.
30. King, *Autobiography*, 574.
31. King, *Testament of Hope*, 241.

32. The quotation is taken from Hawken, *Blessed Unrest*, 186. See also Mieder, "*Making a Way*," 346.

33. Carson and Shepard, eds., *Call to Conscience*, 143.

34. Bingham and Wallace, *Ali's Greatest Fight*, 143.

35. Carson, Lapsansky-Werner, and Nash, *African American Lives*, 487.

36. Oates, *Trumpet Sound*, 413.

37. Carson, Lapsansky-Werner, and Nash, *African American Lives*, 487.

38. Hine, Hine, and Harrold, *African American Odyssey*, 547.

39. King, *Testament of Hope*, 240.

40. Carmichael and Hamilton, *Black Power*, xi.

41. King, *Testament of Hope*, 589.

42. Sugrue, *Sweet Land of Liberty*, 353.

43. Lawson, *Running for Freedom*, 289.

44. Anderson, *Pursuit of Fairness*, 88.

45. Hine, Hine, and Harrold, *African American Odyssey*, 552.

46. King, *Papers 6*, 169.

47. King, *Testament of Hope*, 65–66, 72.

48. Behnken, *Fighting Their Own Battles*, 150.

49. Garrow, *Bearing the Cross*, 621.

4. "So Let It Be Done"

1. Hampton, Frayer, and Flynn, eds., *Voices of Freedom*, 564.

2. Perlstein, *Nixonland*, 255.

3. Goodwin, *Johnson and the American Dream*, 251.

4. Westheider, *Fighting on Two Fronts*, 18.

5. Baraka and Harris, *Jones/Baraka Reader*, 167; Leitch, *Cultural Criticism*, 86.

6. Rabaka, *Hip Hop's Inheritance*, 105.

7. Baldwin, "Autobiographical Notes," 9.

8. Hine, Hine, and Harrold, *African American Odyssey*, 560.

9. Hine, Hine, and Harrold, *African American Odyssey*, 560.

10. Hine, Hine, and Harrold, *African American Odyssey*, 560.

11. Hine, Hine, and Harrold, *African American Odyssey*, 560.

12. Bloom, *Ellison's Invisible Man*, 43.

13. Milner, "Black Magic," 12.

14. Boyd, *Black Enough*, 8.

15. Brown, *Godfather of Soul*, 200.

16. Reeves, *Calling Out*, 56.

17. Reed, *Holy Profane*, 122.

18. Watkins, "Richard Pryor," *New York Times*.

19. Watkins, "Richard Pryor," *New York Times*.

20. Watkins, "Richard Pryor," *New York Times*.

21. Watkins, "Richard Pryor," *New York Times*.

22. Watkins, "Richard Pryor," *New York Times*.

23. Shayon, "'Julia': Breakthrough or Letdown?," *Saturday Review*.

24. The Archive of American Television, "The Jeffersons," unpaginated.

25. The Archive of American Television, "The Jeffersons," unpaginated.

26. Whitaker, "A Nation within a Nation," unpaginated.

27. Whitaker, "A Nation within a Nation," unpaginated.

28. Whitaker, "A Nation within a Nation," unpaginated.

29. Whitaker, "A Nation within a Nation," unpaginated.

30. Graham, *By His Own Rules*, 93.

31. Office of Policy Planning and Research, *Negro Family*, 29.

32. King and Smith, *Still a House Divided*, 151.

33. Lawson, *Running for Freedom*, 113.

34. Hampton, Fayer, and Flynn, *Voices of Freedom*, 566.

35. Hampton, Fayer, and Flynn, *Voices of Freedom*, 568–69.

36. "Conservatism and the Rise of Ronald Regan," unpaginated.

5. *"To the Break of Dawn"*

1. Reagan, *Tear Down This Wall*, 142.

2. Kweit and Kweit, *People and Politics*, 409.

3. Golson, *Playboy Interview*, 268.

4. cbs News, "Clarence Thomas: The Justice Nobody Knows."

5. Hine, Hine, and Harrold, *African American Odyssey*, 582.

6. cbs News, "Anita Hill vs. Clarence Thomas."

7. cbs News, "Anita Hill vs. Clarence Thomas."

8. Hornblower, "Taking It All Back," *Time*.

9. Lewis, "Barbara Jordan," unpaginated.

10. Lewis, "Barbara Jordan," unpaginated.

11. Lewis, "Barbara Jordan," unpaginated.

12. Wyman, "Did 'Thriller' Really Sell," unpaginated.

13. *Michael Jackson BlogSpot*, "Michael Jackson Biography," unpaginated; *MichaelJacksonDeceased.com*, "The Passing of a Superstar," unpaginated.

14. *MichaelJacksonDeceased.com*, "The Passing of a Superstar," unpaginated.

15. *MichaelJacksonDeceased.com*, "The Passing of a Superstar," unpaginated.

16. *MichaelJacksonDeceased.com*, "The Passing of a Superstar," unpaginated.

17. *The Arena*, "Jesse Jackson," unpaginated.

18. Sabato, "Jackson's 'Hymietown' Remark," unpaginated.

19. *The Arena*, "Jesse Jackson," unpaginated.

20. Viscount, "Jackson, Jesse," unpaginated.

21. Viscount, "Jackson, Jesse," unpaginated.

22. Viscount, "Jackson, Jesse," unpaginated.

23. Viscount, "Jackson, Jesse," unpaginated.

24. Lester, *Fire in My Soul*, 229.

25. Carson, Lapsansky-Werner, and Nash, *African American Lives*, 517.
26. Clemons, *Global Affairs*, 79.
27. Mariner, *No Escape*, 157.
28. Gray, "LA Riots," unpaginated.
29. Gray, "LA Riots," unpaginated.
30. Whitaker, *Race Work*, 249–50.
31. "Sharpton Slams NYC Cops," *Michigan Daily*.
32. Baron, *Web of Urban Racism*, 1–35.
33. Carson, Lapsansky-Werner, and Nash, *African American Lives*, 535.
34. Bancroft, *Human Sexuality*, 183.
35. West, *Race Matters*, xii.
36. Harris-Lacewell, "Clinton Fallacy," unpaginated.
37. Berry, "Diluting the Vote," 436–43.
38. Berry, "Diluting the Vote," 436–43.

  6. *"The Audacity of Hope"*

1. Butler, "Colin Powell," unpaginated.
2. Butler, "Colin Powell," unpaginated.
3. Weaver, "Making the Case for Public Education," 22.
4. Alexander and Benet, "Believe in Magic," *People*, unpaginated.
5. Hine, Hine, and Harrold, *Concise History*, 530.
6. NAACP, "Focus on Minority Health Disparities," 55.
7. Hood, "Why Should Minorities Be Concerned," 55.
8. Salzberger and Turck, *Reparations*, 70.
9. Robinson, *Debt*, 221.
10. Asante, *Erasing Racism*, 330.
11. Hine, Hine, and Harrold, *Concise History*, 490.
12. Hine, Hine, and Harrold, *African American Odyssey*, 602.
13. Hazen, Hausman, Straus, and Chihara, eds., *After 9/11*, 64.
14. Barras, "Complexity of African-American Views of the 'War,'" *Washington Post*.
15. Leonard Pitts Jr., "Sept. 12, 2001: We'll Go Forward from this Moment," *Miami Herald*.
16. Marable, *Great Wells*, 316.
17. Price, *Barack Obama*, 33.
18. Obama, "Against Going to War in Iraq," unpaginated.
19. Obama, "Against Going to War in Iraq," unpaginated.
20. Obama, "American Promise," unpaginated.
21. Portions of this chapter were previously published as pp. 1–10 in Levitt and Whitaker, eds., *Hurricane Katrina*.
22. Dyson, *Hell or High Water*, 2.
23. West, "Exiles," unpaginated.
24. Dyson, *Hell or High Water*, 87.

25. Frey, *Three Quarter Cadillac*, 89.

26. Christian, "Black Leaders Sound Off," *Jet*.

27. White, *Modernity*, 180.

28. Dyson, *Is Bill Cosby Right?*, 1.

29. Dyson, *Is Bill Cosby Right?*, xv.

30. Jackson, "U.S. Economy Forces Many Black Americans," unpaginated.

31. Painter, *Creating Black Americans*, 355.

32. Smiley, *Covenant*, 9.

33. King, *Down Low*, 13.

7. Contemporary Black America

1. Wurts, "Dave Chappelle," *Inside the Actors Studio*.

2. Farley, "Dave Speaks," *Time*, unpaginated.

3. Farley, "Dave Speaks," *Time*, unpaginated.

4. Kelley, *Race Rebels*, 185.

5. Pollock, *By the Time*, 239.

6. Hine, Hine, and Harrold, *African American Odyssey*, 667–80.

7. Hine, Hine, and Harrold, *African American Odyssey*, 667–80.

8. Grandmaster Flash and the Furious Five, "The Message."

9. Hine, Hine, and Harrold, *African American Odyssey*, 667–80.

10. Hine, Hine, and Harrold, *African American Odyssey*, 667–80.

11. Sharpley-Whiting, *Pimps Up*, 12.

12. Hine, Hine, and Harrold, *African American Odyssey*, 667–80.

13. Hine, Hine, and Harrold, *African American Odyssey*, 667–80.

14. The Biography Channel, "Tupac Shakur Biography," unpaginated.

15. The Biography Channel, "Tupac Shakur Biography," unpaginated.

16. "Tupac Shakur Biography," *Rolling Stone*, unpaginated.

17. Powell, "Ready To Live," 45–52.

18. Berube, "The 2Pac and Notorious B.I.G. Feud," unpaginated.

19. Berube, "The 2Pac and Notorious B.I.G. Feud," unpaginated.

20. Tate, *Everything but the Burden*, 2.

21. Hine, Hine, and Harrold, *African American Odyssey*, 670–80.

22. Hine, Hine, and Harrold, *African American Odyssey*, 670–80.

23. Pellett and Nelson, PBS.

24. LaBlaine and Bigelow, *Contemporary Black Biography*, 6.

25. Asante, *Afrocentric Idea*, 32.

26. Hine, Hine, and Harrold, *African American Odyssey*, 596.

27. Hutchinson, "Diversity," unpaginated.

28. Schlesinger, *ISOC Internazionale*, 39.

29. Alexander, *Farrakhan Factor*, 106.

30. Magida, *Prophet*, xxi.

31. Farrakhan, "Why A Million Man March," unpaginated.

32. Quoted in Kelley, *Yo' Mama's Disfunktional!*, 88.

33. Brown, *Taste of Power*, 357.

34. Cole and Guy-Sheftall, *Gender Talk*, 96.

35. Crenshaw, "Whose Story," 405.

36. Coretta Scott King, welcoming remarks at 13th Annual Creating Change Conference, Atlanta GA, November 14, 2000.

37. Whitaker, "A Nation within a Nation," unpaginated.

8. Hope and Change

1. Parts of this chapter have been hewn from Matthew C. Whitaker, "Barack Obama and American Democracy," Barack Obama and American Democracy Conference Program (unpublished), Arizona State University, March 24–25, 2011. Also found online at http://shprs.clas.asu.edu/BOAD.

2. Whitaker, "Barack Obama and American Democracy," unpaginated.

3. Murray, *Autobiography*, 36.

4. Whitaker, "Barack Obama and American Democracy," unpaginated.

5. Sharpley-Whiting, ed., *The Speech*, 201–2.

6. Henry, Allen, and Chrisman, *Obama Phenomenon*, 131.

7. Henry, Allen, and Chrisman, *Obama Phenomenon*, 241.

8. "Fox Anchor Calls Obama Fist Pound a 'Terrorist Fist Jab,'" *Huffington Post*.

9. Spaulding, "Obama Daughters Labeled 'Nappy Headed Hos,'" unpaginated.

10. Gutgold, *Almost Madam President*, 45.

11. Formisano, *Tea Party*, 43.

12. Whitaker, "Barack Obama and American Democracy," unpaginated.

13. Whitaker, "Barack Obama and American Democracy," unpaginated.

14. Obama, "First Inaugural Address," unpaginated.

15. Joseph, *Dark Days*, 217.

16. Whitaker, "Racist Taunts at Obama Should Worry Us All," unpaginated.

17. Joseph, *Dark Days*, 377.

18. Joseph, *Dark Days*, 221.

19. Joseph, *Dark Days,* 221–22.

20. Olbermann, *Pitchforks and Torches*, 168.

21. Watson, "Confederate 'Swastika' under Attack," BBC.

22. Joseph, *Dark Days*, 228.

23. Galston, "Obama's First Two Years," unpaginated.

24. Mann, "American Politics," unpaginated.

25. Galston, "Obama's First Two Years," unpaginated.

26. Baker, "Whose President Is He, Anyway?" *New York Times*.

27. Galston, "Obama's First Two Years," unpaginated.

28. Baker, "Education of a President," *New York Times*.

29. Galston, "Obama's First Two Years," unpaginated.

30. Wolf, "Obama Reaches Three-Year Mark," USA *Today*.

31. Feldmann, "Gabrielle Giffords Shooting," *Christian Science Monitor.*

32. Nicholas and Parsons, "Obama Mocks Trump's Presidential Ambitions," *USA Today.*

33. Nicholas and Parsons, "Obama Mocks Trump's Presidential Aspirations," *West Australian.*

34. Nicholas and Parsons, "Obama's Poker Face."

35. Nicholas and Parsons, "Obama's Poker Face."

36. Stengel, "The Next America," *Time.*

37. Whitaker, "Change Blossoming," *Arizona Republic.*

BIBLIOGRAPHY

Abdul-Jabbar, Kareem, and Alan Steinberg. *Black Profiles in Courage: A Legacy of African-American Achievement*. New York: HarperCollins, 1996.

Alexander, Amy, ed. *The Farrakhan Factor: African-American Writers on Leadership, Nationhood, and Minister Louis Farrakhan*. New York: Grove Press, 1998.

Alexander, Benita, and Lorenzo Benet. "Believe in Magic," *People* 26, no. 20 (November 25, 1991). http://www.people.com/people/archive/article/ 0,,20111343,00.html. Accessed December 4, 2011.

Allen, Robert L. *Black Awakening in Capitalist America: An Analytic History*. New York: Anchor Books, 1970.

———. *The Port Chicago Mutiny*. New York: Warner Books, 1989.

Anderson, Jervis. *A. Philip Randolph: A Biographical Portrait*. Berkeley: University of California Press, 1986.

Anderson, Talmadge, ed. *Black Studies: Theory, Method, and Cultural Perspectives*. Pullman: Washington State University Press, 1990.

Anderson, Terry H. *The Pursuit of Fairness: A History of Affirmative Action*. New York: Oxford University Press, 2005.

Andrews, William L., Frances Smith Foster, and Trudier Harris, eds. *The Oxford Companion to African American Literature*. New York: Oxford University Press, 1997.

Angelou, Maya. *I Know Why the Caged Bird Sings*. New York: Ballantine, 2009. First published 1969 by Random House.

Appiah, Anthony, and Amy Gutmann. *Color Conscious: The Political Morality of Race*. Princeton NJ: Princeton University Press, 1996.

Aptheker, Herbert, ed. *A Documentary History of the Negro People in the United States*. 7 vols. New York: Citadel Press, 1951–94.

The Archive of American Television. "The Jeffersons," *EmmyTVLegends.org*, http:// emmytvlegends.org/interviews/shows/jeffersons-the.

The Arena. "Jesse Jackson," http://www.politico.com/arena/bio/jesse_jackson.html, 2011.

Asante, Molefi K. *African American History: A Journey of Liberation*. Maywood NJ: Peoples Publishing Group, 1995.

———. *The Afrocentric Idea*. Philadelphia: Temple University Press, 1987.

———. *Erasing Racism: The Survival of the American Nation*. Amherst NY: Prometheus Books, 2003.

Baker, Lori K. "Lincoln Ragsdale: The Man Who Refused to Be Invisible." *Phoenix Magazine* (January 1993): 96–99.

Baker, Peter . "Education of a President." *New York Times*, October 12, 2010. http://www.nytimes.com/2010/10/17/magazine/17obama-t.htom?pagewanted=all.

———. "Whose President Is He, Anyway?" *New York Times*, November 18, 2008. http://www.nytimes.com/2008/11/16/weekinreview/16baker.html?pagewanted -all&r=0. Accessed November 15, 2008.

Baldwin, James. "Autobiographical Notes." In *James Baldwin: Collected Essays, Volume 2*. New York: Library of America, 1998.

———. *Nobody Knows My Name: More Notes of a Native Son*. New York: Dial Press, 1961.

———. *Notes of a Native Son*. New York: Dial Press, 1955.

Bancroft, J. H. *Human Sexuality and Its Problems*, 3rd. ed. Amsterdam: Elsevier Health Sciences, 2009.

Baraka, Amiri, and William J. Harris. *The LeRoi Jones/Amiri Baraka Reader*. New York: Basic Books, 1999.

Baraka, Amiri, and Larry Neal, eds. *Black Fire: An Anthology of Afro-American Writing*. New York: Black Classic Press, 2007. First published 1968 by Morrow.

Baraka, Imamu Amiri. *The Autobiography of LeRoi Jones*. New York: Freundlich Books, 1984.

———. *Blues People: Negro Music in White America*. New York: W. Morrow, 1963.

Bardolph, Richard. *The Civil Rights Record: Black Americans and the Law, 1849–1970*. New York: Crowell, 1970.

Barlow, William. *Voice Over: The Making of Black Radio*. Philadelphia: Temple University Press, 1999.

Baron, Harold M. *The Web of Urban Racism*. Chicago: Chicago Urban League, 1968.

Barr, Alwyn. *Black Texans: A History of African Americans in Texas, 1528–1995*. Norman: University of Oklahoma Press, 1996.

Barras, Jonetta Rose. "The Complexity of African-American Views of the 'War.'" *Washington Post*, October 28, 2001.

Barrett, Paul. *The Good Black: A True Story of Race in America*. New York: Dutton, 1999.

Bartley, Numan V. *The Rise of Massive Resistance: Race and Politics in the South during the 1950s*. Baton Rouge: Louisiana State University Press, 1969.

Bates, Daisy. *The Long Shadow of Little Rock: A Memoir*. New York: David McKay, 1962.

Behnken, Brian. *Fighting Their Own Battles: Mexican Americans, African Americans, and the Struggle for Civil Rights in Texas.* Chapel Hill: University of North Carolina Press, 2011.

Bell, Derrick A. *Faces at the Bottom of the Well: The Permanence of Racism.* New York: Basic Books, 1992.

Benjamin, Lois. *The Black Elite: Facing the Color Line in the Twilight of the Twentieth Century.* Chicago: Nelson-Hall, 1991.

Bennett, Lerone. *Before the Mayflower: A History of Black America.* 8th ed. Chicago: Johnson Publishing, 2008.

———. *The Shaping of Black America.* New York: Viking Penguin, 1993.

Berman, William C. *The Politics of Civil Rights in the Truman Administration.* Columbus: Ohio State University Press, 1970.

Bernal, Martin. *Black Athena: The Afroasiatic Roots of Classical Civilization.* London: Free Association Books, 1987.

Berry, Mary Frances. "Commission Reports Minorities Penalized in 2000 Election; Calls for Probe by Justice Dept.," *Jet* 100, no. 2 (June 25, 2001): 6.

———. "Diluting the Vote: The Irony of Bush v. Gore," *Journal of American History* 88, no. 2 (September 2001): 436–43.

———. *My Face Is Black Is True: Callie House and the Struggle for Ex-Slave Reparations.* New York: Alfred A. Knopf, 2005.

Berry, Mary Frances, and John W. Blassingame. *Long Memory: The Black Experience in America.* New York: Oxford University Press, 1982.

Berube, Jennifer. "The 2Pac and Notorious B.I.G. Feud: Theories Surrounding the Murders of the Hottest Rivalling Rappers." *Rap/Hip Hop Music@suite101*, http://suite101.com/article/the-2pac-and-notorious-big-feud-a211291.

Billingsley, Andrew. *Climbing Jacob's Ladder: The Enduring Legacy of African-American Families.* New York: Simon and Schuster, 1992.

Bingham, Howard, and Max Wallace. *Muhammad Ali's Greatest Fight: Cassius Clay vs. the United States of America.* Ann Arbor MI: M. Evans, 2000.

The Biography Channel. "Tupac Shakur Biography," http://www.biography.com/people/tupac-shakur-206528.

Blaustein, Albert P., and Robert L. Zangrando, eds. *Civil Rights and African Americans: A Documentary History.* Evanston IL: Northwestern University Press, 1991.

Bloom, Harold. *Ralph Ellison's Invisible Man.* New York: Chelsea House Publications, 2009.

Bluestone, Barry, and Bennett Harrison. *The Deindustrialization of America: Plant Closings, Community Abandonment, and the Dismantling of Basic Industry.* New York: Basic Books, 1982.

Blum, John Morton. *V Was for Victory: Politics and American Culture during World War II.* New York: Harcourt Brace Jovanovich, 1996.

Bogues, Anthony. *Black Heretics, Black Prophets: Radical Political Intellectuals.* New York: Routledge, 2003.

Boyd, Todd. E. *Am I Black Enough for You? Popular Culture from the Hood and Beyond*. Bloomington: Indiana University Press, 1997.

Branch, Taylor. *Parting the Waters: America in the King Years, 1954–63*. New York: Simon and Schuster, 1988.

——— . *Pillar of Fire: America in the King Years, 1963–65*. New York: Simon and Schuster, 1998.

Brazile, Donna. *Cooking with Grease: Stirring the Pots in American Politics*. New York: Simon and Schuster, 2004.

Broussard, Albert S. *Black San Francisco: The Struggle for Racial Equality in the West, 1900–1954*. Lawrence: University Press of Kansas, 1993.

Brown, Elaine. *A Taste of Power: A Black Woman's Story*. New York: Pantheon Books, 1992.

Brown, James. *James Brown: The Godfather of Soul*. New York: Da Capo Press, 2003. First published 1986 by Macmillan.

Brown, Michael K. *Race, Money, and the American Welfare State*. Ithaca NY: Cornell University Press, 1999.

Bullard, Robert D., Glenn S. Johnson, and Angel O. Torres, eds. *Highway Robbery: Transportation Racism and New Routes to Equity*. Cambridge MA: South End Press, 2004.

Bunche, Ralph J. "The Negro's Stake in the World Crisis," a speech given to the Association of Colleges and Secondary School for Negroes, Montgomery, Alabama, December 6, 1940. Bunche Papers, Department of Special Collections, Charles E. Young Research Library, University of California, Los Angeles.

Burk, Robert Fredrick. *The Eisenhower Administration and Black Civil Rights*. Knoxville: University of Tennessee Press, 1984.

Burner, Eric. *And Gently He Shall Lead Them: Robert Parris Moses and Civil Rights in Mississippi*. New York: New York University Press, 1994.

Burns, Stewart. *Daybreak of Freedom: The Montgomery Bus Boycott*. Chapel Hill: University of North Carolina Press, 1997.

Butler, Gerry. "Colin Powell (1937–)," TheBlackPast.org. http://www.blackpast.org/?q=aah/powell-colin-1937.

Capeci, Dominic J. *The Harlem Riot of 1943*. Philadelphia: Temple University Press, 1977.

——— . *Race Relations in Wartime Detroit: The Sojourner Truth Housing Controversy of 1942*. Philadelphia: Temple University Press, 1984.

Capeci, Dominic J., and Martha Frances Wilkerson. *Layered Violence: The Detroit Rioters of 1943*. Jackson: University of Mississippi, 1991.

Carmichael, Stokely, and Charles V. Hamilton. *Black Power: The Politics of Liberation in America*. New York: Random House, 1967.

Carnoy, Martin. *Faded Dreams: The Politics and Economics of Race in America*. New York: Cambridge University Press, 1994.

Carson, Clayborne. "The Civil Rights Movement," in Leonard W. Levy, Kenneth

Karst, and John West, eds., *Encyclopedia of the American Constitution*. New York: Macmillan, 1992.

——. *In Struggle: SNCC and the Black Awakening of the 1960s*. Cambridge MA: Harvard University Press, 1981.

Carson, Clayborne, Emma J. Lapsansky-Werner, and Gary B. Nash. *African American Lives: The Struggle for Freedom*. Combined vol. New York: Longman, 2004.

Carson, Clayborne, and Kris Shepard, eds. *A Call to Conscience: The Landmark Speeches of Dr. Martin Luther King, Jr.* New York: Warner, 2001.

CBS News. "Anita Hill vs. Clarence Thomas: The Backstory." October 20, 2010. http://www.cbsnews.com/stories/2010/10/20/national/main69755679.stml.

——. "Clarence Thomas: The Justice Nobody Knows." *60 Minutes*, New York: CBS News, September 30, 2007.

Chang, Jeff. *Can't Stop, Won't Stop: A History of the Hip-Hop Generation*. New York: St. Martin's Press, 2005.

Chrisman, Robert L., and Robert L. Allen. *Court of Appeal: The Black Community Speaks Out on the Racial and Sexual Politics of Thomas vs. Hill*. New York: Ballantine Books, 1992.

Christian, Charles Melvin. *Black Saga: The African American Experience*. Boston: Houghton Mifflin, 1995.

Christian, Margiena A. "Black Leaders Sound Off: Did Race Delay Relief to Disaster Areas?" *Jet* 108, no. 13 (September 26, 2005).

Clark, Septima Poinsette. *Ready from Within: Septima Clark and the Civil Rights Movement*. Edited with an introduction by Cynthia Stokes Brown. Navarro CA: Wild Trees Press, 1986.

Cleaver, Eldridge. *Eldridge Cleaver: Post-Prison Writings and Speeches*. Edited by Robert Scheer. New York: Random House, 1969.

Clegg, Claude Andrew. *An Original Man: The Life and Times of Elijah Muhammad*. New York: St. Martin's Press, 1997.

Clemons, Michael L. *African Americans in Global Affairs: Contemporary Perspectives*. Lebanon NH: University Press of New England, 2010.

Cohen, Cathy J. *The Boundaries of Blackness: AIDS and the Breakdown of Black Politics*. Chicago: University of Chicago Press, 1999.

Colburn, David R., and Elizabeth Jacoway, eds. *Southern Businessmen and Desegregation*. Baton Rouge: Louisiana State University Press, 1982.

Cole, Johnnetta B., and Beverly Guy-Sheftall. *Gender Talk: The Struggle for Women's Equality in African American Communities*. New York: One World/Ballantine Books, 2003.

Cone, James H. *Martin and Malcolm and America: A Dream or a Nightmare*. Maryknoll NY: Orbis Books, 1991.

Conley, Dalton. *Being Black, Living in the Red: Race, Wealth, and Social Policy in America*. Berkeley: University of California Press, 1999.

Conniff, Michael, and Thomas J. Davis. *Africans in the Americas: A History of the Black Diaspora*. New York: Bedford St. Martin's, 1993.

"Conservatism and the Rise of Ronald Regan," *American History: From Revolution to Reconstruction and Beyond*, http://www.let.rug.nl/usa/outlines/history-1994/ toward-the-21st-century/conservatism-and-the-rise-of-ronald-reagan.php.

CORE. "Making Equality a Reality." Congress of Racial Equality, CORE, 2013. http:// www.core-online/History/history/htm. Accessed April 18, 2013.

Cowan, Thomas Dale, and Jack Maguire. *Timelines of African-American History: 500 Years of Black Achievement*. New York: Berkley, 1994.

Crawford, Vicki L., Jacqueline Anne Rouse, and Barbara Woods, eds. *Women in the Civil Rights Movement: Trailblazers and Torchbearers, 1941–1965*. Brooklyn NY: Carlson, 1990.

Crenshaw, Kimberlé W. "Whose Story Is It, Anyway? Feminist and Antiracist Appropriations of Anita Hill," in *Race-ing Justice, En-gendering Power: Essays on Anita Hill, Clarence Thomas, and the Construction of Social Reality*, edited by Toni Morrison, 402–40. New York: Pantheon, 1992.

Cripps, Thomas. *Making Movies Black: The Hollywood Message Movie from World War II to the Civil Rights Era*. New York: Oxford University Press, 1993.

Cross, Theodore L. *The Black Power Imperative: Racial Inequality and the Politics of Nonviolence*. New York: Faulkner, 1984.

Dalfiume, Richard M. *Desegregation of the U.S. Armed Forces: Fighting on Two Fronts, 1939–1953*. Columbia: University of Missouri Press, 1969.

Dallek, Robert. *Flawed Giant: Lyndon Johnson and His Times, 1961–1973*. New York: Oxford University Press, 1998.

———. *Ronald Reagan: The Politics of Symbolism*. Cambridge MA: Harvard University Press, 1984.

Davis, F. James. *Who is Black?: One Nation's Definition*. University Park: Pennsylvania State University Press, 1991.

DeGraaf, Lawrence B. "Significant Steps on an Arduous Path: The Impact of World War II on Discrimination against African Americans in the West." *Journal of the West* 35, no. 1 (1996): 25–26.

D'Emilio, John. *Lost Prophet: The Life and Times of Bayard Rustin*. New York: Free Press, 2003. First published 1985 by Temple University Press.

DeVeaux, Scott Knowles. *The Birth of Bebop: A Social and Musical History*. Berkeley: University of California Press, 1997.

Dickerson, Dennis C. *Militant Mediator: Whitney M. Young Jr*. Lexington: University Press of Kentucky, 1998.

Dittmer, John. *Local People: The Struggle for Civil Rights in Mississippi*. Urbana: University of Illinois Press, 1994.

Drake, St. Clair, and Horace Cayton. *Black Metropolis: A Study of Negro Life in a Northern City*. New York: Harcourt Brace, 1945.

Drake, Willie Avon, and Robert D. Holsworth. *Affirmative Action and the Stalled Quest for Black Progress*. Urbana: University of Illinois Press, 1996.

Dryden, Charles W. *A-Train: Memoirs of a Tuskegee Airman*. Tuscaloosa: University of Alabama Press, 1997.

DuBois, W. E. B. "Returning Soldiers." *Crisis* 18 (May 1919): 13.

Ducas, George, and Charles Van Doren, eds. *Great Documents in Black American History*. New York: Praeger , 1970.

Dudziak, Mary L. *Cold War Civil Rights: Race and the Image of American Democracy*. Princeton NJ: Princeton University Press, 2000.

Duff, Alan. *What Becomes of the Broken Hearted?* Auckland, NZ: Vintage, 1996.

Dulaney, W. Marvin. *Black Police in America*. Bloomington: Indiana University Press, 1996.

Dyson, Michael Eric. *April 4, 1968: Martin Luther King Jr.'s Death and How It Changed America*. New York: Basic Books, 2008.

———. *Come Hell or High Water: Hurricane Katrina and the Color of Disaster*. New York: Basic Civitas Books, 2006.

———. *I May Not Get There With You: The True Martin Luther King, Jr.* New York: Free Press, 2000.

———. *Is Bill Cosby Right? Or Has the Black Middle Class Lost Its Mind?.* New York: Basic Civitas Books, 2005.

Eagles, Charles W., ed. *The Civil Rights Movement in America*. Jackson: University Press of Mississippi, 1986.

Earley, Charity Adams. *One Woman's Army: A Black Officer Remembers the WAC*. College Station: Texas A&M University Press, 1989.

Ellison, Ralph. *A Biography*. New York: Alfred A. Knopf. Reprint 2007.

Emanuel, James A., and Theodore L. Gross, eds. *Dark Symphony: Negro Literature in America*. New York: Free Press, 1968.

Emerson, Michael O. *People of the Dream: Multiracial Congregations in the United States*. Princeton NJ: Princeton University Press, 2010.

Exum, William H. *Paradoxes of Protest: Black Student Activism in a White University*. Philadelphia: Temple University Press, 1985.

Fairclough, Adam. *Better Day Coming: Blacks and Equality, 1890–2000*. New York: Viking, 2001.

———. *To Redeem the Soul of America: The Southern Christian Leadership Conference and Martin Luther King, Jr.* Athens: University of Georgia Press, 1987.

Farley, Christopher John. "Dave Speaks," *Time*, May 14, 2005, http://www.time.com/time/magazine/article/0,9171,1061512,00.html. Accessed May 12, 2013.

Farmer, James. *Lay Bare the Heart: An Autobiography of the Civil Rights Movement*. New York: Arbor House, 1985.

Farrakhan, Louis. "Why A Million Man March," unpublished program distributed at the Million Man March. In author's possession.

Feldmann, Linda. "Gabrielle Giffords Shooting: A Leadership Moment for Obama, Boehner," *Christian Science Monitor*, January 10, 2011.

Findlay, James F. *Church People in the Struggle: The National Council of Churches and the Black Freedom Movement, 1950–1970*. New York: Oxford University Press, 1993.

Fine, Sidney. *Violence in the Model City: The Cavanagh Administration, Race Relations, and the Detroit Riot of 1967*. Ann Arbor: University of Michigan Press, 1989.

"First Ladies of Color in America." *Crisis* (September 1942): 383–86.

Fishel, Leslie H., Jr., and Benjamin Quarles, eds. *The Black American: A Documentary History*. Glenview IL: Scott, Foresman, 1976.

Fleming, Cynthia Griggs. *Soon We Will Not Cry: The Liberation of Ruby Doris Smith Robinson*. Lanham MD: Rowman and Littlefield, 1998.

Foner, Philip Sheldon, ed. *The Black Panthers Speak*. Philadelphia: Lippincott, 1970.

——— . *Organized Labor and the Black Worker, 1619–1981*. 2nd ed. New York: International Publishers, 1982.

Foner, Philip Sheldon, and Ronald L. Lewis, eds. *The Black Worker: A Documentary History from Colonial Times to the Present*. 8 vols. Philadelphia: Temple University Press, 1978–84.

Formisano, Ronald P. *The Tea Party: A Brief History*. Baltimore: Johns Hopkins University Press, 2012.

Formwalt, Lee W. "Albany Movement," Organization of American Historians, December 2, 2003, http://www.georgiaencyclopedia.org/nge/Article.jsp?id =h-1057.

"Fox Anchor Calls Obama Fist Pound a 'Terrorist Fist Jab.'" *Huffington Post*, June 9, 2008. www.huffingtonpost.com/2008/06/09/fox-anchor-calls-obama-fi_n _106027.html. Accessed May 12, 2013.

Frady, Marshall. *Jesse: The Life and Pilgrimage of Jesse Jackson*. New York: Random House, 1996.

Franklin, Jimmie Lewis. *Back to Birmingham: Richard Arrington, Jr. and His Times*. Tuscaloosa: University of Alabama Press, 1989.

Franklin, John Hope, and August Meier, eds. *Black Leaders in the Twentieth Century*. Urbana: University of Illinois Press, 1982.

Franklin, John Hope, and Alfred A. Moss, Jr. *From Slavery to Freedom: A History of African Americans*. 8th ed. New York: Alfred A. Knopf, 2000.

Frazier, Thomas R., Jr., ed. *Afro-American History: Primary Sources*. Rev. ed. Chicago: Dorsey Press, 1988.

Frey, Jerry. *Three Quarter Cadillac*. Sandy UT: ECKO Publishing, 2008.

Gaillard, Frye. *The Dream Long Deferred*. Chapel Hill: University of North Carolina Press, 1988.

Galston, William A. "President Barack Obama's First Two Years: Policy Accomplishments, Political Difficulties." Brookings Institution. http://www .brookings.edu.research/articles/2010/11/04-obama-galston. Accessed May 11, 2013.

Garfinkel, Herbert. *When Negroes March: The March on Washington Movement in the Organizational Politics for FEPC*. Glencoe IL: Free Press, 1959.

Garrow, David J. *Bearing the Cross: Martin Luther King, Jr., and the Southern Christian Leadership Conference*. New York: W. Morrow, 1986.

————. *The* FBI *and Martin Luther King, Jr.: From "Solo" to Memphis*. New York: W. W. Norton, 1981.

Gates, Henry Louis, Jr., ed. *A Chronology of African American History from 1445–1980*. New York: Amistad, 1980.

Gates, Henry Louis, Jr., and Evelyn Brooks Higginbotham, eds. *African American Lives*. New York: Oxford University Press, 2004.

Germany, Kent B. *New Orleans after the Promises: Poverty, Citizenship, and the Search for the Great Society*. Athens: University of Georgia Press, 2007.

Giddings, Paula. *When and Where I Enter: The Impact of Black Women on Race and Sex in America*. New York: William Morrow, 1984.

Gilens, Martin. *Why Americans Hate Welfare: Race, Media, and the Politics of Antipoverty Policy*. Chicago: University of Chicago Press, 1999.

Gillespie, Dizzy, and Al Fraser. *To Be, or Not . . . to Bop: Memoirs*. Garden City NY: Doubleday, 1979.

Giovanni, Nikki. *Black Feeling, Black Talk*. New York: Harper Perennial, 1971.

Glasgow, Douglas G. *The Black Underclass: Poverty, Unemployment, and Entrapment of Ghetto Youth*. San Francisco: Jossey-Bass Publishers, 1980.

Goings, Kenneth W., and Raymond A. Mohl, eds. *The New African American Urban History*. Thousand Oaks CA: Sage Publications, 1996.

Gold, Susan Dudley. *The Civil Rights Act of 1964*. Salt Lake City UT: Benchmarks Books, 2010.

Goldfield, David R. *Black, White, and Southern: Race Relations and Southern Culture, 1940 to the Present*. Baton Rouge: Louisiana State University Press, 1990.

Golson, G. Barry. *The Playboy Interview*. New York: Putnam, 1981.

Gooding-Williams, Robert, ed. *Reading Rodney King/Reading Urban Uprising*. New York: Routledge, 1993.

Goodwin, Doris Kearns. *Lyndon Johnson and the American Dream*. New York: Harper & Row, 1976.

Gordon, Jacob U., ed. *Narratives of African Americans in Kansas, 1870–1992: Beyond the Exodus Movement*. Lewiston NY: Edwin Mellen Press, 1993.

Gorn, Elliott J., ed. *Muhammad Ali, the People's Champ*. Urbana: University of Illinois Press, 1995.

Graham, Bradley. *By His Own Rules: The Ambitions, Successes, and Ultimate Failures of Donald Rumsfeld*. New York: Public Affairs Books, 2009.

Grandmaster Flash and the Furious Five. "The Message." Warner/Chappell Music, Sony/ATV Music Publishing LLC, EMI Music Publishing, 1982.

Gray, Madison. "The LA Riots: 15 Years After Rodney King." *Time*. http://www.time.com/time/specials/2007/article/0,28804,1614117_1614084_1614831,00.html. Accessed May 11, 2013.

Green, Adam. *Selling the Race: Culture, Community, and Black Chicago, 1940–1955*. Chicago: University of Chicago Press, 2007.

Greenhaw, Wayne, *Fighting the Devil in Dixie: How Civil Rights Activists Took On the Ku Klux Klan in Alabama*. Chicago: Review Press, 2011.

Guinier, Lani. *The Tyranny of the Majority: Fundamental Fairness in Representative Democracy*. New York: Free Press, 1994.

Gutgold, Nichola P. *Almost Madam President: Why Hillary Clinton "Won" in 2008*. Lanham MD: Lanham Books, 2009.

Hacker, Andrew. *Two Nations: Black and White, Separate, Hostile, Unequal*. Rev ed. New York: Ballantine Books, 1995.

Ham, Debra Newman, ed. *The African-American Mosaic: A Library of Congress Resource Guide for the Study of Black History and Culture*. Washington DC: U.S. Government Printing Office, 1994.

Hamilton, Charles V. *Adam Clayton Powell, Jr.: The Political Biography of an American Dilemma*. New York: Atheneum, 1991.

Hampton, Henry, Steve Fayer, and Sarah Flynn, eds. *Voices of Freedom: An Oral History of the Civil Rights Movement from the 1950s through the 1980s*. New York: Bantam Books, 1990.

Hardin, Vincent, Robin D. G. Kelley, and Earl Lewis. *We Changed the World: African Americans, 1945–1970*. New York: Oxford University Press, 1997.

Harley, Sharon. *The Timetables of African-American History: A Chronology of the Most Important People and Events in African-American History*. New York: Simon and Schuster, 1995.

Harris, Joseph E. *African-American Reactions to War in Ethiopia, 1936–1941*. Baton Rouge: Louisiana State University Press, 1994.

Harris, William H. *The Harder We Run: Black Workers Since the Civil War*. New York: Oxford University Press, 1982.

Harris-Lacewell, Melissa Victoria. *Barbershops, Bibles, and BET: Everyday Talk and Black Political Thought*. Princeton NJ: Princeton University Press, 2004.

———. "The Clinton Fallacy: Did Blacks Really Make Big Economic Gains During the 90s?" *Slate*, January 28, 2008, http://www.slate.com/articles/news_and _politics/politics/2008/01/the_clinton_fallacy.html. Accessed April 2, 2013.

Hartman, Chester W., ed. *Double Exposure: Poverty and Race in America*. Armonk NY: M. E. Sharpe, 1997.

Hatch, James V., and Ted Shine, eds. *Black Theatre USA: Plays by African Americans 1847 to Today*. New York: Free Press, 1996.

Hawken, Paul. *Blessed Unrest: How the Largest Movement in the World Came into Being, and Why No One Saw It Coming*. New York: Penguin, 2007.

Hayes, Floyd W., III, ed. *A Turbulent Voyage: Readings in African American Studies*. 3rd ed. Lanham MD: Rowman and Littlefield, 2000.

Haygood, Wil. *King of the Cats: The Life and Times of Adam Clayton Powell, Jr.* Boston: Houghton Mifflin, 1993.

Hazen, Don, Tate Hausman, Tamara Straus, and Michelle Chihara, eds. *After 9/11: Solutions for a Saner World*. N.p.: Independent Media Institute and AlterNet, 2001.

Henry, Charles P. *Jesse Jackson: The Search for Common Ground*. Oakland CA: Black Scholar Press, 1991.

———. *Long Overdue: The Politics of Racial Reparations*. New York: New York University Press, 2007.

Henry, Charles P., Robert L. Allen, and Robert Chrisman, eds. *The Obama Phenomenon: Toward a Multiracial Democracy*. Champaign: University of Illinois Press, 2011.

Higginbotham, Evelyn Brooks, Leon F. Litwack, Darlene Clark Hine, and Randall K. Burkett, eds. *The Harvard Guide to African-American History*. Cambridge MA: Harvard University Press, 2001.

Hill, Anita Faye, and Emma Coleman Jordan, eds. *Race, Gender, and Power in America: The Legacy of the Hill-Thomas Hearings*. New York: Oxford University Press, 1995.

Hill, Lance E. *The Deacons for Defense: Armed Resistance and the Civil Rights Movement*. Chapel Hill: University of North Carolina Press, 2004.

Hill, Patricia Liggins, Bernard W. Bell, Trudier Harris, William J. Harris, R. Baxter Miller, and Sondra A. O'Neale, eds. *Call and Response: The Riverside Anthology of the African American Literary Tradition*. Boston: Houghton Mifflin, 1998.

Hill Collins, Patricia. *Black Feminist Thought: Knowledge, Consciousness, and the Politics of Empowerment*. New York: Routledge, 2008.

Hine, Darlene Clark, ed. *Black Women in United States History*. 16 vols. Brooklyn NY: Carlson, 1990.

———. *Black Women in White: Racial Conflict and Cooperation in the Nursing Profession, 1890–1950*. Bloomington: Indiana University Press, 1989.

———. *Hine Sight: Black Women and the Re-Construction of American History*. Brooklyn NY: Carlson, 1994.

———, ed. *The State of Afro-American History: Past, Present, and Future*. Baton Rouge: Louisiana State University Press, 1986.

Hine, Darlene Clark, Elsa Barkley Brown, and Rosalyn Terborg-Penn, eds. *Black Women in America: An Historical Encyclopedia*. 2 vols. Brooklyn NY: Carlson, 1993.

Hine, Darlene Clark, William C. Hine, and Stanley Harrold. *The African American Odyssey*. Combined vol. 2nd ed. Upper Saddle River NJ: Prentice Hall, 2005.

———. *African Americans: A Concise History*. 1st ed. Upper Saddle River NJ: Prentice Hall, 2004.

Hine, Darlene Clark, Steven F. Lawson, and Merline Pitre. *Black Victory: The Rise and Fall of the White Primary in Texas*. 2nd ed. Columbia: University of Missouri Press, 2003.

Hine, Darlene Clark, and Kathleen Thompson. *A Shining Thread of Hope: The History of Black Women in America*. New York: Broadway Books, 1998.

Holt, Thomas C., and Elsa Barkley Brown, eds. *Major Problems in African-American History*. Vol. 2, *From Freedom to "Freedom Now" 1865–1990s*. Boston: Houghton Mifflin, 2000.

Hood, Rodney. "Why Should Minorities Be Concerned About Cultural Competence in Health Care?" *The Crisis* 110, no. 6 (November/December 2003): 55.

hooks, bell. *Outlaw Culture: Resisting Representations*. New York: Routledge, 1994.

Hornblower, Margot. "Taking It All Back: At Pete Wilson's Urging, the University of California Says No to Racial Preferences." *Time* 146 (July 31, 1995): 34.

Horne, Gerald. *Black and Red: W. E. B. Du Bois and the Afro-American Response to the Cold War, 1944–1963*. Albany: State University of New York Press, 1986.

Hornsby, Alton, Jr. *Chronology of African-American History: Significant Events and People from 1619 to the Present*. Detroit: Gale Research, 1991.

Horton, James Oliver, and Lois E. Horton, eds. *A History of the African American People: The History, Traditions and Culture of African Americans*. Detroit: Wayne State University Press, 1997.

Huggins, Nathan, Martin Kilson, and Daniel M. Fox, eds. *Key Issues in the Afro-American Experience*. Vol. 2, *Since 1865*. New York: Harcourt Brace Jovanovich, 1971.

Hull, Gloria T., Patricia Bell Scott, and Barbara Smith, eds. *All the Women Are White, All the Blacks Are Men, but Some of Us Are Brave: Black Women's Studies*. Old Westbury NY: Feminist Press, 1982.

———. *But Some of Us Are Brave: All the Women Are White, All the Blacks Are Men: Black Women's Studies*. New York: Feminist Press at CUNY, 2000.

Hutchinson, Earl Ofari. "Diversity: Celebrate Blacks' Accomplishments Across the Board, Not in One 'Official' Month or Textbook Chapter." *LA Times*, February 24, 1997.

Jackson, Michael. *Moonwalk*. Rev. ed. New York: Crown Archetype, 2009.

Jackson, Phillip. "U.S. Economy Forces Many Black Americans into Third-World Status." *Black Star Journal*. http://www.blackstarjournal.org/?p=1166. Accessed July 18, 2012.

Jackson, Thomas F. *From Civil Rights to Human Rights: Martin Luther King, Jr., and the Struggle for Economic Justice*. Philadelphia: University of Philadelphia Press, 2006.

James, Joy. *Transcending the Talented Tenth: Black Leaders and American Intellectuals*. New York: Routledge, 1996.

Jaynes, Gerald David, and Robin M. Williams, Jr., eds. *A Common Destiny: Blacks and American Society*. Washington DC: National Academy Press, 1989.

Jencks, Christopher. *Rethinking Social Policy: Race, Poverty, and the Underclass*. Cambridge MA: Harvard University Press, 1992.

Jennings, James. *Welfare Reform and the Revitalization of Inner City Neighborhoods*. East Lansing: Michigan State University Press, 2003.

Jewsiewicki, Bogumil, and David Newbury, eds. *African Historiographies: What History for Which Africa?* Beverly Hills CA: Sage, 1986.

Johnson, John H., ed. *Negro Digest* vol. 6., p. 87 Chicago: Johnson Publishing Company, 1945.

Jones, Jacqueline. *American Work: Four Centuries of Black and White Labor*. New York: W. W. Norton, 1998.

———. *Labor of Love, Labor of Sorrow: Black Women, Work, and the Family from Slavery to the Present*. New York: Basic Books, 1985.

Joseph, Peniel E. *Black Power Movement: Rethinking the Civil Rights–Black Power Era*. New York: Routledge, 2006.

——. *Dark Days, Bright Nights: From Black Power to Barack Obama*. New York: Basic Civitas Books, 2010.

——. *Waiting 'Til the Midnight Hour: A Narrative History of Black Power in America*. New York: Henry Holt, 2006.

Kapur, Sudarshan. *Raising Up a Prophet: The African-American Encounter with Gandhi*. Boston: Beacon Press, 1992.

Katz, Michael B. *The Undeserving Poor: From the War on Poverty to the War on Welfare*. New York: Pantheon, 1989.

Kelley, Norman. *The Head Negro in Charge Syndrome: The Dead End of Black Politics*. New York: Nation Books, 2004.

Kelley, Robin D. G. *Freedom Dreams: The Black Radical Imagination*. Boston: Beacon Press, 2003.

——. *Race Rebels: Culture, Politics, and the Black Working Class*. New York: Free Press, 1994.

——. *Yo' Mama's Disfunktional! Fighting the Culture Wars in Urban America*. Boston: Beacon Press, 1997.

Kelley, Robin D. G., and Earl Lewis, eds. *To Make Our World Anew: A History of African Americans*. New York: Oxford University Press, 2000.

Kennedy, Randall. "Martin Luther King's Constitution: A Legal History of the Montgomery Bus Boycott." *Yale Law Journal* 98 (April 1989): 999–1067.

Kersten, Andrew Edmund. *Labor's Home Front: The American Federation of Labor during World War II*. New York: New York University Press, 2006.

——. *Race, Jobs, and the War: The FEPC in the Midwest, 1941–46*. Urbana: University of Illinois Press, 2000.

Keto, C. Tsehloane. *Vision and Time: Historical Perspective of an Africa-Centered Paradigm*. Lanham MD: University Press of America, 2001.

Keyes, Cheryl Lynette. *Rap Music and Street Consciousness*. Urbana: University of Illinois Press, 2002.

Kindred, Dave. *Sound and Fury: Two Powerful Lives, One Remarkable Friendship*. New York: Simon and Schuster, 2006.

King, Coretta Scott. Welcoming Remarks at 13th Annual Creating Change Conference, Atlanta GA, November 14, 2000.

King, Desmond, and Rogers M. Smith. *Still a House Divided: Race and Politics in Obama's America*. Princeton NJ: Princeton University Press, 2011.

The King Encyclopedia. "The Civil Rights Act (1964)," http://mlkkpp01.stanford .edu/kingweb/about_king/encyclopedia/enc_civil_rights_bill.htm.

King, J. P. *On the Down Low: A Journey in the Land of "Straight" Men Who Sleep with Men*. New York: Broadway Books, 2004.

King, Martin Luther, Jr. *The Autobiography of Martin Luther King, Jr*. New York: Grand Central, 1998. Reprinted 2001 by Warner NY.

——. "I Have A Dream," *Ebony*, January 1986, 40–42.

———. "Letter from Birmingham Jail." The Martin Luther King, Jr., Research and Education Institute, http://www.mlk-kpp01.stanford.edu/index.php.letter_from _birmingham_jail/. Accessed April 19, 2013.

———. Carson, Clayborne, Ralph E. Luker, Penny A. Russell, eds. *The Papers of Martin Luther King, Jr.* 6 vols. Berkeley: University of California Press, 1992–2007.

———. *Stride toward Freedom: The Montgomery Story.* New York: Harper, 1958.

———. *A Testament of Hope: The Essential Writings and Speeches of Martin Luther King, Jr.* New York: HarperCollins, 1990.

Klarman, Michael J. *From Jim Crow to Civil Rights: The Supreme Court and the Struggle for Racial Equality.* New York: Oxford University Press, 2004.

Kluger, Richard. *Simple Justice: The History of Brown v. Board of Education and Black America's Struggle for Equality.* Rev. ed. New York: Knopf, 2004.

Kofsky, Frank. *John Coltrane and the Jazz Revolution of the 1960s.* 2nd ed. New York: Pathfinder, 1998.

Kozol, Jonathan. *Savage Inequalities: Children in America's Schools.* New York: Crown, 1991.

Kusmer, Kenneth L., ed. *Black Communities and Urban Development in America, 1720–1990.* 10 vols. Hamden CT: Garland, 1991.

Kweit, Robert W., and Mary G. Kweit. *People and Politics in Urban America.* 2nd ed. New York: Taylor and Francis, 1999.

LaBlaine, Michael, and Barbara Carlisle Bigelow, eds. *Contemporary Black Biography* 2. Farmington Hills MI: Gale Research, 1992.

Landry, Bart. *The New Black Middle Class.* Berkeley: University of California Press, 1987.

Lawson, Steven F. *Black Ballots: Voting Rights in the South, 1944–1969.* New York: Columbia University Press, 1976.

———. *In Pursuit of Power: Southern Blacks and Electoral Politics, 1965–1982.* New York: Columbia University Press, 1985.

———. *Running for Freedom: Civil Rights and Black Politics in America since 1941.* 2nd ed. New York: McGraw-Hill, 1997.

Lawson, Steven F., and Charles Payne. *Debating the Civil Rights Movement, 1945– 1968.* 2nd ed. Lanham MD: Rowman and Littlefield, 2006.

Lee, Chana Kai. *For Freedom's Sake: The Life of Fannie Lou Hamer.* Urbana: University of Illinois Press, 1999.

Lee, Ulysses. *The Employment of Negro Troops.* Washington DC: Center of Military History, United States Army, 1966.

Leitch, Vincent B. *Cultural Criticism, Literary Theory, and Poststructuralism.* New York: Columbia University Press, 1992.

Lerner, Gerda, ed. *Black Women in White America: A Documentary History.* New York: Vintage Books, 1973.

Lester, Joan. *Fire in My Soul: The Life of Eleanor Holmes Norton.* New York: Simon and Schuster, 2003.

Levenson, Jacob. *The Secret Epidemic: The Story of* AIDS *and Black America*. New York: Pantheon Books, 2004.

Levine, Ellen S. *Freedom's Children: Young Civil Rights Activists Tell Their Own Stories*. New York: Puffin, 2000.

Levitt, Jeremy I., and Matthew C. Whitaker, eds. *Hurricane Katrina: America's Unnatural Disaster*. Lincoln: University of Nebraska Press, 2009.

Lewis, Catherine M., and J. Richard Lewis, eds. *Race, Politics, and Memory: A Documentary History of the Little Rock School Crisis*. Fayetteville: University of Arkansas Press, 2007.

Lewis, David Levering. *King: A Biography*. Urbana: University of Illinois Press, 2013.

———. *King: A Critical Biography*. New York: Praeger, 1970.

———. *W. E. B. DuBois, 1919–1963: The Fight for Equality and the American Century*. New York: Henry Holt, 2000.

———. *W. E. B. DuBois: A Biography*. New York: Henry Holt, 2009.

Lewis, Jone Johnson. "Barbara Jordan." About.com Women's History. http://womenshistory.about.com/od/congress/p/barbara_jordan.html.

Lincoln, C. Eric, ed. *The Black Muslims in America*. Boston: Beacon Press, 1961.

Lipsitz, George. *Rainbow at Midnight: Labor and Culture in the 1940s*. Urbana: University of Illinois Press, 1994.

Lott, Tommy Lee. *The Invention of Race: Black Culture and the Politics of Representation*. Malden MA: Blackwell, 1999.

Luckingham, Bradford. *Minorities in Phoenix: A Profile of Mexican American, Chinese American, and African American Communities, 1860–1992*. Tucson: University of Arizona Press, 1994.

Lukas, J. Anthony. *Common Ground: A Turbulent Decade in the Lives of Three American Families*. New York: Knopf, 1985.

Mack, Dwayne. "Freedom Rides (1961)." *TheBlackPast.org*. http://www.blackpast.org/?q=aah/freedom-rides-1961.

MacLean, Nancy. *Freedom is Not Enough: The Opening of the American Workplace*. New York: R. Sage, 2006.

Madhubuti, Haki R. *Black Men: Obsolete, Single, Dangerous?: Afrikan American Families in Transition: Essays in Discovery, Solution, and Hope*. Chicago: Third World Press, 1990.

Magida, Arthur J. *Prophet of Rage: A Life of Louis Farrakhan and His Nation*. New York: Basic Books, 1997.

Mann, Thomas E. "American Politics on the Eve of the Midterm Elections." Brookings Institution, http://www.brookings.edu/research/articles/2010/10/11-midterm-elections-mann. Accessed May 11, 2013.

Marable, Manning. *The Great Wells of Democracy: The Meaning of Race in American Life*. New York: Basic Civitas, 2002.

———. *How Capitalism Underdeveloped Black America: Problems in Race, Political Economy and Society*. Boston: South End Press, 1983.

———. *Malcolm X: A Life of Reinvention*. New York: Viking, 2011.

———. *Race, Reform, and Rebellion: The Second Reconstruction and Beyond in Black America, 1945–2006*. 3rd ed. Jackson: University Press of Mississippi, 2007.

Mariner, Joann E. *No Escape: Male Rape in U.S. Prisons*. New York: Human Rights Watch, 2001.

Massey, Douglas S., and Nancy A. Denton. *American Apartheid: Segregation and the Making of the Underclass*. Cambridge MA: Harvard University Press, 1993.

McAdam, Doug. *Freedom Summer*. New York: Oxford University Press, 1988.

McCartney, John T. *Black Power Ideologies: An Essay in African-American Political Thought*. Philadelphia: Temple University Press, 1992.

McClain, William B. *Black People in the Methodist Church: Whither Thou Goest?* Cambridge MA: Schenkman, 1984.

McCormick, Richard Patrick. *The Black Student Protest Movement at Rutgers*. New Brunswick NJ: Rutgers University Press, 1990.

McKenzie, Steven L. *All God's Children: A Biblical Critique of Racism*. Louisville KY: Westminster John Knox Press, 1997.

McLaurin, Melton A. *The Marines of Montford Point: America's First Black Marines*. Chapel Hill: University of North Carolina Press, 2007.

McMillan, Terry, et al. *Five for Five: The Films of Spike Lee*. New York: Stewart, Tabori and Chang, 1991.

McMillen, Neil R. *The Citizens' Council: Organized Resistance to the Second Reconstruction, 1954–64*. Urbana: University of Illinois Press, 1971.

———, ed. *Remaking Dixie: The Impact of World War II on the American South*. Jackson: University Press of Mississippi, 1997.

McNeil, Genna Rae. *Groundwork: Charles Hamilton Houston and the Struggle for Civil Rights*. Philadelphia: University of Pennsylvania Press, 1983.

McPherson, James M., Laurence R. Holland, James M. Banner, Nancy J. Weiss, and Michael D. Bell, eds. *Blacks in America: Bibliographical Essays*. Garden City NY: Doubleday, 1971.

McQuillar, Tannayah Lee, and Fred Johnson. *Tupac Shakur: The Life and Times of an American Icon*. New York: Da Capo Press, 2010.

Meier, August, and Elliott M. Rudwick. *Black History and the Historical Profession*. Urbana: University of Illinois Press, 1986.

———. *CORE: A Study in the Civil Rights Movement, 1942–1968*. New York: Oxford University Press, 1973.

———. *From Plantation to Ghetto*. 3rd ed. New York: Hill and Wang, 1976.

———, eds. *The Making of Black America: Essays in Negro Life and History*. 2 vols. New York: Atheneum, 1969.

Meier, August, Elliott Rudwick, and Francis L. Broderick, eds. *Black Protest Thought in the Twentieth Century*. Indianapolis: Bobbs-Merrill, 1971.

Mendenhall, Stan. "Everett Dirksen and the Civil Rights Act of 1964." *Illinois History Teacher* 3, no. 1 (1996): 48–55.

Michael Jackson BlogSpot. "Michael Jackson Biography." http://michaeljacksonmm
.blogspot.com.

MichaelJacksonDeceased.com. "The Passing of a Superstar." http://www.michael
jacksondeceased.com/Bio.html (now defunct).

Mieder, Wolfgang. *"Making a Way out of No Way": Martin Luther King's Sermonic Proverbial Rhetoric*. New York: Peter Lang, 2010.

Milner, Ronald. "Black Magic, Black Art." *Negro Digest* 14, no. 4 (April 1967): 8–12.

Moody, Anne. *Coming of Age in Mississippi*. New York: Dial Press, 1968.

Morgan, Joan. *When Chickenheads Come Home to Roost: My Life as a Hip-Hop Feminist*. New York: Simon and Schuster, 1999.

Morris, Aldon D. *The Origins of the Civil Rights Movement: Black Communities Organizing for Change*. New York: Free Press, 1984.

Morrison, Toni, ed. *To Die for the People: The Writings of Huey P. Newton*. New York: Writers and Readers, 1995.

Moses, Wilson Jeremiah. *Afrotopia: The Roots of African American Popular History*. New York: Cambridge University Press, 1998.

Motley, Mary Penick. *The Invisible Soldier: The Experience of the Black Soldier, World War II*. Detroit: Wayne State University Press, 1975.

Mullane, Deirdre, ed. *Crossing the Danger Water: Three Hundred Years of African-American Writing*. New York: Anchor Books, 1993.

Mullings, Leith. *On Our Own Terms: Race, Class, and Gender in the Lives of African American Women*. New York: Routledge, 1997.

Murray, Pauli. *Pauli Murray: The Autobiography of a Black Activist Feminist Lawyer*. Knoxville: University of Tennessee Press, 1989.

NAACP. "NAACP to Focus on Minority Health Disparities." *Crisis* 110, no. 6 (November–December 2003).

National Park Service. "Little Rock Nine," Central High School National Historic Site. *The Encyclopedia of Arkansas History and Culture*. http://www.encyclopedia ofarkansas.net/encyclopedia/entry-detail.aspx?search=1&entryID=723.

Neal, Larry. *Visions of a Liberated Future: Black Arts Movement Writings, Poetry and Prose*. New York: Thunder's Mouth Press, 1989.

Neal, Mark Anthony. *New Black Man*. New York: Routledge, 2005.

Neale, Caroline. *Writing "Independent" History: African Historiography, 1960–1980*. Westport CT: Greenwood Press, 1985.

Nelson, Jack, and Jack Bass. *The Orangeburg Massacre*. 2nd ed. Macon GA: Mercer, 1984.

Nelson, William E., Jr., and Philip J. Meranto. *Electing Black Mayors: Political Action in the Black Community*. Columbus: Ohio State University Press, 1977.

Nicholas, Peter, and Christi Parsons. "Obama Mocks Trump's Presidential Ambitions." *USA Today*. May 1, 2011.

———. "Obama Mocks Trump's Presidential Aspirations." *West Australian*. May 1, 2011.

———. "Obama's Poker Face Was Sorely Tested." *Los Angeles Times*, May 2, 2011.

Nieman, Donald G. *Promises to Keep: African-Americans and the Constitutional Order, 1776 to the Present*. New York: Oxford University Press, 1991.

Norrell, Robert J. *Reaping the Whirlwind: The Civil Rights Movement in Tuskegee*. New York: Knopf, 1985.

Norton, Mary Beth, and Pamela Gerardi, eds. *The American Historical Association's Guide to Historical Literature*. 2 vols. 3rd ed. New York: Oxford University Press, 1995.

Oates, Stephen B. *Let the Trumpet Sound: A Life of Martin Luther King, Jr.* New York: HarperCollins, 2009.

Obama, Barack. "Against Going to War in Iraq." Information Clearing House, October 2, 2002, http://www.informationclearinghouse.info/article19440.htm.

———. "The American Promise." Democratic National Convention, August 28, 2008, Denver, Colorado.

———. *The Audacity of Hope: Thoughts on Reclaiming the American Dream*. New York: Crown, 2006.

———. *Dreams from My Father: A Story of Race and Inheritance*. New York: Times Books, 1995.

———. First Inaugural Address. *White House Blog*, January 20, 2008. http://www.whitehouse.gov/blog/inaugural-address/. Accessed April 15, 2008.

O'Brien, Gail Williams. *The Color of the Law: Race, Violence, and Justice in the Post–World War II South*. Chapel Hill: University of North Carolina Press, 1999.

Office of Policy Planning and Research, U.S. Department of Labor Books. *The Negro Family: The Case for National Action*. Westport CT: Greenwood, 1981.

Olbermann, Keith. *Pitchforks and Torches: The Worst of the Worst, from Beck, Bill, and Bush to Palin and Other Posturing Republicans*. Hoboken NJ: John Wiley and Sons, 2010.

O'Meally, Robert G. *The Craft of Ralph Ellison*. Cambridge MA: Harvard University Press, 1980.

O'Reilly, Kenneth. *Nixon's Piano: Presidents and Racial Politics from Washington to Clinton*. New York: Free Press, 1995.

———. *Racial Matters: The FBI's Secret File on Black America, 1960–1972*. New York: Free Press, 1989.

Orfield, Gary. *Must We Bus? Segregated Schools and National Policy*. Washington DC: Brookings Institution, 1978.

Osofsky, Gilbert, ed. *The Burden of Race: A Documentary History of Negro-White Relations in America*. New York: Harper and Row, 1967.

Osur, Alan M. *Blacks in the Army Air Forces during World War II: The Problem of Race Relations*. Washington DC: Office of Air Force History, 1977.

Painter, Nell Irvin. *Creating Black Americans: African American History and Its Meanings, 1619 to the Present*. New York: Oxford University Press, 2005.

Palmer, Colin A., ed. *Encyclopedia of African American Culture and History: The Black Experience in the Americas*. 6 vols. 2nd ed. Detroit: Macmillan Reference, 2006.

——— *Passageways: An Interpretive History of Black America*. Vol. 2. Fort Worth: Harcourt Brace College, 1998.

Parker, Frank R. *Black Votes Count: Political Empowerment in Mississippi After 1965*. Chapel Hill: University of North Carolina Press, 1990.

Patterson, James T. *Brown v. Board of Education: A Civil Rights Milestone and its Troubled Legacy*. New York: Oxford University Press, 2001.

Pattillo, Mary E., David F. Weiman, and Bruce Western, eds. *Imprisoning America: The Social Effects of Mass Incarceration*. New York: Russell Sage Foundation, 2004.

Payne, Charles M. *I've Got the Light of Freedom: The Organizing Tradition and the Mississippi Freedom Struggle*. Berkeley: University of California Press, 1995.

Pellett, Gail, and Stanley Nelson. *Shattering the Silences: Minority Professors Break into the Ivory Tower*. Public Broadcasting Service Documentary. Arlington VA, 1997.

Perlstein, Rick. *Nixonland: The Rise of a Presidency and the Fracturing of America*. New York: Simon and Schuster, 2010.

Phibbs, Cheryl Fisher. *The Montgomery Bus Boycott: A History and Reference Guide*. New York: Greenwood, 2009.

Pitts, Leonard, Jr. "Sept. 12, 2001: We'll Go Forward from this Moment." *Miami Herald*, September 12, 2001.

Plummer, Brenda Gayle. *Rising Wind: Black Americans and U.S. Foreign Affairs, 1935–1960*. Chapel Hill: University of North Carolina Press, 1996.

———, ed. *Window on Freedom: Race, Civil Rights, and Foreign Affairs, 1945–1988*. Chapel Hill: University of North Carolina Press, 2003.

Pollock, Bruce. *By the Time We Got to Woodstock: The Great Rock 'n' Roll Revolution of 1969*. Milwaukee, WI: Hal Leonard, 2009.

Potter, Lou, William Miles, and Nina Rosenblum. *Liberators: Fighting on Two Fronts in World War II*. New York: Harcourt Brace Jovanovich, 1992.

Powell, Kevin. *The Black Male Handbook: A Blueprint for Life*. New York: Atria, 2008.

———. "Ready To Live." In Vibe Magazine, *Tupac Shakur*, 45–52. New York: Three Rivers Press, 1998.

———. *Who's Gonna Take the Weight? Manhood, Race, and Power in America*. New York: Three Rivers Press, 2003.

Powell, Richard J. *Black Art: A Cultural History*. Rev. ed. London: Thames and Hudson, 2002.

Powledge, Fred. *Free at Last? The Civil Rights Movement and the People Who Made It*. Boston: Little, Brown, 1991.

Pratt, Robert A. *The Color of their Skin: Education and Race in Richmond, Virginia, 1954–89*. Charlottesville: University Press of Virginia, 1992.

Price, Joanne. *Barack Obama: The Voice of an American Leader.* Santa Barbara CA: ABC-CLIO, 2008.

Quarles, Benjamin. *The Negro in the Making of America.* 3rd ed. New York: Macmillan, 1987.

Rabaka, Reiland. *Hip Hop's Inheritance: From the Harlem Renaissance to the Hip Hop Feminist Movement.* New York: Lexington Books, 2011.

Raines, Howell. *My Soul Is Rested: Movement Days in the Deep South Remembered.* New York: Putnam, 1977.

Ralph, James, Jr. *Northern Protest: Martin Luther King, Jr., Chicago, and The Civil Rights Movement.* Cambridge MA: Harvard University Press, 1993.

Ransby, Barbara. *Ella Baker and the Black Freedom Movement: A Radical Democratic Vision.* Chapel Hill: University of North Carolina Press, 2003.

Ravitch, Diane. *The Great School Wars, New York City, 1805–1973: A History of the Public Schools as Battlefield of Social Change.* New York: Basic Books, 1974.

Rawn, James. *The Double V: How Wars, Protest, and Harry Truman Desegregated America's Military.* New York: Bloomsbury Press, 2013.

Reagan, Ronald. *Tear Down This Wall: The Reagan Revolution: A National Review History.* New York: Continuum, 2004.

Reed, Adolph L., Jr. *The Jesse Jackson Phenomenon: The Crisis of Purpose in Afro-American Politics.* New Haven CT: Yale University Press, 1986.

Reed, Ishmael. *Airing Dirty Laundry.* Reading MA: Addison-Wesley, 1993.

Reed, Linda. *Simple Decency and Common Sense: The Southern Conference Movement, 1938–1963.* Bloomington: Indiana University Press, 1991.

Reed, Teresa. *Calling Out Around the World: A Motown Reader.* London: Helter Skelter, 2001.

Reeves, Martha. *The Holy Profane: Religion in Black Popular Music.* Lexington: University of Kentucky Press, 2004.

Remnick, David. *King of the World: Muhammad Ali and the Rise of an American Hero.* New York: Random House, 1998.

Rich, Wilbur C. *Coleman Young and Detroit Politics: From Social Activist to Power Broker.* Detroit: Wayne State University Press, 1989.

———. *Defending the Spirit: A Black Life in America.* New York: Dutton, 1998.

Richardson, Riché. *Black Masculinity and the U.S. South: From Uncle Tom to Gangsta.* Athens: University of Georgia Press, 2007.

Roberts, Randy, and James S. Olson. *Winning Is the Only Thing: Sports in America since 1945.* Baltimore: Johns Hopkins University Press, 1991.

Robeson, Paul, Jr. *The Undiscovered Paul Robeson: Quest for Freedom, 1939–1976.* New York: John Wiley & Sons, 2009.

Robinson, Jo Ann Gibson, and David J. Garrow. *The Montgomery Bus Boycott and the Women Who Started It: The Memoir of Jo Ann Gibson Robinson.* Knoxville: University of Tennessee Press, 1987.

Robinson, Randall. *The Debt: What America Owes to Blacks.* New York: Dutton, 2000.

Robnett, Belinda. *How Long? How Long?: African-American Women in the Struggle for Civil Rights.* New York: Oxford University Press, 1997.

Rogers, Mary Beth. *Barbara Jordan: American Hero.* New York: Bantam Books, 1998.

Rose, Tricia. *Black Noise: Rap Music and Black Culture in Contemporary America.* Hanover NH: Wesleyan University Press, 1994.

Ryan, William. *Blaming the Victim.* New York: Vintage, 1976.

Sabato, Larry. "Jesse Jackson's 'Hymietown' Remark—1984." *Washington Post.* http://www.washingtonpost.com/wp-srv/politics/special/clinton/frenzy/jackson.htm. Accessed May 27, 2010.

Salter, Daren. "Stokely Carmichael (Kwame Ture) (1941–1998)," *BlackPast.org,* http://www.blackpast.org/?q=aah/carmichael-stokely-kwame-ture-1941-1998.

Salzberger, Ronald Paul, and Mary C. Turck. *Reparations for Slavery: A Reader.* New York: Rowman and Littlefield, 2004.

Salzman, Jack, David Lionel Smith, and Cornel West, eds. *Encyclopedia of African American Culture and History.* 5 vols. New York: Simon and Schuster Macmillan, 1996.

Sandler, Stanley. *Segregated Skies: Black Combat Squadrons of World War II.* Washington DC: Smithsonian Institution, 1992.

Savage, Barbara Dianne. *Broadcasting Freedom: Radio, War, and the Politics of Race, 1938–1948.* Chapel Hill: University of North Carolina Press, 1999.

Savoy, Lauret. "A Stone's Throw." *Terrain.org: A Journal of the Built & Natural Environments* (2013). http:\\www.terrain.org/columns/23/savoy.htm. Accessed April 30, 2013.

Schlesinger, Arthur M., Jr. *The Disuniting of America.* New York: Norton, 1992.

———. *ISOC Internazionale* 22–23 (1991): 39.

Schwerin, Jules Victor. *Got to Tell It: Mahalia Jackson, Queen of Gospel.* New York: Oxford University Press, 1992.

Scott, Daryl Michael. *Contempt and Pity: Social Policy and the Image of the Damaged Black Psyche, 1880–1996.* Chapel Hill: University of North Carolina Press, 1997.

Scott, William R. *The Sons of Sheba's Race: African-Americans and the Italo-Ethiopian War, 1935–1941.* Bloomington: Indiana University Press, 1993.

Seale, Bobby. *Seize the Time: The Story of the Black Panther Party and Huey P. Newton.* New York: Random House, 1970.

Sellers, Cleveland, with Robert L. Terrell. *The River of No Return: The Autobiography of a Black Militant and the Life and Death of SNCC.* New York: Morrow, 1973.

Sharpley-Whiting, T. Denean. *Pimps Up, Ho's Down: Hip Hop's Hold on Young Black Women.* New York: New York University Press, 2007.

———. *The Speech: Race and Barack Obama's "A More Perfect Union".* New York: Bloomsbury, 2009.

Sharpton, Al, with Karen Hunter. *Al on America*. New York: Kensington, 2002.

"Sharpton Slams NYC Cops after Shooting." *Michigan Daily*, November 27, 2006.

Shayon, Robert Lewis. "'Julia': Breakthrough or Letdown?" *Saturday Review* 51, April 20, 1968: 49.

Shogan, Robert, and Tom Craig. *The Detroit Race Riot: A Study in Violence.* Philadelphia: Chilton Books, 1964.

"Shooting Down Racism: Civic Leader Recalls Battle to Win Dignity." *Arizona Republic*, ca. 1985.

Shulman, Steven, ed. *The Impact of Immigration on African Americans*. New Brunswick NJ: Transaction, 2004.

Simba, Malik. "Malcolm X (1925–1965)," *BlackPast.org*, http://www.blackpast.org/ ?q=aah/x-malcolm-1925-1965.

Simpson, Andrea Y. *The Tie that Binds: Identity and Political Attitudes in the Post–Civil Rights Generation.* New York: New York University Press, 1998.

Singh, Nikhil Pal. *Black Is a Country: Race and the Unfinished Struggle for Democracy.* Cambridge MA: Harvard University Press, 2004.

Skinner, Elliott P. "Afro-Americans, Africa, and America," in *Theory and Practice: Essays Presented to Gene Weltfish*, 125–52. Berlin: Walter de Gruyter, 1980.

Smallwood, Arwin D., and Jeffrey M. Elliot. *The Atlas of African-American History and Politics: From the Slave Trade to Modern Times.* Boston: McGraw-Hill, 1998.

Smiley, Tavis. *The Covenant with Black America.* Chicago: Third World Press, 2006.

Smith, Jessie Carney, Casper L. Jordan, and Robert L. Johns, eds. *Black Firsts: 2,000 Years of Extraordinary Achievement.* Detroit: Visible Ink, 1994.

Smith, Robert Charles. *We Have No Leaders: African-Americans in the Post–Civil Rights Era.* Albany: State University of New York Press, 1996.

Sowell, Thomas. *Preferential Policies: An International Perspective.* New York: W. Morrow, 1990.

Spaulding, Pam. "Obama Daughters Labeled 'Nappy Headed Hos' in Art Exhibit." pamshouseblend.firedoglake.com/2008/6/13/obama-daughters-labeled-nappy -headed-hos-in-art-exhibit/. Accessed May 12, 2013.

Stabile, Carol A. *White Victims, Black Villains: Gender, Race, and Crime News in U.S. Culture.* New York: Routledge, 2006.

Steele, Shelby. *The Content of Our Character: A New Vision of Race in America.* New York: Harper Perennial, 1991.

———. *A Dream Deferred: The Second Betrayal of Black Freedom in America.* New York: HarperCollins, 1998.

Stengel, Richard. "From the Editor's Desk: The Next America: Against the Odds, the President Built a New Majority." *Time*, December 31, 2012–January 7, 2013: 14.

Sterling, Dorothy, ed. *We Are Your Sisters: Black Women in the Nineteenth Century.* New York: W. W. Norton, 1984.

Stillwell, Paul, ed. *The Golden Thirteen: Recollections of the First Black Naval Officers.* Annapolis MD: Naval Institute Press, 1993.

Strickland, William. *Malcolm X: Make it Plain*. New York: Penguin, 1995.

Sugrue, Thomas J. *The Origins of the Urban Crisis: Race and Inequality in Postwar Detroit*. Princeton NJ: Princeton University Press, 1996.

———. *Sweet Land of Liberty: The Forgotten Struggle for Civil Rights in the North*. New York: Random House, 2009.

Tate, Greg. *Everything but the Burden: What White People Are Taking from Black Culture*. New York: Broadway Books, 2003.

———. *Flyboy in the Buttermilk: Essays on Contemporary America*. New York: Fireside, 1992.

Taylor, Quintard, Jr. *In Search of the Racial Frontier: African Americans in the American West, 1528–1990*. New York: W. W. Norton, 1998.

Taylor, Quintard, Jr., and Shirley Ann Wilson Moore, eds. *African American Women Confront the West, 1600–2000*. Norman: University of Oklahoma Press, 2003.

Terkel, Studs, ed. *"The Good War": An Oral History of World War Two*. New York: Pantheon Books, 1984.

Terry, Wallace. *Bloods: An Oral History of the Vietnam War*. New York: Random House, 1984.

Thomas, J. C. *Chasin' the Trane: The Music and Mystique of John Coltrane*. Garden City NY: Doubleday, 1975.

"Tupac Shakur Biography." *Rolling Stone*, http://www.rollingstone.com/music/artists/tupac-shakur/biography.

Tushnet, Mark V. *Making Civil Rights Law: Thurgood Marshall and the Supreme Court, 1936–1961*. New York: Oxford University Press, 1994.

Tyson, Timothy B. *Radio Free Dixie: Robert F. Williams and the Roots of Black Power*. Chapel Hill: University of North Carolina Press, 1999.

United States Institute of Medicine Committee on Understanding and Eliminating Racial and Ethnic Disparities in Health Care. *Unequal Treatment: Confronting Racial and Ethnic Disparities in Health Care*. vol. 2. Atlanta GA: National Academic Press, 2003.

Urquhart, Brian. *Ralph Bunche: An American Life*. New York: W. W. Norton, 1993.

Viscount, Nelson H. "Jackson, Jesse Louis, Sr. (1941–)," *BlackPast.org*, 2012, http://www.blackpast.org/?q=aah/jackson-jessie-louis-1941.

Walker, Clarence Earl. *Deromanticizing Black History: Critical Essays and Reappraisals*. Knoxville: University of Tennessee Press, 1991.

———. *We Can't Go Home Again: An Argument About Afrocentrism*. New York: Oxford University Press, 2001.

Walker, Juliet E. K. *The History of Black Business in America: Capitalism, Race, Entrepreneurship*. New York: Macmillan Library Reference, 1998.

Walters, Ronald W. *Freedom Is Not Enough: Black Voters, Black Candidates, and American Presidential Politics*. Lanham MD: Rowman and Littlefield, 2005.

Walton, Hanes. *Black Politics: A Theoretical and Structural Analysis*. Philadelphia: Lippincott, 1972.

Ward, Brian. *Just My Soul Responding: Rhythm and Blues, Black Consciousness, and Race Relations.* Berkeley: University of California Press, 1998.

Washburn, Patrick Scott. *A Question of Sedition: The Federal Government's Investigation of the Black Press during World War II.* New York: Oxford University Press, 1986.

Washington, James Melvin. *Frustrated Fellowship: The Black Baptist Quest for Social Power.* Macon GA: Mercer, 1986.

Watkins, Mel. "Richard Pryor, Iconoclastic Comedian, Dies at 65." *New York Times,* December 11, 2005.

Watson, Rob. "World: America's Confederate 'Swastika' under Attack." BBC *News,* November 3, 1999. http://www.news.bbc.co.uk.12/hi.americas/503579.stm. Accessed May 12, 2013.

Weaver, Reginald. "Making the Case for Public Education." *Black Issues in Higher Education* 20, no. 25 (January 29, 2004).

Webb, Wellington. *Wellington Webb: The Man, the Mayor, and the Making Of Modern Denver: An Autobiography with Cindy Brovsky.* Golden CO: Fulcrum Publishing, 2006.

Weiss, Nancy J. *Whitney M. Young, Jr., and the Struggle for Civil Rights.* Princeton NJ: Princeton University Press, 1989.

Werner, Craig Hansen. *Playing the Changes: From Afro-Modernism to the Jazz Impulse.* Urbana: University of Illinois Press, 1994.

West, Cornel. *Democracy Matters: Winning the Fight against Imperialism.* New York: Penguin Press, 2004.

——. "Exiles from a City and from a Nation," *Observer,* http://www.guardian.co .uk.world.2005.sep/11/hurricanekatrina.comment. Accessed September 16, 2005.

——. *Race Matters.* Boston: Beacon Press, 1993.

Westheider, James. *Fighting on Two Fronts: African Americans and the Vietnam War.* New York: New York University Press, 1997.

Wexler, Laura. *Fire in a Canebrake: The Last Mass Lynching in America.* New York: Scribner, 2003.

Whitaker, Matthew C., ed. *African American Icons of Sport: Triumph, Courage, and Excellence.* Westport CT: Greenwood, 2008.

——. "Barack Obama and American Democracy." Unpublished Barack Obama and American Democracy Conference Program, Arizona State University, March 24–25, 2011, http://shprs.clas.asu.edu/BOAD.

——. "Change Blossoming in 'Age of Obama.'" *Arizona Republic,* February 17, 2013. http:www.azcentral.com/opinions/articles/20130214matthew-whitaker-era -obama.html. Accessed February 17, 2013.

——. "A Nation within a Nation." In *The American Mosaic: The African American Experience.* ABC-CLIO, 2010. http://africanamerican2.abc-clio.com.

——. *Race Work: The Rise of Civil Rights in the Urban West.* Lincoln: University of Nebraska Press, 2005.

———. "Racist Taunts at Obama Should Worry Us All," http://www.cnn.com/2013/08/08/opinion/whitaker-obama-arizona-race/index.html. Accessed August 8, 2013.

White, Elsa Joy. *Modernity, Freedom, and the African Diaspora: Dublin, New Orleans, Paris*. Bloomington: Indiana University Press, 2012.

Wilkins, Roy, with Tom Mathews. *Standing Fast: The Autobiography of Roy Wilkins*. New York: Viking Press, 1982.

Williams, Delores S. *Sisters in the Wilderness: The Challenge of Womanist God-Talk*. Maryknoll NY: Orbis Books, 1993.

Williams, Juan. *Enough: The Phony Leaders, Dead-End Movements, and Culture of Failure that Are Undermining Black America—and What We Can Do About It*. New York: Crown Publishers, 2006.

———. *Eyes on the Prize: America's Civil Rights Years, 1954–1965*. New York: Viking, 1987.

———. *Thurgood Marshall: American Revolutionary*. New York: Times Books, 1998.

Williams, Robert F. *Negroes with Guns*. Edited by Marc Schleifer. New York: Marzani and Munsell, 1962.

Willibys-corruptJustice.blogspot.com. "The Johannes Mehserle Trial—2010—Part III." http://willibys-corruptjustice.blogspot.com/2010/06/johannes-mehserle-trial-2010-part-iii.html.

Wilmore, Gayraud S. *Black Religion and Black Radicalism: An Interpretation of the Religious History of African Americans*. 3rd ed. Maryknoll NY: Orbis Books, 1998.

Wilson, William J. *The Bridge Over the Racial Divide: Rising Inequality and Coalition Politics*. Berkeley: University of California Press, 1999.

———. *The Truly Disadvantaged: The Inner City, the Underclass, and Public Policy*. Chicago: University of Chicago Press, 1987.

Wolf, Richard. "Obama Reaches Three-Year Mark with Big Wins, but Much Undone." *USA Today*, January 20, 2012.

Wurts, Jeff. "Dave Chappelle." Interviewed by James Lipton on Inside the Actors Studio, No. 10, Season 12. *Bravo*, February 12, 2006.

Wyman, Bill. "Did 'Thriller' Really Sell a Hundred Million Copies?" *New Yorker*, January 4, 2013. http://www.newyorker.com/online/blogs/culture/2013/01/did-michael-jacksons-thriller-really-sell-a-hundred-millioncopies.html. Accessed May 10, 2013.

Young, Andrew. *An Easy Burden: The Civil Rights Movement and the Transformation of America*. New York : HarperCollins, 1996.

Young, Marilyn. *Vietnam Wars 1945–1990*. New York: Harper Perennial, 1991.

INDEX

*Page numbers in italics refer to
photographs.*

Aaron, Hank, 46
Abacha, Sani, 269
Abernathy, Ralph, 70, 82, 130–31; and
    Montgomery Bus Boycott, 60, 66, 68
Abraham Lincoln Battalion, 9–10
actors, black, 43–44, 115, 248–49, 251–
    53, 262
Adams, Charity E., *20*
affirmative action, 160, 172, 180,
    207; *Bakke* case and, 166–67, 178;
    California debate over, 179–80; cuts
    in, 169, 180, 244–45; in military, 139;
    supporters' argument for, 178–79;
    Supreme Court's upholding of, 180–81
Afghanistan, 224, 226, 299
African American history, 2, 263–64.
    See also black studies programs
The Afrocentric Idea (Asante), 266
Afrocentricity, 265–67
Agnew, Spiro, 125
Aid to Families with Dependent
    Children (AFDC), 158
Alabama Christian Movement for
    Human Rights (ACMHR), 69, 90
Albany, Ga., 87–89
Alcindor, Lew (Kareem Abdul-Jabbar),
    112

Alexander, Clifford, Jr., 167
Alhamisi, Ahmed, 142
Ali, Muhammad, *111*; and Nation of
    Islam, 110; opposition to Vietnam
    War by, 111, 112
All in the Family, 152
American Federation of Labor (AFL),
    10, 30
American Recovery and Reinvestment
    Act, 287, 296
Anderson, W. G., 88
Angelou, Maya, 140
Anniston, Ala., 81–82
antiapartheid movement, 194–96
Appiah, Anthony, 263
The Arena, 191, 193
Aresenio Hall Show, 206
Asante, Molefi Kete, 155, 222; and
    Afrocentricity, 265–67
Assad, Hafez al-, 193
Association of Black Women
    Historians, 265
athletes, black, 237, 247–48; Jackie
    Robinson, 44–46; Michael Jordan,
    238, 240–41; Muhammad Ali, 110–11;
    and 1968 Olympics, 111–12
Atlanta, Ga., 75
Attica, 134–35
Ayers, William "Bill," 283–84

Badu, Erykah, 253
Baia, Ashley, 331–32
Baker, Ella, 35, 67
Bakke case, 166–67, 178, 180
Baldwin, James, 141, 263
Bambaataa, Afrika "Bam," 255
Bambara, Toni Cade, 250
Baraka, Amiri, 124, 143, 213; background of, 125; and Black Arts Movement, 139, 140; at National Black Political Convention, 162, 163
—works: *Black Fire*, 140; *The Dutchman*, 125; *Preface to a Twenty Volume Suicide Note*, 125
Barkley, Charles, 248
Barnett, Ross, 90
Baron, Harold M., 203
baseball, 44–46
Beale, Frances, 274
bebop, 43
Beckwith, Byron de la, 93
Belafonte, Harry, 92
Bell, Sean, 200
Bell, William, 172, 173
Beloved (Morrison), 249–50
Berlin, Germany, 41
Bernstein, Carl, 161
Berry, Delores, 275
Berry, Halle, 248
Berry, Marion, 75, 80
Berry, Mary Frances, 167, 172–73, 195, 223
Berube, Jennifer, 259
Beval, James, 92
Biden, Joseph, 283
bin Laden, Osama, 226, 303–4
Birmingham, Ala.: campaign of 1963 in, 90–93; church bombing in, 95, 97
Bittker, Boris, 221–22
Black Arts Movement (BAM), 131, 139–43; Amiri Baraka and, 139, 140; cultural nationalism within, 140, 143; legacy of, 143

Black Arts Repertory Theater, 140
Black Community Development and Defense Organization, 125
Black Dialogue, 141, 142
Black Dragon Society, 33
Black Fire (Baraka and Neal), 140
Black History Month, 289
black liberation theology, 76, 132
"Black Manifesto" (Forman), 108, 221
Black Methodists for Church Renewal, 108
black nationalism, 6, 33, 77, 164, 255; during 1960s, 83, 110, 120, 125, 141, 142. *See also* cultural nationalism
Black Panther Party (BPP), *121*; government campaign against, 125, 133–34; rise of, 120–21
black power movement, 5, 109, 131–32, 162, 163; Black Arts Movement and, 139; COINTELPRO program against, 125, 143; Martin Luther King Jr. and, 107, 117, 123; Stokely Carmichael and, 106–7, 123–24; supplanting of civil rights movement by, 107
Black Power (Carmichael and Hamilton), 123–24
Black Presbyterians United, 108
The Black Scholar, 142
black scholars, 155, 158, 281; as public intellectuals, 263–67
black studies programs, 153–55, 265
black-white gap, 305; in criminal justice system, 197–98; in health, 221, 245–46; in housing, 53, 242–43; in income, 165–66, 170, 203, 209–10, 214, 242–43
Black Women in America (Hine), 263
Blair, Izell, 74
Blaming the Victim (Ryan), 157–58
Blanco, Kathleen, 235
The Bluest Eye (Morrison), 249
Bond, Julian, 75
Borosage, Robert, 299

Bostic, Joe, 43
Boston busing fight, 159
Boyton v. Virginia, 81
Bradley, Mamie, 56, *57*
Bradley, Thomas, 165
Braun, Carol Moseley, 227
Brewer, Jan, 301
Briggs v. Elliot, 47, 48
Broadside Press, 142
Brooke, Edward W., 115, 126
Brooks, Gwendolyn, 43, 51, 141, 142
Brotherhood of Sleeping Car Porters, 11, 59
Brown, Elaine, 273
Brown, Foxy, 262
Brown, H. Rap, 109, 117; and black power movement, 107
Brown, James, *124*, 213; "Say It Loud, I'm Black and I'm Proud!," 114, 144–45
Brown, Jesse, 206
Brown, Michael, 232–33, 235
Brown, Minnijean, 72–73
Brown, Ronald H., 181, 206
Brown, Sterling A., 142
Brown v. Topeka Board of Education, *50*, 51; about, 48–49; resistance to, 54–55; text of decision, 311
Brown II, 54
Bryant, Roy, 55–56
Buckley, William F., Jr., 171
Buffalo Soldiers, 19
Bullins, Ed, 141
Bunche, Ralph, 38, 51, 70
Burks, Mary Frances Fair, 59
Bush, George H. W., 170, 172, 197, 204; appointment of African Americans by, 216, 218
Bush, George W., 137, 177, 211–12, 218, 227, 284; and Hurricane Katrina, 231, 234–36; and Iraq and Afghanistan wars, 226–27
Bush v. Gore, 211–12

busing, school, 219; Boston struggle around, 159; opposition to, 158–59
Byrnes, James, 54

Cabin in the Sky, 43
Cambridge, Md., 107
Campbell, Abbie N., *20*
Carlos, John, 112, *113*
Carmichael, Stokely (Kwame Ture), 109, *123*, 133, 213; background of, 104; on black power, 106–7, 123–24; and Martin Luther King Jr., 117, 119; on Vietnam, 111
Carroll, Diahann, 150
Carter, Jimmy, 167–68
Carter, Robert L., 47
The Case for Black Reparations (Bittker), 221–22
Castro, Fidel, 193
Cayton, Horace, 27
Central Intelligence Agency (CIA), 37
Chandler, Happy, 45
Chaney, James, 99, 171–72
Chapelle, David, 251–53
Chapelle's Show, 252
Charles, Ray, 43, 144, 188; "I Got a Woman," 144; "Let's Go Get Stoned," 144; "(Night Time Is) The Right Time," 144
Chenault, Kenneth I., 242
Chicago, Ill., 56, 134, 165; Martin Luther King Jr.'s campaign in, 119–20
Chionesu, Phile, 269
Chisholm, Shirley, 5, 164, 183
Chrisman, Robert, 142, 143
Christian Front, 33
Christmas, William, 117
churches, black, 108
Civil Rights Act (1957), 71, 126
Civil Rights Act (1964), 131; amendment of 1991 to, 185; and gender, 166, 272; Lyndon Johnson and, 97–98, 126; text of, 313–16

Civil Rights Act (1968), 130
Civil Rights Act (1982), 184
Civil Rights Act (1991), 185
Civil Rights Division (Justice
    Department), 71–72, 87
civil rights movement, 4–5; Albany,
    Ga., movement, 87–89; Birmingham
    campaign, 90–93; black power
    movement supplanting of, 107;
    and economic justice, 119, 128;
    freedom rides, 80–83, 85; Freedom
    Summer, 98–100; growth of,
    after Montgomery, 69–76; and
    international politics, 7, 37, 70;
    lasting effects of, 85, 131, 213;
    March on Washington, 13, 94–95;
    Montgomery Bus Boycott, 59–69;
    national and international support
    for, 66–68, 84; self-defense efforts
    in, 83; and Selma, Ala., 102–4; stu-
    dent sit-ins, 74–75, 76, 93
Civil Rights Restoration Act (1988), 184
civil rights workers, murder of, 99,
    171–72
Clark, Kenneth, 47
Clark, Mark, 134
Clark, Septima, 61
Clarke, Richard A., 226
class divisions, African American, 165–
    66, 237
Cleaver, Eldridge, 120
Cleveland, Ohio, 115, 162
Clinton, Bill, 137, 179, 197, 203–11;
    African Americans and, 203–4,
    206–7, 209–10; Republican opposi-
    tion to, 208, 210; and 2008 election
    campaign, 281, 283; and welfare
    reform, 208–9
Clinton, Hillary Rodham, 208; and
    2008 election campaign, 279–80,
    281–82
Club 662, 259
Clutchette, John, 117

Cochran, Johnnie, 201
COINTELPRO, 125, 143
Cold War, 87; African Americans and,
    36–42; anticommunist witch-hunt
    during, 39–40, 51; containment
    policy in, 36; rise of, 36–38, 41
Cole, Johnetta B., 237
Cole, Nat "King," 43
Coleman, Bessie, 24
Coleman, Ornette, 144
Collins, Cardiss, 183
The Color Purple, 238, 250–51
Coltrane, John, 144
Colvin, Claudette, 60
Combs, Sean "Diddy," 261; and hip-
    hop, 258, 259–61
comedians, black, 147–50, 251–53
Commission on Civil Rights (CCR), 71–
    72, 172–73
Committee of Racial Equality (CRE), 31
Committee on Equal Employment
    Opportunity, 87
Common (rapper), 262
Communist Party, 42, 67, 109, 114, 115;
    anticommunist witch-hunt and,
    39–40
Community Action Programs (CAPS),
    127
Comprehensive Anti-Apartheid Act, 196
Confederate battle flag, 138, 290, 324
Congressional Black Caucus (CBC),
    139, 195
Congress of Industrial Organizations
    (CIO), 30
Congress of Racial Equality (CORE),
    85, 98, 107, 125; early years of, 34–35;
    and freedom rides, 80, 82
Connerly, Ward, 174, 179–80
Connor, Eugene "Bull," 92
Constitution, U.S., 63, 323; excerpts
    from, 307–8; Fourteenth
    Amendment to, 48, 49; Thirteenth
    Amendment to, 276

Conyers, John, 222
Cook, Mercer, 87
Cornell University, 155
Cosby, Bill, 236–37
Cose, Ellis, 207
Council of Federated Organizations
    (COFO), 98–99
Council on Civic Unity (Los Angeles),
    35
The Covenant with Black America
    (Smiley), 245
Crenshaw, Kimberlé, 274
Crenshaw, Milton, 26
crime, 201–2
Crisis, 22, 33
The Crisis of the Negro Intellectual
    (Cruse), 114
Cruse, Harold, 114
Cuba, 83, 125, 193
cultural nationalism, 114, 115, 125, 140,
    143
Custis, Lemuel, 25
Czechoslovakia, 40

Daley, Phyllis, 23
Daley, Richard J., 120
Daley, William, 301
Damon, Matt, 293
Daniels, John, 26
Dave Chapelle's Block Party, 253
Davis, Angela, *114*, 198; and black
    power politics, 112, 114; legal case
    against, 117; and Marxism, 109, 115
Davis, Benjamin O., Jr., 25–26
Davis, George, 116–17
Davis, Jefferson, 172
Davis, John W., 48
Davis, Miles, 144
Davis, Ossie, 105, 248
Dawson, William L., 46
Days, Drew, III, 167
Deacons for Defense and Justice, 125
Dead Prez, 262

De Bow, Charles, 25
The Debt (Robinson), 222
decolonization movement, 38, 70,
    79–80
Dee, Ruby, 248
Def Jam Records, 260
Def Poetry, 260
Dellums, Ronald, 196
Democratic Party, 128, 169, 181; Barack
    Obama and, 284, 293–94; diversity
    in, 210–11, 227; Jesse Jackson and,
    193–94; and 1968 election, 156; and
    2008 election, 280–82, 284–85
Denny, Reginald, 199
Denver, Colo., 29
Department of Homeland Security
    (DHS), 224
desegregation: of interstate travel, 81,
    84; of schools, 46–47, 72–74, 90, 159;
    of U.S. military, 42
Detroit, Mich., 32, 165; 1943 riot in, 32–
    33; 1967 riot in, 122–23
Diallo, Amadou, 200
Diggs, Charles, 162
Dinkins, David, 181
diversity, 217; affirmative action and,
    166, 178, 181; African Americans
    and, 215, 271, 304–5; in Democratic
    Party, 210–11, 227
Divine, Annie, 100
Dixon (Kelly), Sharon Pratt, 181–82
Doar, John, 72
Doby, Larry, 46
Donilon, Tom, 303–4
Dophy, Eric, 144
Dorismond, Patrick, 200
Double V campaign, 3, 11, 33, 35, 138
Dove, Rita, 249
Drake, St. Clair, 27
Dre, Dr., 259
Dreams from My Father (Obama), 229–
    30, 325–26
Dred Scott decision, 211

Driven from Within (Jordan), 241
Drumgo, Fleeta, 117
Du Bois, W. E. B., 21, 263; denunciation of imperialism by, 38, 39; on double consciousness, 213, 214–15, 276; and McCarthyism, 39–40, 51
Dukakis, Michael, 193–94, 197
The Dutchman (Baraka), 125
Dylan, Bob, 188
Dyson, Michael Eric, 233, 237, 263

Earl, Nancy, 184
Eastland, James O., 54
Eckford, Elizabeth, 72
Edelman, Marian Wright, 207, 209
education: attack on affirmative action in, 166–67, 180, 244–45; *Brown* decision and, 48–49, 311; continuing difficulties for blacks in, 244–45, 327; desegregation fights in, 46–47, 72–74, 90, 159; No Child Left Behind program, 218–19; "separate but equal" doctrine in, 47, 48, 49, 311; voucher system in, 218
Edwards, Harry, 112
Eisenhower, Dwight D., 27, 48, 136; and civil rights struggle, 54, 71, 72, 73
Elders, Jocelyn, 206
elected officials, black, 115, 162, 163, 164–65, 181; women as, 182–84
Ellis, Opal, 35, 74
Ellison, Ralph, 143–44, 263
Episcopal Union of Black Clergy and Laity, 108
Equal Employment Opportunity Commission (EEOC), 167, 175
Equal Rights Amendment, 156, 273
Ervin, Sam, Jr., 55
Espy, Mike, 206
Essien, Essien, 266
Ethiopia, 9
Evans, Faith, 259
Evers, Medgar, 93

Evers, Myrlie, 56
Everything But the Burden (Tate), 262
Executive Order #8802, 13, 22, 30, 51; text of, 309–10
Executive Order #9346, 30
Executive Order #9981, 42, 51
Executive Order #11063, 87

Fair Employment Practices Commission (FEPC), 13, 14, 30
Fair Housing Act (1988), 184–85; text of, 321–22
Falwell, Jerry, 54
Family Assistance Plan (FAP), 158
Farmer, James, 31, 34, 80, 92
Farrakhan, Louis: international travels of, 269; on Jews, 268; and Malcolm X, 105, 268; and Million Man March, 268–69; NOI leadership by, 267–68
Faubus, Orville, 72, 73
Faulkner, William, 327
Fauntroy, Walter, 195
Federal Bureau of Investigation (FBI), 21–22, 141; and Angela Davis, 117; and Black Panther Party, 133–34; COINTELPRO program of, 125; and Martin Luther King Jr., 67, 119, 224
Federal Emergency Management Agency (FEMA), 30, 232–33, 235–36
Fellowship of Reconciliation (FOR), 31
feminism, black, 144, 177, 272–74
Ferraro, Geraldine, 326
film industry, 43–44; black directors in, 248; stereotyping of blacks by, 34, 43
financial crisis, 243, 284
Finch, Robert, 159
The Fire Next Time (Baldwin), 141
Fisher, Bernice, 34
Fitzgerald, Ella, 43, 51
Fleischer, Ari, 234
Flemming, Arthur S., 172
Fletcher, Alphonse, Jr., 242

Florida: during civil rights movement, 69; and 2000 election, 211–12

food stamps, 158

Ford, Gerald, 161, 167

Ford, Louis Henry, *57*

Forman, James, 108, 221

Formwalt, Lee W., 87

Fort Huachuca, Ariz., 19, 23

4 Little Girls (Lee), 248

Foxx, Jamie, 248

Foxx, Redd, 149

Franco, Francisco, 9

Franklin, Aretha, 144

Franklin, John Hope, 47, 207, 237, 263, *264*

Frazier, E. Franklin, 158, 263

freedom rides, 80–82, 84

Freedom Summer, 98–100

Freeman, Morgan, 248

Free South Africa Movement, 196

The Fresh Prince of Bel-Air, 248

Frick, Ford, 45

Fruit of Islam (FOI), 77, 267

Fugees, 253

Fuller, Hoyt, 142

Furious Five, 255–56

Galston, William A., 291, 292, 298

Gandhi, Mahatma, 31, 34, 66

gangs, 202, 259

gangsta rap, 256, 257, 260

Garrity, W. Arthur, 159

Garvey, Marcus, 77

Gary, Indiana, 115, 162

Gates, Henry Louis, 237, 263

Gaye, Marvin, 114, 145–46; "Inner City Blues," 145; "What's Going On," 145

Gayle v. Browder, 68

gays and lesbians, 31, 171; fight for rights by, 274–76; in military, 294

Germany, 8, 41; POWs from, 17

Giffords, Gabrielle, 299–300, 301

Gillespie, Dizzy, 20–21, 43

Giovanni, Nikki, 139–40, 142; *Black Feeling, Black Talk*, 139–40; *We a BaddDDD People*, 140

Glover, Danny, 251

Goldberg, Whoopi, 250–51

Goldwater, Barry, 100

Goodman, Andrew, 99, 171–72

Goodman, Robert, 183

Good Times, 151

Gordy, Berry, 145, 146

Gore, Albert, Jr., 211–12

gospel music, 43, 144

Graetz, Robert, 66

Grandmaster Flash (Joseph Saddler), 255–56

Granger, Lester, 11, 19

Gratz v. Bollinger, 180–81

Gray, Victoria, 100

Gray, William H., III, 181, 207

Great Migration, 4, 13–14, 28–29, 162

Great Society: Johnson campaign for, 126–28; neoconservative dismantling of, 203; Vietnam undermining of, 126, 128, 129, 136

Green, Ernest, 72–74, 167

Greenberg, Hank, 45

Greenberg, Jack, 47

Greensboro, N.C., 74

Gregory, Dick, 147, 149

Grutter v. Bollinger, 180–81

Guantanamo Bay prison, 299

Guihard, Paul, 90

Guinier, Lani, 206

Guinn, Joe, 34

Gulf of Tonkin incident, 136

Gulf War (1991), 204, 216

Haley, Harold, 117

Hamer, Fannie Lou, 100, *101*, 102

Hamilton, Bobb, 141–42

Hamilton, Charles, 123–24

Hampton, Fred, 134

Hansberry, Lorraine, 115, 141

Hare, Nathan, 142
Harlem Renaissance, 139, 143
Harrell, Andre, 259
Harris, Patricia, 167
Harrold, Stanley, 175, 176–77
Harvard University, 155, 265
Hatcher, Richard G., 115, 162, 163
"The Hate That Hate Produced" (documentary), 79
Hayes, George E. C., 50
Hayes, Isaac, 146; "Shaft," 146; "Soulsville," 146–47
Head Start, 127, 171
health and health care: black-white disparity in, 221, 245–46; HIV-AIDS crisis and, 171, 219–21, 245–46; reform efforts in, 208, 291, 297–98
Hemsley, Sherman, 152
Henry, Aaron, 100
Herc DJ Kool (Clive Campbell), 254–55
Hermann, Susan, 82
Highlander Folk School, 61
Hill, Anita, 176; and Clarence Thomas, 175–77
Hill, Lauryn, 253
Hill, Oliver, 47
Hill, Sylvia, 224
Hill, T. Arnold, 11, 12, 19
Hine, Darlene Clark, 237; on Anita Hill, 175, 176–77; on black women's history, 263, 265
Hine, William C., 175, 176–77
hip-hop, 253–62; and fashion, 261–62; national spread of, 261; women's treatment in, 256–57; youth and, 256
Hitler, Adolf, 8
HIV-AIDS crisis, 171, 219–21, 245–46
Holder, Eric, 299, 300; speech on race by, 288–89, 290
Holiday, Billie, 43
Holliday, George, 199
Hood, Rodney, 220, 221
Hoover, J. Edgar, 67, 119, 125, 224

Hornblower, Margot, 179
Horne, Lena, 22, 43
Horton, Willie, 197
House, Callie, 223
Houser, George, 34
House Un-American Activities Committee (HUAC), 39–40, 46
housing: black-white gap in, 53, 242–43; Chicago campaign against discrimination in, 119–20; Fair Housing Act, 184–85, 321–22; financial crisis and, 243; Open Housing Act, 130; Sojourner Truth Housing Project violence, 32
Houston, Charles Hamilton, 47
Howard University, 31–32
Hudson, Hosea, 42
Hudson, Jennifer, 251
Hughes, Allen, 258
Hughes, Langston, 39, 141
Hull, Blair, 231
Humphrey, Hubert H., 42, 100, 156
Hussein, Saddam, 226, 230
Hutchinson, Earl Ofari, 267
Hynes, Daniel, 231

Ice-T, 256
I Know Why the Caged Bird Sings (Angelou), 140
immigrants, 211; African, 271–72, 276–77
Immortal Technique, 262
Imus, Don, 257
In Friendship, 67
Inside the Actors Studio, 253
interracial marriage, 113, 115, 270
Interstate Commerce Commission (ICC), 84, 89
Introduction to Black Studies (Karenga), 155
Iraq War (2003): Barack Obama and, 230–31, 299; Bush administration and, 225–27

Irvin, Monte, 46
Is Bill Cosby Right? (Dyson), 237

Jack, Homer, 34
Jackmon, Marvin, 141
Jackson, George, 117
Jackson, Janet, 189, 258
Jackson, Jesse, 179, *192*, 227, 234–35, 257, 275; about, 191, 193–94; on HIV-AIDS crisis, 220; international mediation efforts by, 193, 194; and Operations Breadbasket and PUSH, 120, 146, 191; presidential bids by, 193–94, 267, 281; and Rainbow Coalition, 193, 204
Jackson, Jesse, Jr., 210
Jackson, Jimmie Lee, 102
Jackson, Jonathan, 117
Jackson, Mahalia, 43
Jackson, Michael, 185, *186*, 187–90, 237; death and legacy of, 190; rumors and scandals around, 188–90
—albums and videos: *Bad*, 188; *Ben*, 186; *Dangerous*, 189; *Got to Be There*, 186; *HIStory: Past, Present, and Future, Book I*, 189; *Invincible*, 189; *Off the Wall*, 186; *Thriller*, 187; *Victory*, 188
Jackson, Miss., 82
Jackson-Lee, Sheila, 183
Jagger, Mick, 188
James, Daniel "Chappie," Jr., 139
jazz, 8, 143–44
The Jeffersons, 151–52
Jeffries, Edward, Jr., 33
Jemison, Mae, 249
Jews, 8; blacks and, 108–9, 128, 267–68
Jim Crow, 9, 15, 49, 53, 224, 256, 276; characterization of blacks under, 287–88; legacy of, 157, 179, 221, 222, 266; in Southwest, 29; and "states' rights," 171
Johnson, Ervin "Magic," 219–20, 248
Johnson, Hazel Winifred, 139

Johnson, John, 142
Johnson, Lyndon B., 65, 71, 87, 100, 115, 125; and Civil Rights Act of 1964, 97–98, 169; Great Society campaign of, 126–28; and Martin Luther King Jr., 118, 128, 135; and Vietnam, 135, 136–37; and Voting Rights Act, 103, 104
Johnson, Robert L., 241–42
Jones, Billy, 275
Jones, Quincy, *186*
Jordan, Barbara, 183–84, 207
Jordan, Michael, 237, *240*, 248; career of, 238, 240–41
Jordan, Vernon, 161–62, 206–7
Joseph, Peniel, 286, 287–88, 290–91
Journal of Black Poetry, 142
Julia, 150–51
Julian, Hubert, 24

Karenga, Maulana, 125, 155, 163
Karim, Abdul, 141
Katrina, Hurricane, 231–36, 330; devastation of, 231–32, 235; federal government and, 232–33, 234, 235–36
Katzenbach, Nicholas, 104
Kelley, Alfred, 47
Kelley, Robin D. G., 254, 263
Kennedy, John F., 86–87; assassination of, 97, 105; and civil rights struggle, 84, 85, 86–87, 90, 92, 93–94; and Vietnam, 136
Kennedy, Robert F., 5, 156; and civil rights struggle, 82, 86, 87, 90
Kent State University, 160
Kerner Commission, 125–26
Kerry, John F., 227
Keyes, Alan, 174, 231
Kind of Blue (Davis), 144
King, A. D., 93
King, Albert, 146
King, Coretta Scott, 86, 162, 196; on gay and lesbian rights, 275–76; and Martin Luther King Jr., 58–59, 92

King, C. W., 87
King, Ed, 100
King, J. L., 246
King, Lonnie, 75
King, Martin Luther, Jr., 65, 67, 73, 75, 82, 96, 100, 158; about, 56–59; and Albany movement, 88–89; assassination of, 5, 130, 131, 135; and Birmingham campaign, 91–93; on Birmingham church bombing, 97; and black power, 107, 117, 123; Chicago campaign of, 119–20; commitment to nonviolence by, 91, 99, 119, 123, 124, 129, 130; on decolonization movement, 70; and economic justice fight, 119, 128; FBI surveillance of, 67, 119, 224; federal holiday around, 190–91, 207; John Kennedy and, 86–87; Lyndon Johnson and, 118, 128; March on Washington speech by, 13, 95; and Memphis sanitation strike, 129–30; and Montgomery Bus Boycott, 60, 63–64, 66, 68–69; and Poor People's Campaign, 128–29; and SCLC, 69–71; and Selma, Ala., 102, 103, 104; and SNCC, 88–89, 117; and Vietnam, 117–19, 128
King, Rodney, 198–99, 290
King Holiday and Service Act (1994), 207
Kissinger, Henry, 160
Kitchen Table: Woman of Color Press, 250
Knight, Etheridge, 142
Knight, Marion "Suge," 259
Knights of the White Camelia, 33
Kosovo, 194
KRS-1, 262
Ku Klux Klan (KKK), 33, 68, 93
Kweli, Talib, 262

labor, organized, 10, 30, 158

Labrie, Aubrey, 141
Lackey, D. H., 61
The Lady of Rage, 262
Landis, John, 187
Lassiter, James, 249
Last Poets, 141, 146, 254, 255
Latifah, Queen (Dana Elaine Owens), 262
Latinos, 210, 255, 299; and multiracial identity, 271
Lawson, James, 74–75
Leadership Conference on Civil Rights, 46
League for Non-Violent Civil Disobedience against Military Segregation (NCDAMS), 41, 42
Lear, Norman, 151–52
Lee, Don L. (Haki R. Madhubuti), 139, 142
Lee, Spike, 248, 287
Legal Defense and Educational Fund (LDEF), 47
"Letter from Birmingham Jail" (King), 91–92
Levison, Stanley, 66, 67
Lewinsky, Monica, 208
Lewis, John, 75, 81, 102, 119, 207, 275; and Birmingham campaign, 90–91; and March on Washington, 94–95
Lewis, Jone Johnson, 183–84
LGBTQ community, 171, 275
Lil' Kim, 262
Lincoln, Abraham, 279
Liston, Sonny, 111
Little Richard, 43
Little Rock, Ark., 72–74
Lockett, Clayborne, 26
Loeb, Henry, 129
Los Angeles, Calif., 28, 29, 165, 200–201; Rodney King case in, 198–99, 290–91; Watts riot in, 122
Loughner, Jared, 299, 301
Louima, Abner, 200

Loving v. Virginia, 115, 270
Lowndes County Freedom
    Organization (LCFO), 106
Lumumba, Mamadou, 141–42
lynching, 41, 46, 224; of Emmett Till,
    55–56

Mabley, Gene, 57
Mack, Dwayne, 84
Major, Clarence, 142
Malcolm X, 77, 78, 79–80, 213, 224;
    assassination of, 105, 125, 268; influ-
    ence of, 104, 106, 120; on March
    on Washington, 95; and Nation
    of Islam, 77, 78–79, 105, 268; and
    Organization for Afro-American
    Unity, 105
Mallet, Edward, 199–200
Mandela, Nelson, 195, 196, *197*
Mandela, Winnie, 270
Mann, Thomas, 292
Marable, Manning, 225–26
March on Washington (1963), 13, 94–
    95, *96*
March on Washington Movement
    (MOWM), 12–13, 30
Marshall, Burke, 72, 92
Marshall, Thurgood, 18, 39, 46, 47, *50*,
    87, 119; and *Brown* case, 48–49; as
    Supreme Court justice, 115, 166, 174
Marshall Plan, 37
Martin, Louis, 167
Martinez, Clarissa, 299
Marxism, 10, 108, 109, 115, 120
Mayfield, Curtis, 146
Mays, Willie, 46
McCain, Franklin, 74
McCain, John, 191; and 2008 election
    campaign, 283–84, 330
McCarthy, Eugene, 155–56
McCarthy, Joseph, and McCarthyism,
    37, 39–40
McCartney, Paul, 186–87

McClain, James, 117
McCloud, John, 103
McCree, Wade, 167
McGovern, George, 161
McKinney, Cynthia, 183
McLaurin v. Oklahoma, 47
MC Lyte, 262
McMillan, Terry, 251
McNair, Chris, 97
McNeil, Joseph, 74
McQueen, Butterfly, 43
McWhorter, John, 223
Medicaid, 126, 158
Melton, William, 26
Memphis, Tenn., 129–30
Meredith, James, 90, 106
The Message (Furious Five), 256
Mexico City, 112
Michigan State University, 155, 265
middle class, black, 5, 7, 207, 236–37,
    276
Milam, J. W., 55–56
military-industrial complex, 37
Miller, Doris "Dorie," 15, *16*
Million Man March (1995), 268–69, 276
Million Woman March (1997), 269–70,
    276
Milner, Ronald, 141, 144
Milosevic, Slobodan, 194
Ming, Robert, 47
Mississippi: Emmett Till lynching
    in, 55–56; and freedom rides, 82;
    Freedom Summer in, 98–100; mur-
    der of civil rights workers in, 99,
    171–72
Mississippi Freedom Democratic Party
    (MFDP), 100–102
Missouri ex rel. Gaines v. Canada, 47
Missy Elliot, 262
Mitchell, Michael, 281
Momyer, William M., 26
Mondale, Walter, 193
Monk, Thelonious, 43, 144

Monroe, N.C., 83

Montgomery, Ala., 56, 82

Montgomery Bus Boycott, 59–69; attacks on, 66, 68; Martin Luther King Jr.'s leadership in, 63–64, 68–69; national and international support for, 66–68; Rosa Parks's arrest and, 61–62

Montgomery Improvement Association (IA), 63, 64, 68

Moore, Jimmy, 25

Morgan v. the Commonwealth of Virginia, 81

Morris, Aldon, 97

Morrison, Toni, 204, 250, 251; background and career of, 249–50

—works: *Beloved*, 249–50; *The Bluest Eye*, 249; *Song of Solomon*, 249; *Sula*, 249; *Tar Baby*, 249

Mos Def, 253, 262

Moses, Robert "Bob," 98–99

Mothershed, Thelma, 72–73

Motley, Constance Baker, 47

Motown Records, 145–46

Moynihan, Daniel Patrick, 157–58

Mueller, Robert, 300

Muhammad, Elijah, 22, 76, 267; Malcolm X and, 79, 105

Muhammad, Wallace D., 267

Muhammad, Wallace Fard, 76

multiracial identity, 270–71

Murphy, Eddie, 251

Murray, Pauli, 30–32, 273, 280

music, 43, 114, 143–47; hip-hop and rap, 253–62; jazz, R&B, and gospel, 8, 143–45; Michael Jackson, 185–90

Music Television (MTV), 188, 261

Mussolini, Benito, 8

My Face Is Black Is True (Berry), 223

Nabrit, James M., 47, 50

Nagin, Ray, 235

Nash, Diane, 75

Nashville, Tenn., 74–75

National Association for the Advancement of Colored People (NAACP), 19, 33, 94; in Albany, Ga., 87, 88; banning in South of, 55, 69; and Double V campaign, 11, 33; and Montgomery, Ala., 59–60, 68; school segregation challenges by, 46–47, 72; and strategic and tactical differences with SCLC, 33–34, 71, 75–76

National Association of Colored Graduate Nurses (NACGN), 23

National Black Convention (Little Rock, 1974), 164

National Black Feminist Organization (NBFO), 274

National Black Political Convention (Gary, 1972), 162–64

National Coalition of Black Lesbians and Gays (NCBLG), 275

National Conference on Black Power (1967), 124

National Council of Churches (NCC), 108

National Organization for Women, 273

National Urban League (NUL), 11, 94, 175

National Workers Leagues, 33

Nation of Islam (NOI), 22, 125; under Louis Farrakhan, 267–68; and Malcolm X, 77, 78–79, 105, 268; rise of, 76–77

Neal, Larry, 140, 142

Neal, Mark Anthony, 257

Negro American Labor Council, 94

Negro Digest/Black World, 142

"The Negro Family" (Moynihan Report), 157–58

Negro Gospel and Religious Music Festival, 43

Negroes with Guns (Williams), 83

Nelson, Willie, 188

neoconservatives, black, 173–74, 223

Neshoba County, Miss., 171, 172
Newark, N.J., 122
New Careers program, 127
New Orleans, La., 81; and Hurricane Katrina, 231–36
New Right, 169–71, 177–78
Newton, Huey P., 120, 133–34
New York, N.Y., 181, 288; police brutality in, 200
New York Post, 287–88
New York Times, 134–35, 147, 295, 298
Nicholas, Peter, 303
Niggaz wit Attitude (NWA), 256
"Niggers Are Scared of Revolution" (Last Poets), 146
Nixon, E. D., 59–60, 62–63, 66, 67
Nixon, Richard M., 86, 156, 157, 158; and Martin Luther King Jr., 70; racism of, 156–57; and school busing, 158–59; and Vietnam, 160–61; and Watergate, 161
Nkrumah, Kwame, 70
No Child Left Behind program, 218–19
nonviolence, 61, 92, 196; black power critique of, 104, 123–24, 131, 141, 146; in civil rights actions, 13, 31, 34, 35, 71, 74–75, 88, 100; Gandhian principles of, 31, 34, 66; Malcolm X on, 105; Martin Luther King Jr.'s commitment to, 91, 99, 119, 123, 124, 129, 130; Robert F. Williams on, 83; SNCC and, 80, 104
North Atlantic Treaty Organization (NATO), 36
Northwestern University, 155, 265
Norton, Eleanor Holmes, 195, 275; as D.C. delegate, 183, 207; as EEOC head, 167, 172
nurses, black, 23, 139

Obama, Barack, 229, 237, 279–84, 285, 286–305; accomplishments of, 295, 299; African American reaction to, 280–81; ambiguity in rhetoric of, 295; and auto industry bailout, 287, 291, 296, 298; background and history of, 229–31; and birther movement, 301–3; and health care reform, 291, 297–98; and Eric Holder's speech on race, 289, 290; inauguration of, 285–86; and killing of Osama bin Laden, 303–4; leadership style of, 296–98; left-liberal criticisms of, 293–94, 299; popularity slippage of, 291–94; presidential election of (2008), 279–84; racially charged criticisms and depictions of, 282, 287–88, 289–90, 291; reelection of (2012), 304; speech on race relations by, 281, 323–32; and Tucson, Ariz., shooting, 299–301
Obama, Michelle, 230, 282, 291
O'Clark, Lawrence, 26
O'Connor, Sandra Day, 180, 181
Office of Emergency Management (OEM), 30
Ogletree, Charles, 281
O'Leary, Hazel, 206
Olympic Project for Human Rights, 112
Omar, Mullah, 226
O'Neal, E. Stanley, 242
O'Neal, Shaquille, 248
On the Down Low (King), 246
Open Housing Act, 130
Operation Breadbasket, 119, 120, 191
Operation PUSH, 146, 191
Oprah Winfrey Show, 238
Orangeburg, S.C., 152–53
O'Reilly, Bill, 282
Organization of Afro-American Unity, 105
Osborn, Sidney P., 19
Overbrook Entertainment, 249

Paige, Rod, 218
Paige, Satchel, 46

Painter, Nell Irvin, 20, 245, 263
Palestinians, 193
Palin, Sarah, 283, 284, 301
pan-Africanism, 38
Parker, Charlie, 43, 144
Parks, Rosa, 35, *61*, 196, 202; and
    Montgomery Bus Boycott, 61–62, 66
Parsons, Christi, 303
Parsons, Richard, 242
Patient Protection and Affordable Care
    Act, 291
patriotism, 225
Patterson, John, 82
Pattillo, Melba, 73
Payton, Benjamin, 108
Pearl Harbor, 9, 15
Peekskill, N.Y., 40
Pendleton, Clarence, 172, 173
Perle, Richard, 230
Perry, Tyler, 237
Personal Responsibility and Work
    Opportunity Reconciliation Act
    (1996), 208–9
Philadelphia Plan, 160
*Phillips v. the Phoenix Union High
    School District*, 47–48
Phoenix, Ariz., 28, 35, 74; police brutal-
    ity in, 199–200; race riot in, 18–19;
    segregation in, 29, 47–48
Pitts, Leonard, Jr., 225
Pittsburgh Courier, 11, 20
Plessy v. Ferguson, 47, 48–49, 211
Plouffe, David, 296–97
poets, black, 141–42, 249
Poitier, Sidney, 115, *116*
—films: *Cry, the Beloved Country*, 115;
    Guess Who's Coming to Dinner, 115;
    In the Heat of the Night, 115; *No Way
    Out*, 115; *A Raisin in the Sun*, 115
police brutality and violence, 33, *197*,
    201; in Chicago, 134; in Los Angeles,
    198–99, 290; in New York City, 200;
    in Phoenix, 199–200

Poor People's Campaign, 128–29,
    130–31
Port Chicago Mutiny, 17–18
poverty, 170, 233; African Americans
    in, 5, 165–66, 203, 207–8, 243; War
    on, 127–28, 157
Powell, Adam Clayton, Jr.: in Congress,
    46, 109–10; and fight against dis-
    crimination, 11, 19, 41, 46
Powell, Colin L., *205*, 215–17, 237; mili-
    tary career of, 138, 206, 215–16; as
    secretary of state, 217, 226
presidential elections: of 1948, 42; of
    1960, 86; of 1964, 100–102; of 1968,
    155–56; of 1972, 158, 161; of 1976, 167;
    of 1980, 168; of 1984, 193, 267; of
    1988, 193–94, 197; of 1992, 197, 204;
    of 2000, 211–12; of 2004, 227; of
    2008, 279–84; of 2012, 304
Price, Cecil, 99
Price, Vincent, 187
Prince Edward County, Va., 54–55
prisoners' rights movement, 117, 134;
    and Attica rebellion, 134–35
prison system, 197–98, 244
Pritchett, Laurie, 88, 89
Proposition 209 (California), 179–80
Pryor, Richard, *148*; career of, 147,
    149–50
—films and albums: *Greased Lightning*,
    150; *Is It Something I Said*, 150;
    Richard Pryor, 149; *Richard Pryor:
    Live in Concert*, 150; *Silver Streak*,
    150; *That Nigger's Crazy*, 149–50
Public Enemy, 262
Public Works Employment Act, 167–68

Quayle, Dan, 137

Race Matters (West), 207
racial profiling, 197, 201, 224
The Rage of a Privileged Class (Cose),
    207

Ragsdale, Lincoln J., 15–17, 28, 199
Rainbow Coalition, 193, 204
Randall, Dudley, 142
Randolph, A. Philip, 70; and fight
    against discrimination, 11, 19, 21,
    41, 42; and March on Washington
    (1963), 94; and March on
    Washington Movement, 12–13, 30
rap music, 254–57, 262; about, 254;
    crossover legitimacy of, 255–56;
    feuding and murders in, 257–60;
    gangsta, 256, 257, 260
"Rapper's Delight" (Sugar Hill Gang),
    255
Raspberry, William, 223
Ray, Gloria, 72–73
Ray, James Earl, 130
Rayburn, Sam, 71
Reagan, Ronald, 161, 168; and African
    Americans, 171–72, 190–91; on HIV-
    AIDS epidemic, 171; and rise of New
    Right, 169–70; and South African
    apartheid, 194–95, 196
The Real Roxanne, 262
Redding, Louis, 47
Redding, Otis, 144
Reeb, James, 103
Reed, Adolph, 263, 269
Reese, Pee Wee, 45
reparations, 221–23
Republican Party, 168, 210; black neo-
    conservatives within, 173–74; New
    Right within, 169–70; and Obama
    administration, 293, 294, 297; south-
    ern strategy of, 157, 158, 169
"R.E.S.P.E.C.T.," 144
Reynolds, Grant, 42
rhythm and blues (R&B), 43, 143, 144
Rice, Condoleezza, 26, 205, 217–18, 237
Richards, Ann, 184
Richardson, Elliot, 159
Richmond, David, 74
Rickey, Branch, 44

riots, 4, 32; after King assassination
    (1968), 130, 133; in Chicago (1966),
    119; in Detroit (1943), 32–33; in
    Detroit (1967), 122–23; in Los
    Angeles (1991), 199, 290–91; in
    Newark (1967), 122; in Phoenix
    (1942), 18–19; Watts (1965), 122
Ritchie, Lionel, 188
Roberts, George S., 25
Roberts, Isiak, 57
Roberts, Terrence, 72–73
Robeson, Paul, 40, 51
Robinson, Bill, 43
Robinson, Eddie, 43
Robinson, Jackie, 22, 45; and integra-
    tion of baseball, 44–46, 51
Robinson, James R., 34
Robinson, Jo Ann Gibson, 59, 60, 62,
    64
Robinson, Randall, 195, 222
Rock, Chris, 251
Rock Hill, S.C., 81
Roe v. Wade, 273
Romney, Mitt, 304
Roosevelt, Eleanor, 23
Roosevelt, Franklin D., 10, 12, 30, 33;
    Executive Order #8802 issued by, 13,
    22, 309–10
The Roots, 253, 262
Ross, Mac, 25
Roundtree, Richard, 146
Rowan, Carl, 87
Run-DMC, 261
Rustin, Bayard, 22, 31, 34, 100; and
    March on Washington, 94; and
    Montgomery Bus Boycott, 66–67
Ryan, William, 157–58

Sanchez, Sonia, 139, 142
Sanders, Pharoah, 144
San Francisco, Calif., 28
Saturday Review, 151
Schimmel, Michael, 253

Schlesinger, Arthur, Jr., 267
Schuyler, George, 20, 76
Schwerner, Michael, 99, 171–72
Scott, Jill, 253
Scott-Heron, Gil, 141, 146, 254; *Free Will*, 146; *Pieces of a Man*, 146; *Small Talk at 125th & Lenos*, 146; *Winter in America*, 146
Seale, Bobby, 120
Seigenthaler, John, 82
self-defense, 77, 79, 106; Robert F. Williams and, 83
Sellers, Cleveland, 153
Selma, Ala., 102–4
"separate but equal" doctrine, 47, 48, 49, 311
September 11 attacks, 223–26
sexism, 273–74; within black rights movement, 107, 164; within hip-hop and rap, 256–57
sexual orientation, 245–46. *See also* gays and lesbians
Shabazz, Betty, 162
Shabazz, Qubilah Bahiyah, 268
Shakur, Afeni, 257–58
Shakur, Tupac, 257–59; murder of, 259
—songs, films, and albums: "All Eyez on Me," 259; "Hit 'Em Up," 259; "How Do You Want It," 259; "Me Against the World," 258–59; *Poetic Justice*, 258
Shapiro, Thomas, 243
Sharpley-Whiting, T. Denean, 257
Sharpton, Al, 200, 227, 257, 287
Shepp, Archie, 144
Sheridan, Arthur A., 141
Shuttlesworth, Fred, 66, 69, 82
Simmons, Russell, 242, 260, *261*
Simmons, Ruth, 223
Simone, Nina: "Mississippi Goddam," 114; "Young, Gifted, and Black," 145
Simpson, O. J., 200–201, 330
Sipuel v. Oklahoma, 47

sit-ins, 31, 35; during civil rights movement, 74–75, 76, 93
Smalls, Biggie (Notorious B.I.G.), 257, 259–60
Smith, Barbara, 250
Smith, Eleanor, 265
Smith, Ruby Doris, 75
Smith, Tommie, 112, *113*
Smith, Will, 237; career of, 248–49
Sojourner Truth Housing Project (Detroit), 32
Soledad brothers, 117
Song of Solomon (Morrison), 249
Sotomayor, Sonia, 299
Soulbook, 141–42
Soul Children, 146
Souljah, Sister, 270
Soul on Ice (Cleaver), 120, 123
The Souls of Black Folk (Du Bois), 213
South Africa, 193; antiapartheid movement, 194–96
South Carolina State College, 152–53
Southern Christian Leadership Conference (SCLC), 90, 94, 102; decline of, 131; founding of, 69–70; Martin Luther King Jr. and, 70–71; and NAACP, 71; and Poor People's Campaign, 128–29; youth conflicts with, 75–76, 80
"The Southern Manifesto," 55, 126
Southern Regional Council (SRC), 34
Southern Voters League, 33
Soviet Union, 8, 36–38, 41
Sowell, Thomas, 174
Spanish civil war, 9–10
Spielberg, Steven, 238, 250
sports. *See* athletes, black
Spriggs, Edward, 141, 142
Springsteen, Bruce, 188
Stanford, Karin, 194
Staple Singers, 146; "Respect Yourself," 145
states' rights, 171, 212

Staupers, Mabel K., 11, 19, 23
Steele, C. K., 69
Steele, Shelby, 174, 263
Stengel, Richard, 304
stereotyping, 150, 180, 214, 253; of
    African immigrants, 272; Barack
    Obama on, 326, 327; in Hollywood,
    34, 43; by *New York Post*, 287–88;
    after 9/11, 224
Stokes, Carl, 115, 162, 163
Stone Mountain, Ga., 172
Stonewall riots, 274
Stormy Weather, 43
strategy and tactics, 5; differences over,
    33–34, 71, 75–76, 83, 123–24; growing
    militancy in, 104, 109–10
Student Executive Committee for
    Justice (Greensboro), 74
student movement and protests: dur-
    ing Birmingham campaign, 92;
    and fight for black studies, 153–55;
    and Orangeburg massacre, 152–53;
    and sit-in campaign, 74–75, 76, 93;
    against South African apartheid,
    196; during World War II, 31–32, 35
Student Nonviolent Coordinating
    Committee (SNCC), 82, 85, 94, 102,
    125, 137, 144; and Albany, Ga., move-
    ment, 88–89; and Birmingham,
    Ala., campaign, 90–91, 92; birth of,
    80; decline of, 107; and Freedom
    Summer, 98, 99; and Martin Luther
    King Jr., 88–89, 117; radicalization
    of, 104, 106, 112
suburbanization, 53
Sugar Hill Gang, 255–56
Sula (Morrison), 249
superrich African Americans, 237–38,
    241–42
Supreme Court decisions: *Brown
    v. Topeka Board of Education*,
    48–49, 311; *Brown II*, 54; *Bush v.
    Gore*, 211–12; *Gayle v. Browder*, 68;

Gratz v. Bollinger, 180–81; *Loving
    v. Virginia*, 115, 270; *Morgan v. the
    Commonwealth of Virginia*, 81;
    Plessy v. Ferguson, 47, 48–49; *Roe v.
    Wade*, 273; *University of California
    Regents v. Bakke*, 166–67, 178, 180
Supremes, 114
Sweatt v. Painter, 47
Syria, 193

Taliban, 226
Tallahassee, Fla., 69
Tar Baby (Morrison), 249
Tate, Gregg, 262
Tea Party, 293, 294, 301
television sitcoms, 150–52
Temple University, 155, 265
Terborg-Penn, Rosalyn, 265
Third World Press, 142
Thirteenth Amendment, 276
Tho, Le Duc, 160
Thomas, Carla, 146
Thomas, Clarence, *173*, 198; affirmative
    action opposed by, 172, 180; as black
    neoconservative, 173, 174; nomina-
    tion of, to Supreme Court, 174–77
Thomas, Gary, 117
Thomas, Jefferson, 72–73
Thomas, Rufus, 146
Thompson, James C., 11
Thurmond, Strom, 42
Till, Emmett, 55–56
TIME Magazine, 199
Title IX, 273
TLC, 262
Topeka, Kans., 48
To Secure These Rights (report), 41–42
Touré, Askia, 142
Townes, Jeff, 248
Trans-Africa, 195
Travis, Dempsey, 17
trickle-down economics, 170
Trina, 262

Truman, Harry S., 39, 41, 42
Trump, Donald, 301, 302–3
Tucson, Ariz., 299–301
Turner, Ike, 43
Turner, Tina, 188
Tuskegee, Ala., 15–17
Tuskegee Airmen, 24–26, 27–28
Tuskegee Institute, 24
Tutu, Desmond, 196
Tyson, Mike, 259

unemployment, 5, 53, 170, 203
United Automobile Workers (UAW),
    30, 32
United Nations, 36, 38, 226
United States v. Paradise, et al., 179
Universal Negro Improvement
    Association (UNIA), 77
University of California at Berkeley,
    180, 265
University of Massachusetts, 265
University of Michigan, 180–81
University of Mississippi, 90
Upward Bound, 127
Urban League. See National Urban
    League (NUL)
U.S. Employment Service (USES), 10
U.S. military, 41; affirmative action
    within, 139; blacks in combat during
    World War II, 24–26, 27–28; black
    women in, 22–23; desegregation of,
    42; discrimination against blacks
    during World War II, 10–11, 14–21,
    22, 24–25; and draft, 22, 41, 110, 111,
    137; during Vietnam, 137–39
U.S. population and demographics:
    African Americans and, 28–29, 333,
    335, 337; multiracial identity, 270–71.
    See also black-white gap

Vann, Robert, 11, 19
Vasquez, Anthony, 200
Vaughn, Sarah, 43

Vietnam War, 110, 111, 135–39; about,
    135–36; African American casualties
    in, 137–38; Great Society derailment
    by, 126, 128, 129, 136; Martin Luther
    King Jr. on, 117–19, 128; radicaliza-
    tion of black soldiers during, 138–
    39; Richard Nixon and, 160–61
Volunteers in Service to America
    (VISTA), 127
voter registration, 71–72, 102, 191;
    Freedom Summer efforts around,
    98–99; Voting Rights Act impact on,
    104, 161–62
Voting Rights Act (1965), 97–98, 103,
    104, 126, 131; amendments to, 164,
    184; impact of, 104, 161–62; text of,
    317–20
Voting Rights Act (1982), 184

Walker, Alice, 250–51
Walker, Margaret, 142
Wallace, George, 102
Wallace, Henry, 42
Wallace, Michele, 263
Wallace, Mike, 79
Walls, Carlotta, 72–73
Walters, Ronald, 162, 163, 225
Ware, Charlie, 88
War on Poverty, 127–28, 157
Warren, Earl, 49
Washington, Booker T., 24
Washington, D.C., 181–82
Washington, Denzel, 248
Washington, Harold, 165
Watergate scandal, 161
Waters, Ethel, 43
Waters, Maxine, 183, 270
Watkins, Mel, 147
Watts riot (1965), 122
Watts Summer Festival (1972), 146–47
Wayne, John, 172
Weaver, George L. P., 87
Weaver, Reginald, 219

Weaver, Robert, 87
welfare programs, 158, 168, 327; black neoconservatives on, 174; Clinton reform of, 208–9; Reagan and New Right on, 169, 170, 171, 191
West, Cornel, 234, 237, 263; *Race Matters*, 207
West, Kanye, 235, 253
West, U.S., 28–29
Weston, Kim, 146
Whitaker, Forrest, 251
White, Walter, 11, 12, 19, 39
White Citizens Councils, 54, 66
Wichita, Kans., 74
Wicker, Tom, 134–35
Wideman, John Edgar, 263
Wilbur, Susan, 82
Wilder, L. Douglas, 164
Wilkins, Roy, 94, 126, 133, 158, 162–63; and Maritn Luther King Jr., 117, 119
Williams, Anthony, 219
Williams, Hosea, 102
Williams, Juan, 223
Williams, Robert F., 83, 104
Williams, Venus and Serena, 247
Williams, Walter, 174
Wilson, August, 249
Wilson, Joe, 289–90
Wilson, Pete, 179
Wilson, William Julius, 263
Winchell, Walter, 17
Winfrey, Oprah, 238, *239*; in *Beloved*, 249; in *The Color Purple*, 238, 251; *Oprah Winfrey Show*, 238; wealth of, 237, 238
Wolfowitz, Paul, 230
women, black, 35, 171; in Black Arts Movement, 140; black feminism and, 144, 177, 272–74; as elected legislators, 182–84; hip-hop depiction of, 256–57; history of, 263, 265; and Million Woman March, 269–70; in Montgomery Bus Boycott, 64; movement sexism toward, 107, 164; during World War II, 10–11, 22–23, 29–30, 31–32
Women's Auxiliary Army Corps (WAAC), 19, *20*
women's history, 2, 263, 265
Women's Political Council (WPC), 59
Wonder, Stevie, 145–46, 196
Woods, Eldrick "Tiger," 237, 248
Woodward, Bob, 161
Woodward, C. Vann, 47
World War II: blacks in combat during, 24–26, 27–28; blacks in industry during, 4, 10, 13–14, 29–30; discrimination against blacks in armed forces during, 10–11, 14–21, 22, 24–25; Double V campaign during, 3, 11, 33, 35, 138; events of, 8–9, 36; German POWs during, 17; impact on African Americans of, 3, 4, 7; March on Washington Movement during, 12–13, 30; migration of blacks during, 4, 13–14, 28–29
Wright, Jeremiah, 284, 324–30
Wright, Mose, 56
Wright, Richard, 39, 263
writers and playwrights, black, 43, 249–51
Wygant v. Jackson Board of Education, 179

Yale University, 265
Yorkin, Bud, 151
Young, Andrew, 167
Young, Coleman, 165
Young, Whitney, 94, 117, 158

Zulu Nation, 255

CPSIA information can be obtained at www.ICGtesting.com
Printed in the USA
BVOW08s0133071113

335622BV00001B/1/P